MW00769883

Parent Training
for Autism Spectrum Disorder

Parent Training
for Autism Spectrum Disorder

Improving the Quality of Life for
Children and Their Families

Edited by
**Cynthia R. Johnson, Eric M. Butter,
and Lawrence Scahill**

AMERICAN PSYCHOLOGICAL ASSOCIATION
Washington, DC

Published by
American Psychological Association
750 First Street, NE
Washington, DC 20002
www.apa.org

APA Order Department
P.O. Box 92984
Washington, DC 20090-2984
Phone: (800) 374-2721; Direct: (202) 336-5510
Fax: (202) 336-5502; TDD/TTY: (202) 336-6123
Online: http://www.apa.org/pubs/books
E-mail: order@apa.org

In the U.K., Europe, Africa, and the Middle East, copies may be ordered from
Eurospan Group
c/o Turpin Distribution
Pegasus Drive
Stratton Business Park
Biggleswade, Bedfordshire
SG18 8TQ United Kingdom
Phone: +44 (0) 1767 604972
Fax: +44 (0) 1767 601640
Online: https://www.eurospanbookstore.com/apa
E-mail: eurospan@turpin-distribution.com

Typeset in Goudy by Circle Graphics, Inc., Columbia, MD

Printer: Maple Press, York, PA
Cover Designer: Naylor Design, Washington, DC

Library of Congress Cataloging-in-Publication Data

Names: Johnson, Cynthia R. (Cynthia Rheney), editor. | Butter, Eric M.,
  editor. | Scahill, Lawrence, editor. | American Psychological Association, issuing body.
Title: Parent training for autism spectrum disorder : improving the quality of life for children and
  their families / edited by Cynthia R. Johnson, Eric M. Butter, and Lawrence Scahill.
Description: First edition. | Washington, DC : American Psychological Association, [2019] |
  Includes bibliographical references and index.
Identifiers: LCCN 2018018541 (print) | LCCN 2018022033 (ebook) | ISBN 9781433829727
  (eBook) | ISBN 143382972X (eBook) | ISBN 9781433829710 (hbk.) | ISBN 1433829711 (hbk.)
Subjects: | MESH: Autism Spectrum Disorder—therapy | Parents—education | Parenting |
  Problem Behavior | Child
Classification: LCC RJ506.A9 (ebook) | LCC RJ506.A9 (print) | NLM WS 350.8.P4
  | DDC 618.92/85882—dc23
LC record available at https://lccn.loc.gov/2018018541

British Library Cataloguing-in-Publication Data
A CIP record is available from the British Library.

Printed in the United States of America
First Edition

http://dx.doi.org/10.1037/0000111-000

10 9 8 7 6 5 4 3 2 1

We dedicate this book to the memory of Tristram Smith, who was a pioneer in moving the practice and research of applied behavior analysis into the mainstream. He offered a quiet yet persuasive voice on the need for rigorous testing of behavioral interventions for children with autism spectrum disorder.

CONTENTS

CONTRIBUTORS

Courtney A. Aponte, PhD, Interventionist/Assessor, Department of Pediatrics, University of Rochester Medical Center, Rochester, NY

Karen Bearss, PhD, Psychologist, Seattle Children's Autism Center, and Assistant Professor, Department of Psychiatry and Behavioral Sciences, University of Washington, Seattle

T. Lindsey Burrell, PhD, Psychologist, Pediatric Feeding Disorders Program, Marcus Autism Center, Children's Healthcare of Atlanta, and Assistant Professor, Department of Pediatrics, Emory University School of Medicine, Atlanta, GA

Eric M. Butter, PhD, Chief, Department of Pediatric Psychology and Neuropsychology, Nationwide Children's Hospital, and Associate Professor, Departments of Pediatrics and Psychology, The Ohio State University, Columbus

Nathan A. Call, PhD, Clinical Director, Marcus Autism Center, Children's Healthcare of Atlanta, and Associate Professor, Department of Pediatrics, Emory University School of Medicine, Atlanta, GA

Rachel M. Fenning, PhD, Associate Professor, Department of Child and Adolescent Studies, and Cofounder and Codirector, Center for Autism, California State University, Fullerton

Richard M. Foxx, PhD, Professor Emeritus of Psychology, Department of Social Sciences and Psychology, The Pennsylvania State University, Harrisburg, and Adjunct Professor of Pediatrics, College of Medicine, The Pennsylvania State University, Hershey

Benjamin L. Handen, PhD, Professor of Psychiatry and Pediatrics, University of Pittsburgh School of Medicine, and Director of Research and Clinical Services, Center for Autism and Developmental Disorders, Western Psychiatric Institute and Clinic, Pittsburgh, PA

Cynthia R. Johnson, PhD, Director, Cleveland Clinic Center for Autism, and faculty, Lerner College of Medicine, Case Western Reserve University, Cleveland, OH

Luc Lecavalier, PhD, Professor of Psychology and Psychiatry, Nisonger Center, The Ohio State University, Columbus

Beth A. Malow, MS, MD, Burry Chair in Cognitive Childhood Development, Professor of Neurology and Pediatrics, and Director of the Vanderbilt Sleep Disorders Division, Vanderbilt University, Nashville, TN

Joanna Lomas Mevers, PhD, Director, Severe Behavior Program, Marcus Autism Center, Children's Healthcare of Atlanta, and Assistant Professor, Department of Pediatrics, Emory University School of Medicine, Atlanta, GA

Daniel W. Mruzek, PhD, Associate Professor, Department of Pediatrics, University of Rochester Medical Center, Rochester, NY

Colin Muething, PhD, Psychologist, Severe Behavior Program, Marcus Autism Center, Children's Healthcare of Atlanta, and Assistant Professor, Department of Pediatrics, Emory University School of Medicine, Atlanta, GA

Valentina Postorino, PhD, Postdoctoral Psychology Fellow, Brain and Body Integration Mental Health Clinic, Denver, CO

Lawrence Scahill, MSN, PhD, Director of Clinical Trials, Marcus Autism Center, Children's Healthcare of Atlanta, and Professor, Department of Pediatrics, Emory University School of Medicine, Atlanta, GA

Mindy Scheithauer, PhD, Program Manager, Severe Behavior Program, Marcus Autism Center, Children's Healthcare of Atlanta, and Assistant Professor, Department of Pediatrics, Emory University School of Medicine, Atlanta, GA

William Sharp, PhD, Director, Feeding Disorders Program, Marcus Autism Center, Children's Healthcare of Atlanta, and Associate Professor, Department of Pediatrics, Emory University School of Medicine, Atlanta, GA

Stephanie Y. Shire, PhD, Assistant Professor, Department of Special Education and Clinical Sciences, University of Oregon, Eugene

Tristram Smith, PhD, Haggerty-Friedman Professor of Developmental/Behavioral Pediatric Research, Department of Pediatrics, University of Rochester Medical Center, Rochester, NY

Cristina Whitehouse, PhD, BCBA-D, Clinical Supervisor, Florida Autism Center, University of Florida, Gainesville

Parent Training for Autism Spectrum Disorder

INTRODUCTION

CYNTHIA R. JOHNSON, ERIC M. BUTTER, AND LAWRENCE SCAHILL

Children with autism spectrum disorder (ASD) present many challenges to their parents. Caring for children with ASD can be expensive, exhausting, and more burdensome than parenting children with other disabilities (Hayes & Watson, 2013). One of the emerging empirically supported interventions available for helping parents and children with ASD is behavioral parent training (PT). PT is a psychotherapeutic intervention that targets parent behavior to change noncompliant and disruptive behavior in the child (American Academy of Child and Adolescent Psychiatry, 2007). The goal of PT is to transfer knowledge to parents, thus helping them acquire new parenting skills so they can promote and sustain behavioral improvements in children with ASD. PT for children with ASD is a family-based psychotherapy intended to decrease functional impairment and improve the quality of life for affected children and their families.

http://dx.doi.org/10.1037/0000111-001
Parent Training for Autism Spectrum Disorder: Improving the Quality of Life for Children and Their Families,
C. R. Johnson, E. M. Butter, and L. Scahill (Editors)

The collective science supporting PT for disruptive behavior in children, including those with ASD, is built on hundreds of research publications over the past 60 years. With potential for widespread implementation and dissemination, PT for children with ASD is poised to become one of the most widely used evidence-based practices for ASD treatment. PT as a treatment modality offers many advantages (Bearss, Burrell, Stewart, & Scahill, 2015). PT manuals are readily available, it is a time-limited and relatively low-cost intervention, and it has solid empirical support. Social learning theory and applied behavior analysis (ABA) provide the theoretical and practical foundations for PT in ASD. Training clinicians to implement PT is relatively straightforward and can be provided in multiple service settings (Johnson et al., 2007).

Despite these advantages and the empirical support for PT, it is not just a forum for parenting skill development. The therapeutic relationship between parent and clinician helps to define PT as a psychotherapy. In 2006, the American Psychological Association (APA) Presidential Task Force on Evidence-Based Practice (2006) put forth a policy statement on evidence-based practice as "the integration of the best available research with clinical expertise in the context of patient characteristics, culture, and preferences" (p. 280). Evidence-based practice focuses first on the patient and the appropriate application of psychotherapeutic technique. However, evidence-based practice also attends to a broader set of factors, including empathy and therapeutic alliance (Messer, 2004). The goal of this book is to summarize the current state of scientific support for PT for children with ASD and to promote implementation of PT by competent, committed clinicians. Each chapter describes PT interventions that are relevant to specific deficits and behavioral problems in children with ASD. An overriding principle is that these interventions are most effective when delivered within a psychotherapeutic framework.

OVERVIEW OF AUTISM SPECTRUM DISORDER AND APPLIED BEHAVIOR ANALYSIS

ASD is a neurodevelopmental disorder characterized by deficits in social communication and presence of repetitive and restrictive behaviors (American Psychiatric Association, 2013; World Health Organization, 2013). ASD is usually a lifelong disability but with widespread agreement that early treatment can greatly improve prognosis and functional outcomes (Reichow, 2012). Current prevalence estimates of ASD range from 6.2 to 14.7 per 1,000 (Christensen et al., 2016; Elsabbagh et al., 2012). In addition to the diagnostic features of ASD, as many as 70% of children with ASD have additional behavioral problems, such as disruptive behavior, hyperactivity, anxiety, depression, sleep disturbances, feeding problems, difficulty with toileting, and unsafe wandering away from adult supervision (Anderson et al., 2012; Johnson et al., 2013; Kroeger & Sorensen-Burnworth, 2009; Lecavalier, 2006; Seiverling, Williams, Ward-Horner, & Sturmey, 2011). Fortunately, empirically supported treatments are emerging for a range of problems in children with ASD and their families. Although there is no cure for ASD, available evidence supports behavioral approaches; comprehensive educational programs; traditional interventions, such as speech and occupation therapies; medications; and alternative/complementary approaches (Lofthouse, Hendren, Hurt, Arnold, & Butter, 2012; McDougle & Posey, 2011; Rogers & Vismara, 2008). A cursory Google search of "autism and treatment" in early 2017 resulted in more than 48 million hits. For many treatments, however, the evidence supporting efficacy is inadequate.

The behavioral treatment approaches borne of ABA have been the most researched treatments for ASD. Within the field of ABA, there are several treatment paradigms, including discrete trial training (DTT), pivotal response training (PRT), and verbal behavior (VB). However, many of the behaviorally based treatments rely on highly trained therapists to provide the one-to-one intervention to the child. This is not only costly, but trained therapists are not available in every community to work directly with the child. Moreover, although intensive one-to-one treatment with a child is necessary in some cases, this level of care may not be required for all children with ASD. Alternatively, parents are central to the lives of their children with ASD and potentially the most influential people for the child over time. It also is parents who face the daily challenges of promoting the development of a child with ASD. Clinicians—many already familiar with the expertise involved in providing PT to other populations—could offer PT to children with ASD as an effective treatment model.

PT that is grounded in the principles of ABA offers the potential for parents to make use of effective techniques for behavioral management and skill development (Bearss et al., 2015; Johnson et al., 2007). PT is accessible and can play a central role in empowering a parent to be the agent of change in the child. PT is not proposed as a replacement for more comprehensive, child-focused ABA interventions, such as DTT, PRT, or VB. Instead, PT offers a supplemental and/or stand-alone intervention designed to reduce behavioral problems and promote daily living skills in the child, as well as improve quality of life for the family. Research over the past 20 years has demonstrated that parents can be taught to implement a range of behavioral techniques to address targeted behaviors and skills. In addition to single-subject design studies showing that several PT techniques are effective, a growing number of randomized controlled trials have demonstrated efficacy for various PT programs (Bearss et al., 2015; Kasari et al., 2014; McConachie & Diggle, 2007).

OVERVIEW OF THE BOOK'S CONTENTS

This book focuses on behaviorally based PT as a treatment model for addressing disruptive behavior and skill deficits in children with ASD. Chapter 1 provides a historical account and theoretical basis for the PT model, including the central tenets of PT, as well as its advantages and limitations. The emergence of PT for children with ASD and PT's roots in ABA also is presented.

Next is a chapter on clinical assessment and decision making when selecting children for PT. Chapter 2 reviews a range of assessment tools for diagnosis of ASD and pretreatment measurement as a starting point in the treatment planning process. The chapter also covers assessment tools designed to determine the impact of treatment for the parent and child. The chapter describes measures and procedures that have been used in previous treatment studies and shown sensitivity to change with treatment.

Chapter 3 reviews the importance of parent engagement and adherence, which are essential to the success of PT—including child outcomes. This chapter reviews prior research on variables associated parent engagement and, conversely, with parent resistance. Conceptual models of treatment barriers and practical strategies to promote parent engagement also are presented.

Chapter 4 covers the PT literature on social communication deficits in children with ASD. It begins with a review of toddler and early childhood interventions. Afterward is a comprehensive review of empirically tested PT models for social communication deficits, as well as assessment tools for these deficits. The chapter offers considerations for practitioners who work with parents of children with ASD.

In Chapter 5, the authors review the expanding literature on PT for disruptive behavior in children with ASD. The chapter provides information on the prevalence, impact, and predisposing factors for disruptive behavior in children with ASD. It also offers descriptions of the practical techniques used in the treatment of disruptive behavior in this population.

Chapter 6 discusses PT for sleep disturbances most commonly observed in children with ASD. Similar in format to the previous chapter, this chapter provides an overview of the types of sleep disturbances in children with ASD, specific sleep assessment tools, and the behavioral procedures used in PT targeting sleep disturbances.

In Chapter 7, the authors describe PT for children with food selectivity. They review the clinical presentation and impact of feeding problems in children with ASD. In addition to potential health impacts of feeding problems in children with ASD, the authors provide a thorough review of the literature on PT for feeding problems in ASD.

Chapter 8 describes the challenges of bowel and bladder training in children with ASD. Specific assessment strategies are followed by PT techniques to address both initial toileting, as well as bladder and bowel accidents.

Chapter 9 takes on the treatment of wandering and elopement in children with ASD. Wandering and bolting away from parent supervision are dangerous behaviors that have been chronicled in several tragic stories in the press over the past few years. The chapter presents descriptions and possible motivations of wandering and bolting from caregivers and thoroughly discusses an assessment of this class of behaviors. Afterward is an examination of available literature on PT for wandering or elopement. Practical suggestions are made along with a case example.

The concluding chapter offers a summary and recommendations for future directions for PT in ASD.

This edited book brings together clinicians and clinical investigators who have dedicated many years to developing, testing, revising, and testing again PT programs across a gamut of issues facing parents of children with ASD. Our intended audience is the wide range of professionals providing care for children with ASD and their families. We offer these chapters as conceptual and practical guides to practitioners and trainees, including psychologists, behavior analysts, mental health counselors, early intervention therapists, special educators, child psychiatrists, psychiatric nurse practitioners, and others serving children with ASD. Given the broadening of the ASD phenotype and resulting increase in the prevalence of the diagnosis, we are convinced that practitioners across a number of settings will benefit from a comprehensive discussion of PT for children with ASD. Based on the collective experience of the book's authors, we also are convinced that collaboration with parents is an effective way to promote skill acquisition and reduce behavioral problems in children with ASD. We offer this book as a foundation for practitioners and trainees who want to learn the nuts and bolts of PT and the growing empirical basis of this treatment model for children with ASD.

REFERENCES

American Academy of Child and Adolescent Psychiatry. (2007). Practice parameter for the assessment and treatment of children and adolescents with oppositional defiant disorder. *Journal of the American Academy of Child and Adolescent Psychiatry*, 46, 126–141.

American Psychiatric Association. (2013). *Diagnostic statistical manual of mental disorders* (5th ed.). Arlington, VA: Author.

American Psychological Association Presidential Task Force on Evidence-Based Practice. (2006). Evidence-based practice in psychology. *American Psychologist, 61*, 271–285. http://dx.doi.org/10.1037/0003-066X.61.4.271

Anderson, C., Law, J. K., Daniels, A., Rice, C., Mandell, D. S., Hagopian, L., & Law, P. A. (2012). Occurrence and family impact of elopement in children with autism spectrum disorders. *Pediatrics, 130*, 870–877. http://dx.doi.org/10.1542/peds.2012-0762

Bearss, K., Burrell, T. L., Stewart, L., & Scahill, L. (2015). Parent training in autism spectrum disorder: What's in a name? *Clinical Child and Family Psychology Review, 18*, 170–182. http://dx.doi.org/10.1007/s10567-015-0179-5 (Erratum published 2015, *Clinical Child and Family Psychology Review, 18*, p. 183. http://dx.doi.org/10.1007/s10567-015-0183-9)

Christensen, D. L., Baio, J., Van Naarden Braun, K., Bilder, D., Charles, J., Constantino, J. N., . . . Yeargin-Allsopp. (2016, Summer). Prevalence and characteristics of autism spectrum disorder among children aged 8 years—Autism and developmental disabilities monitoring network, 11 sites, United States, 2012. *Morbidity and Mortality Weekly Report Surveillance Summaries, 65*, 1–23. http://dx.doi.org/10.15585/mmwr.ss6503a1 (Erratum published 2016, *Morbidity and Mortality Weekly Report, 65*, 404.)

Elsabbagh, M., Divan, G., Koh, Y. J., Kim, Y. S., Kauchali, S., Marcín, C., . . . Fombonne, E. (2012). Global prevalence of autism and other pervasive developmental disorders. *Autism Research, 5*, 160–179. http://dx.doi.org/10.1002/aur.239

Hayes, S. A., & Watson, S. L. (2013). The impact of parenting stress: A meta-analysis of studies comparing the experience of parenting stress in parents of children with and without autism spectrum disorder. *Journal of Autism and Developmental Disorders, 43*, 629–642. http://dx.doi.org/10.1007/s10803-012-1604-y

Johnson, C. R., Handen, B. L., Butter, E., Wagner, A., Mulick, J., Sukhodolsky, D. G., . . . Smith, T. (2007). Development of a parent training program for children with pervasive developmental disorders. *Behavioral Interventions, 22*, 201–221. http://dx.doi.org/10.1002/bin.237

Johnson, C. R., Turner, K. S., Foldes, E., Brooks, M. M., Kronk, R., & Wiggs, L. (2013). Behavioral parent training to address sleep disturbances in young children with autism spectrum disorder: A pilot trial. *Sleep Medicine, 14*, 995–1004. http://dx.doi.org/10.1016/j.sleep.2013.05.013

Kasari, C., Lawton, K., Shih, W., Barker, T. V., Landa, R., Lord, C., . . . Senturk, D. (2014). Caregiver-mediated intervention for low-resourced preschoolers with autism: An RCT. *Pediatrics, 134*, e72–e79. http://dx.doi.org/10.1542/peds.2013-3229

Kroeger, K. A., & Sorensen-Burnworth, R. (2009). Toilet training individuals with autism and other developmental disabilities: A critical review. *Research in Autism Spectrum Disorders, 3*, 607–618. http://dx.doi.org/10.1016/j.rasd.2009.01.005

Lecavalier, L. (2006). Behavioral and emotional problems in young people with pervasive developmental disorders: Relative prevalence, effects of subject characteristics, and empirical classification. *Journal of Autism and Developmental Disorders, 36,* 1101–1114. http://dx.doi.org/10.1007/s10803-006-0147-5

Lofthouse, N., Hendren, R., Hurt, E., Arnold, L. E., & Butter, E. (2012). A review of complementary and alternative treatments for autism spectrum disorders. *Autism Research and Treatment.* Advance online publication. http://dx.doi.org/10.1155/2012/870391

McConachie, H., & Diggle, T. (2007). Parent implemented early intervention for young children with autism spectrum disorder: A systematic review. *Journal of Evaluation in Clinical Practice, 13,* 120–129. http://dx.doi.org/10.1111/j.1365-2753.2006.00674.x

McDougle, C. J., & Posey, D. J. (2011). Assessment and treatment of autistic and pervasive developmental disorders. In A. Martin, L. Scahill & C. J. Kratochvil (Eds.), *Pediatric psychopharmacology: Principles and practice* (pp. 547–560). New York, NY: Oxford University Press.

Messer, S. B. (2004). Evidence-based practice: Beyond empirically supported treatments. *Professional Psychology: Research and Practice, 35,* 580–588. http://dx.doi.org/10.1037/0735-7028.35.6.580

Reichow, B. (2012). Overview of meta-analyses on early intensive behavioral intervention for young children with autism spectrum disorders. *Journal of Autism and Developmental Disorders, 42,* 512–520. http://dx.doi.org/10.1007/s10803-011-1218-9

Rogers, S. J., & Vismara, L. A. (2008). Evidence-based comprehensive treatments for early autism. *Journal of Clinical Child and Adolescent Psychology, 37,* 8–38. http://dx.doi.org/10.1080/15374410701817808

Seiverling, L. J., Williams, K. E., Ward-Horner, J., & Sturmey, P. (2011). Interventions to treat feeding problems in children with autism spectrum disorders: A comprehensive review. In J. L. Matson & P. Sturmey (Eds.), *International handbook of autism and pervasive developmental disorders* (pp. 491–508). New York, NY: Springer. http://dx.doi.org/10.1007/978-1-4419-8065-6_31

World Health Organization. (2013). *ICD–11 beta draft: Mortality and morbidity statistics.* Retrieved from https://icd.who.int/dev11/l-m/en

1

HISTORY AND THEORETICAL FOUNDATIONS OF PARENT TRAINING

KAREN BEARSS

In child mental health services, the term *parent training* (PT) refers to an evidence-based treatment for children with disruptive behavior. The efficacy of PT in treating disruptive behavior in children with oppositional defiant disorder and attention-deficit/hyperactivity disorder from preschool to adolescence is supported by decades of research (Dretzke et al., 2009; Michelson, Davenport, Dretzke, Barlow, & Day, 2013). Indeed, clinicians can choose from one of several well-established, structured programs, including Webster-Stratton's (n.d.) Incredible Years, Kazdin's (2005) PT, Barkley's (2013) Defiant Children, and Eyberg's Parent–Child Interaction Therapy (McNeil & Hembree-Kigin, 2011). This body of evidence has influenced international dissemination of PT and has prompted several clinical practice guidelines in the United States, United Kingdom, and elsewhere in an effort to raise standards of mental health care for youths (American Academy of Child and Adolescent Psychiatry, 2007; National Institute for Health and Care Excellence, 2006).

http://dx.doi.org/10.1037/0000111-002
Parent Training for Autism Spectrum Disorder: Improving the Quality of Life for Children and Their Families,
C. R. Johnson, E. M. Butter, and L. Scahill (Editors)

PARENT TRAINING IN AUTISM SPECTRUM DISORDER

PT as a mode of treatment in autism spectrum disorder (ASD) has taken a different and somewhat multifaceted path for obvious reasons: The complexity of the disorder, with deficits in social communication, imitation, and play, requires a more expansive approach. Due to the child's multiple needs, best practices for children with ASD historically have involved intensive, child-focused, school-based services that target core symptoms of ASD. Parent participation is included as one of the six main tenets of the Individuals With Disabilities Education Act of 2004. In practice, PT may be viewed as a supplement to those comprehensive school-based programs. In this context, PT is designed to play a supporting role in the promotion of continued skill acquisition and generalization from class to the home and community.

ROLE OF PARENT TRAINING

Challenges associated with caring for a child with ASD do not end when the child leaves the educational or therapeutic setting. Studies have confirmed the burden and stress parents face when raising a child with ASD (Hayes & Watson, 2013; Kogan et al., 2008; Tonge et al., 2006). With insufficient resources available through the educational system, parents have to look elsewhere for support and guidance on managing the challenges of raising a child with ASD. Unfortunately, access to quality community-based services is limited. Although children with ASD represent 10% to 14% of psychiatrically referred populations (Joshi et al., 2010), only 5% of community mental health therapists consider themselves to have expertise in ASD (Brookman-Frazee, Drahota, & Stadnick, 2012). In addition, parents have reported frustration about the slow pace of progress in treatment and a lack of practical "tools" to manage children with ASD (Brookman-Frazee et al., 2012). As a result, the demand for parent support in caring for children with ASD, both within the school and community systems, is far outpacing the availability of services by skilled providers. This lack of access may result in long delays in securing effective behavioral intervention. Some families may resort to obtaining services in specialty clinics. Other children may go without needed services (Wacker et al., 2013).

The recognized struggles parents face in rearing a child with ASD have prompted increased interest in the development and empirical testing of parent-focused interventions for ASD. PT warrants interest as a frontline intervention model because it traditionally is a time-limited approach (typically 10–20 sessions) delivered during brief (60–90 minutes) weekly sessions.

As such, it may be applicable in a wide range of service settings. PT also emphasizes the role of parents as the change agents. Furthermore, there is increased recognition that intensive, school-based or therapist-based interventions are costly (Solomon, Necheles, Ferch, & Bruckman, 2007), and such specialized, intensive services may not be available in all communities (Croen, Grether, Hoogstrate, & Selvin, 2002). Teaching parents to be the therapist for their child allows for delivery of treatment across settings and contexts (Burrell & Borrego, 2012).

WHAT IS PARENT TRAINING IN AUTISM SPECTRUM DISORDER?

PT in the general child mental health field refers predominantly to a systematic approach designed to reduce disruptive child behaviors. In the field of ASD, however, PT is attached to a variety of treatments that may not share common features. The ambiguity of the term *parent training* in ASD may be due to differences in the targets of intervention: skill deficits in language, social reciprocity, joint attention versus disruptive behavior, and other co-occurring behavioral issues. Thus, although *parent training* is a clear label for describing an empirically supported treatment for children with disruptive behavior uncomplicated by ASD, the application of this term within the ASD field requires clarification (Nevill, Lecavalier, & Stratis, 2018; Oono, Honey, & McConachie, 2013; Postorino et al., 2017). Given this broad application of the label *parent training* in ASD, it is not surprising that clinicians (even those well versed in ASD) offer different definitions. Confusion about the label *parent training* in ASD also may extend to parents, clinic administrators, insurance companies, and policymakers. Thus, given the ambiguities of terminology used to describe PT programs in ASD, clarification is overdue (see Figure 1.1).

PARENT TRAINING: CHARACTERIZING THE LABEL

Initially, PT programs can be characterized in two ways: whether the program focuses on imparting information to the parent that promotes understanding of ASD versus whether it promotes skill acquisition in the child or management of maladaptive behavior (Bearss, Burrell, Stewart, & Scahill, 2015). Figure 1.1 highlights the differences in these two broad categories. This first classification schema can be broadened to include programs within four main categories: care coordination, psychoeducation, parent-mediated interventions (PMIs) for core symptoms, and PMIs for maladaptive behavior.

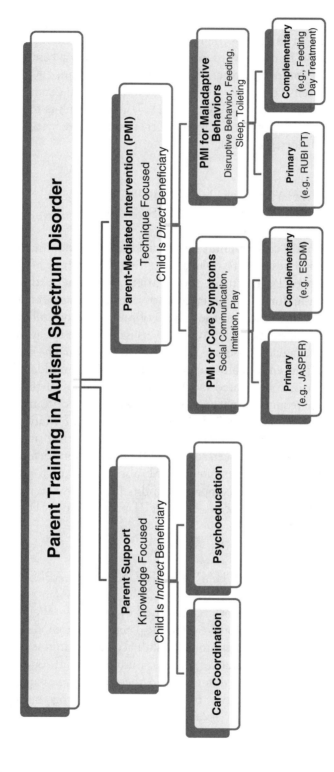

Figure 1.1. Taxonomy of parent training (PT) in autism spectrum disorder (ASD). JASPER = joint attention, symbolic play, engagement, and regulation; ESDM = early start Denver model; RUBI = The RUBI [Research Units in Behavioral Intervention] Autism Network. From "Erratum to: Parent Training in Autism Spectrum Disorder: What's in a Name?," by K. Bearss, T. L. Burrell, L. Stewart, and L. Scahill, 2015, *Clinical Child and Family Psychology Review, 18,* p. 19. Copyright 2015 by Springer. Reprinted with permission.

Each of these modalities has a tradition and a history. Moreover, each has varying levels of research support from case reports through rigorous single-subject design and, rarely, randomized controlled trials (RCTs) with structured interventions.

PT also can be characterized by the program's format, intensity, location, duration, and target age group of the child (Beaudoin, Sébire, & Couture, 2014; Oono et al., 2013; Schultz, Schmidt, & Stichter, 2011; Steiner, Koegel, Koegel, & Ence, 2012). *Format* refers to how information is presented to the parent. Self-guided material may be available online or in self-help books. Alternatively, therapist-guided programs may be offered in groups or one-to-one. The most common and most complex format involves therapist-guided parent–child interactions (Schultz et al., 2011). PT programs also may range from low to high intensity. *Low-intensity programs* may include brief consultation with a care coordinator or bimonthly meetings with a therapist. Other more intensive programs may include 60- to 90-minute weekly out-patient or in-home sessions (Bearss, Johnson, Handen, Smith, & Scahill, 2013; Hardan et al., 2015; Kasari et al., 2014). *High-intensity programs* may involve multiple sessions per week or day treatment (Dawson et al., 2010; Sharp, Jaquess, Morton, & Miles, 2011; Wong & Kwan, 2010). In their review of parenting programs for children with ASD, Schultz et al. (2011) reported that intensity of treatments ranged from 1 hour to 25 hours a week. *Location* is where the intervention takes place and may include clinic, school, home-based services, or, in recent years, online presentation or delivery via tele-health (Wacker et al., 2013). *Duration* reflects the length of time for the parent intervention. The range of PT programs for young children with ASD varies widely from 1 week to 2 years (Oono et al., 2013). Programs may focus on specific *target age groups*: For example, in younger or newly diagnosed children, services may focus on increasing parent understanding of their child's diagnosis and how to navigate educational and treatment planning. Treatments targeting parents of young children commonly focus on addressing core skill deficits, such as communication, socialization, and joint attention (Dawson et al., 2010; Kasari et al., 2014). Conversely, parents of older children and transition-age youths may benefit instead from programs targeting long-term planning (L. E. Smith, Greenberg, & Mailick, 2014).

PARENT SUPPORT

Parent support encompasses programs intended to provide indirect benefit to the child by providing support to the parent and increasing parental knowledge about ASD. Parent support can be categorized as care coordination or psychoeducation.

Care Coordination

The Agency for Healthcare Research and Quality (AHRQ; 2014) defined *care coordination* as "the deliberate organization of patient care activities between two or more participants involved in a patient's care to facilitate the appropriate delivery of health care services" (p. 41). Given the complex medical and educational requirements of children with ASD, care coordination is an essential element in overall clinical management. Indeed, children with ASD use more health care resources than the general pediatric population (Gurney, McPheeters, & Davis, 2006; Liptak, Stuart, & Auinger, 2006). Parental effort required to coordinate multiple services is substantial, which results in parents' reducing working hours or discontinuing work outside the home to meet service demands (Kogan et al., 2008). For example, in a sample of 2,088 families from the 2005–2006 National Survey of Children with Special Health Care Needs, 25% of families reported spending 10 or more hours per week coordinating the child's care (Kogan et al., 2008). This burden of care could be reduced if access to appropriate services and better integration of available services were available (Parellada et al., 2013).

The goal of care coordination is to connect families to services and to bridge gaps along a care pathway. Such coordination often involves assisting parents to navigate the complicated array of medical, behavioral, alternative, educational, and medical treatments. Care coordination tends to be a brief and time-limited consultative service delivered by a social worker or case manager. State and local agencies also may provide care coordination services. For example, in Pennsylvania, families can register their child with the Office of Developmental Programs to obtain services from a support coordinator, who serves as an advocate and develops an individual support plan (Lubetsky, Handen, Lubetsky, & McGonigle, 2014).

Although there are accepted recommendations for educational and medical services for children with ASD (e.g., National Research Council, 2001; Wilczynski et al., 2009), empirical support for current models of care coordination in ASD is sparse. A major barrier to rigorous testing of care coordination models is the wide range of regional differences in available services. In addition, the services indicated for children with ASD across the range of severity and age pose a challenge for care coordination. As in many areas in ASD, one size does not fit all.

One model of care coordination for individuals with ASD and their families was described by Parellada et al. (2013). The program, Comprehensive Medical Care for Autism Spectrum Disorders, developed in Spain, aims to provide centralized care for medical, developmental, and behavioral problems in individuals with ASD. In this model, the care coordinator facilitates care by organizing appointments for the families, accompanying the family to appointments, and communicating with relevant practitioners regarding the individual's needs (Parellada et al., 2013).

The program described by Parellada et al. (2013) is consistent with the concept of the medical home model articulated by the American Academy of Pediatrics (Medical Home Initiatives for Children With Special Needs Project Advisory Committee, American Academy of Pediatrics, 2002; see also Hyman & Johnson, 2012). Medical homes are intended to provide coordinated, accessible, continuous, and culturally competent care that includes screening, education, referrals, and follow-up for children with ASD (Lubetsky et al., 2014; Medical Home Initiatives, 2002; Murphy, Carbone, & the Council on Children With Disabilities, 2011). Available research findings have suggested that care coordination under the rubric of the medical home results in improved health status for children with ASD (Homer et al., 2008) and that participation in a medical home also may reduce costs of medical care (Kogan et al., 2008).

Psychoeducation

One of the most frequently expressed unmet needs by parents of children with ASD at the point of the child's diagnosis is access to quality information about ASD (Hamilton, 2008; Whitaker, 2002). By providing parents with up-to-date information about ASD, effective psychoeducational programs can help parents adjust expectations for the child's future and advocate for appropriate services. For example, psychoeducation can help parents prepare for the challenges in the development of an individualized education plan. Parents of newly diagnosed children need guidance about interventions with empirical support, interventions without solid evidence that are promising, and interventions that are unfounded and unsafe. Psychoeducation also can be beneficial as new challenges unfold throughout the child's lifetime, such as the onset of puberty or transition to independent living.

There are many self-guided psychoeducational resources available to parents, such as Volkmar and Wiesner's (2009) book *A Practical Guide to Autism: What Every Parent, Family Member, and Teacher Needs to Know*, and web-based resources, such as the Autism Speaks 100-Day Kit (http://www.autismspeaks.org/family-services/tool-kits/100-day-kit). Informal psychoeducation also occurs as a part of regular clinical practice (e.g., within the primary care or mental health setting). A structured psychoeducational program is likely to be more intensive than care coordination in the number of visits and can be delivered by case managers, social workers, psychiatric nurse practitioners, or psychologists. Structured psychoeducational programs generally are short term (i.e., 6–12 sessions) and can be conducted in group or individual formats. Group programs have the added value of promoting mutual support and opportunities to share personal experiences with other parents (Daley, Singhal, Weisner, Barua, & Brezis, 2013; Farmer & Reupert, 2013).

Common outcomes for psychoeducational programs in ASD include increased parental knowledge, enhanced competence in advocating for the child, decreased parental stress, and a reduced sense of isolation (Daley et al., 2013; Farmer & Reupert, 2013; L. E. Smith et al., 2014; Tonge et al., 2006). Psychoeducation also may include a few sessions on behavioral management strategies or techniques to enhance communication. Given the brief coverage of these topics within a broader psychoeducation program (Farmer & Reupert, 2013; L. E. Smith et al., 2014), these few sessions may increase parental knowledge on behavioral techniques but are unlikely to provide adequate guidance on management of moderate or greater behavioral problems.

To date, research on psychoeducation in ASD has been limited. A few pilot studies have examined psychoeducation as a stand-alone intervention for ASD (Daley et al., 2013; Farmer & Reupert, 2013; L. E. Smith et al., 2014) or as a control condition (Bearss, Johnson, et al., 2015; Hardan et al., 2015; Tonge et al., 2006; Tonge, Brereton, Kiomall, Mackinnon, & Rinehart, 2014). In their pilot study of parents of 10 adolescents with ASD, L. E. Smith et al. (2014) described a structured parent psychoeducational program called Transitioning Together. The 10-session program included two individual family sessions focused on goal setting for the adolescent. Those sessions were followed by eight multifamily group sessions that covered a range of topics, including the developmental course of ASD, negotiation of service systems, exploration of behavioral management strategies, advocacy, parental well-being, and long-term planning for the adolescent. The study provided encouraging results on parental understanding of the child's disability and service system, as well as improvements in the parent–child relationship (L. E. Smith et al., 2014).

PARENT-MEDIATED INTERVENTIONS

PMIs are *technique focused* in which the parent is the agent of change and the child is the direct beneficiary of treatment (Bearss, Burrell, Stewart, & Scahill, 2015). As shown in Figure 1.1, PMIs may focus on the treatment of core features of ASD or maladaptive behavior.

Programs that fall within PMIs may be divided further into primary or complementary interventions. This distinction is based on whether the parent is the primary change agent or a team member in a therapist-led intervention. *Primary programs* actively engage the parent from the outset to facilitate the child's acquisition of specific skills (e.g., joint attention; Kasari et al., 2014) or the reduction of the child's maladaptive behavior (Bearss et al., 2013). In *complementary programs*, the treatment, at least initially, involves the child's working with a therapist. The therapist then may work with the parent to promote generalization of techniques from therapist to parent (e.g., early start Denver model; Dawson et al., 2010) or from clinic into the home and community (e.g., Marcus Autism Center feeding program; Sharp et al., 2011). Although this distinction is useful for classifying interventions, hybrid programs have emerged in which interventions initially designed as complementary have expanded to include primary programs (e.g., early start Denver model; Rogers et al., 2012).

PMIs for Core Symptoms

PMIs for core symptoms include treatments that focus on teaching parents how to promote social interaction, communication, imitation and play skills. Although there are self-guided PMI resources for parents (e.g., *Teaching Social Communication to Children With Autism: A Manual For Parents* [Ingersoll & Dvortcsak, 2010]; *More Than Words: A Parent's Guide to Building Interaction and Language Skills for Children With Autism Spectrum Disorder or Social Communication Difficulties* [Sussman, 2012]), most PMI programs for core symptoms involve the therapist's working with the parent–child dyad (Oono et al., 2013; Schultz et al., 2011). PMIs can be delivered in the home and community settings. Those locations may be preferred because interactions and skill acquisition occur in a naturalistic setting (Carter et al., 2011; Dawson et al., 2010; Drew et al., 2002; J. Roberts et al., 2011; Siller, Hutman, & Sigman, 2013; T. Smith, Groen, & Wynn, 2000). Most programs run 2 to 3 hours per session, but the frequency ranges widely from twice daily to monthly (Oono et al., 2013). Duration varies, too. Although many structured PMIs targeting core symptoms are over 1 year in length (Casenhiser, Shanker, & Stieben, 2013; Dawson et al., 2010; Drew et al., 2002; Green et al., 2010; J. Roberts et al., 2011), a few programs teach skills to parents within 1 to 2 weeks (Nefdt, Koegel, Singer, & Gerber, 2010; Wong & Kwan, 2010). PMIs may be delivered by a variety of professionals, including special educators, speech pathologists, psychologists, psychiatric nurse practitioners, and board-certified behavior analysts.

Currently, most parenting interventions for core features of ASD focus on socialization and communication or imitation skills (Oono et al., 2013). In their review, Schultz et al. (2011) noted that nearly half of the 30 studies on PT they examined focused on communication as the primary target for intervention. In the Beaudoin et al. (2014) review on parenting interventions for toddlers with ASD, communication was a main goal in all 15 included studies. Nevill et al. (2018) recently completed a meta-analysis of 19 RCTs targeting core symptoms of ASD, with sample sizes ranging from 20 to 152.

An example of a primary PMI for core symptoms is the Joint Attention Symbolic Play Engagement and Regulation (JASPER) program developed and tested by Kasari et al. (2014). JASPER targets social communication skills in disadvantaged preschoolers (ages 2–5 years). The intervention, delivered in the home or school, uses a structured intervention. Therapists teach parents how to cultivate engagement with the child during play and everyday activities (e.g., chores, grooming). The active instruction aims to promote joint attention, play skills, and language.

The early start Denver model (ESDM) is an example of a complementary PMI for core features of ASD (Dawson et al., 2010). This comprehensive, child-focused intervention for children ages 12 to 48 months involves therapist-led treatment 20 hours per week (e.g., 4 hours per day, 5 days a week) for 2 years in the home. The treatment also includes twice monthly parent consultation during which the principles and specific techniques of ESDM are taught to parents. Parents are then encouraged to apply ESDM strategies during everyday activities, such as feeding, bath time, and play. ESDM integrates developmental and relationship-based approaches with techniques from applied behavior analysis (ABA) to promote interpersonal exchange and shared engagement with real-life activities in the child. It also promotes parental sensitivity to the child's cues and verbal and nonverbal communication.

PMI for Maladaptive Behavior

In addition to core features of ASD, clinically significant disruptive behavior problems are common and may include tantrums, aggression, noncompliance with routine demands, self-injury, property destruction, and hyperactivity (Kaat & Lecavalier, 2013; Kanne & Mazurek, 2011; Mayes et al., 2012; Mazurek, Kanne, & Wodka, 2013), as well as more focal concerns, such as food refusal (Sharp et al., 2013), sleep disturbance (Hoffman, Sweeney, Gilliam, & Lopez-Wagner, 2006; Johnson et al., 2014), toileting problems (Maskey, Warnell, Parr, Le Couteur, & McConachie, 2013; Simonoff et al., 2008) and elopement (Anderson et al., 2012). These maladaptive behaviors may interfere with a child's response to educational intervention, lead to further isolation from peers, and increase caregiver stress due to disruptions in daily activities (Brereton, Tonge, & Einfeld, 2006; Hayes & Watson, 2013; Herring et al., 2006; Simonoff et al., 2008; Tonge et al., 2006). Children with ASD with disruptive behavior who actively resist acquiring new skills or performing already acquired skills likely will fall behind in adaptive functioning (Scahill et al., 2016). Indeed, on measures of adaptive functioning, children with ASD often are a full standard deviation below their assessed cognitive ability (Kanne et al., 2011; Perry, Flanagan, Dunn Geier, & Freeman, 2009).

This connection between disruptive behavior and impaired adaptive functioning provides a compelling rationale for PMIs designed to reduce the child's behavioral problems and improve daily living skills.

Until recently, most studies on training parents to reduce disruptive behavior used single-subject designs (Campbell, 2003). Those studies offered proof of concept for specific parent-mediated techniques for children with ASD and maladaptive behavior. However, the individualized approach may hinder replication (T. Smith et al., 2007). In addition, study samples often were inadequately characterized, thus making generalization difficult. More recently, several open prospective case series (Bearss et al., 2013; Brookman-Frazee et al., 2012; Dababnah & Parish, 2016; Okuno et al., 2011; Research Units on Pediatric Psychopharmacology [RUPP] Autism Network, 2007; D. Roberts & Pickering, 2010; Wacker et al., 2013) and quasiexperimental trials (Lindgren et al., 2016; Tonge et al., 2014) using structured manuals have been published, supporting the efficacy of behavioral PT in reducing behavioral problems in children with ASD. PT also has been shown to be an effective adjunct treatment to medication in youths with ASD: atomoxetine in the treatment of attention-deficit/hyperactivity disorder and noncompliance (Handen et al., 2015) and risperidone in the treatment of serious behavioral problems (Aman et al., 2009).

Six (sample sizes ranged from 26 to 180) RCTs of PT as a stand-alone treatment have been published to date (Bearss, Johnson, et al., 2015; Ginn, Clionsky, Eyberg, Warner-Metzger, & Abner, 2015; Reitzel et al., 2013; Sofronoff, Leslie, & Brown, 2004; Tellegen & Sanders, 2014; Whittingham, Sofronoff, Sheffield, & Sanders, 2009; see Postorino et al., 2017, for a review). For example, Sofronoff et al. (2004) compared a 1-day workshop ($n = 18$) and six-session individual PT program ($n = 18$) to wait-list control ($n = 15$) in 6- to 12-year-old children with Asperger's disorder. Whittingham et al. (2009) randomized children with ASD (ages 2–9) to the Stepping Stones Triple P PT program ($n = 29$) or a wait-list control ($n = 30$). Both studies showed significant reductions of parent-reported child behavioral problems for PT programs compared with wait-list. In the Sofronoff et al. (2004) study, individually delivered PT was superior to the 1-day workshop and wait-list. Behavioral improvements were maintained at the 3-month (Sofronoff et al., 2004) and 6-month (Whittingham et al., 2009) follow-up. The Cochrane review of PT programs for children 6 years and under reported inconsistent results for reduction in maladaptive behavior (Oono et al., 2013).

The RUBI [Research Units in Behavioral Intervention] Autism Network PT program illustrates a primary PMI program designed to reduce disruptive behavior and improve adaptive skills in young children with ASD (Aman et al., 2009; Bearss et al., 2013; Bearss, Johnson, et al., 2015; Johnson et al., 2007; Research Units on Pediatric Psychopharmacology [RUPP] Autism

Network, 2007; Scahill et al., 2012, 2016). The program consists of 11 core and up to two optional focal-problem sessions (e.g., toileting or sleep problems), as well as two telephone booster calls and two home visits delivered over the course of 6 months. The intervention is based on the principles and techniques of ABA. In this model, disruptive, noncompliant, and aggressive behaviors are presumed to serve a function for the child. The function may be access to a tangible item (e.g., certain food, preferred toy), attention, escape from a demand, or self-stimulatory in nature. The key to changing a behavior is first to identify the function and then modify the situations that precede the behavior and the consequences that follow the behavior. Because therapists set out to teach parents how to modify the child's behavior, parents are the change agents. The program targets daily activities, such as getting dressed, getting ready for bed, or managing trips to the grocery store that often are daily struggles for parents of children with ASD.

In comparison, the intensive feeding day treatment program at the Marcus Autism Center in Atlanta, Georgia, is a model of a complementary PMI for maladaptive behavior in the form of extreme food refusal and food selectivity in children with ASD (Sharp et al., 2011). The intervention involves four, 45-minute meals presented each day, 5 days a week for 8 weeks. An individualized treatment protocol is developed for each child using common behavioral intervention components, such as stimulus fading (e.g., gradual increase of bite size), escape extinction (i.e., no longer allowing disruptive behavior to serve as an escape from meal demand), and positive reinforcement (Sharp et al., 2011). Although caregivers are involved in the selection of foods in the treatment and they observe the intervention strategies, the therapist implements all aspects of the treatment protocol until the child's short-term feeding goals are met. Once these goals are met, the therapist conducts in vivo parent–child training to promote reliable application of the interventions developed and implemented by the therapist. Once trained, parents implement the intervention in the home.

THEORETICAL FOUNDATIONS OF PARENT TRAINING

Understanding the development and maintenance of behavior problems (e.g., feeding, sleep difficulties, disruptive behavior, elopement) has been aided by social learning theory (Bandura, 1971) and operant conditioning (Skinner, 1963). *Social learning theory* describes the processes by which children develop a behavioral repertoire through direct experience, observation, and modeling. For example, a child may hit another child on the playground to gain access to a ball after observing that aggression was successful when used by another child. This process of observing and imitating also occurs in the family. Rather than implying that the child or the parent is independently responsible for the child's maladaptive behavior, social learning theory directs attention to the interactions between family members as a source of child behavioral problems.

A child initially may engage in disruptive behavior through observation and imitation of others. Whether or not the child *continues* to engage in that behavior can be explained through principles of operant conditioning. The organizing principle of *operant conditioning* is that a behavior can be modified (i.e., increased or decreased) through the manipulation of its antecedents and/or consequences. An *antecedent* is the stimulus that cues an organism to perform a learned behavior. When an organism perceives the antecedent stimulus, it behaves in a way that is designed to maximize the reinforcing consequences and minimize punishing consequences. A *consequence* is the event that immediately follows the behavior. The consequences of reinforcement and punishment are the core tools through which operant behavior is modified. Positive reinforcement (e.g., providing praise for cleaning up toys) and negative reinforcement (e.g., taking an aspirin to "remove" a headache) increase the probability of a behavior. In contrast, positive punishment (e.g., scolding for not following directions) and negative punishment (e.g., removing a favorite toy for hitting) reduce the probability of a behavior that each follows.

Operant conditioning is a core component of ABA, which is defined as the systematic application of learning theory. ABA is a mainstay treatment for individuals with ASD. First developed in the 1970s, ABA for children with ASD found its roots in the work of psychologist Ivar Lovaas, who published a landmark study in 1987 that demonstrated the impact of up to 40 hours per week of one-on-one teaching on improvements in child cognitive functioning and functional learning (Lovaas, 1987). Called discrete trial training or the "Lovaas Method," programming includes a highly individualized curriculum, home-based intervention, and active parent involvement. Stemming from Lovaas's (1987) work on discrete trial training, intervention packages based on principles of ABA have expanded to include approaches, such as incidental teaching (Fenske, Krantz, & McClannahan, 2001), pivotal response teaching/training (Hardan et al., 2015), and the Picture Exchange Communication System (Frost & Bondy, 1994).

The aims of ABA in the field of ASD are to teach skills to address core deficits along with other developmentally appropriate behaviors and reduce co-occurring behavioral concerns and demonstrate that the interventions used are responsible for the improvement in behavior (Baer, Wolf, & Risley, 1968). ABA postulates that by understanding a behavior's antecedents and consequences, one can determine its purpose, or *function*. Common functions of maladaptive behavior include access to a tangible item (e.g., food or a favorite toy), attention from others (e.g., positive reinforcement), escape from a demand or an aversive stimulus (e.g., negative reinforcement), or sensory or other internal stimulation (e.g., automatic reinforcement; Iwata & Worsdell, 2005). By understanding the function of the behavior problem, parents learn to modify their usual response to teach the child a more appropriate behavior (Horner, Carr, Strain, Todd, & Reed, 2002). For example, a child may learn that a tantrum will result in escape from a routine demand (e.g., household chore). In such a case, the parent can be taught to (a) ensure the child is not allowed to escape the routine demand and (b) implement strategies to promote compliance (e.g., a reward for completing chores).

Naturalistic developmental behavioral interventions (NDBIs; Schreibman et al., 2015) are emerging as a common framework for many PMIs for core symptoms of ASD. NDBIs are founded on both principles of ABA and developmental science. NDBIs use operant teaching techniques and target socially significant goals. Outcomes are objectively evaluated before, during, and after intervention. NDBIs commonly use ABA strategies, such as modeling, shaping, chaining, prompting, and differential reinforcement as tools for behavioral change and skill development; more centrally, though, NDBIs incorporate developmental perspectives. First, child development follows regular sequences across several domains (Piaget, 1966). Second, children most easily learn skills that are just beyond their present knowledge, suggesting value in assessing the child's current skill levels and choosing intervention targets that fall within what Vygotsky (1962) called the child's "zone of proximal development." Third, children learn best when they are active participants in learning (Gibson, 1973). Fourth, child learning is facilitated by affective exchanges with a social partner (Kuhl, 2007).

NDBIs are designed to target the broad range of developmental domains (e.g., cognition, social skills, language, play, motor skills), and intervention approaches use learning experiences that promote development of social, language, and cognitive skills. This focus on a broad range of developmental domains is counter to more traditional discrete trial approaches in which skills may be taught one at a time and in isolation. The starting point and choice of intervention targets are informed by the child's chronological *and* developmental readiness, which is consistent with the value of promoting foundational skills that are precursors to language, such as joint attention and gestures, as well as skills (e.g., imitation, shared affect, social engagement) that are critical prerequisites for learning a range of other higher level skills. Additional hallmarks of NDBIs include the delivery of services in naturalistic and interactive social contexts, such as play and daily routines. Child-directed activities may be used as the entry point for engagement so that the child is an active participant rather than a passive learner. NDBIs encourage parents to implement strategies in the natural environment to promote functional skills used in everyday life (Schreibman et al., 2015).

SPECIAL CONSIDERATIONS FOR PARENTS OF CHILDREN WITH ASD

Unsurprisingly, the inconsistent use of the term *parent training* for children with ASD has promulgated confusion among professionals, parents, administrators and third-party payers on its meaning. The simple division of parent support programs and PMIs for children with ASD illustrated in Figure 1.1 is a starting point for placing a given intervention into the broader treatment landscape. For example, within PMI for core symptoms, NDBI is an emerging label being used to characterize a cluster of early interventions (e.g., JASPER, ESDM) that address deficits in communication and cognition in young children.

Beyond the growing list of brand names (e.g., NDBIs, JASPER, ESDM), the diverse nature of programs involving parents requires the field to avoid using labels that do not elucidate the program content. In practical terms, this implies that saying a program is a PMI is insufficient. The label should promote distinction between a PMI for communication versus a PMI for imitation skills. Although this expanded description may seem unnecessary or burdensome, it may be especially useful to insurance companies, policymakers, and clinic administrators. These stakeholders may be unfamiliar with the similarities and differences across various PT programs—but they play an important role in determining program viability. Moreover, parents, who are the primary consumer of these services, often are inundated with information and may be overwhelmed by treatment choices. Clear descriptions will help parents decipher treatment options.

ADDITIONAL CONSIDERATIONS

The delineation of PMIs implies that the resulting categories are mutually exclusive. In clinical settings, however, the demarcation may not be so firm, and there may be overlap across the four areas (i.e., care coordination, psychoeducation, PMI for core symptoms, PMI for maladaptive behavior). In some settings, clinicians provide a combination of supportive and skill-based treatments by necessity. Alternatively, there may be programs that are designed primarily to address core symptoms or behavioral issues in children with ASD but also may include, as part of the program, sessions on enhancing language acquisition.

CLINICAL IMPLICATIONS

Within the field of ASD, emerging evidence suggests PMIs can be helpful in reducing disruptive, noncompliant behaviors in children and improving social communication skills. Applying a treatment manual into clinical practice, however, can be challenging. Successful implementation occurs when treatment systematically introduces parents to a range of techniques designed to shift the balance of negative parent–child interactions to positive ones. Although programs include a range of strategies that have been effective, not every strategy fits every child and parent. When it comes to specific PT techniques, what works for one parent–child dyad may not work for another parent–child dyad. The clinical challenge is to equip the parent with the tools to fit with the individual child.

When initiating a PMI, parents initially may struggle to understand why they are being asked to attend treatment when their child has the skill deficit or behavioral problem. In clinical settings, some clinicians may raise the same question. Some parents also may silently wonder if their need for PT implies that the child's skill deficits or behavioral problems are the parents' fault. It often is useful to address these concerns up front. For example, it can be noted that children with disruptive behavior require the application of specific parenting techniques that most other children do not require. An easy and potentially illustrative contrast can be offered to parents who have other children without ASD. This contrast may help parents see that particular parenting strategies may work with one child but not another. Therapists also should reinforce the notion that because parents are on the frontline with the child day in and day out, they are attending treatment to become the agents of change for the child's behavior. A positive rephrasing of this principle is that the therapist is providing parents with the skills to change the child's behavior. Mastery of effective parenting strategies increases opportunities for success in multiple settings (e.g., home, grocery store, playground) and contexts (e.g., morning routine, homework, mealtimes, bedtime). This discussion is all about the delicate balance of engaging the parent in the treatment while simultaneously avoiding the suggestion that the parent is to blame for the child's difficulties.

Balancing Parent Expectations and Child Ability in Parent Training

In PT, parents are encouraged to consider the child's development and to keep expectations in accordance with the child's abilities. Difficulties may emerge if a parent holds unrealistic expectations about the child's skill level. For example, a child with impaired receptive language would affect the child's understanding of verbal commands and predictably reduce engagement and compliance if commands are too complex. Conversely, parents may have lowered expectations about a child's abilities and refrain from placing appropriate demands on the child. Although lower demands on the child may reduce noncompliance, lower demands also may interfere with the acquisition of new skills and the regular performance of current skills. Thus, effective PT finds a balance between increasing parental demands or expectations for the child at a pace that fits with the child's development.

FUTURE DIRECTIONS

PMIs for core symptoms of ASD have been an area of active research. In a recent Cochrane review (Oono et al., 2013), improvement in proximal outcomes, such as shared attention between parent and child, and distal improvements in child language skills and reduction in core features of ASD were noted. Improvements in child social initiations, adaptive skills, maladaptive behavior, and parent stress, however, were inconclusive. Of the 19 RCTs reviewed, only one study (Green et al., 2010) was deemed adequately powered (Oono et al., 2013). Thus, although there is a growing body of evidence for PMIs focused on core features of ASD, additional research is needed to test existing and new models.

As the empirical foundation for PT expands, there will be a concomitant need for dissemination (i.e., spreading the word about the evidence-based intervention) and implementation (i.e., taking deliberate steps to incorporate evidence-based treatments into real-world settings). Training demands for empirically supported interventions for children with ASD vary with the complexity of the treatment (Postorino et al., 2017). For example, PT for disruptive behavior in young children with ASD is likely to require less training than the early start Denver model. Due to the complexity of some interventions, implementation may be selective to centers that have the capacity to adopt more specialized treatments.

Finally, expansion of the autism spectrum diagnosis and improved methods of assessment have contributed to an increase in the prevalence of ASD (Elsabbagh et al., 2012). The term *autism spectrum* implies that those affected have a range of treatment needs. Some children may need intensive intervention to address severe challenging behaviors; for others, less intensive PMI may be appropriate. The challenges for the field are to continue building the evidence base and to implement treatments that are supported empirically.

REFERENCES

Agency for Healthcare Research and Quality. (2014). Chapter 2: What is care coordination? In *Care Coordination Measures Atlas Update*. Retrieved from http://www.ahrq.gov/professionals/prevention-chronic-care/improve/coordination/atlas2014/chapter2.html

Aman, M. G., McDougle, C. J., Scahill, L., Handen, B., Arnold, L. E., Johnson, C., . . . Wagner, A. (2009). Medication and parent training in children with pervasive developmental disorders and serious behavior problems: Results from a randomized clinical trial. *Journal of the American Academy of Child & Adolescent Psychiatry, 48*, 1143–1154. http://dx.doi.org/10.1097/CHI.0b013e3181bfd669

American Academy of Child and Adolescent Psychiatry. (2007). Practice parameter for the assessment and treatment of children and adolescents with oppositional defiant disorder. *Journal of the American Academy of Child and Adolescent Psychiatry, 46*, 126–141.

Anderson, C., Law, J. K., Daniels, A., Rice, C., Mandell, D. S., Hagopian, L., & Law, P. A. (2012). Occurrence and family impact of elopement in children with autism spectrum disorders. *Pediatrics, 130*, 870–877. http://dx.doi.org/10.1542/peds.2012-0762

Baer, D. M., Wolf, M. M., & Risley, T. R. (1968). Some current dimensions of applied behavior analysis. *Journal of Applied Behavior Analysis, 1*, 91–97. http://dx.doi.org/10.1901/jaba.1968.1-91

Bandura, A. (1971). *Social learning theory*. Morristown, NJ: General Learning Press.

Barkley, R. A. (2013). *Defiant children: A clinician's manual for assessment and parent training* (3rd ed.). New York, NY: Guilford Press.

Bearss, K., Burrell, T. L., Stewart, L., & Scahill, L. (2015). Parent training in autism spectrum disorder: What's in a name? *Clinical Child and Family Psychology Review, 18*, 170–182. http://dx.doi.org/10.1007/s10567-015-0179-5 (Erratum published 2015, *Clinical Child and Family Psychology Review, 18*, p. 183. http://dx.doi.org/10.1007/s10567-015-0183-9)

Bearss, K., Johnson, C., Handen, B., Smith, T., & Scahill, L. (2013). A pilot study of parent training in young children with autism spectrum disorders and disruptive behavior. *Journal of Autism and Developmental Disorders, 43*, 829–840. http://dx.doi.org/10.1007/s10803-012-1624-7

Bearss, K., Johnson, C., Smith, T., Lecavalier, L., Swiezy, N., Aman, M., . . . Scahill, L. (2015). Effect of parent training vs parent education on behavioral problems in children with autism spectrum disorder: A randomized clinical trial. *JAMA, 313*, 1524–1533. http://dx.doi.org/10.1001/jama.2015.3150

Beaudoin, A. J., Sébire, G., & Couture, M. (2014). Parent training interventions for toddlers with autism spectrum disorder. *Autism Research and Treatment, 2014*, Article ID 839890. Retrieved from http://dx.doi.org/10.1155/2014/839890

Brereton, A. V., Tonge, B. J., & Einfeld, S. L. (2006). Psychopathology in children and adolescents with autism compared to young people with intellectual disability. *Journal of Autism and Developmental Disorders, 36*, 863–870. http://dx.doi.org/10.1007/s10803-006-0125-y

Brookman-Frazee, L. I., Drahota, A., & Stadnick, N. (2012). Training community mental health therapists to deliver a package of evidence-based practice strategies for school-age children with autism spectrum disorders: A pilot study. *Journal of Autism and Developmental Disorders, 42*, 1651–1661. http://dx.doi.org/10.1007/s10803-011-1406-7

Burrell, T. L., & Borrego, J., Jr. (2012). Parents' involvement in ASD treatment: What is their role? *Cognitive and Behavioral Practice, 19*, 423–432. http://dx.doi.org/10.1016/j.cbpra.2011.04.003

Campbell, J. M. (2003). Efficacy of behavioral interventions for reducing problem behavior in persons with autism: A quantitative synthesis of single-subject research. *Research in Developmental Disabilities, 24*, 120–138. http://dx.doi.org/10.1016/S0891-4222(03)00014-3

Carter, A. S., Messinger, D. S., Stone, W. L., Celimli, S., Nahmias, A. S., & Yoder, P. (2011). A randomized controlled trial of Hanen's "More Than Words" in toddlers with early autism symptoms. *Journal of Child Psychology and Psychiatry, 52*, 741–752. http://dx.doi.org/10.1111/j.1469-7610.2011.02395.x

Casenhiser, D. M., Shanker, S. G., & Stieben, J. (2013). Learning through interaction in children with autism: Preliminary data from asocial-communication-based intervention. *Autism, 17*, 220–241. http://dx.doi.org/10.1177/1362361311422052

Croen, L. A., Grether, J. K., Hoogstrate, J., & Selvin, S. (2002). The changing prevalence of autism in California. *Journal of Autism and Developmental Disorders, 32*, 207–215. http://dx.doi.org/10.1023/A:1015453830880

Dababnah, S., & Parish, S. L. (2016). Feasibility of an empirically based program for parents of preschoolers with autism spectrum disorder. *Autism, 20*, 85–95. http://dx.doi.org/10.1177/1362361314568900

Daley, T. C., Singhal, N., Weisner, T., Barua, M., & Brezis, R. S. (2013, May). *Evaluation of an acceptance and empowerment parent training model: Evidence from an intervention in India.* Paper presented as a part of an Integrated Educational Session on Parent Training and Parent Mediated Intervention in Diverse Contexts at the annual meeting of the International Meeting for Autism Research, San Sebastian, Spain.

Dawson, G., Rogers, S., Munson, J., Smith, M., Winter, J., Greenson, J., . . . Varley, J. (2010). Randomized, controlled trial of an intervention for toddlers with autism: The early start Denver model. *Pediatrics, 125*, e17–e23. http://dx.doi.org/10.1542/peds.2009-0958

Dretzke, J., Davenport, C., Frew, E., Barlow, J., Stewart-Brown, S., Bayliss, S., . . . Hyde, C. (2009). The clinical effectiveness of different parenting programmes for children with conduct problems: A systematic review of randomised controlled trials. *Child and Adolescent Psychiatry and Mental Health, 3,* 1–10. http://dx.doi.org/10.1186/1753-2000-3-7

Drew, A., Baird, G., Baron-Cohen, S., Cox, A., Slonims, V., Wheelwright, S., . . . Charman, T. (2002). A pilot randomised control trial of a parent training intervention for pre-school children with autism. *European Child & Adolescent Psychiatry, 11,* 266–272. http://dx.doi.org/10.1007/s00787-002-0299-6

Elsabbagh, M., Divan, G., Koh, Y. J., Kim, Y. S., Kauchali, S., Marcín, C., . . . Fombonne, E. (2012). Global prevalence of autism and other pervasive developmental disorders. *Autism Research, 5,* 160–179. http://dx.doi.org/10.1002/aur.239

Farmer, J., & Reupert, A. (2013). Understanding autism and understanding my child with autism: An evaluation of a group parent education program in rural Australia. *Australian Journal of Rural Health, 21,* 20–27. http://dx.doi.org/10.1111/ajr.12004

Fenske, E. C., Krantz, P. J., & McClannahan, L. E. (2001). Incidental teaching: A not-discrete-trial teaching procedure. In C. Maurice, G. Green, & R. M. Foxx (Eds.), *Making a difference: Behavioral interventions for autism* (pp. 75–82). Austin, TX: PRO-ED.

Frost, L. A., & Bondy, A. (1994). *The picture exchange communication system training manual.* Cherry Hill, NJ: Pyramid Educational Consultants.

Gibson, E. J. (1973). *Principles of perceptual learning and development.* New York, NY: Appleton-Century-Crofts.

Ginn, N. C., Clionsky, L. N., Eyberg, S. M., Warner-Metzger, C., & Abner, J. P. (2015). Child-directed interaction training for young children with autism spectrum disorders: Parent and child outcomes. *Journal of Clinical Child and Adolescent Psychology, 46,* 101–109. http://dx.doi.org/10.1080/15374416.2015.1015135

Green, J., Charman, T., McConachie, H., Aldred, C., Slonims, V., Howlin, P., . . . the PACT Consortium. (2010). Parent-mediated communication-focused treatment in children with autism (PACT): A randomised controlled trial. *The Lancet, 375,* 2152–2160. http://dx.doi.org/10.1016/S0140-6736(10)60587-9

Gurney, J. G., McPheeters, M. L., & Davis, M. M. (2006). Parental report of health conditions and health care use among children with and without autism: National Survey of Children's Health. *Archives of Pediatrics & Adolescent Medicine, 160,* 825–830. http://dx.doi.org/10.1001/archpedi.160.8.825

Hamilton, L. M. (2008). *Facing autism: Giving parents reasons for hope and guidance for help.* New York, NY: Random House Digital.

Handen, B. L., Aman, M. G., Arnold, L. E., Hyman, S. L., Tumuluru, R. V., Lecavalier, L., . . . Smith, T. (2015). Atomoxetine, parent training, and their combination in children with autism spectrum disorder and attention-deficit/hyperactivity disorder. *Journal of the American Academy of Child & Adolescent Psychiatry, 54,* 905–915. http://dx.doi.org/10.1016/j.jaac.2015.08.013

Hardan, A. Y., Gengoux, G. W., Berquist, K. L., Libove, R. A., Ardel, C. M., Phillips, J., . . . Minjarez, M. B. (2015). A randomized controlled trial of pivotal response treatment Group for parents of children with autism. *Journal of Child Psychology and Psychiatry, 56,* 884–892. http://dx.doi.org/10.1111/jcpp.12354

Hayes, S. A., & Watson, S. L. (2013). The impact of parenting stress: A meta-analysis of studies comparing the experience of parenting stress in parents of children with and without autism spectrum disorder. *Journal of Autism and Developmental Disorders, 43,* 629–642. http://dx.doi.org/10.1007/s10803-012-1604-y

Herring, S., Gray, K., Taffe, J., Tonge, B., Sweeney, D., & Einfeld, S. (2006). Behaviour and emotional problems in toddlers with pervasive developmental disorders and developmental delay: Associations with parental mental health and family functioning. *Journal of Intellectual Disability Research, 50,* 874–882. http://dx.doi.org/10.1111/j.1365-2788.2006.00904.x

Hoffman, C. D., Sweeney, D. P., Gilliam, J. E., & Lopez-Wagner, M. C. (2006). Sleep problems in children with autism and in typically developing children. *Focus on Autism and Other Developmental Disabilities, 21,* 146–152. http://dx.doi.org/10.1177/10883576060210030301

Homer, C. J., Klatka, K., Romm, D., Kuhlthau, K., Bloom, S., Newacheck, P., . . . Perrin, J. M. (2008). A review of the evidence for the medical home for children with special health care needs. *Pediatrics, 122,* e922–e937. http://dx.doi.org/10.1542/peds.2007-3762

Horner, R. H., Carr, E. G., Strain, P. S., Todd, A. W., & Reed, H. K. (2002). Problem behavior interventions for young children with autism: A research synthesis. *Journal of Autism and Developmental Disorders, 32,* 423–446. http://dx.doi.org/10.1023/A:1020593922901

Hyman, S. L., & Johnson, J. K. (2012). Autism and pediatric practice: Toward a medical home. *Journal of Autism and Developmental Disorders, 42,* 1156–1164. http://dx.doi.org/10.1007/s10803-012-1474-3

Individuals With Disabilities Education Act, 34 C.F.R.§ 300.321 (2004).

Ingersoll, B., & Dvortcsak, A. (2010). *Teaching social communication to children with autism: A manual for parents.* New York, NY: Guilford Press.

Iwata, B. A., & Worsdell, A. S. (2005). Implications of functional analysis methodology for the design of intervention programs. *Exceptionality, 13,* 25–34. http://dx.doi.org/10.1207/s15327035ex1301_4

Johnson, C. R., Handen, B. L., Butter, E., Wagner, A., Mulick, J., Sukhodolsky, D. G., . . . Smith, T. (2007). Development of a parent training program for children with pervasive developmental disorders. *Behavioral Interventions, 22,* 201–221. http://dx.doi.org/10.1002/bin.237

Johnson, C. R., Turner, K., Stewart, P. A., Schmidt, B., Shui, A., Macklin, E., . . . Hyman, S. L. (2014). Relationships between feeding problems, behavioral characteristics and nutritional quality in children with ASD. *Journal of Autism and Developmental Disorders, 44,* 2175–2184. http://dx.doi.org/10.1007/s10803-014-2095-9

Joshi, G., Petty, C., Wozniak, J., Henin, A., Fried, R., Galdo, M., . . . Biederman, J. (2010). The heavy burden of psychiatric comorbidity in youth with autism spectrum disorders: A large comparative study of a psychiatrically referred population. *Journal of Autism and Developmental Disorders*, *40*, 1361–1370. http://dx.doi.org/10.1007/s10803-010-0996-9

Kaat, A. J., & Lecavalier, L. (2013). Disruptive behavior disorders in children and adolescents with autism spectrum disorders: A review of the prevalence, presentation, and treatment. *Research in Autism Spectrum Disorders*, *7*, 1579–1594. http://dx.doi.org/10.1016/j.rasd.2013.08.012

Kanne, S. M., Gerber, A. J., Quirmbach, L. M., Sparrow, S. S., Cicchetti, D. V., & Saulnier, C. A. (2011). The role of adaptive behavior in autism spectrum disorders: Implications for functional outcome. *Journal of Autism and Developmental Disorders*, *41*, 1007–1018. http://dx.doi.org/10.1007/s10803-010-1126-4

Kanne, S. M., & Mazurek, M. O. (2011). Aggression in children and adolescents with ASD: Prevalence and risk factors. *Journal of Autism and Developmental Disorders*, *41*, 926–937. http://dx.doi.org/10.1007/s10803-010-1118-4

Kasari, C., Lawton, K., Shih, W., Barker, T. V., Landa, R., Lord, C., . . . Senturk, D. (2014). Caregiver-mediated intervention for low-resourced preschoolers with autism: An RCT. *Pediatrics*, *134*, e72–e79. http://dx.doi.org/10.1542/peds.2013-3229

Kazdin, A. E. (2005). *Parent management training: Treatment for oppositional, aggressive, and antisocial behavior in children and adolescents.* New York, NY: Oxford University Press.

Kogan, M. D., Strickland, B. B., Blumberg, S. J., Singh, G. K., Perrin, J. M., & van Dyck, P. C. (2008). A national profile of the health care experiences and family impact of autism spectrum disorder among children in the United States, 2005–2006. *Pediatrics*, *122*, e1149–e1158. http://dx.doi.org/10.1542/peds.2008-1057

Kuhl, P. K. (2007). Is speech learning "gated" by the social brain? *Developmental Science*, *10*, 110–120. http://dx.doi.org/10.1111/j.1467-7687.2007.00572.x

Lindgren, S., Wacker, D., Suess, A., Schieltz, K., Pelzel, K., Kopelman, T., . . . Waldron, D. (2016). Telehealth and autism: Treating challenging behavior at lower cost. *Pediatrics*, *137*(Suppl. 2), S167–S175. http://dx.doi.org/10.1542/peds.2015-2851O

Liptak, G. S., Stuart, T., & Auinger, P. (2006). Health care utilization and expenditures for children with autism: Data from U.S. national samples. *Journal of Autism and Developmental Disorders*, *36*, 871–879. http://dx.doi.org/10.1007/s10803-006-0119-9

Lovaas, O. I. (1987). Behavioral treatment and normal educational and intellectual functioning in young autistic children. *Journal of Consulting and Clinical Psychology*, *55*, 3–9. http://dx.doi.org/10.1037/0022-006X.55.1.3

Lubetsky, M. J., Handen, B. L., Lubetsky, M., & McGonigle, J. J. (2014). Systems of care for individuals with autism spectrum disorder and serious behavioral disturbance through the lifespan. *Child and Adolescent Psychiatric Clinics of North America*, *23*, 97–110. http://dx.doi.org/10.1016/j.chc.2013.08.004

Maskey, M., Warnell, F., Parr, J. R., Le Couteur, A., & McConachie, H. (2013). Emotional and behavioural problems in children with autism spectrum disorder. *Journal of Autism and Developmental Disorders, 43*, 851–859. http://dx.doi.org/ 10.1007/s10803-012-1622-9

Mayes, S. D., Calhoun, S. L., Aggarwal, R., Baker, C., Mathapati, S., Anderson, R., & Petersen, C. (2012). Explosive, oppositional and aggressive behavior in children with autism compared to other clinical disorders and typical children. *Research in Autism Spectrum Disorders, 6*, 1–10. http://dx.doi.org/10.1016/ j.rasd.2011.08.001

Mazurek, M. O., Kanne, S. M., & Wodka, E. L. (2013). Physical aggression in children and adolescents with autism spectrum disorders. *Research in Autism Spectrum Disorders, 7*, 455–465. http://dx.doi.org/10.1016/j.rasd.2012.11.004

McNeil, C. B., & Hembree-Kigin, T. L. (2011). *Parent–child interaction therapy* (2nd ed.). New York, NY: Springer.

Medical Home Initiatives for Children With Special Needs Project Advisory Committee, American Academy of Pediatrics. (2002). The medical home. *Pediatrics, 110*, 184–186.

Michelson, D., Davenport, C., Dretzke, J., Barlow, J., & Day, C. (2013). Do evidence-based interventions work when tested in the "real world?" A systematic review and meta-analysis of parent management training for the treatment of child disruptive behavior. *Clinical Child and Family Psychology Review, 16*, 18–34. http://dx.doi.org/10.1007/s10567-013-0128-0

Murphy, N. A., Carbone, P. S., & the Council on Children With Disabilities. (2011). Parent–provider–community partnerships: Optimizing outcomes for children with disabilities. *Pediatrics, 128*, 795–802. http://dx.doi.org/10.1542/ peds.2011-1467

National Institute for Health and Care Excellence. (2006). *Parent-training/education programs in the management of children with conduct disorders.* London, England: National Institute for Clinical Excellence.

National Research Council, Committee on Educational Interventions for Children With Autism. (2001). *Educating children with autism.* Washington, DC: National Academy Press.

Nefdt, N., Koegel, R., Singer, G., & Gerber, M. (2010). The use of a self-directed learning program to provide introductory training in pivotal response treatment to parents of children with autism. *Journal of Positive Behavior Interventions, 12*, 23–32. http://dx.doi.org/10.1177/1098300709334796

Nevill, R. E., Lecavalier, L., & Stratis, E. A. (2018). Meta-analysis of parent-mediated interventions for young children with autism spectrum disorder. *Autism, 22*, 84–98. http://dx.doi.org/10.1177/1362361316677838

Okuno, H., Nagai, T., Sakai, S., Mohri, I., Yamamoto, T., Yoshizaki, A., . . . Taniike, M. (2011). Effectiveness of modified parent training for mothers of children with pervasive developmental disorder on parental confidence and children's behavior. *Brain & Development, 33*, 152–160. http://dx.doi.org/10.1016/j.braindev.2010.03.007

Oono, I. P., Honey, E. J., & McConachie, H. (2013). Parent-mediated early intervention for young children with autism spectrum disorders (ASD). *Cochrane Database of Systematic Reviews, 2013*(4), 1–98. http://dx.doi.org/10.1002/14651858.CD009774.pub2

Parellada, M., Boada, L., Moreno, C., Llorente, C., Romo, J., Muela, C., & Arango, C. (2013). Specialty care programme for autism spectrum disorders in an urban population: A case-management model for health care delivery in an ASD population. *European Psychiatry, 28*, 102–109. http://dx.doi.org/10.1016/j.eurpsy.2011.06.004

Perry, A., Flanagan, H. E., Dunn Geier, J., & Freeman, N. L. (2009). Brief report: The Vineland Adaptive Behavior Scales in young children with autism spectrum disorders at different cognitive levels. *Journal of Autism and Developmental Disorders, 39*, 1066–1078. http://dx.doi.org/10.1007/s10803-009-0704-9

Piaget, J. (1966). *Psychology of intelligence.* Totowa, NJ: Littlefield Adams.

Postorino, V., Sharp, W. G., McCracken, C. E., Bearss, K., Burrell, T. L., Evans, A. N., & Scahill, L. (2017). A systematic review and meta-analysis of parent training for disruptive behavior in children with autism spectrum disorder. *Clinical Child and Family Psychology Review, 20*, 391–402. http://dx.doi.org/10.1007/s10567-017-0237-2

Reitzel, J., Summers, J., Lorv, B., Szatmari, P., Zwaigenbaum, L., Georgiades, S., & Duku, E. (2013). Pilot randomized controlled trial of a functional behavior skills training program for young children with autism spectrum disorder who have significant early learning skill impairments and their families. *Research in Autism Spectrum Disorders, 7*, 1418–1432. http://dx.doi.org/10.1016/j.rasd.2013.07.025

Research Units on Pediatric Psychopharmacology (RUPP) Autism Network. (2007). Parent training for children with pervasive developmental disorders: A multisite feasibility trial. *Behavioral Interventions, 22*, 179–199. http://dx.doi.org/10.1002/bin.236

Roberts, D., & Pickering, N. (2010). Parent training programme for autism spectrum disorders: An evaluation. *Community Practitioner, 83*, 27–30.

Roberts, J., Williams, K., Carter, M., Evans, D., Parmenter, T., Silove, N., . . . Warren, A. (2011). A randomized controlled trial of two early intervention programs for young children with autism: Centre-based with parent program and home-based. *Research in Autism Spectrum Disorders, 5*, 1553–1566. http://dx.doi.org/10.1016/j.rasd.2011.03.001

Rogers, S. J., Estes, A., Lord, C., Vismara, L., Winter, J., Fitzpatrick, A., . . . Dawson, G. (2012). Effects of a brief early start Denver model (ESDM)-based parent intervention on toddlers at risk for autism spectrum disorders: A randomized controlled trial. *Journal of the American Academy of Child & Adolescent Psychiatry, 51*, 1052–1065. http://dx.doi.org/10.1016/j.jaac.2012.08.003

Scahill, L., Bearss, K., Lecavalier, L., Smith, T., Swiezy, N., Aman, M. G., . . . Johnson, C. (2016). Effect of parent training on adaptive behavior in children with autism spectrum disorder and disruptive behavior: Results of a randomized trial. *Journal of the American Academy of Child & Adolescent Psychiatry, 55,* 602–609.e3. http://dx.doi.org/10.1016/j.jaac.2016.05.001

Scahill, L., McDougle, C. J., Aman, M. G., Johnson, C., Handen, B., Bearss, K., . . . Vitello, B. (2012). Effects of risperidone and parent training on adaptive functioning in children with pervasive developmental disorders and serious behavioral problems. *Journal of the American Academy of Child & Adolescent Psychiatry, 51,* 136–146. http://dx.doi.org/10.1016/j.jaac.2011.11.010

Schreibman, L., Dawson, G., Stahmer, A. C., Landa, R., Rogers, S. J., McGee, G. G., . . . Halladay, A. (2015). Naturalistic developmental behavioral interventions: Empirically validated treatments for autism spectrum disorder. *Journal of Autism and Developmental Disorders, 45,* 2411–2428. http://dx.doi.org/10.1007/s10803-015-2407-8

Schultz, T. R., Schmidt, C. T., & Stichter, J. P. (2011). A review of parent education programs for parents of children with autism spectrum disorders. *Focus on Autism and Other Developmental Disabilities, 26,* 96–104. http://dx.doi.org/10.1177/1088357610397346

Sharp, W. G., Berry, R. C., McCracken, C., Nuhu, N. N., Marvel, E., Saulnier, C. A., . . . Jaquess, D. L. (2013). Feeding problems and nutrient intake in children with autism spectrum disorders: A meta-analysis and comprehensive review of the literature. *Journal of Autism and Developmental Disorders, 43,* 2159–2173. http://dx.doi.org/10.1007/s10803-013-1771-5

Sharp, W. G., Jaquess, D. L., Morton, J. F., & Miles, A. G. (2011). A retrospective chart review of dietary diversity and feeding behavior of children with autism spectrum disorder before and after admission to a day-treatment program. *Focus on Autism and Other Developmental Disabilities, 26,* 37–48. http://dx.doi.org/10.1177/1088357609349245

Siller, M., Hutman, T., & Sigman, M. (2013). A parent-mediated intervention to increase responsive parental behaviors and child communication in children with ASD: A randomized clinical trial. *Journal of Autism and Developmental Disorders, 43,* 540–555. http://dx.doi.org/10.1007/s10803-012-1584-y

Simonoff, E., Pickles, A., Charman, T., Chandler, S., Loucas, T., & Baird, G. (2008). Psychiatric disorders in children with autism spectrum disorders: Prevalence, comorbidity, and associated factors in a population-derived sample. *Journal of the American Academy of Child & Adolescent Psychiatry, 47,* 921–929. http://dx.doi.org/10.1097/CHI.0b013e318179964f

Skinner, B. F. (1963). Operant behavior. *American Psychologist, 18,* 503–515. http://dx.doi.org/10.1037/h0045185

Smith, L. E., Greenberg, J. S., & Mailick, M. R. (2014). The family context of autism spectrum disorders: Influence on the behavioral phenotype and quality of life.

Child and Adolescent Psychiatric Clinics of North America, 23, 143–155. http://dx.doi.org/10.1016/j.chc.2013.08.006

Smith, T., Groen, A. D., & Wynn, J. W. (2000). Randomized trial of intensive early intervention for children with pervasive developmental disorder. *American Journal on Mental Retardation, 105,* 269–285. http://dx.doi.org/10.1352/0895-8017(2000)105<0269:RTOIEI>2.0.CO;2

Smith, T., Scahill, L., Dawson, G., Guthrie, D., Lord, C., Odom, S., . . . Wagner, A. (2007). Designing research studies on psychosocial interventions in autism. *Journal of Autism and Developmental Disorders, 37,* 354–366. http://dx.doi.org/10.1007/s10803-006-0173-3

Sofronoff, K., Leslie, A., & Brown, W. (2004). Parent management training and Asperger syndrome: A randomized controlled trial to evaluate a parent based intervention. *Autism, 8,* 301–317. http://dx.doi.org/10.1177/1362361304045215

Solomon, R., Necheles, J., Ferch, C., & Bruckman, D. (2007). Pilot study of a parent training program for young children with autism: The PLAY project home consultation program. *Autism, 11,* 205–224. http://dx.doi.org/10.1177/1362361307076842

Steiner, A. M., Koegel, L. K., Koegel, R. L., & Ence, W. A. (2012). Issues and theoretical constructs regarding parent education for autism spectrum disorders. *Journal of Autism and Developmental Disorders, 42,* 1218–1227. http://dx.doi.org/10.1007/s10803-011-1194-0

Sussman, F. (2012). *More than words: A parent's guide to building interaction and language skills for children with autism spectrum disorder or social communication difficulties.* Toronto, Ontario, Canada: The Hanen Centre.

Tellegen, C. L., & Sanders, M. R. (2014). A randomized controlled trial evaluating a brief parenting program with children with autism spectrum disorders. *Journal of Consulting and Clinical Psychology, 82,* 1193–1200. http://dx.doi.org/10.1037/a0037246

Tonge, B., Brereton, A., Kiomall, M., Mackinnon, A., King, N., & Rinehart, N. (2006). Effects on parental mental health of an education and skills training program for parents of young children with autism: A randomized controlled trial. *Journal of the American Academy of Child & Adolescent Psychiatry, 45,* 561–569. http://dx.doi.org/10.1097/01.chi.0000205701.48324.26

Tonge, B., Brereton, A., Kiomall, M., Mackinnon, A., & Rinehart, N. J. (2014). A randomised group comparison controlled trial of 'preschoolers with autism': A parent education and skills training intervention for young children with autistic disorder. *Autism, 18,* 166–177. http://dx.doi.org/10.1177/1362361312458186

Volkmar, F. R., & Wiesner, L. A. (2009). *A practical guide to autism: What every parent, family member, and teacher needs to know.* Hoboken, NJ: Wiley.

Vygotsky, L. S. (1962). *Thought and language.* Cambridge, MA: MIT Press. http://dx.doi.org/10.1037/11193-000

Wacker, D. P., Lee, J. F., Padilla Dalmau, Y. C., Kopelman, T. G., Lindgren, S. D., Kuhle, J., . . . Waldron, D. B. (2013). Conducting functional communication training via telehealth to reduce the problem behavior of young children with autism. *Journal of Developmental and Physical Disabilities*, 25, 35–48. http://dx.doi.org/10.1007/s10882-012-9314-0

Webster-Stratton, C. (n.d.). *The Incredible Years parent, teacher and child programs fact sheet*. Retrieved from http://www.incredibleyears.com

Whitaker, P. (2002). Supporting families of preschool children with autism: What parents want and what helps. *Autism*, 6, 411–426. http://dx.doi.org/10.1177/1362361302006004007

Whittingham, K., Sofronoff, K., Sheffield, J., & Sanders, M. R. (2009). Stepping Stones Triple P: An RCT of a parenting program with parents of a child diagnosed with an autism spectrum disorder. *Journal of Abnormal Child Psychology*, 37, 469–480. http://dx.doi.org/10.1007/s10802-008-9285-x (Erratum published 2014, *Journal of Abnormal Child Psychology*, 42, p. 1249. http://dx.doi.org/10.1007/s10802-014-9927-0)

Wilczynski, S., Green, G., Ricciardi, J., Boyd, B., Hume, A., Ladd, M., & Rue, H. (2009). *National standards report: The national standards project—Addressing the need for evidence-based practice guidelines for autism spectrum disorders*. Randolph, MA: The National Autism Center.

Wong, V. C. N., & Kwan, Q. K. (2010). Randomized controlled trial for early intervention for autism: A pilot study of the Autism 1-2-3 project. *Journal of Autism and Developmental Disorders*, 40, 677–688. http://dx.doi.org/10.1007/s10803-009-0916-z

2

CLINICAL ASSESSMENT OF CHILDREN WITH AUTISM SPECTRUM DISORDER BEFORE AND AFTER PARENT TRAINING

VALENTINA POSTORINO AND LAWRENCE SCAHILL

Disruptive behaviors, including tantrums, aggression, and self-injury, are common complaints by parents of young children with autism spectrum disorder (ASD; Mazurek, Kanne, & Wodka, 2013). These behaviors hinder the child's development of social, communication, and daily living skills, and often undermine parental sense of competence. Persistence of these disruptive behaviors in school-age children may result in restrictive educational placement and use of potent medications (Aman et al., 2009). There is a growing body of evidence that structured parent training (PT) programs can reduce disruptive behavior, improve daily living skills, and promote parental self-efficacy (Bearss et al., 2015; Iadarola et al., 2017; Postorino et al., 2017; Scahill, Bearss, Lecavalier, et al., 2016). PT uses direct instruction, role play, and homework assignments to build behavior management strategies in a relatively time-limited program (e.g., 6 months). PT programs vary in content, target age group, number of visits, and instructional methods. Common components

http://dx.doi.org/10.1037/0000111-003
Parent Training for Autism Spectrum Disorder: Improving the Quality of Life for Children and Their Families,
C. R. Johnson, E. M. Butter, and L. Scahill (Editors)

include education about the nature of disruptive behavior followed by strategies for prevention and for altering consequences.

PT is gradually moving out of the research environment and into practice (Bearss et al., 2018; Brookman-Frazee, Drahota, & Stadnick, 2012; Stadnick, Drahota, & Brookman-Frazee, 2013). In clinical practice, treatment begins with assessment. The information gathered during the initial evaluation is used to determine whether PT is a good fit for the parent and child. The decision on whether PT is a good fit for the child is based on the child's age, developmental level, severity of disruptive behavior, and review of previous treatments. For example, a 10-year-old child with severe aggression and tantrums may warrant a consultation for medication. For the parent, essential considerations include current level of psychosocial adversity for the family, as well as the parent's intellectual and language capacity. For example, a parent who is facing marked psychosocial adversity may need support through the current crisis before initiating PT. A parent who recently participated in PT that was not helpful may not be ready to try again—even if the prior program was not well delivered. Pretreatment assessment also is essential for monitoring progress over time (e.g., midtreatment, at the end of the treatment, and posttreatment).

This chapter describes contemporary assessment practices that can be used to determine whether the child with ASD is an appropriate candidate for PT that targets disruptive behavioral problems. The aim is to provide the essential elements of child and family history, as well as feasible diagnostic, cognitive, adaptive, and language assessments that can guide implementation of PT in clinical settings. This chapter describes methods of identifying and sorting out target behaviors to plan treatment and evaluate the child's progress overtime. A case vignette illustrates our approach to assessment.

COMPONENTS OF ASSESSMENT

An accurate assessment of the child and family situation is a prerequisite for well-informed treatment planning (Aman, 2005; Rutter, 2003). In clinical practice and research, information from multiple informants (e.g., parents, teachers) is commonly recommended because a child's behavior may vary in school compared with home. Children also may respond differently to limit-setting from mothers compared with fathers (Korsch & Petermann, 2014; Youngstrom, Loeber, & Stouthamer-Loeber, 2000). Along with informant-based measures, multiple data collection methods (e.g., interviews, observation, standardized tests) also are recommended.

In addition to gathering information about the child's behavior across settings, a detailed review of the child's medical, developmental, and treatment histories, as well as family composition and history, is warranted. The assessment will establish or confirm a preexisting diagnosis of ASD (i.e., *Diagnostic and Statistical Manual of Mental Disorders* [fifth ed.; *DSM–5*]; American Psychiatric Association, 2013) or pervasive developmental disorder (i.e., *International Classification of Diseases* [10th ed.; ICD–10]; World Health Organization, 2010).

Child and Family History

Child history includes

- prenatal/postnatal course;
- medical or genetic conditions that may affect the child's development; the review of the past medical history and current medical status should cover infectious disease, hospitalizations, surgeries, serious injuries, deafness, blindness, epilepsy, cerebral palsy, and asthma, and should consider specialized medical assessments, such as magnetic resonance imaging, electroencephalogram, or endoscopy;
- child's development: motor milestones and competencies (e.g., age and first walking unaided, status of gross and fine motor skills), language development, cognitive abilities and daily living skills, social skills, social interest, and play skills;
- educational history, current grade, placement, and current services (e.g., speech therapy, occupational therapy, social skills training, academic tutoring);
- evidence of regression (when an established set of developmental milestones were apparently achieved and then deteriorated);
- current and past treatments outside the school setting, including behavioral interventions, medication, speech therapy, and occupational therapy; this review includes the start dates (and stop dates, if not current), dose of the medication, and frequency of other treatments; the primary caregiver should be asked to describe benefits and adverse effects;
- findings from past diagnostic, cognitive, and language assessments;
- current behavioral problems and parental chief concerns; and
- additional areas, which may include sleep problems (see Chapter 6), feeding problems (see Chapter 7), and toileting problems (see Chapter 8).

Family history includes

- family composition, marital status of primary caregiver, racial and ethnic background, parental education, occupation, and a review of financial status and supports;

- psychiatric conditions in immediate family members and parents' first-degree relatives;
- current medical conditions of immediate family members that may affect caregiving;
- the caregiver(s) who would be available for the child's treatment (e.g., in PT, it is strongly preferred that the same caregiver attend each session to ensure continuity);
- parental practices (see Current Parental Practices section); and
- sources and level of parental stress.

Current Clinical Picture

The current clinical picture considers several domains, including psychiatric diagnosis, other medical problems, behavioral problems, and cognitive and language ability, as well as adaptive functioning. Commonly used measures are listed in Table 2.1. A full review of these measures is beyond the scope of this chapter. Here, we review measures that are germane to the clinical decision on whether to recommend PT for a child with ASD.

ASD Diagnosis

Some children referred for assessment and treatment may have already been diagnosed with ASD. Whenever possible, the actual report should be obtained. The Autism Diagnostic Observation Schedule, Second Edition (ADOS-2) and the Autism Diagnostic Interview-Revised (ADI-R) are considered the gold standard ASD diagnostic instruments (Lord et al., 2012; Lord, Rutter, & Le Couteur, 1994). These measures were developed as research tools to differentiate children with ASD from typically developing children and children with developmental delays without ASD. Thus, the application of these gold standard assessments in clinical practice may not be feasible in all settings. For example, the ADI-R is time consuming to administer, requiring 2 to 3 hours. The ADOS takes about 40 to 45 minutes but requires a substantial investment of training time for the clinician. Because the clinical diagnosis of ASD may be used to garner special educational services, however, clinicians in regional referral centers may decide that it is worth the investment to get clinicians trained in the ADOS-2.

In other settings, the assessment could also include informant-based rating scales to assist with the diagnosis, such as the Social Communication Questionnaire (SCQ); Social Responsiveness Scale, Second Edition (SRS-2); and Child and Adolescent Symptom Inventory-5 (CASI-5).

The SCQ is a 40-item parent-report screening questionnaire for ASD, based on ADI-R (Corsello et al., 2007; Rutter, Bailey, & Lord, 2003). It could

TABLE 2.1

Measures Commonly Used for Assessment of Children With ASD

Measure	Format	Age range	Administration time	Training
ASD diagnosis				
ADOS-2 (Lord et al., 2012)	Diagnostic interview	12 months to adult	30–50 min	Intensive
ADI-R (Lord et al., 1994)	Parent Interview	18 months to adult	1–2.5 hr	Intensive
CASI-5 (Gadow & Sprafkin, 2013)	Parent Questionnaire	5–18 years	1–2 hr	Moderate
SCQ (Corsello et al., 2007; Rutter et al., 2003)	Parent Questionnaire	4 years to adult	<10 min	Minimal
SRS-2 (Constantino & Gruber, 2012)	Parent Questionnaire	4 years to adult	<15 min	Minimal
Cognitive evaluation				
MSEL (Mullen, 1995)	Standardized test	Birth to 5 years, 8 months	15 min to 1 hr	Moderate
Leiter-3 (Roid & Miller, 2013)	Standardized test	3 years to adult	20–45 min	Moderate
SB-5 (Bain & Allin, 2005)	Standardized test	2 years to adult	5 min per subtest	Moderate
Adaptive behavior				
Vineland-3 (Sparrow et al., 2016)	Parent Interview	Birth to adult	20–60 min	Moderate
ABAS-3 (Harrison & Oakland, 2015)	Parent Questionnaire	Birth to adult	15–20 min	Minimal

(continues)

TABLE 2.1

Measures Commonly Used for Assessment of Children With ASD   *(Continued)*

Measure	Format	Age range	Administration time	Training
		Language		
MCDI	Questionnaire	8 to 30 months	5 min	Minimal
EVT-2	Standardized test	2 years 6 months to adult	10–20 min	Moderate
REOWPVT-4/EOWPVT-4	Standardized test	2 years to adult	15–25 min	Moderate
CELF-4	Standardized test	5 to 21 years	30–60 min	Moderate
PLS-4	Standardized test	Birth to 6 years 11 months	20–45 min	Moderate
CSBS-screen	Questionnaire	6 to 24 months	5–10 min	Minimal
		Behavior Problems		
ABC (Aman et al., 1985)	Parent questionnaire	3–18 years	10–15 min	—
HSQ-ASD (Chowdhury et al., 2016)	Parent questionnaire	3–14 years	10 min	—
Parent Target Problem list	Parent interview	3–18 years	15–20 min	Moderate

Note. ADOS-2 = Autism Diagnostic Observation Schedule, Second Edition; ADI-R = Autism Diagnostic Interview-Revised; CASI-5 = Child and Adolescent Symptom Inventory-5; SCQ = Social Communication Questionnaire; SRS-2 = Social Responsiveness Scale, Second Edition; MSEL = Mullen Scales of Early Learning; Leiter-3 = Leiter International Performance Scale, Third Edition; SB-5 = Stanford–Binet Intelligence Scales-Fifth Edition; Vineland-3 = Vineland Adaptive Behavior Scales, Third Edition; ABAS-3 = Adaptive Behavior Assessment System, Third Edition; MCDI = MacArthur–Bates Communicative Development Inventories; EVT-4 = Expressive Vocabulary Test, fourth edition; REOWPVT-4/EOWPVT-4 = Receptive and Expressive One-Word Picture Vocabulary Test; CELF-4 = Clinical Evaluation of Language Fundamentals, fourth edition; CSBS-screen = Communication and Symbolic Behavior Scales Developmental Profile Infant-Toddler Checklist-screen; PLS-4 = Preschool Language Scales, fourth edition; ABC = Aberrant Behavior Checklist; HSQ-ASD = Home Situations Questionnaire-Autism Spectrum Disorder.

be used to complement the ADOS or a systematic clinical diagnostic interview. The SCQ asks parents to indicate whether their child shows a particular symptom (current) and whether the symptom was present at age 4 to 5 years (lifetime). Because language items are not relevant for nonverbal children, they can be omitted. Total scores can range from 0 to 39 (the first item is a language screening question and is not included in the total score). Nineteen items rate current behavior, and 20 items rate behavior when the child was 4 to 5 years old. The cutoff score for ASD of ≥ 15 is predictive of an ASD diagnosis (Charman et al., 2007; Corsello et al., 2007). The SRS-2 is a 65-item questionnaire that measures the ability of a child age 4 to 18 years to engage in reciprocal social behavior (Constantino & Gruber, 2012). The SRS-2 has impressive normative data from several large community samples. Although the SRS-2 does not map directly onto *DSM–5* (American Psychiatric Association, 2013), a total score ≥ 65 is predictive of an ASD diagnosis (Charman et al., 2007).

The Child and Adolescent Symptom Inventory-5 (CASI-5) is a 173-item *DSM–5*–based checklist that asks parents to rate the severity of symptoms on the major *DSM–5* (American Psychiatric Association, 2013) diagnostic categories, including ASD (Gadow & Sprafkin, 2013). Each item is rated on a 4-point scale, where 0 = *never*, 1 = *sometimes*, 2 = *often*, and 3 = *very often*. Scores of 2 or higher are regarded a positive symptom. The CASI-5 can assist with the identification of other *DSM–5* conditions.

Cognitive and Adaptive Skills

Although cognitive ability and adaptive skills do not bear directly on the diagnosis of ASD, these domains are essential for assessment and treatment planning of children with ASD. Cognitive evaluation is essential for the clinician to make judgments about school placement, needed educational supports, and long-term outcome (Klin, Saulnier, Tsatsanis, & Volkmar, 2013).

Several commonly used IQ tests are used with children with ASD. The Leiter International Performance Scale, Third Edition (Leiter-3), is a measure of nonverbal intelligence that is appropriate for individuals with a mental age of 3 years or higher (Roid & Miller, 2013). Because the Leiter-3 does not rely on language, it can be used in children with moderate to severe language delay. Although it does not rely on expressive language, it requires the ability to sit at a table, maintain attention and interest, and follow the nonverbal instructions. For younger children, the Mullen Scales of Early Learning (for ages 1–68 months; Mullen, 1995) is commonly used. For children with spoken language, the Stanford–Binet Intelligence Scales-Fifth Edition (SB-5) is widely used to assess intellectual capacity (Bain & Allin, 2005). The abbreviated SB-5 battery, which includes the Nonverbal Fluid

Reasoning and Verbal Knowledge subtests, provides an efficient estimation of general intellectual abilities. This abbreviated battery takes 15 to 20 minutes to complete and has been successfully used in large-scale PT clinical trials (Aman et al., 2009; Bearss et al., 2015). Disadvantages of the abbreviated SB-5 include its reliance on language and its inability to measure IQ below 40. (For reviews on cognition in children with ASD, see Brunsdon & Happé, 2014, and Charman et al., 2011.)

The term *adaptive function* covers a range of behaviors across several domains of everyday life, including use of spoken and written language, capacity and performance in the age-appropriate social milieu, and performance of daily living skills (age-appropriate personal care). As described by the American Association of Intellectual and Developmental Disabilities (n.d.), the classification of intellectual disability requires evidence of intellectual limitation (IQ < 70) and adaptive skill deficits. In treatment planning, the identification of adaptive skill deficits offers a point of intervention. For instance, children with ASD and disruptive behavior are likely to show deficiencies in daily living skills (Scahill, Bearss, Lecavalier, et al., 2016). For example, the mother who regularly faces tantrums and aggression when trying to advance the child's ability to get dressed may understandably back off and complete the task to move on with the day. This pattern interferes with the child's acquisition of new skills, as well as the regular performance of current skills. Initially, PT may focus on reducing disruptive behavior and then offer instruction to parents for skill development (Scahill, Bearss, Lecavalier, et al., 2016).

The most widely used measure of adaptive skill is the Vineland Adaptive Behavior Scales (Vineland, Sparrow, Balla, & Cicchetti, 1984; Sparrow, Cicchetti, & Saulnier, 2016). The Vineland, now in its third edition (Vineland-3), is designed to measure adaptive behavior in children and adults from birth to 90 years of age (Sparrow et al., 2016). The Vineland-3 can be given as a parent-rated questionnaire (Parent/Caregiver Form; takes 20–25 minutes) or as a semistructured parent interview (Interview Form; takes about 35–45 minutes). As in previous versions, the Vineland-3 items are arranged from simple to more complex behaviors across three primary domains: Communication, Socialization, and Daily Living. Standard scores have a mean of 100 and standard deviation of 15. In addition to the standard scores, the Vineland-3 also yields raw scores and age equivalent scores for each domain. In children with intellectual disability without ASD, Vineland and IQ scores tend to be similar. In contrast, it has long been observed that children with ASD have lower Vineland scores than their IQ would predict (Bölte & Poustka, 2002; Green & Carter, 2014; Perry, Flanagan, Dunn Geier, & Freeman, 2009).

The Adaptive Behavior Assessment System, Third Edition, is a norm-referenced, informant questionnaire (e.g., parent or teacher) designed to measure adaptive functioning in individuals from birth to age 89 (Harrison & Oakland, 2015). It provides standard scores of 100 with a standard deviation of 15. The measure takes 15 to 20 minutes to complete and has demonstrated reliability and validity. Both the Vineland-3 and ABA-3 are available in Spanish.

Current Parental Practices

The challenges of raising a child with ASD and disruptive behavior prompt many parents to alter, adjust, and readjust parenting practices in search of what works. Parents of children with ASD and disruptive behavior who are seeking treatment often exclaim, "We've tried everything." It is also common to learn that mothers and fathers view the child's problems differently and adopt strategies that follow from their separate points of view. Thus, thorough, nonjudgmental assessment of parental perception of the problem and current parental management strategies is warranted. This frank discussion provides a starting place for adequate treatment planning. A theme that often emerges during the discussion of parenting practices is blame. The mother, who is often the primary caregiver, may hear from her partner or extended family members that the child's disruptive behavior is due to mother's permissiveness or lack of consistency. Mothers and fathers may hear from friends and relatives that misbehavior should be punished, that the child's tantrums are manipulative, or that using reward to promote positive behavior is bribing the child. These issues of parental self-blame and uncertainty about how to manage the child's disruptive behavior are not unique to ASD (Kazdin, 2008). Recognizing the signs of parental self-blame and perceived incompetence during the assessment can lead to a useful discussion with the parent about the nature of the child's misbehavior. Analogies to the challenges of raising a child with a medical problem, such as diabetes—in which parents must learn multiple management strategies that other parents do not—may help parents get past self-blame. Permission and encouragement to move beyond parental self-blame by the clinician may set the stage for parental readiness to learn new strategies and even retry discarded strategies. PT offers specific strategies delivered in a stepwise manner to achieve behavior change (see Chapter 5).

Parenting Efficacy, Caregiver Strain, and Parent Stress

Parents who struggle with self-blame and uncertainty may not feel ready to meet the daily challenges of the child's seemingly perplexing disruptive behavior. Ironically, this erosion of self-efficacy may contribute to lower parental effectiveness (Jones & Prinz, 2005; Shumow & Lomax, 2002). The Parenting Sense of Competence (PSOC) scale (Johnston & Mash, 1989) is a 16-item scale designed to measure parental efficacy (i.e., confidence in the parenting role) and parental satisfaction (i.e., level of frustration, anxiety, and motivation in parenting role). Items are rated on a 6-point Likert scale with high scores representing higher degree of satisfaction and efficacy. Adoption and mastery of PT strategies promote improvement in parental self-efficacy, as measured on the PSOC (Iadarola et al., 2017).

Parental stress and caregiver strain are closely related to self-efficacy. Caregiver strain reflects self-perceived threat to emotional health, physical health, social life, and financial status as a result of parenting (Arai, 2004). Elevated caregiver strain can adversely affect caregiver health outcomes and caregiving (Khanna et al., 2011; Sales, Greeno, Shear, & Anderson, 2004). The Caregiver Strain Questionnaire (Brannan, Heflinger, & Bickman, 1997) is a 21-item, parent self-reported measure rated on a 5-point scale from 1 (*not at all a problem*) to 5 (*very much a problem*). It consists of three dimensions: Objective Strain, Internalized Strain, and Externalized Strain. It also includes a global score. The Objective subscale includes 11 items that capture the negative consequences of caregiving on personal time, work, family finances, and social isolation. The Internalized Strain subscale includes six items that ask about the caregiver's feelings of worry, guilt, and unhappiness. The four-item Externalized Strain subscale reflects parental anger, embarrassment, and resentment toward the child. The score for each subscale is totaled and then divided by the number of items in the subscale to obtain a per-item mean. Per-item mean scores of 2 or greater on the Objective Strain and Externalized Strain subscales, and scores greater than 3 on the Internalized Strain are worthy of discussion with parents at the start of treatment.

It is well documented that the day-to-day stress for parents of a child with ASD is greater than the stress of raising a typically developing child (Hayes & Watson, 2013). Not surprisingly, children with ASD and disruptive behavior present even greater parenting challenges, which may amplify parental stress and reduce parental effectiveness (Osborne, McHugh, Saunders, & Reed, 2008). The 36-item Parent Stress Index-Short Form (PSI-SF) is a widely used parent self-report designed to measure stress that may be useful in clinical practice and research (Abidin, 1995). The PSI-SF consists of three 12-item subscales: Parental Distress (perceived lack of social support and depression); Parent–Child Dysfunctional Interaction (satisfactory versus unsatisfactory parent–child interactions); and Difficult Child (child's behavior that affects the complexity of caregiving). Each item is rated on a 5-point scale, and some items are reverse scored. The PSI total score is the sum of all items and can be compared with normative data in the PSI manual. The 90th percentile of the total PSI-SF score represents a "clinically significant" level of parenting stress.

Target Behaviors

When describing the child's disruptive behavior, parents often can provide exquisite detail on the child's tantrums, aggression, self-injury, property destruction, and reckless behavior. On initial evaluation, parents may be less sure about the situations and events that precede disruptive behavior. Similarly, parents may not recognize the ways in which their response to the child's disruptive behavior may inadvertently reinforce the behavior. For example, a child may learn that tantrums allow escape from a routine demand. Escape from an unwanted activity serves as a reward and increases the likelihood that the child will have a tantrum in similar future situations. A child who is set on obtaining a specific object (e.g., food or a preferred toy) may learn over time that self-injurious behavior results in obtaining the object of interest. Escape from a routine demand or interest in obtaining a specific object may be considered the purpose or function of the behavior (Beavers, Iwata, & Lerman, 2013; Hanley, Iwata, & McCord, 2003). (For a full discussion of functional analysis and related behavioral interventions, see Chapter 5). The three main types of functional assessment include functional analysis, descriptive assessment, and indirect assessment (Hanley et al., 2003).

Functional analysis involves direct observation of behavior and manipulation of environmental events to identify what is maintaining the behavior (Beavers et al., 2013). It is conducted in controlled settings, is time consuming, and requires specialized training. Therefore, functional analysis may be difficult to apply in clinical practice (Hanley et al., 2003). *Descriptive assessment* involves direct observation of behavior in naturalistic settings (e.g., home or classroom) but without any manipulation of environmental conditions (Beavers et al., 2013; Hanley et al., 2003). *Indirect assessment* relies on interview or rating scales from the primary caregiver (Hanley et al., 2003). The indirect approach is not as detailed as the more formal functional analysis. However, it is less time consuming and may be useful in clinical practice.

Informant-based rating scales (e.g., completed by a parent or teacher) may not identify the function of the child's disruptive behavior but may provide insight into the nature and severity of the child's disruptive behavior. Common informant-based measures with established validity and reliability include the 58-item Aberrant Behavior Checklist (ABC) and the 24-item Home Situations Questionnaire-Autism Spectrum Disorder (HSQ-ASD; see Chapter 5; Aman, Singh, Stewart, & Field, 1985; Chowdhury et al., 2016).

For the assessment of feeding and sleep problems, parent ratings, such as the Brief Autism Mealtime Behavior Inventory (see Chapter 7) and the Family Inventory of Sleep Habits (see Chapter 6), may be useful.

Parent target problems. Although informant-based rating scales can provide useful data in the clinical assessment, focused interviews with a parent may identify child-specific problems that may not be captured in standardized rating scales. The parent target problem (PTP) method involves a semistructured interview to identify the child's two most pressing problems for the parent (Arnold et al., 2003; Scahill, Bearss, Sarhangian, et al., 2016). This interview begins by asking the parent to nominate the top two problems. Through brief discussion, the frequency (for episodic behaviors) or constancy (for problems, such as hyperactivity reflecting more enduring patterns), intensity, and impact of each behavioral problem on the family are established. The findings are summarized in a brief narrative, and parents can be asked to validate the description—making adjustments to the baseline narrative—as necessary (see Table 2.2). At subsequent clinic visits, the baseline narrative can be reviewed and a new narrative can be documented to reflect current behavior. This review can be used to track progress in treatment (Scahill et al., 2015).

Clinical Global Impression scales. The Clinical Global Impression-Severity (CGI-S) and the Clinical Global Impression-Improvement (CGI-I) are clinician-rated measures of overall severity and improvement over time (CGI-I; Guy, 1976). The CGI-S is a 7-point severity scale ranging from 1 to 7 (i.e., 1 = *normal, not at all ill*; 2 = *borderline mentally ill*; 3 = *mildly ill*; 4 = *moderately ill*; 5 = *markedly ill*; 6 = *severely ill*; 7 = *among the most extremely ill patients*). To rate the CGI-S, the clinician considers the degree of social impairment, level of repetitive behavior, presence and degree of language delay, and behavioral problems (e.g., tantrums, aggression, self-injury, hyperactivity). By convention, a child with ASD uncomplicated by high levels of social impairment, repetitive behavior, language delay, or disruptive behavior would be given a CGI-S of 3. A CGI-S of 7 is reserved for extreme cases that likely need inpatient care. In outpatient settings, most children with ASD will fall into moderate (i.e., CGI-S of 4), marked (i.e., CGI-S of 5) or severe (i.e., CGI-S of 6) categories. A 5-year-old, hyperactive, although not aggressive, child who is managed in a structured school classroom but poses more problems at home would fit with a CGI-S of 4. A similar child whose hyperactivity poses a problem at home and school—despite a structured program—would probably warrant a CGI-S of 5. In practice, clinicians base the CGI-S on all available information, including the clinical interview, rating scales, and observation.

The CGI-I is also a 7-point scale (i.e., 1 = *very much improved*; 2 = *much improved*; 3 = *minimally improved*; 4 = *no change from baseline*; 5 = *minimally*

TABLE 2.2
Examples of Parent Target Problem Narratives

Problem	Description
Aggression	Occurs at home, at school, and in public settings (e.g., grocery store) from two to 10 times per day—average lately is five. Includes hitting, pinching, biting, throwing objects. Mother is source of routine demands and aggression mostly directed toward her (she has several bruises). Stressful for family. Mother discouraged and feels resentment sometimes.
Tantrums	Occur two to three times per day, lasting 2–10 minutes. Occur at school and at home. Behaviors include yelling, crying, screaming, protesting, throwing self on the floor. Occur if demands are not met, routine is not followed, or in transitions. Mother at a loss about how to handle it. Reluctant to take him to public places.
Self-injury	Occurs five to seven times per day, lasting seconds to minutes. Hits head against hard surfaces, such as table, doors, etc. Results in bruising, swelling on his forehead. Parents need to be vigilant; they avoid taking child to other people's houses or public places, such as restaurants.
Hyperactivity	On the go most of the time (at least 75% of the time). Can't sit still for more than a few minutes. Is not able to sit through dinner—runs around the table grabbing food. Jumps from one piece of furniture to another. May bolt in public places—doesn't stop on request. Needs close supervision due to his reckless behavior. Mother won't take him to public places by herself. Parents have to plan outings carefully.
Noncompliance	Occurs several times per hour at home whenever a demand (e.g., getting dressed) is placed on him. Episodes last up to 5 minutes. He whines and yells "no" or runs away. It takes a lot of parental effort to calm him down. Parents are stressed; other adult family members (e.g., grandmother) refrain from placing any demands on him to keep things quiet. Mother: "He runs the house."
Food selectivity	Every meal, every day. Only eats dry, crunchy carbohydrates. Insists on certain brands of food (e.g., of granola bars). Parents have to buy these specific brands to avoid protest and refusal to eat. Demand on food preparation is rigid (e.g., toasted bread has to be just right). Foods can't touch on the plate. If food is not right, he'll have a meltdown of screaming and yelling for up to 30 minutes, and refuse to eat. Dominates family life. Family will not go to a restaurant.
Midsleep awakening	Almost every night, gets up in the middle of night between 2 a.m. and 4 a.m.—awake for up to 2 hours. When up, she may go to the bathroom, call for mom (parents' bedroom is upstairs, she is downstairs), may just play in own room with lights on/off, or may wander around the house. Mother is tired—not getting enough sleep. Child's nighttime behavior also may wake up other family members.
Bolting	Whenever he can, he runs away in public places (e.g., grocery store, store parking lot, mall). Will not hold mother's hand. Needs to be in a stroller. Several times a day, tries to leave the house—parents had to add a key lock on the inside to keep him from taking off. If someone comes to the house—have to hold him back so he won't run away. Parents very concerned about potential safety.

TABLE 2.3
Marc's Baseline Test Scores

Abbreviated SB-5	
Nonverbal	106
Verbal	90
Full scale	98
Vineland	
Communication	74
Socialization	59
Daily living	75
ABC	
Irritability	24
Social withdrawal	16
Stereotypy	8
Hyperactivity	28
Inappropriate speech	10
HSQ	3.8

Note. SB-5 = Stanford–Binet Intelligence Scales, Fifth Edition (Bain & Allin, 2005); ABC = Aberrant Behavior Checklist (Aman et al., 1985); HSQ = Home Situations Questionnaire-Autism Spectrum Disorder (Chowdhury et al., 2016).

worse; 6 = *much worse*; 7 = *very much worse*). The CGI-I compares the child's current behavior with baseline. The combined use of PTPs and the CGI-I can help the clinician and parent stay focused on the problems that brought the child into treatment. The baseline PTP narratives can be read to the parent, and a comment elicited on each metric in the baseline narrative (e.g., frequency, intensity and duration, and the impact of the behavior on the family). An example of the combined use of the PTPs and the CGI-I for a child treated with PT at baseline, Weeks 12 and 24, is presented in Table 2.3.

CASE EXAMPLE

Marc[1] is a 4-and-a-half-year-old Caucasian boy who lives with his biological parents and a 2-year-old sister in the family home. He attends an all-day prekindergarten program that is mixed mainstream and special education. He was delivered vaginally at term following an uncomplicated pregnancy. Marc's mother recalls that he did not start speaking single words until 15 months. Marc started walking at 12 months. Marc attended a day

---

[1]Clinical material has been disguised to protect client confidentiality.

care setting at about age 2 and a half years. Within a few months of starting day care, the staff told Marc's mother that he showed a lack of interest in other children and that his language was delayed compared with his classmates. He was not fully toilet trained until 3 years, 6 months. Marc's mother consulted with the pediatrician, who referred Marc to an autism clinic at the regional medical center. Marc was seen there just before his fourth birthday. The team evaluation included interviews about his developmental and medical histories. The assessment included the SCQ, ADOS, abbreviated SB, Vineland, Expressive Vocabulary Test, Second Edition (EVT-2; Williams, 2007), and Clinical Evaluation of Language Fundamentals-Preschool version (CELF-P; Semel, Wiig, & Secord, 2003) version. Marc's mother also completed the ABC and the HSQ-ASD (see Table 2.3). In the current pre-kindergarten program, Marc receives 1 hour, 30 minutes per week of speech therapy (1 hour of individual, 30 minutes of group), and 1 hour per week of occupational therapy.

The findings on the SCQ and ADOS were consistent with the team's clinical impression of ASD. Soon after that assessment, he was placed in his current school program. On the abbreviated SB-5, Marc performed in the average range (full-scale IQ = 98). Vineland scores were 15 to 20 points below that IQ estimate. Marc obtained an EVT-2 standard score of 91, indicating that his ability to name objects was in the average range. In contrast, the score of 71 on the CELF-P indicated that he was nearly two standard deviations below his age mates in his understanding of language structure—how words are put together in sentences.

A CGI-S score of 5 (i.e., marked) was warranted, given the presence, frequency, and intensity of aggression, angry outbursts, and noncompliant behavior; the impact of those behavioral problems on the family's life; and the language delay. Marc was an appropriate candidate for PT focused on disruptive behavior.

Marc's mother attended 11 PT sessions over 16 weeks and two review sessions over the ensuing 4 weeks. Table 2.4 shows the baseline and revised narratives of the PTPs, as well as the Aberrant Behavior Checklist-Irritability subscale, and the per-item mean scores on the HSQ-ASD at Weeks 12 and 24. At Week 12, there was clear movement in the right direction. However, Marc's behaviors still posed a daily challenge to his parents. A CGI-S of 4 (i.e., moderate) and a CGI-I of 3 (i.e., minimally improved) indicated that continued treatment was warranted. By Week 24, there were significant reductions in Marc's aggression, outbursts, and noncompliant behaviors. The family was more willing to go to public places, and Marc's mother also reported a reduction in level of stress. Based on the information provided by the care-givers regarding Marc's target behaviors, a CGI-I score of 2 (i.e., markedly improved) was warranted.

TABLE 2.4
Marc's Baseline, Week 12 and Weeks 24 PTPs, ABC-I, HSQ-ASD, and CGI Scores

PTPs	Baseline	Week 12	Week 24
Aggression	Occurs when angry; other times, hits, and pulls mother's hair when not angry: five times/day at home and one to two times/day at school. Most of the time aggression is in context of demand or with limit-setting. Via mother: His behavior is unpredictable. Family treads lightly most of the time. Household in chaos.	Occurs when angry; only some-times occurs in the absence of anger. Hitting three times/day. Accepts prompts not to hit. No reports of hitting at school lately. With routine demands and limit-setting, may have angry outbursts without aggression. Behavior is unpredictable. Family treads lightly about half the time.	May get angry: Stomps his feet, may whine—a few times a day. No hitting or hair pulling over past few weeks at home or school with limit-setting, or with routine demands. May yell—but outbursts are short lived. Household is not in chaos. Family rarely has to tread lightly.
Noncompliance	Occurs every day—most of the time. Mother has to cajole and work around his noncompliance. He may ignore request or actively protest (e.g., run away, yelling "no"). Everything takes longer; sometimes mother gives up (e.g., forgets about bath). Situation would be worse— if mother placed usual demands on him. Household revolves around him. Tension between parents on how to handle.	Occurs at least a few times a day. Mother is not avoiding all routine demands, but at least once a day she has to work around his noncompliant behavior. He may ignore request or yell and run off to escape. Some daily tasks take longer, may require coaxing. Sometimes mother finishes the job or gives up (e.g., bath). Less tension between parents.	Compliant 50% of the time. When noncompliant, may yell and scream. Short lived. Mother does have to "work around" and cajole to get his compliance. But she often places usual demands of daily living on him with success. Family life does not "revolve around him." No tension between parents.
CGI-S	5	4	4
CGI-I	—[a]	3	2
ABC-I	24	18	12
HSQ-ASD	3.8	3.0	2.2

Note. PTPs = parent target problems; ABC-I = Aberrant Behavior Checklist-Irritability subscale (Aman et al., 1985); HSQ-ASD = Home Situations Questionnaire-Autism Spectrum Disorder (Chowdhury et al., 2016); CGI = Clinical Global Impression (Guy, 1976); CGI-S = Clinical Global Impression-Severity (Guy, 1976); CGI-I = Clinical Global Impression-Improvement (CGI-I; Guy, 1976) scale at baseline because this measure is rated based on the child's improvement in current behavior during treatment. Therefore, this measure compares the child's current behavior with baseline.
[a]The table does not report data for the Clinical Global Impression-Improvement (CGI-I; Guy, 1976) scale at baseline because this measure is rated based on the child's improvement in current behavior during treatment. Therefore, this measure compares the child's current behavior with baseline.

REFERENCES

Abidin, R. R. (1995). *Parenting stress index* (3rd ed.). Odessa, FL: Psychological Assessment Resource.

Aman, M. G. (2005). Treatment planning for patients with autism spectrum disorders. *Journal of Clinical Psychiatry, 66*(Suppl. 10), 38–45.

Aman, M. G., McDougle, C. J., Scahill, L., Handen, B., Arnold, L. E., Johnson, C., . . . Wagner, A. (2009). Medication and parent training in children with pervasive developmental disorders and serious behavior problems: Results from a randomized clinical trial. *Journal of the American Academy of Child & Adolescent Psychiatry, 48,* 1143–1154. http://dx.doi.org/10.1097/CHI.0b013e3181bfd669

Aman, M. G., Singh, N. N., Stewart, A. W., & Field, C. J. (1985). The aberrant behavior checklist: A behavior rating scale for the assessment of treatment effects. *American Journal of Mental Deficiency, 89,* 485–491.

American Association of Intellectual and Developmental Disabilities. (n.d.). *Definition of intellectual disability.* Retrieved from http://aaidd.org/intellectual-disability/definition

American Psychiatric Association. (2013). *Diagnostic and statistical manual of mental disorders* (5th ed.). Arlington, VA: Author.

Arai, Y. (2004). Family caregiver burden in the context of the long-term care insurance system. *Journal of Epidemiology, 14,* 139–142. http://dx.doi.org/10.2188/jea.14.139

Arnold, L. E., Vitiello, B., McDougle, C., Scahill, L., Shah, B., Gonzalez, N. M., . . . Tierney, E. (2003). Parent-defined target symptoms respond to risperidone in RUPP autism study: Customer approach to clinical trials. *Journal of the American Academy of Child & Adolescent Psychiatry, 42,* 1443–1450. http://dx.doi.org/10.1097/00004583-200312000-00011

Bain, S. K., & Allin, J. D. (2005). Book review: Stanford–Binet Intelligence Scales, Fifth Edition. *Journal of Psychoeducational Assessment, 23,* 87–95. http://dx.doi.org/10.1177/073428290502300108

Bearss, K., Burrell, T. L., Challa, S. A., Postorino, V., Gillespie, S. E., Crooks, C., & Scahill, L. (2018). Feasibility of parent training via telehealth for children with autism spectrum disorder and disruptive behavior: A demonstration pilot. *Journal of Autism and Developmental Disorders, 48,* 1020–1030. http://dx.doi.org/10.1007/s10803-017-3363-2

Bearss, K., Johnson, C., Smith, T., Lecavalier, L., Swiezy, N., Aman, M., . . . Scahill, L. (2015). Effect of parent training vs parent education on behavioral problems in children with autism spectrum disorder: A randomized clinical trial. *JAMA, 313,* 1524–1533. http://dx.doi.org/10.1001/jama.2015.3150

Beavers, G. A., Iwata, B. A., & Lerman, D. C. (2013). Thirty years of research on the functional analysis of problem behavior. *Journal of Applied Behavior Analysis, 46,* 1–21. http://dx.doi.org/10.1002/jaba.30

Bölte, S., & Poustka, F. (2002). The relation between general cognitive level and adaptive behavior domains in individuals with autism with and without co-morbid mental retardation. *Child Psychiatry and Human Development, 33,* 165–172. http://dx.doi.org/10.1023/A:1020734325815

Brannan, A. M., Heflinger, C. A., & Bickman, L. (1997). The caregiver strain questionnaire: Measuring the impact on the family of living with a child with serious emotional problems. *Journal of Emotional and Behavioral Disorders, 5,* 212–222. http://dx.doi.org/10.1177/106342669700500404

Brookman-Frazee, L. I., Drahota, A., & Stadnick, N. (2012). Training community mental health therapists to deliver a package of evidence-based practice strategies for school-age children with autism spectrum disorders: A pilot study. *Journal of Autism and Developmental Disorders, 42,* 1651–1661. http://dx.doi.org/10.1007/s10803-011-1406-7

Brunsdon, V. E. A., & Happé, F. (2014). Exploring the "fractionation" of autism at the cognitive level. *Autism, 18,* 17–30. http://dx.doi.org/10.1177/1362361313499456

Charman, T., Baird, G., Simonoff, E., Loucas, T., Chandler, S., Meldrum, D., & Pickles, A. (2007). Efficacy of three screening instruments in the identification of autistic-spectrum disorders. *British Journal of Psychiatry, 191,* 554–559. http://dx.doi.org/10.1192/bjp.bp.107.040196

Charman, T., Jones, C. R. G., Pickles, A., Simonoff, E., Baird, G., & Happé, F. (2011). Defining the cognitive phenotype of autism. *Brain Research, 1380,* 10–21. http://dx.doi.org/10.1016/j.brainres.2010.10.075

Chowdhury, M., Aman, M. G., Lecavalier, L., Smith, T., Johnson, C., Swiezy, N., . . . Scahill, L. (2016). Factor structure and psychometric properties of the revised Home Situations Questionnaire for autism spectrum disorder: The Home Situations Questionnaire-Autism Spectrum Disorder. *Autism, 20,* 528–537. http://dx.doi.org/10.1177/1362361315593941

Constantino, J. N., & Gruber, C. P. (2012). *The Social Responsiveness Scale Manual, Second Edition (SRS-2).* Los Angeles, CA: Western Psychological Services.

Corsello, C., Hus, V., Pickles, A., Risi, S., Cook, E. H., Jr., Leventhal, B. L., & Lord, C. (2007). Between a ROC and a hard place: Decision making and making decisions about using the SCQ. *Journal of Child Psychology and Psychiatry, 48,* 932–940. http://dx.doi.org/10.1111/j.1469-7610.2007.01762.x

Gadow, K. D., & Sprafkin, J. (2013). *Adolescent Symptom Inventory 5: Screening manual.* Stony Brook, NY: Checkmate Plus.

Green, S. A., & Carter, A. S. (2014). Predictors and course of daily living skills development in toddlers with autism spectrum disorders. *Journal of Autism and Developmental Disorders, 44,* 256–263. http://dx.doi.org/10.1007/s10803-011-1275-0

Guy, W. (Ed.). (1976). *ECDEU assessment manual for psychopharmacology* (DHEW Publication No. 76-338). Washington, DC: U.S. Government Printing Office.

Hanley, G. P., Iwata, B. A., & McCord, B. E. (2003). Functional analysis of problem behavior: A review. *Journal of Applied Behavior Analysis, 36,* 147–185. http://dx.doi.org/10.1901/jaba.2003.36-147

Harrison, P. L., & Oakland, T. (2015). *Adaptive Behavior Assessment System* (3rd ed.). Minneapolis, MN: Pearson Assessment.

Hayes, S. A., & Watson, S. L. (2013). The impact of parenting stress: A meta-analysis of studies comparing the experience of parenting stress in parents of children with and without autism spectrum disorder. *Journal of Autism and Developmental Disorders, 43,* 629–642. http://dx.doi.org/10.1007/s10803-012-1604-y

Iadarola, S., Levato, L., Harrison, B., Smith, T., Lecavalier, L., Johnson, C., . . . Scahill, L. (2017). Teaching parents behavioral strategies for autism spectrum disorder (ASD): Effects on stress, strain, and competence. *Journal of Autism and Developmental Disorders, 48,* 1031–1040.

Johnston, C., & Mash, E. J. (1989). A measure of parenting satisfaction and efficacy. *Journal of Clinical Child Psychology, 18,* 167–175. http://dx.doi.org/10.1207/s15374424jccp1802_8

Jones, T. L., & Prinz, R. J. (2005). Potential roles of parental self-efficacy in parent and child adjustment: A review. *Clinical Psychology Review, 25,* 341–363. http://dx.doi.org/10.1016/j.cpr.2004.12.004

Kazdin, A. E. (2008). Evidence-based treatment and practice: New opportunities to bridge clinical research and practice, enhance the knowledge base, and improve patient care. *American Psychologist, 63,* 146–159. http://dx.doi.org/10.1037/0003-066X.63.3.146

Khanna, R., Madhavan, S. S., Smith, M. J., Patrick, J. H., Tworek, C., & Becker-Cottrill, B. (2011). Assessment of health-related quality of life among primary caregivers of children with autism spectrum disorders. *Journal of Autism and Developmental Disorders, 41,* 1214–1227. http://dx.doi.org/10.1007/s10803-010-1140-6

Klin, A., Saulnier, C., Tsatsanis, K., & Volkmar, F. R. (2013). Clinical evaluation in autism spectrum disorders: Psychological assessment within a transdisciplinary framework. In F. R. Volkmar, R. Paul, A. Klin, & D. J. Cohen (Eds.), *Handbook of autism and pervasive developmental disorders: Vol. 2. Assessment, interventions, and policy* (3rd ed., pp. 772–798). Hoboken, NJ: Wiley. http://dx.doi.org/10.1002/9780470939352.ch3

Korsch, F., & Petermann, F. (2014). Agreement between parents and teachers on preschool children's behavior in a clinical sample with externalizing behavioral problems. *Child Psychiatry and Human Development, 45,* 617–627. http://dx.doi.org/10.1007/s10578-013-0430-6

Lord, C., Rutter, M., DiLavore, P. C., Risi, S., Gotham, K., & Bishop, S. L. (2012). *Autism Diagnostic Observation Schedule, Second Edition (ADOS-2) manual (Part I): Modules 1–4.* Torrance, CA: Western Psychological Services.

Lord, C., Rutter, M., & Le Couteur, A. (1994). Autism Diagnostic Interview-Revised: A revised version of a diagnostic interview for caregivers of individuals with possible pervasive developmental disorders. *Journal of Autism and Developmental Disorders, 24,* 659–685. http://dx.doi.org/10.1007/BF02172145

Mazurek, M. O., Kanne, S. M., & Wodka, E. L. (2013). Physical aggression in children and adolescents with autism spectrum disorders. *Research in Autism Spectrum Disorders, 7,* 455–465. http://dx.doi.org/10.1016/j.rasd.2012.11.004

Mullen, E. M. (1995). *Mullen Scales of Early Learning: AGS edition.* Circle Pines, MN: American Guidance Service.

Osborne, L. A., McHugh, L., Saunders, J., & Reed, P. (2008). Parenting stress reduces the effectiveness of early teaching interventions for autistic spectrum disorders. *Journal of Autism and Developmental Disorders, 38,* 1092–1103. http://dx.doi.org/10.1007/s10803-007-0497-7

Perry, A., Flanagan, H. E., Dunn Geier, J., & Freeman, N. L. (2009). Brief report: The Vineland Adaptive Behavior Scales in young children with autism spectrum disorders at different cognitive levels. *Journal of Autism and Developmental Disorders, 39,* 1066–1078. http://dx.doi.org/10.1007/s10803-009-0704-9

Postorino, V., Sharp, W. G., McCracken, C. E., Bearss, K., Burrell, T. L., Evans, A. N., & Scahill, L. (2017). A systematic review and meta-analysis of parent training for disruptive behavior in children with autism spectrum disorder. *Clinical Child and Family Psychology Review, 20,* 391–402. http://dx.doi.org/10.1007/s10567-017-0237-2

Roid, G. M., & Miller, L. J. (2013). *Leiter International Performance Scale-Revised: Examiners manual.* Wood Dale, IL: Stoelting.

Rutter, M. (2003). *Handbook of Assessment and Treatment Planning for Psychological Disorders* [Review of book]. *Psychiatric Services, 54,* 757. http://dx.doi.org/10.1176/appi.ps.54.5.757

Rutter, M., Bailey, A., & Lord, C. (2003). *The Social Communication Questionnaire (SCQ).* Torrance, CA: Western Psychological Services.

Sales, E., Greeno, C., Shear, M. K., & Anderson, C. (2004). Maternal caregiving strain as a mediator in the relationship between child and mother mental health problems. *Social Work Research, 28,* 211–223. http://dx.doi.org/10.1093/swr/28.4.211

Scahill, L., Bearss, K., Lecavalier, L., Smith, T., Swiezy, N., Aman, M. G., . . . Johnson, C. (2016). Effect of parent training on adaptive behavior in children with autism spectrum disorder and disruptive behavior: Results of a randomized trial. *Journal of the American Academy of Child & Adolescent Psychiatry, 55,* 602–609.e3. http://dx.doi.org/10.1016/j.jaac.2016.05.001

Scahill, L., Bearss, K., Sarhangian, R., McDougle, C. J., Arnold, L. E., Aman, M. G., . . . Vitiello, B. (2016). Using a patient-centered outcome measure to test methylphenidate versus placebo in children with autism spectrum disorder. *Journal of Child and Adolescent Psychopharmacology.* Advance online publication. http://dx.doi.org/10.1089/cap.2016.0107

Scahill, L., McCracken, J. T., King, B. H., Rockhill, C., Shah, B., Politte, L., . . . McDougle, C. J. (2015). Extended-release guanfacine for hyperactivity in children with autism spectrum disorder. *American Journal of Psychiatry, 172,* 1197–1206. http://dx.doi.org/10.1176/appi.ajp.2015.15010055

Semel, E., Wiig, E. H., & Secord, W. A. (2003). *Clinical evaluation of language fundamentals* (4th ed.). San Antonio, TX: Psychological Corporation.

Shumow, L., & Lomax, R. (2002). Parental self-efficacy: Predictor of parenting behaviour adolescent outcomes. *Parenting: Science and Practice, 2,* 127–150. http://dx.doi.org/10.1207/S15327922PAR0202_03

Sparrow, S. S., Balla, D. A., & Cicchetti, D. V. (1984). *Vineland Adaptive Behavior Scales.* Circle Pines, MN: American Guidance Service.

Sparrow, S. S., Cicchetti, D. V., & Saulnier, C. A. (2016). *Vineland Adaptive Behavior Scales, Third Edition* (Vineland-3). Circle Pines, MN: American Guidance Service.

Stadnick, N. A., Drahota, A., & Brookman-Frazee, L. (2013). Parent perspectives of an evidence-based intervention for children with autism served in community mental health clinics. *Journal of Child and Family Studies, 22,* 414–422. http://dx.doi.org/10.1007/s10826-012-9594-0

Williams, K. T. (2007). *The Expressive Vocabulary Test* (2nd ed.). Circle Pines, MN: American Guidance Service.

World Health Organization. (2010). *The ICD–10 Classification of Mental and Behavioural Disorders: Clinical descriptions and diagnostic guidelines.* Geneva, Switzerland: Author. Retrieved from http://www.who.int/classifications/icd/en/bluebook.pdf

Youngstrom, E., Loeber, R., & Stouthamer-Loeber, M. (2000). Patterns and correlates of agreement between parent, teacher, and male adolescent ratings of externalizing and internalizing problems. *Journal of Consulting and Clinical Psychology, 68,* 1038–1050. http://dx.doi.org/10.1037/0022-006X.68.6.1038

3

PROMOTING PARENT ENGAGEMENT IN PARENT TRAINING FOR CHILDREN WITH AUTISM SPECTRUM DISORDER

RACHEL M. FENNING AND ERIC M. BUTTER

Parent training (PT) interventions have great utility in children's mental health services (American Academy of Child and Adolescent Psychiatry, 2007) and play a significant role in the treatment of children with autism spectrum disorder (ASD; Nevill, Lecavalier, & Stratis, 2018). PT interventions focus on parents as the critical agents of change. With parents in this central role, greater parental participation in PT interventions has been linked with better treatment effects (e.g., Webster-Stratton, Reid, & Hammond, 2001). Conceptualizing and addressing barriers to parent engagement therefore are fundamental to understanding treatment efficacy and the factors that may moderate outcomes.

http://dx.doi.org/10.1037/0000111-004
Parent Training for Autism Spectrum Disorder: Improving the Quality of Life for Children and Their Families,
C. R. Johnson, E. M. Butter, and L. Scahill (Editors)

IMPORTANCE OF CONSIDERING PARENT ENGAGEMENT

The advantages of PT as a treatment modality are numerous. PT is described easily in manual-based formats and can be disseminated broadly through publication of such manuals. Behavioral PT interventions are theoretically coherent with prevailing professional training models, so many clinical providers can adopt them readily. As a stand-alone or auxiliary intervention, PT can be delivered in traditional outpatient mental health service settings, with visits outlining clear and specific treatment goals. And, as described in other chapters in this book, treatment can focus on a variety of parent-identified issues for children with ASD, such as problems with disruptive and noncompliant behaviors, social communication deficits, feeding problems, toileting difficulties, sleep difficulties, and other challenges. Moreover, PT has been used for many years across a number of childhood psychopathologies with a strong evidence base (Weisz & Jensen, 1999). PT is readily available, relatively low cost to implement, and generally viewed as efficacious. However, if parents are not engaged and involved in the therapeutic process, PT interventions likely will not be effective.

For families of children with ASD, there is a long history of relying on parents to deliver intervention in an effort to capitalize on the integral role parents play in the development, maintenance, and generalization of skills (Lovaas, 1981; Nevill et al., 2018; Zwaigenbaum et al., 2015). Recommended best practice interventions, such as applied behavior analysis (ABA) and early intensive behavioral intervention (EIBI), generally involve a substantial PT component, with some programs designed to be exclusively parent mediated. Stand-alone PT interventions similarly depend centrally on parents to achieve desired treatment outcomes. However, the many unique challenges presented by raising a child with ASD, including intense levels of parenting stress (Barroso, Mendez, Graziano, & Bagner, 2018; Hayes & Watson, 2013), may create added barriers to treatment. The use of methods that effectively enhance parent engagement is likely to be particularly impactful in this population.

To date, relatively limited empirical attention has been devoted to understanding treatment engagement processes in families of children with ASD specifically, despite the clear clinical importance. The present chapter therefore begins with a review of the traditional literature on treatment barriers and relevant intervention approaches. We also discuss the unique needs of families of children with ASD and bridge models of treatment engagement with disability-specific conceptualizations of stress and coping. Given the focus and themes represented in this book, we focus on mechanisms for engaging parents in secondary and stand-alone PT interventions. However, many of the considerations discussed in this chapter are relevant to considering parent engagement in intensive behavioral intervention (i.e., ABA/EIBI), which remains one of the key contexts for parent involvement in treatment for ASD.

CONCEPTUAL MODELS OF ENGAGEMENT AND TREATMENT BARRIERS

Definitions of *treatment engagement* vary in the literature, and some studies operationalize this construct with greater clarity than others. In the present review, we refer to *engagement* as encompassing attendance and persistence, participation during sessions and motivation for treatment, adherence to session content and assignments, and enactment of recommended strategies (Bellg et al., 2004; Eisner & Meidert, 2011; Staudt, 2007). Several models have been proposed to conceptualize components of treatment engagement and factors that may create barriers (Kazdin, Holland, & Crowley, 1997; Kazdin, Holland, Crowley, & Breton, 1997; Snell-Johns, Mendez, & Smith, 2004; Staudt, 2007). These models are complementary and contribute to our current understanding of how to promote parent engagement in PT interventions.

Snell-Johns et al. (2004) applied an ecological systems framework (Bronfenbrenner, 1979) and conceptualized risk at multiple levels of analysis when considering evidence-based approaches to promoting therapeutic engagement. Those levels of analysis included the individual child and the child's immediate family and surroundings (i.e., the microsystem), the community in which a child lives (i.e., the exosystem), and cultural factors impacting each child (i.e., the macrosystem), while alluding to systemic interactions across levels (i.e., the role of the mesosystem). This theoretical approach has helped to generate recommendations for considering access barriers related to transportation and geographic location, parent work commitments, childcare, treatment costs, and other factors that may differentially impact low-income and underserved families. Efforts to consider systemic obstacles to care also have produced service models that have focused on bridging the clinical and home environments, and have emphasized the importance of individualizing treatment by affording greater flexibility in the modality, duration, and setting of intervention delivery. Furthermore, the ability of PT therapists to address expectancies, family strengths, and to provide culturally competent services also have been priorities emerging from an ecological systems framework. For families of children with ASD specifically, consideration of contextual factors additionally underscores the need to understand family relationships and social support, cultural beliefs regarding disability and service-seeking, and the nature and extent of funding and services locally available for children with ASD.

Other models have focused more specifically on clinician behaviors that may influence treatment engagement. Drawing heavily on the work of Kazdin and colleagues (e.g., Kazdin, Holland, & Crowley, 1997; Kazdin, Holland, Crowley, & Breton, 1997; Nock & Kazdin, 2001), Staudt (2007) differentiated behavioral (e.g., attendance, adherence, session participation) and attitudinal components of treatment engagement (e.g., investment, commitment, motivation), and provided a heuristically valuable perspective on potential pathways of clinician influence.

At the most basic, to engage, parents must perceive PT to be acceptable and relevant to their child's problems. Parental attributions and expectancies have been linked with help-seeking behaviors, treatment participation and attendance, and treatment outcome (Mah & Johnston, 2008; Morrissey-Kane & Prinz, 1999). Both very low parent expectancies and very high parent expectancies for treatment have been associated with greater likelihood of treatment completion (Nock & Kazdin, 2001), suggesting that parents who expect much and who need a lot may be particularly strong candidates for improved outcomes following PT. The importance of explicitly targeting father participation in behavioral PT also has been emphasized (Fabiano, 2007) because mothers typically are the primary participants in PT programs. In this vein, it is critical that the clinician address any disagreement among parents or other caregivers regarding the child's presenting problems and the associated utility of treatment. This topic may be a particularly sensitive one for families of children with ASD, given that parents may differ in their reaction to child diagnosis and needs, which may have meaningful consequences for parenting behaviors and involvement (Wachtel & Carter, 2008). Careful joining with the family as a whole and an empathic approach to discussing parental perceptions of the child are required.

Identifying, refining, and enhancing parental expectations early in the treatment process represent important steps that clinicians can take to promote engagement. Beyond addressing treatment relevance, explicitly eliciting perceptions of treatment barriers is important because greater parental perception of barriers and treatment burden have been linked with reduced therapeutic change and increased likelihood of treatment dropout (Kazdin, Holland, & Crowley, 1997; Kazdin, Holland, Crowley, & Breton, 1997; Kazdin & Wassell, 1999). Child characteristics such as older age, greater symptom severity, and the presence of psychiatric comorbidity also may play a role in influencing parental expectancies for treatment and parent attendance, adherence, and persistence (Chronis, Chacko, Fabiano, Wymbs, & Pelham, 2004; Nock & Ferriter, 2005; Nock & Kazdin, 2001). As described later, the use of *motivational interviewing*, an approach that involves eliciting parents' treatment goals, expectations, and readiness and motivation for change, may assist clinicians in identifying and supporting families at risk for limited engagement (Miller & Rollnick, 2002; Morrissey-Kane & Prinz, 1999; Nock & Ferriter, 2005). In the case of stand-alone PT interventions for children with ASD, it is important to help parents identify distinct PT treatment goals, balance PT requirements with other service needs, and understand how PT will interface with existing or prior interventions.

The hassles of everyday life and external sources of stress also must be rendered manageable to permit parents to have the time and mental capacity to participate meaningfully in treatment (Ingoldsby, 2010; Kazdin, Holland, & Crowley, 1997; Nock & Ferriter, 2005; Snell-Johns et al., 2004; Staudt, 2007). Parents may benefit from assistance in addressing financial or insurance limitations and pragmatic issues that may conflict with treatment attendance and participation, such as transportation difficulties, parental job demands, or limited childcare options. Low socioeconomic status, racial and ethnic minority background, parent psychopathology, and parenting stress are associated with reduced treatment adherence and persistence (Ingoldsby, 2010; Nock & Ferriter, 2005; Reyno & McGrath, 2006; Snell-Johns et al., 2004; Staudt, 2007; Webster-Stratton, 1998). In particular, parent psychopathology may be tied to treatment resistance (Patterson & Chamberlain, 1994). Clinicians who carefully assess and monitor parent stress and mental health considerations will be in the best position to integrate additional therapeutic elements (e.g., direct stress reduction techniques) or provide referrals for outside resources, as needed (e.g., case management, individual treatment for parent mental health concerns). For families of children with ASD, it is important for clinicians to recognize that those parents are especially vulnerable to clinically significant levels of parenting stress and psychological distress. To provide beneficial support, clinicians may need to address parents' reluctance to attend to their own well-being in the face of what often are pervasive and consuming child needs.

Developing a strong therapeutic relationship is vital to maintaining parent attendance and adherence, and optimizing treatment response (Kazdin, Holland, & Crowley, 1997; Staudt, 2007). Adopting a nonjudgmental stance, demonstrating sufficient empathy, and using culturally appropriate techniques are key to establishing a strong therapeutic alliance and maintaining treatment engagement (Ingoldsby, 2010; Lau, 2006; Snell-Johns et al., 2004). Ultimately, parents must view the clinician as caring, invested, and committed to the child's and parents' success. It also is important for parents to perceive the clinician as knowledgeable about the presenting problems, which may pose particular challenges for families of children with ASD, given the limited number of expert providers and the geographic disparity of experienced and trained clinicians (Austin et al., 2016).

TRADITIONAL INTERVENTIONS DESIGNED
TO FACILITATE PARENT ENGAGEMENT

A high percentage of families drop out of PT interventions prematurely (Wierzbicki & Pekarik, 1993), and problems with retention may be greater for families at higher risk, thus compounding vulnerability (Ingoldsby, 2010; Snell-Johns et al., 2004). The many pitfalls associated with evidence-based practice, namely, issues related to generalizability, are highly relevant and represent disadvantages of PT interventions. Consequently, many treatment developers have underscored the importance of addressing both practical and psychological barriers to treatment engagement (e.g., Ingoldsby, 2010). Resultant efforts have produced a combination of approaches, including orientation materials and brief modules that explicitly focus on initial participation, as well as programs that address barriers explicitly throughout the intervention.

Brief pretreatment interventions have figured prominently as an initial engagement strategy. One study investigating different ways to promote attendance at the first appointment found that any strategy that involved pretreatment contact (e.g., phone calls, welcome letter, or both) was significantly better than no contact (Kourany, Garber, & Tornusciolo, 1990). Similarly, pretreatment orientation group meetings as a prerequisite to starting treatment have been shown to have a positive influence on attendance at first appointments but not necessarily at subsequent treatment visits (Wenning & King, 1995). More individualized pretreatment engagement approaches also have been shown to be helpful. For instance, a family-systems intervention designed to promote engagement at the initial intake session used a strategic structural systems approach during phone contact to join with the family and to restructure resistance to treatment (Szapocznik et al., 1988). Families that received that intervention were more than twice as likely to attend the initial intake session and completed treatment more often than families in the nonintervention control. McKay, Stoewe, McCadam, and Gonzales (1998) similarly found that a telephone engagement interview in combination with an engagement-oriented initial session was associated with increased treatment attendance.

Similar and more elaborated enhancement strategies embedded throughout treatment have achieved varying degrees of success. Reminder calls have demonstrated inconsistent results and may be more helpful for families of children with higher levels of symptom severity (Kourany et al., 1990; Watt, Hoyland, Best, & Dadds, 2007). *Response-cost contracting*, wherein parents forfeit deposited sums of money for not attending appointments or not completing homework assignments, have been shown to increase attendance and adherence (Aragona, Cassady, & Drabman, 1975; Eyberg & Johnson,

1974). Extrinsic rewards for adherence (i.e., payment to parents) may be especially helpful for engaging low-income families (Fleischman, 1979).

Approaches that involve deliberately integrating adjunctive family support throughout PT to address needs beyond immediate treatment goals also have produced positive results for parent engagement (Ingoldsby, 2010). In a randomized clinical trial, enhanced discussion of family concerns not directly related to treatment targeting challenging child behaviors resulted in greater parental engagement and retention (Prinz & Miller, 1994). Motivational interviewing frameworks also are compatible with those findings. Nock and Kazdin (2005) set the bar by conducting a randomized clinical trial of a structured motivational interviewing module embedded within a PT intervention for families of children with externalizing behavior problems. Delivered at treatment outset and again at two subsequent points, Participant Enhancement Intervention was associated with significantly greater treatment motivation, attendance, and adherence in comparison with PT treatment as usual. These preparatory and continuous enhancement strategies, although not ubiquitous and not always explicitly described, do appear to be important in promoting engagement in PT interventions (Nock & Ferriter, 2005). Evidence that child and family factors may differentially influence treatment barriers over time further underscores the value of embedded strategies (Eisner & Meidert, 2011).

Structure and modality of treatment also may influence participation and retention. In some contexts, group PT interventions have been shown to be associated with increased improvement in child behavior problems compared with traditional individual treatment sessions or a wait-list control (Cunningham, Bremner, & Boyle, 1995). PT interventions that adapt the setting of treatment (e.g., home, community, school) and that explicitly consider the implications for transition to community, rather than clinic-based services, may be particularly important to facilitating treatment acceptability, attendance, and use in low-resource families (Webster-Stratton, 1998). Furthermore, PT packages that integrate explicit maintenance strategies, such as interim and long-term booster sessions, may result in improved parent participation and sustained treatment outcomes (Eyberg, Edwards, Boggs, & Foote, 1998).

UNIQUE BARRIERS TO ENGAGEMENT IN FAMILIES OF CHILDREN WITH ASD

Barriers to treatment engagement are heightened for families of children with intellectual and developmental disabilities (IDD), including ASD. Theoretical conceptualizations of influences on parent involvement in behavioral intervention for children with ASD and IDD have underscored the significance of family demographics, social supports, and external work-related stressors, as well as parental stress and coping, and general family functioning (Gavidia-Payne & Stoneman, 1997). Heightened rates of clinically significant parenting stress and associated parent mental health needs are particularly problematic and further exacerbated for families of children with ASD relative to parents of children with IDD, chronic illness, and typical development (Barroso et al., 2018; Hayes & Watson, 2013). Elevated rates of child behavior problems and co-occurring psychiatric disorders also are uniquely complicating for children with ASD and are likely to impact parent engagement in PT interventions. Rates of disruptive behavior disorders are high among children with ASD and IDD, and occur at 3 to 5 times the rate observed among children with neurotypical development (Baker, Neece, Fenning, Crnic, & Blacher, 2010). Indeed, almost 60% of children with ASD meet criteria for a comorbid disruptive behavior disorder (Simonoff et al., 2008).

The transactional relationship between behavior problems and parenting stress is a significant factor to consider when delivering PT interventions to families of children with ASD. Behavior problems in children with ASD are robustly associated with parenting stress (Davis & Carter, 2008), which in turn predicts escalations in child behavior problems over time (Lecavalier, Leone, & Wiltz, 2006; Osborne & Reed, 2009). Parenting stress also has been linked to negative parenting behaviors, such as harsh discipline and criticism, which are associated with externalizing challenges in children with ASD (Bader & Barry, 2014; Shawler & Sullivan, 2017).

In addition, the process of advocating for and obtaining access to educational, recreational, and treatment services can be remarkably difficult for families impacted by and living with ASD. Significant financial demands, resource needs, and difficulties navigating the service delivery system are present for families of children with ASD in ways that are unique, more intense, and relentlessly persistent compared with families of children with neurotypical development (Hastings & Beck, 2004; Karst & Van Hecke, 2012; Sloper, 1999). Indeed, negative interactions with service providers may be a source of increased stress (Hastings & Beck, 2004). Long wait times for treatment and limited access to highly trained providers remain significant problems in how services are organized and delivered (Austin et al., 2016). In addition, although families involved in gold standard ABA/EIBI programs generally experience significant and lasting treatment benefits across child and parent domains, there can be stressors associated with participating in intensive intervention (Grindle, Kovshoff, Hastings, & Remington, 2009; Smith, Buch, & Gamby, 2000). For clinicians delivering stand-alone PT to families enrolled in ABA/EIBI or other treatments, it is essential to address the complexity and impact of concurrent receipt of services.

The sequelae of ASD can be substantial, refractory, and pervasive at multiple levels, and may affect the functioning of individual family members; parent–child, marital, and sibling relationships; and overall family resources and quality of life (Karst & Van Hecke, 2012). Challenges are further intensified for families with ethnic and racial minority status and low financial resources (Magaña, Parish, Rose, Timberlake, & Swaine, 2012; Simonoff et al., 2008). The accumulated risk of minority stress and ASD has been largely overlooked in prior research. Examining processes related to the development and implementation of effective interventions for diverse and underserved families represents an important area for future investigation.

MANAGING BARRIERS ASSOCIATED WITH PARENT STRESS AND PARENT WELL-BEING

Promoting parents' belief in and trust of the PT treatment process may be especially important in families of children with ASD (Durand, Hieneman, Clarke, & Zona, 2009; Karst & Van Hecke, 2012). Higher levels of parenting self-efficacy typically are associated with better reported parenting behaviors in the general population (Jones & Prinz, 2005). In families of children with ASD, greater parenting self-efficacy predicts more therapist-reported involvement in behavioral intervention (Solish & Perry, 2008), whereas lower perceived control regarding child behavior has been linked to reduced parent-reported usability of PT strategies (Whittingham, Sofronoff, & Sheffield, 2006). Parenting self-efficacy also may help to explain the relationship between child problem behaviors and mental health difficulties in mothers of children with ASD, and may moderate this association for fathers (Hastings & Brown, 2002). Focusing on enhancing parenting self-efficacy in PT interventions with families of children with ASD therefore may be critical to promoting parent well-being and to achieving positive treatment response.

Parenting self-efficacy also has a strong negative relationship with parenting stress. It is not surprising, then, that parenting stress has emerged as a significant barrier to the successful implementation of intervention for families of children with ASD. High parenting stress has been linked with reduced response to early intervention for children with ASD (Osborne, McHugh, Saunders, & Reed, 2008), suggesting that parenting stress may attenuate the effects of evidence-based treatments. Despite these findings, parenting stress rarely has been addressed directly in interventions for this population, and even less so in underserved and underrepresented families in which clinical needs are greater.

Integrating models of stress and coping into PT curriculums and manuals represents an important way to advance the field. The double ABCX model of family adaptation represents a conceptualization having particular relevance to PT in families of children with ASD (Konstantareas, 1991; McCubbin & Patterson, 1983). This model considers the influence of the severity of stressors, the family's internal and external resources, and family members' appraisal of the stressors and prominent coping strategies on parent–child relationship quality, patterns of family interaction, and child outcomes. Several studies have supported the utility of the double ABCX model for understanding variation in family functioning and level of parental distress in families of children with ASD, and have highlighted the important role of social support, active coping, and cognitive reframing in predicting positive adaptation in this population (Bristol, 1987; Manning, Wainwright, & Bennett, 2011; Paynter, Riley, Beamish, Davies, & Milford, 2013).

In particular, the double ABCX model allows for exploration of parental perceptions of the child's developmental disorder, which may meaningfully influence treatment expectancies, goal setting, and the presence of other psychological barriers in families of children with ASD. Research on families of individuals with IDD has indicated that parental positive and negative perceptions regarding the impact of a child's disability are separable constructs, and perceived positive impact appears uniquely predictive of parental well-being (Blacher & Baker, 2007). Perceptions of positive impact also may buffer parents against the adverse effects of child problem behaviors on parental stress and well-being (Blacher & Baker, 2007), although significant cultural differences may exist (Blacher, Begum, Marcoulides, & Baker, 2013), and mothers of children with ASD may be more apt to endorse positive perceptions than fathers (Hastings et al., 2005). Conversely, strong negative conceptualizations of a child's ASD diagnosis and maternal self-blame have been associated with poorer observed parenting quality and difficulties with marital functioning (Bristol, 1987). Collectively, these findings underscore the importance of assessing and addressing parental attributions regarding a child's ASD diagnosis and the perceived impact of the disorder.

Efforts to identify strengths in families of children with IDD and ASD also have focused on parental optimism as a potential protective factor. Parental optimism appears to predict parental depression and marital adjustment more strongly than other powerful child factors, such as behavior problems, and mothers higher in dispositional optimism may experience fewer negative consequences of child behavior problems on parent well-being (Baker, Blacher, & Olsson, 2005). In contrast, parental pessimism has been linked to the exacerbation of child problem behaviors over time, even after considering initial problem severity and child cognitive and adaptive functioning (Durand et al., 2009). Developing strategies to cultivate optimism and encouraging parents to create positive meaning in the context of adversity may promote crucial resilience processes in families of children with ASD (Bayat, 2007; Ekas, Lickenbrock, & Whitman, 2010). Enhancing family social support also may bolster adaptation, given positive associations between social support and parental optimism (Ekas et al., 2010), and inverse relations with perceived negative impact of a child's ASD diagnosis (Bishop, Richler, Cain, & Lord, 2007).

INTERVENTIONS DESIGNED TO FACILITATE ENGAGEMENT IN PARENTS OF CHILDREN WITH ASD

Relatively few systematic investigations of interventions are designed specifically to promote parent engagement in treatment for families of children with ASD. This is an important area for future work in our field.

In the context of stand-alone PT interventions, implementing strategies to address the practical and logistical barriers cited in much of the research and conceptual models of treatment engagement may be a straightforward place to start. Scheduling around parent work commitments, offering incentives, and providing child care during parent sessions are logical interventions based on the research that has been done in other child mental health populations (e.g., Kazdin, Holland, & Crowley, 1997; Kazdin, Holland, Crowley, & Breton, 1997). It seems reasonable that addressing the practical barriers to getting to treatment sessions and helping parents consider when to practice intervention techniques would improve attendance and engagement.

Another avenue for addressing parental engagement in PT includes expanding programming to target parental perceptions of ASD, parental expectancies for treatment, and parenting self-efficacy. *Positive family intervention* (PFI) is a PT intervention that targets parenting self-efficacy directly through adaptation of optimism training (Durand, Hieneman, Clarke, Wang, & Rinaldi, 2013). PFI emphasizes monitoring parents' internal self-talk and using cognitive restructuring to address parental pessimism. In a randomized clinical trial consisting of eight weekly 90-minute sessions, parents of children with IDD participated in either standard PT or the standard program plus PFI. Results revealed significant improvement in problem behaviors in both groups as measured by direct observation and parent report; parents who received the enhanced PFI treatment reported comparatively greater reduction in child problem behavior.

Preliminary evidence also has supported the feasibility and utility of a brief PT module that integrates parent management training with specific content designed to increase parenting self-efficacy in families of children with ASD. Relative to a control group, parents participating in the PT intervention in either a 1-day workshop format or a series of six weekly sessions reported fewer child behavior problems and increased parenting self-efficacy posttreatment (Sofronoff & Farbotko, 2002). Although that study did not compare the self-efficacy–based PT program to a more comprehensive behavioral PT intervention, the findings are important, given the emphasis on addressing self-efficacy specifically and evidence of positive outcomes using both a 1-day workshop and weekly sessions.

Direct support and stress reduction interventions also hold promise for increasing parent engagement in PT. Reviews of the literature that have described how mental health and developmental disabilities systems address parenting stress in families of children with IDD have highlighted several important intervention strategies (Hastings & Beck, 2004; Sloper, 1999). Respite services are a frequent request, and parents who are able to use respite care may experience temporary relief from many practical and even some emotional barriers to treatment engagement. However, respite services are expensive to operate, and resources are quickly saturated. Parent-to-parent supports and parent mentoring programs also are relatively common and may help parents learn how to make the most out of PT interventions. Case management and care coordination services can be effective in reducing unmet needs, particularly for families with limited resources, and may serve to improve relationships with PT providers. Service systems also frequently provide psychoeducational groups and basic stress management programs, which can assist parents with stress reduction and may promote understanding of the relevance of PT interventions. Importantly, there has been no systematic investigation of how these more commonly available resources actually impact parent engagement in parallel or future PT interventions.

Mindfulness interventions represent an intriguing avenue for improving parent engagement and expanding outcomes during PT interventions. These approaches emphasize increasing present-moment awareness and fostering nonreactivity and acceptance of internal experiences to promote acknowledgment of stress while reducing the emotional impact (Gu, Strauss, Bond, & Cavanagh, 2015). Given the pervasive and chronic nature of stress and challenge in families of children with ASD, the focus of mindfulness approaches on managing rather than eliminating stress may make these interventions particularly well suited to this population and a valuable complement to PT.

Of the several versions of mindfulness interventions that exist, mindfulness-based stress reduction (MBSR) is the most empirically tested. MBSR originated as a treatment for adults with chronic pain and anxiety (Kabat-Zinn, 1982) and has been extended to a variety of populations (Grossman, Niemann, Schmidt, & Walach, 2004). Recent studies have been building evidence that MBSR may be an efficacious strategy for reducing stress in parents of children with IDD and ASD (Bazzano et al., 2015; Dykens, Fisher, Taylor, Lambert, & Miodrag, 2014; Neece, 2014), although further rigorous testing—using randomized clinical trials—of MBSR in families of children with ASD is needed. In addition, the use of MBSR or other mindfulness approaches as adjunctive to PT interventions requires further investigation. Integrating mindfulness approaches with traditional behavioral PT programs may enhance treatment efficacy by directly addressing parent strain and underlying psychological barriers to treatment adherence and use. Moreover, although it often is assumed that interventions that improve child functioning and reduce problem behavior will alleviate parenting stress, this is not consistently the case (Oono, Honey, & McConachie, 2013). Remediation of parenting stress may be critical to sustaining long-term treatment gains, given the transactional relationship between parenting stress and child behavior problems. An immediate research need is to examine whether interventions targeting direct stress reduction and parent psychological well-being do improve treatment engagement and PT outcomes.

SPECIAL CONSIDERATIONS

Using strategies to engage parents effectively in PT interventions by reducing treatment barriers and promoting parent well-being has the potential to improve targeted treatment outcomes while benefiting the family system as a whole. In relying on parents to deliver intervention to children with ASD, it is vitally important that our field continues to develop and enhance strategies to support parents in negotiating multiple, complex roles. Given the pervasive needs of many children with ASD, the responsibility of serving as an interventionist in addition to meeting other existing caregiving demands may be overwhelming, even for highly committed and participatory parents. Adopting an interventionist role also may conflict with other valid and important parenting needs, and, for some parents of children with ASD, aspects of a behavioral approach may seem at odds with the relationship-building and warm, sensitive structuring that is the hallmark of positive parenting in typically developing populations. Toward this end, working with families to foster parent–child reciprocity and shared enjoyment while developing skills to implement behavioral strategies effectively may be especially important (e.g., Solomon, Ono, Timmer, & Goodlin-Jones, 2008). Helping parents balance the behavioral and psychological demands of intervention is central to maintaining parent engagement and to achieving long-term adaptive family outcomes.

In addition, for families with multiple parents or caregivers in the home, it is not uncommon for one individual to take on primary involvement in PT, which may have a distancing effect on the other parent and may produce additional tension in the coparenting or marital relationship. Historically, mothers have figured most prominently in studies of PT for children with

ASD, and although increasing attention has been devoted to involving fathers and other caregivers, comparatively little research has been dedicated to understanding the nature of co-parenting dynamics in these families. Developing and disseminating evidence-based approaches to augment PT engagement by addressing the practical and psychological complexity of the interventionist role for parents of children with ASD, and the resultant effects on the family system, represent important research endeavors and a critical clinical need.

CASE EXAMPLE

Gabby[1] is a 32-year-old single mother of two young boys. Her son Michael, age 6, has a diagnosis of ASD. He received ABA/EIBI using discrete trial training interventions for 2 years until services were discontinued following provider concerns that the family's high cancellation rate and difficulty engaging Gabby in parent consultation sessions were compromising the effectiveness of the intervention. At the recommendation of Michael's current school team, Gabby initiated contact with the outpatient treatment clinic to address Michael's ongoing aggression and noncompliance.

The clinic phone coordinator arranged a late evening appointment to avoid conflicting with Gabby's work schedule. The coordinator also obtained information regarding Gabby's preferred timing for phone contact with the treating PT clinician. The clinician engaged in a brief phone-based pretreatment intervention to promote Gabby's attendance at the first session. The clinician explained the purpose of the initial treatment session and encouraged Gabby to ask questions. The clinician made an effort to join with Gabby, listening to and validating her concerns, and linking participation in PT with the opportunity to address and resolve reported challenges. Resistance and potential barriers to initial attendance were addressed. Based on Gabby's admission that she might forget about the scheduled session, Gabby and the clinician decided that the clinic would provide appointment reminder calls several days in advance, as well as the day before the scheduled session. Gabby also entered appointment information in the calendar on her cell phone. The clinician acknowledged and complimented Gabby for taking steps to create desired change, including contacting the clinic, talking with the clinician by phone, and committing to attending the first session. The clinician confirmed the date and time of the first treatment session, and concluded by expressing enthusiasm for working with Gabby.

---

[1]Clinical material has been disguised to protect client confidentiality.

During the first treatment session, the clinician provided an overview of PT procedures and expectations, and prompted Gabby to ask questions. The clinician inquired about Gabby's perspective on prior treatment experiences and engaged in participant enhancement intervention (Nock & Kazdin, 2005). Through this process, the clinician reinforced the rationale for PT intervention, developed therapeutic rapport, and built Gabby's positive expectations for treatment. The clinician elicited self-motivational change statements by asking Gabby to describe the change she would like to see in Michael's behavior and in her own parenting behaviors, her reasons for initiating this change, her expectancies for change, and her planned steps to create change through participation in PT (e.g., attending sessions weekly, completing homework, practicing new skills at home). The clinician also talked with Gabby about potential treatment barriers and involved Gabby in proactive problem solving. For instance, in response to concerns that childcare needs might affect attendance, the clinician helped Gabby to identify a realistic option for extending Michael's care at an existing neighborhood program one night per week. Gabby also decided that it would be helpful to use phone alerts as reminders to complete session homework. The clinician proceeded to gather detailed information regarding Gabby's current concerns and the topography of Michael's challenging behaviors. The clinician reviewed the antecedent-behavior-consequence (A-B-C) model of learning theory and engaged Gabby in completing an A-B-C data sheet to examine contingencies surrounding problem behaviors. Gabby selected one antecedent strategy to attempt in the coming week. She also agreed to collect daily A-B-C data, and she programmed relevant homework reminders into her phone.

The PT clinician contacted Gabby midweek to support adherence and to facilitate attendance at the second treatment session. The clinician praised Gabby for completing the A-B-C log 1 out of 4 days, and for attempting an antecedent intervention twice. The clinician inquired about the utility of strategies Gabby had previously generated to address barriers to homework completion, and additional problem solving ensued. The clinician concluded by describing the purpose and benefits of the second treatment session, and confirming the date and time of the session. As planned, the front desk also provided a reminder call.

The second treatment session began with a review of the previous week and a discussion of homework. Following the midweek phone call, Gabby successfully completed A-B-C data collection on 2 out of 3 days. The clinician underscored Gabby's agency in solution-finding by asking her to describe the strategies that made her increased adherence possible. The clinician also prompted Gabby to share her perspective on the treatment process. Gabby conveyed disappointment and frustration that little had changed with respect to Michael's behavior, despite her efforts to complete homework. After empathizing with Gabby's experience, the clinician sensitively reframed by focusing on positive gains in Gabby's skills and reminding her of the importance of continued learning and practice as a way to attain treatment goals. The clinician also thanked Gabby for her disclosure and emphasized the value of discussing her internal experiences and opinions throughout the treatment process. The clinician further illustrated the association between thoughts, feelings, and actions using an example from Gabby's A-B-C data to explore how her thoughts and feelings influenced antecedent and consequence reactions to Michael's problem behaviors. Monitoring of internal self-talk was added to Gabby's A-B-C data collection to illuminate internal processes that might create barriers to use and implementation of therapeutic techniques. The clinician also modeled acceptance and nonevaluation of negative emotion, and engaged Gabby in in-vivo practice of direct stress reduction techniques (e.g., deep breathing, progressive muscle relaxation). Gabby agreed to expand the homework plan to include practicing self-care strategies.

Acknowledging Gabby's high level of parenting stress, the clinician also assessed the presence and intensity of external sources of stress. The clinician gathered detailed information and linked Gabby with clinic case management services to assist her in accessing needed respite care and in managing a broad range of external stressors. Gabby expressed hope that obtaining additional support would allow her to better focus on PT and supporting Michael's needs. The clinician was careful to save enough time during the session to cover the most fundamental elements of the content in the planned PT training session, despite spending significant time working through stress awareness and stress management with Gabby.

Throughout the duration of PT, the clinician maintained a focus on facilitating Gabby's engagement by monitoring and proactively addressing barriers to attendance, in-session participation, homework completion, skill acquisition, and technique use. In addition to the central focus on directly enhancing parenting skills, the use of motivational interviewing to address goal setting and treatment barriers and the emphasis on facilitating Gabby's own emotion regulation and well-being served to promote her engagement and uptake of treatment strategies over the course of PT. Between-session clinician contact and reminder calls continued to be helpful to Gabby, and referrals for auxiliary supports also were pivotal in facilitating Gabby's PT access. Ultimately, Gabby was successful in attending the majority of her scheduled sessions, and she completed the full treatment dose, which resulted in substantial improvement in parenting behaviors and associated clinically significant reductions in Michael's externalizing behavior problems.

REFERENCES

American Academy of Child and Adolescent Psychiatry. (2007). Practice parameter for the assessment and treatment of children and adolescents with oppositional defiant disorder. *Journal of the American Academy of Child and Adolescent Psychiatry, 46*, 126–141. http://dx.doi.org/10.1097/01.chi.0000246060.62706.af

Aragona, J., Cassady, J., & Drabman, R. S. (1975). Treating overweight children through parental training and contingency contracting. *Journal of Applied Behavior Analysis, 8*, 269–278.

Austin, J., Manning-Courtney, P., Johnson, M. L., Weber, R., Johnson, H., Murray, D., . . . Murray, M. (2016). Improving access to care at autism treatment centers: A system analysis approach. *Pediatrics, 137*(Suppl. 2), S149–S157. http://dx.doi.org/10.1542/peds.2015-2851M

Bader, S. H., & Barry, T. D. (2014). A longitudinal examination of the relation between parental expressed emotion and externalizing behaviors in children and adolescents with autism spectrum disorder. *Journal of Autism and Developmental Disorders, 44*, 2820–2831. http://dx.doi.org/10.1007/s10803-014-2142-6

Baker, B. L., Blacher, J., & Olsson, M. B. (2005). Preschool children with and without developmental delay: Behaviour problems, parents' optimism and well-being. *Journal of Intellectual Disability Research, 49*, 575–590. http://dx.doi.org/10.1111/j.1365-2788.2005.00691.x

Baker, B. L., Neece, C. L., Fenning, R. M., Crnic, K. A., & Blacher, J. (2010). Mental disorders in five-year-old children with or without developmental delay: Focus on ADHD. *Journal of Clinical Child and Adolescent Psychology, 39*, 492–505. http://dx.doi.org/10.1080/15374416.2010.486321

Barroso, N. E., Mendez, L., Graziano, P. A., & Bagner, D. M. (2018). Parenting stress through the lens of different clinical groups: A systematic review & meta-analysis. *Journal of Abnormal Child Psychology, 46*, 449–461. http://dx.doi.org/10.1007/s10802-017-0313-6

Bayat, M. (2007). Evidence of resilience in families of children with autism. *Journal of Intellectual Disability Research, 51*, 702–714. http://dx.doi.org/10.1111/j.1365-2788.2007.00960.x

Bazzano, A., Wolfe, C., Zylowska, L., Wang, S., Schuster, E., Barrett, C., & Lehrer, D. (2015). Mindfulness based stress reduction (MBSR) for parents and caregivers of individuals with developmental disabilities: A community-based approach. *Journal of Child and Family Studies, 24*, 298–308. http://dx.doi.org/10.1007/s10826-013-9836-9

Bellg, A. J., Borrelli, B., Resnick, B., Hecht, J., Minicucci, D. S., Ory, M., . . . Treatment Fidelity Workgroup of the NIH Behavior Change Consortium. (2004). Enhancing treatment fidelity in health behavior change studies: Best practices and recommendations from the NIH Behavior Change Consortium. *Health Psychology, 23*, 443–451. http://dx.doi.org/10.1037/0278-6133.23.5.443

Bishop, S. L., Richler, J., Cain, A. C., & Lord, C. (2007). Predictors of perceived negative impact in mothers of children with autism spectrum disorder. *American Journal on Mental Retardation, 112*, 450–461. http://dx.doi.org/10.1352/0895-8017(2007)112[450:POPNII]2.0.CO;2

Blacher, J., & Baker, B. L. (2007). Positive impact of intellectual disability on families. *American Journal on Mental Retardation, 112*, 330–348. http://dx.doi.org/10.1352/0895-8017(2007)112[0330:PIOIDO]2.0.CO;2

Blacher, J., Begum, G. F., Marcoulides, G. A., & Baker, B. L. (2013). Longitudinal perspectives of child positive impact on families: Relationship to disability and culture. *American Journal on Intellectual and Developmental Disabilities, 118*, 141–155. http://dx.doi.org/10.1352/1944-7558-118.2.141

Bristol, M. M. (1987). Mothers of children with autism or communication disorders: Successful adaptation and the double ABCX model. *Journal of Autism and Developmental Disorders, 17*, 469–486. http://dx.doi.org/10.1007/BF01486964

Bronfenbrenner, U. (1979). *The ecology of human development*. Cambridge, MA: Harvard University Press.

Chronis, A. M., Chacko, A., Fabiano, G. A., Wymbs, B. T., & Pelham, W. E., Jr. (2004). Enhancements to the behavioral parent training paradigm for families of children with ADHD: Review and future directions. *Clinical Child and Family Psychology Review, 7*, 1–27. http://dx.doi.org/10.1023/B:CCFP.0000020190.60808.a4

Cunningham, C. E., Bremner, R., & Boyle, M. (1995). Large group community-based parenting programs for families of preschoolers at risk for disruptive behaviour disorders: Utilization, cost effectiveness, and outcome. *Journal of Child Psychology and Psychiatry, 36*, 1141–1159. http://dx.doi.org/10.1111/j.1469-7610.1995.tb01362.x

Davis, N. O., & Carter, A. S. (2008). Parenting stress in mothers and fathers of toddlers with autism spectrum disorders: Associations with child characteristics. *Journal of Autism and Developmental Disorders, 38*, 1278–1291. http://dx.doi.org/10.1007/s10803-007-0512-z

Durand, V. M., Hieneman, M., Clarke, S., Wang, M., & Rinaldi, M. L. (2013). Positive family interaction for severe challenging behavior I: A multisite randomized clinical trial. *Journal of Positive Behavior Interventions, 15*, 133–143. http://dx.doi.org/10.1177/1098300712458324

Durand, V. M., Hieneman, M., Clarke, S., & Zona, M. (2009). Optimistic parenting: Hope and help for parents with challenging children. In W. Sailor, G. Dulap, G. Sugai, & R. Horner (Eds.), *Handbook of positive behavior support* (pp. 233–256). Boston, MA: Springer. http://dx.doi.org/10.1007/978-0-387-09632-2_10

Dykens, E. M., Fisher, M. H., Taylor, J. L., Lambert, W., & Miodrag, N. (2014). Reducing distress in mothers of children with autism and other disabilities: A randomized trial. *Pediatrics, 134*, e454–e463. http://dx.doi.org/10.1542/peds.2013-3164

Eisner, M., & Meidert, U. (2011). Stages of parental engagement in a universal parent training program. *Journal of Primary Prevention, 32*, 83–93. http://dx.doi.org/10.1007/s10935-011-0238-8

Ekas, N. V., Lickenbrock, D. M., & Whitman, T. L. (2010). Optimism, social support, and well-being in mothers of children with autism spectrum disorder. *Journal of Autism and Developmental Disorders, 40*, 1274–1284. http://dx.doi.org/10.1007/s10803-010-0986-y

Eyberg, S. M., Edwards, D., Boggs, S. R., & Foote, R. (1998). Maintaining the treatment effects of parent training: The role of booster sessions and other maintenance strategies. *Clinical Psychology: Science and Practice, 5*, 544–554. http://dx.doi.org/10.1111/j.1468-2850.1998.tb00173.x

Eyberg, S. M., & Johnson, S. M. (1974). Multiple assessment of behavior modification with families: Effects of contingency contracting and order of treated problems. *Journal of Consulting and Clinical Psychology, 42*, 594–606. http://dx.doi.org/10.1037/h0036723

Fabiano, G. A. (2007). Father participation in behavioral parent training for ADHD: Review and recommendations for increasing inclusion and engagement. *Journal of Family Psychology, 21*, 683–693. http://dx.doi.org/10.1037/0893-3200.21.4.683

Fleischman, M. J. (1979). Using parenting salaries to control attrition and cooperation in therapy. *Behavior Therapy, 10*, 111–116. http://dx.doi.org/10.1016/S0005-7894(79)80014-3

Gavidia-Payne, S., & Stoneman, Z. (1997). Family predictors of maternal and paternal involvement in programs for young children with disabilities. *Child Development, 68*, 701–717. http://dx.doi.org/10.2307/1132120

Grindle, C. F., Kovshoff, H., Hastings, R. P., & Remington, B. (2009). Parents' experiences of home-based applied behavior analysis programs for young children with autism. *Journal of Autism and Developmental Disorders, 39*, 42–56. http://dx.doi.org/10.1007/s10803-008-0597-z

Grossman, P., Niemann, L., Schmidt, S., & Walach, H. (2004). Mindfulness-based stress reduction and health benefits: A meta-analysis. *Journal of Psychosomatic Research, 57*, 35–43. http://dx.doi.org/10.1016/S0022-3999(03)00573-7

Gu, J., Strauss, C., Bond, R., & Cavanagh, K. (2015). How do mindfulness-based cognitive therapy and mindfulness-based stress reduction improve mental health and wellbeing? A systematic review and meta-analysis of mediation studies. *Clinical Psychology Review, 37*, 1–12. http://dx.doi.org/10.1016/j.cpr.2015.01.006 (Corrigendum published 2016, *Clinical Psychology Review, 49*, p. 119. http://dx.doi.org/10.1016/j.cpr.2016.09.011)

Hastings, R. P., & Beck, A. (2004). Practitioner review: Stress intervention for parents of children with intellectual disabilities. *Journal of Child Psychology and Psychiatry, 45*, 1338–1349. http://dx.doi.org/10.1111/j.1469-7610.2004.00357.x

Hastings, R. P., & Brown, T. (2002). Behavior problems of children with autism, parental self-efficacy, and mental health. *American Journal on Mental Retardation, 107*, 222–232. http://dx.doi.org/10.1352/0895-8017(2002)107<0222:BPOCWA>2.0.CO;2

Hastings, R. P., Kovshoff, H., Ward, N. J., degli Espinosa, F., Brown, T., & Remington, B. (2005). Systems analysis of stress and positive perceptions in mothers and fathers of pre-school children with autism. *Journal of Autism and Developmental Disorders, 35*, 635–644. http://dx.doi.org/10.1007/s10803-005-0007-8

Hayes, S. A., & Watson, S. L. (2013). The impact of parenting stress: A meta-analysis of studies comparing the experience of parenting stress in parents of children with and without autism spectrum disorder. *Journal of Autism and Developmental Disorders, 43*, 629–642. http://dx.doi.org/10.1007/s10803-012-1604-y

Ingoldsby, E. M. (2010). Review of interventions to improve family engagement and retention in parent and child mental health programs. *Journal of Child and Family Studies, 19*, 629–645. http://dx.doi.org/10.1007/s10826-009-9350-2

Jones, T. L., & Prinz, R. J. (2005). Potential roles of parental self-efficacy in parent and child adjustment: A review. *Clinical Psychology Review, 25*, 341–363. http://dx.doi.org/10.1016/j.cpr.2004.12.004

Kabat-Zinn, J. (1982). An outpatient program in behavioral medicine for chronic pain patients based on the practice of mindfulness meditation: Theoretical considerations and preliminary results. *General Hospital Psychiatry, 4*, 33–47. http://dx.doi.org/10.1016/0163-8343(82)90026-3

Karst, J. S., & Van Hecke, A. V. (2012). Parent and family impact of autism spectrum disorders: A review and proposed model for intervention evaluation. *Clinical Child and Family Psychology Review, 15*, 247–277. http://dx.doi.org/10.1007/s10567-012-0119-6

Kazdin, A. E., Holland, L., & Crowley, M. (1997). Family experience of barriers to treatment and premature termination from child therapy. *Journal of Consulting and Clinical Psychology, 65*, 453–463. http://dx.doi.org/10.1037/0022-006X.65.3.453

Kazdin, A. E., Holland, L., Crowley, M., & Breton, S. (1997). Barriers to Treatment Participation Scale: Evaluation and validation in the context of child outpatient treatment. *Journal of Child Psychology and Psychiatry, 38*, 1051–1062. http://dx.doi.org/10.1111/j.1469-7610.1997.tb01621.x

Kazdin, A. E., & Wassell, G. (1999). Barriers to treatment participation and therapeutic change among children referred for conduct disorder. *Journal of Clinical Child Psychology, 28*, 160–172. http://dx.doi.org/10.1207/s15374424jccp2802_4

Konstantareas, M. M. (1991). Autistic, learning disabled and delayed children's impact on their parents. *Canadian Journal of Behavioural Science/Revue canadienne des sciences du comportement, 23*, 358–375. http://dx.doi.org/10.1037/h0079022

Kourany, R. F. C., Garber, J., & Tornusciolo, G. (1990). Improving first appointment attendance rates in child psychiatry outpatient clinics. *Journal of the American Academy of Child & Adolescent Psychiatry, 29*, 657–660. http://dx.doi.org/10.1097/00004583-199007000-00022

Lau, A. S. (2006). Making the case for selective and directed cultural adaptations of evidence-based treatments: Examples from parent training. *Clinical Psychology: Science and Practice, 13,* 295–310. http://dx.doi.org/10.1111/j.1468-2850.2006.00042.x

Lecavalier, L., Leone, S., & Wiltz, J. (2006). The impact of behaviour problems on caregiver stress in young people with autism spectrum disorders. *Journal of Intellectual Disability Research, 50,* 172–183. http://dx.doi.org/10.1111/j.1365-2788.2005.00732.x

Lovaas, O. I. (1981). *The ME book: Teaching developmentally disabled children.* Austin, TX: Pro-Ed.

Magaña, S., Parish, S. L., Rose, R. A., Timberlake, M., & Swaine, J. G. (2012). Racial and ethnic disparities in quality of health care among children with autism and other developmental disabilities. *Intellectual and Developmental Disabilities, 50,* 287–299. http://dx.doi.org/10.1352/1934-9556-50.4.287

Mah, J. W., & Johnston, C. (2008). Parental social cognitions: Considerations in the acceptability of and engagement in behavioral parent training. *Clinical Child and Family Psychology Review, 11,* 218–236. http://dx.doi.org/10.1007/s10567-008-0038-8

Manning, M. M., Wainwright, L., & Bennett, J. (2011). The double ABCX model of adaptation in racially diverse families with a school-age child with autism. *Journal of Autism and Developmental Disorders, 41,* 320–331. http://dx.doi.org/10.1007/s10803-010-1056-1

McCubbin, H. I., & Patterson, J. M. (1983). The family stress process: The double ABCX model of adjustment and adaptation. *Marriage & Family Review, 6,* 7–37. http://dx.doi.org/10.1300/J002v06n01_02

McKay, M. M., Stoewe, J., McCadam, K., & Gonzales, J. (1998). Increasing access to child mental health services for urban children and their caregivers. *Health & Social Work, 23,* 9–15. http://dx.doi.org/10.1093/hsw/23.1.9

Miller, W. R., & Rollnick, A. (2002). *Motivational interviewing: Preparing people for change* (2nd ed.). New York, NY: Guilford Press.

Morrissey-Kane, E., & Prinz, R. J. (1999). Engagement in child and adolescent treatment: The role of parental cognitions and attributions. *Clinical Child and Family Psychology Review, 2,* 183–198. http://dx.doi.org/10.1023/A:1021807106455

Neece, C. L. (2014). Mindfulness-based stress reduction for parents of young children with developmental delays: Implications for parental mental health and child behavior problems. *Journal of Applied Research in Intellectual Disabilities, 27,* 174–186. http://dx.doi.org/10.1111/jar.12064

Nevill, R. E., Lecavalier, L., & Stratis, E. A. (2018). Meta-analysis of parent-mediated interventions for young children with autism spectrum disorder. *Autism, 22,* 84–98. http://dx.doi.org/10.1177/1362361316677838

Nock, M. K., & Ferriter, C. (2005). Parent management of attendance and adherence in child and adolescent therapy: A conceptual and empirical review. *Clinical Child and Family Psychology Review, 8,* 149–166. http://dx.doi.org/10.1007/s10567-005-4753-0

Nock, M. K., & Kazdin, A. E. (2001). Parent expectancies for child therapy: Assessment and relation to participation in treatment. *Journal of Child and Family Studies, 10*, 155–180. http://dx.doi.org/10.1023/A:1016699424731

Nock, M. K., & Kazdin, A. E. (2005). Randomized controlled trial of a brief intervention for increasing participation in parent management training. *Journal of Consulting and Clinical Psychology, 73*, 872–879. http://dx.doi.org/10.1037/0022-006X.73.5.872

Oono, I. P., Honey, E. J., & McConachie, H. (2013). Parent-mediated early intervention for young children with autism spectrum disorders (ASD). *Cochrane Database of Systematic Reviews, 2013*(4), 1–98. http://dx.doi.org/10.1002/14651858.CD009774.pub2

Osborne, L. A., McHugh, L., Saunders, J., & Reed, P. (2008). Parenting stress reduces the effectiveness of early teaching interventions for autistic spectrum disorders. *Journal of Autism and Developmental Disorders, 38*, 1092–1103. http://dx.doi.org/10.1007/s10803-007-0497-7

Osborne, L. A., & Reed, P. (2009). The relationship between parenting stress and behavior problems of children with autistic spectrum disorders. *Exceptional Children, 76*, 54–73. http://dx.doi.org/10.1177/001440290907600103

Patterson, G. R., & Chamberlain, P. (1994). A functional analysis of resistance during parent training therapy. *Clinical Psychology: Science and Practice, 1*, 53–70. http://dx.doi.org/10.1111/j.1468-2850.1994.tb00006.x

Paynter, R., Riley, E., Beamish, W., Davies, M., & Milford, T. (2013). The double ABCX model of family adaptation in families of a child with an autism spectrum disorder attending an Australian early intervention service. *Research in Autism Spectrum Disorders, 7*, 1183–1195. http://dx.doi.org/10.1016/j.rasd.2013.07.006

Prinz, R. J., & Miller, G. E. (1994). Family-based treatment for childhood antisocial behavior: Experimental influences on dropout and engagement. *Journal of Consulting and Clinical Psychology, 62*, 645–650. http://dx.doi.org/10.1037/0022-006X.62.3.645

Reyno, S. M., & McGrath, P. J. (2006). Predictors of parent training efficacy for child externalizing behavior problems—A meta-analytic review. *Journal of Child Psychology and Psychiatry, 47*, 99–111. http://dx.doi.org/10.1111/j.1469-7610.2005.01544.x

Shawler, P. M., & Sullivan, M. A. (2017). Parental stress, discipline strategies, and child behavior problems in families with young children with autism spectrum disorders. *Focus on Autism and Other Developmental Disabilities, 32*, 142–151. http://dx.doi.org/10.1177/1088357615610114

Simonoff, E., Pickles, A., Charman, T., Chandler, S., Loucas, T., & Baird, G. (2008). Psychiatric disorders in children with autism spectrum disorders: Prevalence, comorbidity, and associated factors in a population-derived sample. *Journal of the American Academy of Child & Adolescent Psychiatry, 47*, 921–929. http://dx.doi.org/10.1097/CHI.0b013e318179964f

Sloper, P. (1999). Models of service support for parents of disabled children. What do we know? What do we need to know? *Child: Care, Health and Development, 25,* 85–99. http://dx.doi.org/10.1046/j.1365-2214.1999.25220120.x

Smith, T., Buch, G. A., & Gamby, T. E. (2000). Parent-directed, intensive early intervention for children with pervasive developmental disorder. *Research in Developmental Disabilities, 21,* 297–309. http://dx.doi.org/10.1016/S0891-4222(00)00043-3

Snell-Johns, J., Mendez, J. L., & Smith, B. H. (2004). Evidence-based solutions for overcoming access barriers, decreasing attrition, and promoting change with underserved families. *Journal of Family Psychology, 18,* 19–35. http://dx.doi.org/10.1037/0893-3200.18.1.19

Sofronoff, K., & Farbotko, M. (2002). The effectiveness of parent management training to increase self-efficacy in parents of children with Asperger syndrome. *Autism, 6,* 271–286. http://dx.doi.org/10.1177/1362361302006003005

Solish, A., & Perry, A. (2008). Parents' involvement in their children's behavioral intervention programs: Parent and therapist perspectives. *Research in Autism Spectrum Disorders, 2,* 728–738. http://dx.doi.org/10.1016/j.rasd.2008.03.001

Solomon, M., Ono, M., Timmer, S., & Goodlin-Jones, B. (2008). The effectiveness of parent–child interaction therapy for families of children on the autism spectrum. *Journal of Autism and Developmental Disorders, 38,* 1767–1776. http://dx.doi.org/10.1007/s10803-008-0567-5

Staudt, M. M. (2007). Treatment engagement with caregivers of at-risk children: Gaps in research and conceptualization. *Journal of Child and Family Studies, 16,* 183–196. http://dx.doi.org/10.1007/s10826-006-9077-2

Szapocznik, J., Perez-Vidal, A., Brickman, A. L., Foote, F. H., Santisteban, D., Hervis, O., & Kurtines, W. M. (1988). Engaging adolescent drug abusers and their families in treatment: A strategic structural systems approach. *Journal of Consulting and Clinical Psychology, 56,* 552–557. http://dx.doi.org/10.1037/0022-006X.56.4.552

Wachtel, K., & Carter, A. S. (2008). Reaction to diagnosis and parenting styles among mothers of young children with ASDs. *Autism, 12,* 575–594. http://dx.doi.org/10.1177/1362361308094505

Watt, B. D., Hoyland, M., Best, D., & Dadds, M. (2007). Treatment participation among children with conduct problems and the role of telephone reminders. *Journal of Child and Family Studies, 16,* 522–530. http://dx.doi.org/10.1007/s10826-006-9103-4

Webster-Stratton, C. (1998). Parent training with low-income families. In J. R. Lutzker (Ed.), *Handbook of child abuse research and treatment* (pp. 183–210). Boston, MA: Springer. http://dx.doi.org/10.1007/978-1-4757-2909-2_8

Webster-Stratton, C., Reid, M. J., & Hammond, M. (2001). Preventing conduct problems, promoting social competence: A parent and teacher training partnership in head start. *Journal of Clinical Child Psychology, 30,* 283–302. http://dx.doi.org/10.1207/S15374424JCCP3003_2

Weisz, J. R., & Jensen, P. S. (1999). Efficacy and effectiveness of child and adolescent psychotherapy and pharmacotherapy. *Mental Health Services Research, 1*, 125–157. http://dx.doi.org/10.1023/A:1022321812352

Wenning, K., & King, S. (1995). Parent orientation meetings to improve attendance and access at a child psychiatric clinic. *Psychiatric Services, 46*, 831–833. http://dx.doi.org/10.1176/ps.46.8.831

Whittingham, K., Sofronoff, K., & Sheffield, J. K. (2006). Stepping Stones Triple P: A pilot study to evaluate acceptability of the program by parents of a child diagnosed with an Autism Spectrum Disorder. *Research in Developmental Disabilities, 27*, 364–380. http://dx.doi.org/10.1016/j.ridd.2005.05.003

Wierzbicki, M., & Pekarik, G. (1993). A meta-analysis of psychotherapy dropout. *Professional Psychology: Research and Practice, 24*, 190–195. http://dx.doi.org/10.1037/0735-7028.24.2.190

Zwaigenbaum, L., Bauman, M. L., Choueiri, R., Kasari, C., Carter, A., Granpeesheh, D., . . . Natowicz, M. R. (2015). Early intervention for children with autism spectrum disorder under 3 years of age: Recommendations for practice and research. *Pediatrics, 136*(Suppl. 1), S60–S81. http://dx.doi.org/10.1542/peds.2014-3667E

4

PARENT TRAINING FOR SOCIAL COMMUNICATION IN YOUNG CHILDREN WITH AUTISM SPECTRUM DISORDER

STEPHANIE Y. SHIRE AND TRISTRAM SMITH

Signs of autism spectrum disorder (ASD) often emerge at 12 to 18 months of age and become increasingly marked over the next couple of years (Szatmari et al., 2016). Among the first signs are difficulties with prelinguistic social communication (summarized in Exhibit 4.1). Notably, toddlers with ASD have *limited joint engagement*, which occurs when two people share interest in an object—or even are aware of their shared interest and sustain it in a back-and-forth interaction (Szatmari et al., 2016). Toddlers with ASD are less likely than typically developing children to seek to coordinate attention by alternating their gaze between objects and people, and they are less likely to notice when a caregiver does so (Mundy, Sigman, & Kasari, 1990; Mundy, Sigman, Ungerer, & Sherman, 1986; Sigman et al., 1999). They tend not to direct positive affect toward others to show pleasure in interactions (Kasari, Sigman, Mundy, & Yirmiya, 1990; Landa, Holman, & Garrett-Mayer, 2007). Compared with other toddlers, toddlers with ASD are less likely to use gesture

http://dx.doi.org/10.1037/0000111-005
Parent Training for Autism Spectrum Disorder: Improving the Quality of Life for Children and Their Families,
C. R. Johnson, E. M. Butter, and L. Scahill (Editors)

EXHIBIT 4.1
Difficulties in Prelinguistic Social Communication in Autism Spectrum Disorder

Limited joint engagement
   Alternating gaze between objects and people
   Directing positive affect toward others
   Using gesture for back-and-forth social interaction
   Integrating gesture, eye contact, and speech to communicate
Limited imitation
   Mimicry
   Switching back and forth between modeling actions and being modeled
Play
   Make believe or creative activities
   Diverse, flexible, and skillful play acts
   Involvement of peers and caregivers

to initiate joint engagement. Their use of pointing, showing, and giving is diminished or atypical (Baron-Cohen, 1989; Sullivan et al., 2007; Wetherby, Watt, Morgan, & Shumway, 2007), as is their use of *representational gestures*, which depict objects or actions that closely relate to what is conveyed in speech (Wetherby, Prizant, & Hutchinson, 1998). They may display gestures to express wants but not to comment or display interest, and their gestures often are uncoordinated with eye contact and speech (Baron-Cohen, 1989; Goodhart & Baron-Cohen, 1993; Mundy et al., 1986; Wetherby et al., 1998).

Typically developing infants and toddlers learn joint engagement mainly in the context of playful interactions with others, especially caregivers (Adamson, Deckner, & Bakeman, 2010). During those interactions, the child and caregiver often express joy at being together, imitate or build on each other's actions, and make up new variations of games (Adamson et al., 2010). However, toddlers with ASD may be particularly disadvantaged in this type of setting. Along with deficits in coordinating attention, showing pleasure in interactions, and using gestures, toddlers with ASD often have limited imitation skills. Typically developing toddlers use *mimicry* (i.e., automatically copying or mirroring another person's facial expressions and gestures) to facilitate social functioning by establishing rapport and increasing recognition of others' thoughts and feelings; children with ASD rarely do so (McIntosh, Reichmann-Decker, Winkielman, & Wilbarger, 2006). In addition, typically developing toddlers engage in *reciprocal imitation* (i.e., switching back and forth between being the model and imitator), which provides opportunities for monitoring the effect of their actions on others, identifying who is taking which role, and taking on the role of the other person; this also is rare in children with ASD (Nadel, 2014). Moreover, toddlers and children with ASD have deficits in play skills and the ability to share reciprocal play interactions with others. Relying mainly on functional play skills, children with autism seldom engage in creative and imaginative play with objects and people (Jarrold, Boucher, & Smith, 1996; Lewis & Boucher, 1995; Ungerer & Sigman, 1981). The play acts of children with ASD, both functional and symbolic, tend to be less diverse, flexible, and skillful than the play acts of their typically developing peers (Ungerer & Sigman, 1981).

PREVALENCE AND IMPACT OF CORE FEATURES

Difficulties in social communication are a defining feature of ASD (Adamson, Romski, & Barton-Hulsey, 2014) and, as such, are present in all individuals who receive an ASD diagnosis. The early difficulties in joint engagement, imitation, and play are believed to be present in all toddlers with ASD (Mundy & Crowson, 1997), and often remain present in pre-schoolers. Approximately 30% of children with ASD continue to be minimally verbal into later childhood and beyond (Tager-Flusberg & Kasari, 2013), with ongoing difficulties in prelinguistic social communication skills. Other children with ASD learn to use language and even may develop above-average skills for their age in some areas, such as vocabulary. These children may acquire adequate prelinguistic social communication skills but almost always still have difficulties with other aspects of social communication, such as engaging in back-and-forth conversations, understanding implied meanings, or recognizing nonverbal cues (e.g., body language or tone of voice; Adamson et al., 2014).

Early social communication difficulties in ASD appear to have important implications for later functioning. Joint attention skill assessed in the preschool years predicts language outcome 1 year (Kasari, Paparella, Freeman, & Jahromi, 2008; Mundy et al., 1990; Stone & Yoder, 2001), 2 years (Sullivan et al., 2007), 5 years (Charman et al., 2005; Kasari, Gulsrud, Freeman, Paparella, & Hellemann, 2012) and 8 years later (Sigman et al., 1999). Research on typically developing children has suggested that joint attention also is vital for learning to share experiences with others and for recognizing that others may have a different perspective from one's own (Carpenter, Nagell, Tomasello, Butterworth, & Moore, 1998). Thus, difficulties in joint attention could contribute to later difficulties with social reciprocity in children with ASD (Mundy & Crowson, 1997). Imitation also predicts subsequent language (Dawson, 2008; Stone & Yoder, 2001), and symbolic play predicts superior peer social interaction skills during school-aged years (Sigman et al., 1999). These findings suggest that intervening to improve prelinguistic social communication skills could be highly beneficial for toddlers with ASD.

EMPIRICALLY-BASED MODELS FOR TARGETING
SOCIAL COMMUNICATION IN PARENT TRAINING

Because interactions between toddlers and caregivers are crucial to learning prelinguistic social communication skills, many intervention programs have been formulated to teach parents strategies to improve these skills. Table 4.1 describes some of the best-known programs. Most provide 10 to 25 hours of intervention with the parent over 3 to 6 months (Smith & Iadarola, 2015), but some offer more than 100 hours (e.g., Wetherby et al., 2014). Depending on the program, clinicians meet with groups of parents (e.g., Hardan et al., 2015), work with parents individually (e.g., Kasari, Gulsrud, Wong, Kwon, & Locke, 2010), or combine group and individual sessions (e.g., Keen, Couzens, Muspratt, & Rodger, 2010). They may provide didactic instruction to the parent without the child present (e.g., Tonge, Brereton, Kiomall, Mackinnon, & Rinehart, 2014), coach the parent on intervention strategies while the parent is interacting with the child (e.g., Solomon, Van Egeren, Mahoney, Quon Huber, & Zimmerman, 2014), or both (e.g., Keen et al., 2010). Instruction or coaching may occur in a clinic (e.g., Hardan et al., 2015) or in the family home (e.g., Kasari, Lawton, et al., 2014).

Most parent training (PT) programs for social communication emphasize one or both of two theoretical frameworks: applied behavior analysis (ABA; Smith, 2011) and developmental social-pragmatic (DSP) models (also called interactive, transactional, or interpersonal models; Ingersoll, Dvortcsak, Whalen, & Sikora, 2005). ABA programs are based on the view that ASD is a learning difficulty that can be addressed with operant conditioning strategies, such as systematically reinforcing target behaviors and teaching children to distinguish between different cues (Smith, 2011). Strategies are designed to increase children's success in obtaining reinforcement by either simplifying instruction or capitalizing on strengths that children with ASD tend to have. An example of simplified instruction is discrete trial training (DTT), which involves breaking skills down into small steps and teaching them systematically in parent-led, structure sessions that take place in a one-to-one, distraction-free environment. This arrangement may enable children with ASD to pick up new skills rapidly. An example of an approach that aims to capitalize on children's strengths is pivotal response training (PRT). PRT aims to teach "pivotal" responses that, when acquired, have the potential to improve performance across many other skill areas. In PRT, an important pivotal response for communication is learning how to speak in words to make requests. This skill can increase a child's success in gaining access to preferred objects or activities and, as such, may increase the child's overall motivation to communicate (Koegel & Koegel, 2006). Moreover, requesting in words may be easier to teach than other forms of communication

TABLE 4.1
Examples of Parent Training Programs for Social Communication

Program	Sessions	Goals	Strategies	Outcomes
Early social interaction	3 sessions per week (2 home, 1 clinic) individually with parent and child for 6 months; 2 individual sessions per week (1 home, 1 community)	Communication: • initiating, using, and comprehending gestures, sounds, and words; • initiating and responding to joint attention; • increasing functional object use and pretend play; and • interacting reciprocally. Emotional regulation: • expressing emotion; • using calming strategies and communication; and • using regulatory strategies to stay engaged and handle new and changing situations;	• Matching child's preferences and communication level; • designing motivating activities (e.g., providing temptations to communicate in the context of preferred play activities); and • organizing supportive environments (e.g., using visual cues and schedules).	In an RCT of 82 toddlers with ASD, improvements observed in social communication, adaptive behavior, and receptive language; no change observed in expressive language or ASD symptoms (Wetherby et al., 2014)

(continues)

TABLE 4.1
Examples of Parent Training Programs for Social Communication   (Continued)

Program	Sessions	Goals	Strategies	Outcomes
Hanen's more than words	8 group sessions at a clinic intermixed with 3 individual sessions with the parent and child in the family home	• Two-way interaction; and • receptive and expressive communication, particularly for social purposes.	• Responding to communicative attempts; • following the child's lead; • engaging in joint action routines in play; • interacting during daily routine; • using books and play as contexts for communication; • using visual cues and schedules using visual supports; and • arranging opportunities for peer interaction.	No benefits observed in an RCT of 62 toddlers with ASD (Carter et al., 2011)
JASPER[a]	10 one-to-one, weekly sessions with the parent and child	Increasing joint engagement, spontaneous prelinguistic and spoken social communication, play skills, and emotion regulation	• Matching child's pacing and affect; • arranging play environment; • establishing expanding play routines; • creating opportunities and prompting communication; and • responding to and expanding on communication.	Increased joint engagement observed in 4 RCTs of parent-mediated intervention ($N = 38$ [Kasari et al., 2010]; Ns = 66 and 112 [Kasari et al., 2015; Kasari, Kaiser, et al., 2014; Kasari, Lawton, et al., 2014]); inconsistent effects on other outcomes

P-ESDM	12 individual, weekly, 1-hour sessions with the parent and child at a clinic	• Increasing attention and motivation; • enhancing nonverbal and verbal communication, joint attention, and imitation; and • decreasing interfering behaviors.	• Using positive affect; • engaging in joint activity routines with imitation, modeling, and turn-taking; • being sensitive and responsive to child cues; and • assessing function of behavior and using function-based interventions to reduce interfering behaviors.	No benefits observed in an RCT of 98 toddlers with ASD (Rogers et al., 2012)
Parent-mediated communication-focused treatment in children with autism (i.e., PACT)	12 individual, 2-hour group sessions with the parent and child at a clinic over 6 months; 6 2-hour booster sessions over next 6 months	• Shared attention; • communication; • intentionality (awareness of communication partner and attempts to obtain partner's attention); and • pragmatics (using communication for a range of purposes or functions).	• Establishing shared attention; • being synchronous and sensitive; • using language at child's level; • creating routines; • increasing communication functions; and • increasing communication skills.	In an RCT of 144 toddlers with ASD, gains found in parent–child interaction but not in scores on standardized measures of language and ASD symptoms (Green et al., 2010)
PRTG	Eight 90-minute group sessions for parents, intermixed with four 60-minute sessions with child present, weekly	Increasing frequency and complexity of verbal communication	• Structuring learning opportunities; • teaching during naturally occurring routines; • following child's lead and sharing control; • varying instructional tasks; and • responding to communicative attempts.	In an RCT of 53 toddlers and preschoolers with ASD, increase observed in frequency of communication utterances and parent-reported use of communication in everyday situations; no change observed on other measures (Hardan et al., 2015)

(continues)

TABLE 4.1

Examples of Parent Training Programs for Social Communication   (Continued)

Program	Sessions	Goals	Strategies	Outcomes
PLAY project	12 3-hour sessions monthly with parent and child in the home	Increased developmental level of social communication and interaction	• Assessing child's preferences for interactions and sensory input, and developmental level; selecting activities for parent–child interaction; • following child's lead; and • increasing length and complexity of back-and-forth interaction.	In an RCT of 128 preschoolers with ASD, increase observed in parent–child interaction and in development of social communication and interaction; no change observed in language or cognitive development (Solomon et al., 2014)
ImPACT	1–2 1-hour sessions per week for approximately 18 weeks with parent and child at a clinic	• Social engagement; • language; • imitation; and • play.	• Following child's lead (i.e., letting child choose activity, staying at eye level, joining in or imitating); • modeling and expanding language; • creating opportunities for communication; and • pacing interaction to maintain child's motivation.	In RCT (N = 29) of one component (30 sessions of reciprocal imitation training), increase in initiation of joint attention (Ingersoll, 2012)

Note. RCT = randomized controlled trial; ASD = autism spectrum disorder; JASPER = joint attention, symbolic play, engagement, and regulation; P-ESDM = parent delivery of the early start Denver model; PACT = preschool autism communication trial; PRTG = pivotal response treatment group; PLAY = play and language for autistic youngsters; ImPACT = project improving parents as communication teachers.
[a]See Case Example: Bethany section and Table 4.2 for additional information.

because many toddlers with ASD are already better at using prelinguistic communication for requesting than for other purposes, such as *commenting*, that is, language for the purpose of social sharing (Sigman, Mundy, Sherman, & Ungerer, 1986).

DSP interventions are designed to focus more directly on core deficits in ASD in areas such as joint attention and symbolic play, based on evidence (reviewed in the previous section) that these deficits portend a cascade of other problems with social communication and interaction (Mundy & Crowson, 1997). DSP intervention strategies are derived from findings in developmental psychology that show a strong association between caregivers' responsivity to their young children and the children's subsequent acquisition of skills for communicating and interacting with others (Prizant & Wetherby, 2005). Emphasizing strategies similar to ones used in interventions to help caregivers be more sensitive to their young, typically developing children (Wallace & Rogers, 2010), DSP PT programs aim to promote social communication and interaction by helping parents be responsive to their child in ways such as imitating, expanding on, and joining into play activities that the child initiates (Ingersoll et al., 2005). Parents are guided to show positive affect during these activities (Solomon et al., 2014).

Some PT programs explicitly combine ABA and DSP strategies. For example, one program contains seven sessions that focus on DSP strategies, followed by three sessions on ABA strategies and two sessions to help parents generalize and maintain their use of these strategies (Davlantis & Rogers, 2016; Rogers et al., 2012). Such programs have been described as naturalistic developmental behavioral interventions (Schreibman et al., 2015).

PT programs for social communication have been evaluated in more randomized controlled trials (RCTs) than any other psychosocial intervention for ASD. At this writing, more than a dozen RCTs have been published (Smith & Iadarola, 2015). Although some RCTs have been small feasibility trials, others have had samples of more than 100 participants, with exemplary research designs and analysis plans (e.g., Green et al., 2010). However, DTT-based PT has been evaluated only in studies of interventions that include other components or studies that have focused on skills other than social communication (Smith, 2011). For this reason, DTT-based PT programs for social communication are still experimental. A 12-session, PRT-based program in which parents met in groups produced modest increases in total communicative utterances relative to a control group; however, benefits were not found on more global measures of language use (Hardan et al., 2015). Because no other RCTs of PRT-based PT have been published, additional research is needed. Findings from RCTs of DSP-based programs are mixed. Some studies have described benefits for both parent and child (e.g., Wetherby et al., 2014), whereas others have reported gains for the parent but not the child (e.g., Keen et al., 2010), or neither the parent nor the child (Oosterling et al., 2010). When positive effects are seen in the child, they include gains in social communication during interactions with the parent, and they may extend to more global measures of language (e.g., increased scores on standardized tests of language skill or everyday use of language; Wetherby et al., 2014).

Overall, DSP-based PT programs for social communication have been evaluated more broadly than ABA-based programs. The mixed results across studies complicate appraisals of the strength of evidence for DSP-based programs. Nevertheless, reviews have suggested that the evidence is predominately favorable, especially for improving social communication during parent–child interaction. One review designated these programs as "probably efficacious" (Smith & Iadarola, 2015, p. 899), and others have reached similar conclusions (Kendall et al., 2013). Hence, the remainder of this chapter focuses on DSP-based programs.

ASSESSMENT

Direct behavioral assessment is the primary method for evaluating early social communication skills and monitoring progress with treatment in toddlers with ASD (Paul & Fahim, 2014; Tager-Flusberg et al., 2009). Parent report can provide complementary information. Language samples are valuable for evaluating speech used for social communication and can be drawn from the behavioral assessment (Tager-Flusberg et al., 2009). Standardized tests tap a wider range of language skills, such as comprehension, vocabulary, and emergence of language concepts (e.g., attributes, opposites). These tests can be useful for characterizing a child's level of language development at entry into intervention but may be too broad to be sensitive to change that occurs in intervention.

A commercially available behavioral assessment is the Communication and Symbolic Behavior Scales (CSBS; Wetherby & Prizant, 2002a), which is intended for children with developmental levels between 8 and 24 months of age. The CSBS involves interactions between an examiner and child with a standard set of toys; it takes about an hour to administer and another hour to score. It yields scores in seven areas: communicative functions, gestural communicative means, vocal communicative means, verbal communicative means, reciprocity, social-affective signaling, and symbolic behavior. A shorter behavioral assessment involves observing caregiver–child interaction (Adamson & Bakeman, 1984). There are many different protocols for conducting the observation, but most involve 10- to 15-minute sessions that include opportunities for the caregiver and child to freely choose play activities from a standard set of varied toys. Sessions also may include more structured activities in which the caregiver presents different types of toys intended to encourage different types of communication from the child (Adamson, Bakeman, Deckner, & Nelson, 2012). Scoring of the child's social communication usually includes a frequency count of particular behaviors, such as alternating gaze and using gesture for joint attention and requesting. Scoring also may include ratings of the child's level of engagement with others, ranging from completely unengaged (e.g., wandering, repetitive behavior) through coordinated joint engagement (e.g., initiating a play act, commenting on the act, and giving a toy to invite the caregiver to participate). Examples include the Communication Play Protocol (Adamson et al., 2012) and the Communication Intention Inventory (Paul & Norbury, 2012).

Another short behavioral assessment that is under development and will become commercially available is the Brief Observation of Social Communication Change (BOSCC; Grzadzinski et al., 2016). The BOSCC is intended for children with ASD between 18 months and 5 years old. It involves a 12-minute interaction between the child and an evaluator who uses a prespecified set of toys designed to encourage comments and interaction from the child. The evaluator rates 12 items on a 6-point Likert scale, including nine items to assess ASD symptoms in social communication and three items to assess restricted or repetitive behaviors.

Other behavioral assessments focus on particular aspects of social communication. For example, the Early Social Communication Scales involve a semistructured, 15- to 20-minute interaction in which the child and tester sit facing each other at a table with a set of toys in view but out of reach of the child (Mundy et al., 2003). Included are several small windup and hand-operated mechanical toys, as well as a hat, comb, glasses, ball, car, balloon, and book. The administration is recorded on videotape and later scored. Raters count frequencies of both initiations and responses of joint attention behaviors (e.g., coordinated looking, pointing and showing, following points). The Motor Imitation Scale involves rating the quality of the child's imitation of eight actions with objects (e.g., walking a toy dog across the table) and eight gestures (e.g., clapping hands) on a 4-point Likert scale (Stone, Ousley, & Littleford, 1997); half the actions and gestures are conventional movements that children have probably seen before, while the other half are novel. Another measure of imitation is the Imitation Battery (Rogers, Hepburn, Stackhouse, & Wehner, 2003), which consists of 16 tasks (seven manual acts, four actions on objects, and five oral-facial movements), rated on a 3-point Likert scale. In the 15- to 20-minute Structured Play Assessment (SPA; Ungerer & Sigman, 1981), the child is seated at a table and presented with a series of toy sets. The child's play behaviors are later coded from video recordings. All of these instruments have well-established psychometric properties but require specialized training that is difficult for community providers to obtain (training is available mostly in research centers).

Language samples can be obtained by transcribing speech from video- or audio recordings of any of the foregoing behavioral assessments. The transcription process is laborious, but, once complete, the transcripts can be analyzed using software that is either free (Long, 2008; MacWhinney, 2000) or inexpensive (Miller & Chapman, 2008). The analysis provides detailed information on how the child communicates using speech in the context of a play-based, social interaction with an adult, such as how many different words the child uses, how many words are contained in each utterance, and how many different ways the child communicates (e.g., to request, label, comment, or converse; Blume & Lust, 2017).

The most widely used parent rating scale is the MacArthur–Bates Communicative Development Inventories (Fenson, Marchman, Thal, Reznick, & Bates, 2007), which is a 20- to 40-minute checklist for children with language levels between 8 and 37 months old. The inventories ask parents to rate the presence or absence of vocabulary words, early phrase speech, use of gestures, and imitation. Studies have indicated that the inventories correlate well with the results of standardized tests in children with ASD (Tager-Flusberg et al., 2009). Other parent-rating scales that may be considered are the 24-item CSBS DP Infant-Toddler Checklist (Wetherby & Prizant, 2002b) and the 20- to 30-minute Language Use Inventory (O'Neill, 2009), although little is known about their psychometric properties when administered for young children with ASD.

To assess the child's everyday use of communication skills, the Vineland Adaptive Behavior Scales, Third Edition (Sparrow, Cicchetti, & Saulnier, 2016), administered as either a 30-minute parent rating scale or 30- to 60-minute parent interview, yields norm-referenced standard scores and age equivalents for comprehension and production of language. For children who speak communicatively in words, standardized tests of the child can be given to assess level of language development. Examples of tests that may be useful are the Preschool Language Scales, Fifth Edition (Zimmerman, Steiner, & Pond, 2011), and the Reynell Developmental Language Scales (Reynell & Gruber, 1990).

SPECIFIC PARENT TRAINING STRATEGIES

Active Ingredients

The umbrella term *parent training* captures a variety of models that vary in approach, intensity, focus, and delivery, as reviewed in the Empirically-Based

Models for Targeting Social Communication in Parent Training section. Identifying which of these components are "active ingredients" or "mechanisms of change" for improving children's social communication is necessary to optimize interventions and help children achieve the best possible outcomes. Research on this topic is especially important because of the mixed findings across studies (noted in the Empirically-Based Models for Targeting Social Communication in Parent Training section). At present, however, the influence of different components of PT models is not well understood. Comparison of findings across studies suggests that, in general, PT programs may be most successful when they are relatively lengthy (> 20 sessions), include direct coaching of the parent with the child, and conduct sessions in the family home, rather than a clinic (Wetherby et al., 2014). Two articles have provided more direct tests of active ingredients. The first examined whether improvements in parent–child interactions led to improvements in children's communication (Pickles et al., 2015) in the Preschool Autism Communication Trial (PACT; Green et al., 2010), whereas the second sought to distill the active ingredients of joint attention, symbolic play, engagement, and regulation (JASPER) with toddlers (Gulsrud, Hellemann, Shire, & Kasari, 2016)

Pickles et al. (2015) demonstrated that both child behavior (i.e., children's communicative initiations) and parents' behavior (i.e., *parental synchrony*, defined as the proportion of parent's verbal or nonverbal communicative acts that follow the child's focus of attention) mediated the effect of PACT (Green et al., 2010) treatment on a measure of ASD symptom severity.

Gulsrud et al. (2016) conducted a more fine-grained analysis that involved examining four domains of parents' JASPER interaction strategies: (a) environmental arrangement (e.g., developmentally appropriate toy selection, moving face to face, creating clear choices), (b) mirrored pacing (e.g., timing of play act and communication including imitation and modeling), (c) communication, and (d) prompting. These investigators found that mirrored pacing, environmental arrangement, and assignment to JASPER treatment together accounted for 42% of the change in *joint engagement*— the ability to notice both the interaction partner (i.e., the parent) and the shared activity.

Together, those two articles preliminarily linked parents' interaction style and strategies to their children's social communication outcomes. Parental synchrony (in the study by Pickles et al., 2015) and mirrored pacing (in the study by Gulsrud et al., 2016) both required that parents provide contingent timely responses to their children's communication attempts. This skill is emphasized in many DSP PT models and, as such, may be an important similarity among them. Parceling out similarities and differences to test the unique contributions of these components to children's social communication outcomes may aid in selection of intervention approaches based on data-supported components, rather than the "brand name" of an intervention.

Example Intervention: Joint Attention, Symbolic Play, Engagement, and Regulation

JASPER (Kasari, Freeman, & Paparella, 2006; Kasari et al., 2008, 2012) is a targeted social communication module that is delivered in the context of play. RCTs indicate that various agents of change can implement JASPER effectively, including clinicians and parents (Kasari et al., 2010; Kasari, Lawton, et al., 2014; Kasari, Gulsrud, Paparella, Hellemann, & Berry, 2015), as well as preschool teachers and paraprofessionals (Chang, Shire, Shih, Gelfand, & Kasari, 2016). The intervention focuses on coordinating between a play partner and a shared activity (i.e., joint engagement), initiating prelinguistic and spoken social communication skills, and increasing the level and diversity of children's play. To identify developmentally appropriate social communication and play skill targets, clinicians conduct a short initial assessment to identify the child's current skill level and next step. In parent-mediated JASPER, clinicians briefly discuss the information obtained from the assessments with the parent and establish a starting place for the intervention, as illustrated later in the case example (in the section Case Example: Bethany).

Following the assessment, a clinician works individually with a parent and child over the course of 10 sessions of up to 1 hour in length. The clinician aims to teach the parent to select developmentally appropriate materials and set up the play space, respond to and expand children's social communication bids, imitate and expand children's appropriate play acts to build developmentally appropriate play routines, and program explicit opportunities for social communication. The seven core segments of the intervention are described in Table 4.2.

JASPER strategies are introduced to parents in a layered approach: The basic foundations are provided first (e.g., identifying children's current play level and social communication skills; setting up the environment for success) and new steps are introduced weekly until the parent is practicing the full package of JASPER strategies. Brief discussion to introduce the week's topic and to check in with the parent occur at the start of the session, followed by live practice with the child. Live coaching may include modeling strategies with the child while the parent observes, codelivery of the strategies by parent and interventionist, or delivery of the strategies by the parent with verbal and environmental support from the interventionist. The balance of these components is flexible, depending on the parent's needs and learning style. For example, parents who are eager to be active in the session

TABLE 4.2
Key Strategies in Joint Attention, Symbolic Play,
Engagement, and Regulation (JASPER)

Strategies	Description
Supporting engagement and regulation	Appropriately matching child's pacing and affect during play; appropriately applying behavioral strategies when the child is unengaged or dysregulated
Setting up the environment	Setting up the environment to facilitate joint engagement, including environmental arrangement; selecting developmentally appropriate toys and placing them within reach and view of the child; and facing the child at eye level
Following the child's lead	Following the child's interest during the interaction by imitating and modeling at appropriate times
Establishing play routines	Establishing a clear play routine or sequence of steps that is developmentally appropriate
Expanding play routines	Adding timely and developmentally appropriate steps to existing play routines or following a child's appropriate expansion
Programming for joint attention and requesting skills	Modeling and creating opportunities for requesting and joint attention, and responding to the child's joint attention and requesting bids
Language strategies	Talking at the child's level, leaving space to communicate; responding to the child's communication; and expanding communication

may receive more verbal coaching and spend less time observing the interventionist model the strategies, whereas a parent who learns best through observation may observe for a longer portion of the session before practicing the strategies with verbal feedback. Although a sequence of topics is provided for the 10 weeks, the interventionist has the flexibility to alter the sequence, depending on the family's needs (e.g., giving more time to a particularly challenging topic, addressing strategies for dysregulation early rather than late in the sequence for a child struggling with regulation).

SPECIAL CONSIDERATIONS

Implementation of parent-mediated interventions (PMIs) in real-world settings requires attention to a numerous special considerations related to the needs and characteristics of the child, caregiver, and setting, among other factors, particularly for families that typically are underrepresented in ASD research. Three examples are discussed in this section: families that (a) live in underresourced areas, (b) reside far away from research centers but can be reached with technology, or (c) have school-age children with minimal expressive language.

Families Living in Low-Resource Areas

As far as epidemiologists can determine, ASD is present in regions around the globe, regardless of socioeconomic status. The scarcity of human and financial resources, their inequitable distribution among regions, and the inefficiency of delivery to those in need plague mental health services (Saxena, Thornicroft, Knapp, & Whiteford, 2007). Two studies have specifically addressed the delivery of PMIs for preschool-age children with ASD in low-resource settings. The first study focused on underresourced families living in the United States (Kasari, Lawton, et al., 2014). The second examined the adaptation and delivery of the PACT intervention with families in India and Pakistan (Rahman et al., 2016).

Building on data from prior caregiver-mediated trials focusing on toddlers in clinic-based settings, Kasari, Lawton, et al. (2014) enrolled 147 families who had children with ASD, age 3 to 5, and limited home resources (e.g., meeting the state definition of "low income," unemployed primary caregiver, receiving government assistance). The children were highly diverse: 66% identified as a racial/ethnic minority and 15% as speaking a language other than English. Families were randomized to 24 hour-long coaching sessions (i.e., caregiver-mediated JASPER) or 12 two-hour-long small group sessions held in the community; the sessions focused on routines, communication, and behavior management (i.e., caregiver education). Adaptations for low-resource families included conducting sessions in the family home or community, rather than a clinic, and offering flexible scheduling of sessions. Children in caregiver-mediated JASPER demonstrated gains in time jointly engaged with their caregiver and initiations of joint attention captured on the Early Social Communication Scales (ESCS; Mundy et al., 2003) over children with caregivers participating in the small group education sessions.

Similarly, Divan et al. (2015) adapted the PACT intervention to meet the needs of low-resource settings. Examples of adaptations included a mix of clinic and home settings, rather than clinic only; inclusion of grandparents and nannies as participants in the training; and use of nonspecialist interventionists (i.e., college-educated health workers with no prior experience in mental health) who were supervised by specialists. The intervention consisted of 12 hours of discussion and video feedback to support caregivers' interaction with their child. In an RCT of 65 children with ASD, age 2 to 9 years (Rahman et al., 2016), children receiving the adapted PACT intervention increased the proportion of their communication identified as initiations, rather than responses. No changes in parents' report of child skills or parents' report of their own mental health were found.

Both the JASPER caregiver-mediated intervention and PACT trials were conducted one on one with caregivers. Although methods to coach the families in working with their children differed between the two interventions (e.g., live coaching with the dyad versus video review with no coaching), the resource-intensive model of individual sessions in the home/clinic in both interventions led to gains in children's outcome and changes in parents' behavior after relatively brief intervention.

Using Technology to Reach Families at Distance

Research is beginning to emerge on using technology to deliver PT for social communication in children with ASD. One method to reach families living in geographic areas without intervention services is to provide Web-based telehealth programming. Other mental health fields have demonstrated success with online parent education or coaching over the web (e.g., attention-deficit/hyperactivity disorder [Myers, Vander Stoep, Zhou, McCarty, & Katon, 2015], disruptive behaviors [Jones et al., 2013]). Research in ASD is more preliminary, consisting almost entirely of single-subject studies. However, one RCT obtained initial evidence for telehealth coaching (Ingersoll, Wainer, Berger, Pickard, & Bonter, 2016). After 24 30-minute sessions, children with parents who received telehealth coaching demonstrated marginally significant gains in language during interactions with their parent over children with parents who participated in the self-directed condition, which provided unrestricted access to the intervention content via a website but no direct involvement with a clinician. Because of the complexity of coaching, moving from live coaching to a web-based platform poses considerable challenges. However, this adaptation has the potential to increase access to intervention and reduce costs and travel time, especially for families in remote areas. Therefore, further exploration is warranted.

Focusing on Children Who Are Minimally Verbal

School-age children with ASD who continue to have few or no words are underrepresented in the intervention literature, including research on PMIs. However, two randomized trials (Kasari, Kaiser, et al., 2014; Paul, Campbell, Gilbert, & Tsiouri, 2013) focused explicitly on school-age children who were minimally verbal, using fewer than 20 spontaneous functional words at study entry (Tager-Flusberg & Kasari, 2013). Together, the two studies indicated that coaching parents in developmental approaches (JASPER, Kasari, Kaiser, et al., 2014; responsivity training, Paul et al., 2013) in addition to direct clinician–child services can improve social communication outcomes, including spontaneous communicative utterances (Kasari, Lawton, et al., 2014) and words produced (Paul et al., 2013) in semistructured play-based communication assessments, such as the CSBS or language samples. However, those studies did not provide information on the effectiveness of PMI as a stand-alone intervention for minimally verbal children with ASD.

For children who have limited functional spoken communication, augmentative and alternative communication (AAC) systems can provide another modality to communicate (Ganz, 2015). Supporting parents' ability to navigate, program, and communicate via AAC devices could help parents give their children vital access to communication across settings (Shire & Jones, 2015). However, only one RCT has examined whether PMIs can teach parents to use AAC. Kasari, Kaiser, et al. (2014) found that parents successfully incorporated speech-generating AAC devices to target both spoken and augmented language. Social communication outcomes with AAC require further examination not only in PMI trials but throughout the ASD intervention literature.

Unlike caregivers of very young children, families with school-age children with ASD who are minimally verbal have many years of experience with their child and may have received a variety of services, including prior parent education or coaching. Therefore, they already may be using several interaction strategies when they enter a study. Those strategies may influence children's engagement in the interaction. In a study of 61 parent–child dyads, including school-age children with ASD who were minimally verbal, parents averaged 46% fidelity in the intervention strategies at baseline but still had mixed success engaging their children in play-based interactions (Shire et al., 2015). A better understanding of what strategies parents are using already and an understanding of how these strategies fit with those taught in the intervention may help tailor the intervention to caregivers' existing strengths, style, and goals.

CASE EXAMPLE: BETHANY

Bethany[1] is a 5-and-a-half-year-old girl. At intake, her mother reported that Bethany was diagnosed with ASD at age 3 and had been enrolled in publicly funded early intervention and preschool services for the past 2 years. Bethany rarely initiates the use of words for commenting or other forms of

---

[1]Clinical material has been disguised to protect client confidentiality.

communication, but she can echo an adult's words when prompted to request for highly motivating items (e.g., favorite gummies at snack time).

Bethany spends her time wandering around the house or looking out the window. She also plays alone with animal figures for long periods; she likes to line the figures up along the windowsill. She also spends long periods watching her favorite television shows about animals and playing games on her iPad. Her interest in these activities is intense. When others try to play with her or ask her to do something else, she protests with loud vocalizations. Bethany's mother expressed a desire to learn how to play with her daughter. Therefore, the interventionist selected play as their primary routine.

Initial Assessment: Play and Social Communication

The clinician assessed Bethany's play and social communication skills using two semistructured behavioral assessments: SPA (Ungerer & Sigman, 1981) and ESCS (Mundy et al., 2003). During the play assessment (i.e., SPA), Bethany lined up some of the toys and completed simple combinations of play actions (e.g., put all the pieces in the puzzle or shape sorter), and then insisted on cleaning up the toys once she had finished playing with them. During the social communication assessment (i.e., ESCS), Bethany enjoyed the balloons. She spontaneously gave the balloon to request that the assessor blow the balloon up again. She also showed interest in the windup toys by reaching for them when they stopped moving across the table. Bethany also used coordinated joint looks to share her excitement about some of the toys at several points throughout the assessment. Thus, she demonstrated some prelinguistic requesting and joint attention skills.

JASPER Target Skill Planning

Using the assessment information gathered, the interventionist selected the following target skills based on the developmental progression of skills in each domain:

- Requesting: Because Bethany spontaneously gave or reached to request but had not yet pointed to request, the clinician selected "point to request" as the child's requesting target skill.
- Joint attention: Bethany demonstrated coordinated joint looks to share but did not gesture to share during the assessment. Therefore, the clinician selected "show to share" because it is the first of the three gestures (i.e., show, point, give) emphasized in JASPER to emerge in development.

- Play: Bethany was proficient in a beginning type of combination play (i.e., presentation combination play), as shown by her success with the puzzle and shape sorter during the SPA. The next step in play development is to build and combine objects in more flexible ways, such as putting toys into a box or building with blocks (i.e., general combination). Therefore, the clinician selected "general combination play" as Bethany's target play level.

JASPER Session Planning

To prepare for the JASPER sessions, the interventionist focused on how she would set up the play setting to help Bethany engage with both the interventionist herself and Bethany's mother. The goal of the first session was to start to establish play routines, build rapport with the child, and try to support the child's joint engagement in the session. During this session, the interventionist also reassessed the skills that she had targeted for Bethany based on the initial assessment. She decided on the following.

Play Area

The interventionist examined Bethany's home environment and worked together with Bethany's mother in the first session to identify and set up their play area. They focused on identifying a place for Bethany and her mother to sit, selecting furniture to add structure, and identifying developmentally appropriate toys for their first session:

- The interventionist wanted to set up a clear space for the three of them to play. She chose a small rug to place on the floor and a child-sized table and chair. The interventionist planned to start the session wherever Bethany would like to play but set up a table and chair in the room, in case more structure was needed to help Bethany stay focused and engaged.
- The interventionist intended to work together with Bethany's mother to select three to four sets of toys that she has at home. The toys were to include two at the mastered presentation combination level (e.g., nesting boxes, wooden stacker) and two general combination toys (e.g., plastic building blocks, plastic food made of Velcro pieces that could be taken apart and put together).
- The interventionist planned to remove items that could be disruptive or distracting. She knew that Bethany was interested in animals. She included blocks with animals on them to incorpo-

rate Bethany's interest but decided to put away animal figures that Bethany would likely line up. The interventionist planned to try to introduce the animal figures into a later session once she had established play routines. She planned to show Bethany a new way to play with the animals (e.g., put them on top of the box tower after they built it together).

Regulation

The interventionist planned to have activities available to help the child regulate (stay calm, attentive, and ready to learn) if needed:

- The interventionist had access to toys that Bethany could use with ease: toys at her mastered play level (e.g., a puzzle, stacker).
- The interventionist also asked Bethany's mother what types of interactive games that she likes to play with her child. Bethany's mom reported that Bethany enjoys the songs "Wheels on the Bus" and "Head and Shoulders" with actions.

Augmentative and Alternative Communication

The interventionist decided to include a speech-generating application on an electronic tablet because Bethany had not shown that she initiated words to communicate:

- Because the interventionist was not sure if Bethany could discriminate among different picture symbols, she chose to use concrete images (i.e., photographs of objects) and a field of only four photographs on a page in the application. When the photograph was touched, the tablet generated the corresponding spoken word.
- The interventionist picked four words that were a mix of simple nouns and verbs (e.g., block) which she and Bethany could use to talk about the things they were playing with.
- The interventionist planned to model by pairing spoken language with AAC. For example, when she took an action (e.g., stacked a block), she intended on saying the word *block* and pressing the button "block" on the speech-generating device.
- The interventionist was ready to change the number of symbols on the page either by adding more if Bethany appeared to understand and be ready for more words or using fewer (i.e., 1–2) photographs per page if she discovered that she needed to help Bethany learn to discriminate between the photographs.

Monitoring Progress

Weeks 1 to 2

In the first 2 weeks, the interventionist focused on building rapport with Bethany and her mother. She and Bethany's mother selected a small table and chair that they placed in the corner of the family's living room. The interventionist introduced the targets of the intervention (i.e., engagement, social communication, play). Together the interventionist and Bethany's mother looked through the toys at their home to find toys at Bethany's target level (i.e., general combination) and a couple of easier routines to help Bethany stay regulated (i.e., presentation combination). To start to create stacking/building routines, they decided on blocks, nesting cups, and stacking cups as the general routines; they selected a coin bank and peg board as their mastered presentation combination backup routines. After selecting the toys, setting up the play area, and discussing play and engagement, the interventionist used the final 30 minutes of the session to model the intervention strategies with Bethany. As she played, she verbally highlighted the topics they had discussed, including Bethany's engagement, play level, and spontaneous initiations.

In the second session, the interventionist briefly introduced social communication and Bethany's requesting and joint attention target skills, and responded to the Bethany's communication with her mother. Together, Bethany's mother and the interventionist set up the play area. Bethany's mother asked to observe one more session, so the interventionist modeled the strategies with Bethany.

Weeks 3 to 5

These 3 weeks focused on introducing imitating and modeling play acts as strategies to establish play routines. In Week 3, the interventionist introduced imitation, and Bethany's mother began to take turns alongside the interventionist, imitating Bethany's appropriate play acts in routines established by the interventionist. Bethany's mother picked up imitation quickly, and in Weeks 4 and 5 began to engage in familiar routines with Bethany (e.g., stacking blocks, nesting and stacking the cups) with verbal support from the interventionist. The interventionist continued to provide support to expand and maintain the routines, as well as to develop new routines.

Weeks 6 to 8

These three sessions focused on helping Bethany's mother maintain and expand their play routines (i.e., adding complexity, diversity, length), and introducing ways to use modeling to expand communication and joint attention skills. Bethany established stacking routines within the first couple of weeks. The interventionist had been modeling adding extra steps, such as adding other materials to the block tower (e.g., build with cups and then boxes on top), making a variety of structures with blocks (i.e., increasing the diversity of the general combination level play), and then adding figures to their structure (i.e., increasing the level of the play). Because Bethany's joint attention target is a joint attention show, the interventionist highlighted moments during which Bethany's mother could model the show gesture during their routines. For example, before imitating stacking, she would model showing the cup to Bethany paired with the word "cup."

Weeks 9 to 10

The last two sessions focused on supporting the parent's implementation of the full package of JASPER strategies. The interventionist had faded her support to largely verbal suggestions while Bethany's mother led the session with her daughter. Bethany had made clear progress in play, particularly in building and stacking. Therefore, the interventionist helped Bethany's mother to include higher level combination play (e.g., building houses and castles, instead of just stacking the blocks) and the next level of play (i.e., presymbolic play) by adding figures to the houses and castles they built. The interventionist also helped Bethany's mother identify other materials at Bethany's target play level so that she could continue to build new routines in the future.

At the end of Week 10, Bethany's mother was able to successfully establish five to six different routines at her daughter's developmental play level. She had ideas for new routines and new steps for her existing routines from her last two sessions. At the beginning, Bethany's mother found that she wanted to talk a lot and ask her daughter a lot of questions. By the end, she was focused on listening for and responding to Bethany's initiations, including attempts at words and unclear joint attention show gestures. Sometimes she still asked questions and directed Bethany to play the way she wanted her to, but she had learned to notice that Bethany started to become highly focused on the objects, line them up, and stop looking at or communicating with her mother. These cues reminded Bethany's mother to focus on modeling nonverbal gestures and verbal comments, and on presenting choices to see what her daughter was interested in playing with and sharing with her. She also reminded herself that she could support Bethany's initiations through timely addition of materials for new steps in her play routines, modeling language at Bethany's level, and leaving Bethany's play turns open for her to initiate communication.

REFERENCES

Adamson, L. B., & Bakeman, R. (1984). Mothers' communicative acts: Changes during infancy. *Infant Behavior & Development, 7* 467–478. http://dx.doi.org/10.1016/S0163-6383(84)80006-5

Adamson, L. B., Bakeman, R., Deckner, D. F., & Nelson, P. B. (2012). Rating parent–child interactions: Joint engagement, communication dynamics, and shared topics in autism, Down syndrome, and typical development. *Journal of Autism and Developmental Disorders, 42,* 2622–2635. http://dx.doi.org/10.1007/s10803-012-1520-1

Adamson, L. B., Deckner, D. F., & Bakeman, R. (2010). Early interests and joint engagement in typical development, autism, and Down syndrome. *Journal of Autism and Developmental Disorders, 40,* 665–676. http://dx.doi.org/10.1007/s10803-009-0914-1

Adamson, L. B., Romski, M., & Barton-Hulsey, A. (2014). Early language acquisition in autism spectrum disorders: A developmental view. In V. Patel & C. Martin (Eds.), *Comprehensive guide to autism* (pp. 1061–1080). New York, NY: Springer.

Baron-Cohen, S. (1989). The autistic child's theory of mind: A case of specific developmental delay. *Journal of Child Psychology and Psychiatry, 30,* 285–297. http://dx.doi.org/10.1111/j.1469-7610.1989.tb00241.x

Blume, M., & Lust, B. (2017). *Research methods in language acquisition: Principles, procedures, and practices.* Washington, DC: American Psychological Association. http://dx.doi.org/10.1515/9783110415339

Carpenter, M., Nagell, K., Tomasello, M., Butterworth, G., & Moore, C. (1998). Social cognition, joint attention, and communicative competence from 9 to 15 months of age. *Monographs of the Society for Research in Child Development, 63,* i–vi, 1–143. http://dx.doi.org/10.2307/1166214

Carter, A. S., Messinger, D. S., Stone, W. L., Celimli, S., Nahmias, A. S., & Yoder, P. (2011). A randomized controlled trial of Hanen's "more than words" in toddlers with early autism symptoms. *Journal of Child Psychology and Psychiatry, 52,* 741–752. http://dx.doi.org/10.1111/j.1469-7610.2011.02395.x

Chang, Y. C., Shire, S. Y., Shih, W., Gelfand, C., & Kasari, C. (2016). Preschool deployment of evidence-based social communication intervention: JASPER in the classroom. *Journal of Autism and Developmental Disorders, 46,* 2211–2223. http://dx.doi.org/10.1007/s10803-016-2752-2

Charman, T., Taylor, E., Drew, A., Cockerill, H., Brown, J. A., & Baird, G. (2005). Outcome at 7 years of children diagnosed with autism at age 2: Predictive validity of assessments conducted at 2 and 3 years of age and pattern of symptom change over time. *Journal of Child Psychology and Psychiatry, 46,* 500–513. http://dx.doi.org/10.1111/j.1469-7610.2004.00377.x

Davlantis, K. S., & Rogers, S. J. (2016). The early start Denver model: A play-based intervention for young children with autism spectrum disorders. In L. A. Reddy,

T. M. Files-Hall, & C. E. Schaefer (Eds.), *Empirically based play interventions for children* (2nd ed., pp. 205–222). Washington, DC: American Psychological Association. http://dx.doi.org/10.1037/14730-011

Dawson, G. (2008). Early behavioral intervention, brain plasticity, and the prevention of autism spectrum disorder. *Development and Psychopathology, 20,* 775–803. http://dx.doi.org/10.1017/S0954579408000370

Divan, G., Hamdani, S. U., Vajartkar, V., Minhas, A., Taylor, C., Aldred, C., . . . Patel, V. (2015). Adapting an evidence-based intervention for autism spectrum disorder for scaling up in resource-constrained settings: The development of the PASS intervention in South Asia. *Global Health Action, 8,* 27278. http://dx.doi.org/10.3402/gha.v8.27278

Fenson, L., Marchman, V., Thal, D., Reznick, S., & Bates, E. (2007). *MacArthur–Bates Communicative Development Inventories: User's guide and technical manual* (2nd ed.). Baltimore, MD: Brookes.

Ganz, J. B. (2015). AAC interventions for individuals with autism spectrum disorders: State of the science and future research directions. *Augmentative and Alternative Communication, 31,* 203–214. http://dx.doi.org/10.3109/07434618.2015.1047532

Goodhart, F., & Baron-Cohen, S. (1993). How many ways can the point be made? Evidence from children with and without autism. *First Language, 13,* 225–233. http://dx.doi.org/10.1177/014272379301303804

Green, J., Charman, T., McConachie, H., Aldred, C., Slonims, V., Howlin, P., . . . Pickles, A., & the PACT Consortium. (2010). Parent-mediated communication-focused treatment in children with autism (PACT): A randomised controlled trial. *The Lancet, 375,* 2152–2160. http://dx.doi.org/10.1016/S0140-6736(10)60587-9

Grzadzinski, R., Carr, T., Costanza, C., McGuire, K., Dufek, S., Pickles, A., & Lord, C. (2016). Measuring changes in social communication behaviors: Preliminary development of the Brief Observation of Social Communication Change (BOSCC). *Journal of Autism and Developmental Disorders, 46,* 2464–2479. http://dx.doi.org/10.1007/s10803-016-2782-9

Gulsrud, A. C., Hellemann, G., Shire, S., & Kasari, C. (2016). Isolating active ingredients in a parent-mediated social communication intervention for toddlers with autism spectrum disorder. *Journal of Child Psychology and Psychiatry, 57,* 606–613. http://dx.doi.org/10.1111/jcpp.12481

Hardan, A. Y., Gengoux, G. W., Berquist, K. L., Libove, R. A., Ardel, C. M., Phillips, J., . . . Minjarez, M. B. (2015). A randomized controlled trial of pivotal response treatment group for parents of children with autism. *Journal of Child Psychology and Psychiatry, 56,* 884–892. http://dx.doi.org/10.1111/jcpp.12354

Ingersoll, B. (2012). Brief report: Effect of a focused imitation intervention on social functioning in children with autism. *Journal of Autism and Developmental Disorders, 42,* 1768–1773. http://dx.doi.org/10.1007/s10803-011-1423-6

Ingersoll, B., Dvortcsak, A., Whalen, C., & Sikora, D. (2005). The effects of a developmental, social—pragmatic language intervention on rate of expressive language production in young children with autistic spectrum disorders. *Focus on Autism and Other Developmental Disabilities, 20,* 213–222. http://dx.doi.org/10.1177/10883576050200040301

Ingersoll, B., Wainer, A. L., Berger, N. I., Pickard, K. E., & Bonter, N. (2016). Comparison of a Self-directed and therapist-assisted telehealth parent-mediated intervention for children with ASD: A pilot RCT. *Journal of Autism and Developmental Disorders, 46,* 2275–2284. http://dx.doi.org/10.1007/s10803-016-2755-z

Jarrold, C., Boucher, J., & Smith, P. K. (1996). Generativity deficits in pretend play in autism. *British Journal of Developmental Psychology, 14,* 275–300. http://dx.doi.org/10.1111/j.2044-835X.1996.tb00706.x

Jones, D. J., Forehand, R., Cuellar, J., Kincaid, C., Parent, J., Fenton, N., & Goodrum, N. (2013). Harnessing innovative technologies to advance children's mental health: Behavioral parent training as an example. *Clinical Psychology Review, 33,* 241–252. http://dx.doi.org/10.1016/j.cpr.2012.11.003

Kasari, C., Freeman, S., & Paparella, T. (2006). Joint attention and symbolic play in young children with autism: A randomized controlled intervention study. *Journal of Child Psychology and Psychiatry, 47,* 611–620. http://dx.doi.org/10.1111/j.1469-7610.2005.01567.x

Kasari, C., Gulsrud, A., Freeman, S., Paparella, T., & Hellemann, G. (2012). Longitudinal follow-up of children with autism receiving targeted interventions on joint attention and play. *Journal of the American Academy of Child & Adolescent Psychiatry, 51,* 487–495. http://dx.doi.org/10.1016/j.jaac.2012.02.019

Kasari, C., Gulsrud, A., Paparella, T., Hellemann, G., & Berry, K. (2015). Randomized comparative efficacy study of parent-mediated interventions for toddlers with autism. *Journal of Consulting and Clinical Psychology, 83,* 554–563. http://dx.doi.org/10.1037/a0039080

Kasari, C., Gulsrud, A. C., Wong, C., Kwon, S., & Locke, J. (2010). Randomized controlled caregiver mediated joint engagement intervention for toddlers with autism. *Journal of Autism and Developmental Disorders, 40,* 1045–1056. http://dx.doi.org/10.1007/s10803-010-0955-5

Kasari, C., Kaiser, A., Goods, K., Nietfeld, J., Mathy, P., Landa, R., . . . Almirall, D. (2014). Communication interventions for minimally verbal children with autism: A sequential multiple assignment randomized trial. *Journal of the American Academy of Child & Adolescent Psychiatry, 53,* 635–646. http://dx.doi.org/10.1016/j.jaac.2014.01.019

Kasari, C., Lawton, K., Shih, W., Barker, T. V., Landa, R., Lord, C., . . . Senturk, D. (2014). Caregiver-mediated intervention for low-resourced preschoolers with autism: An RCT. *Pediatrics, 134,* e72–e79. http://dx.doi.org/10.1542/peds.2013-3229

Kasari, C., Paparella, T., Freeman, S., & Jahromi, L. B. (2008). Language outcome in autism: Randomized comparison of joint attention and play interventions.

Journal of Consulting and Clinical Psychology, 76, 125–137. http://dx.doi.org/10.1037/0022-006X.76.1.125

Kasari, C., Sigman, M., Mundy, P., & Yirmiya, N. (1990). Affective sharing in the context of joint attention interactions of normal, autistic, and mentally retarded children. *Journal of Autism and Developmental Disorders, 20,* 87–100. http://dx.doi.org/10.1007/BF02206859

Keen, D., Couzens, D., Muspratt, S., & Rodger, S. (2010). The effects of a parent-focused intervention for children with a recent diagnosis of autism spectrum disorder on parenting stress and competence. *Research in Autism Spectrum Disorders, 4,* 229–241. http://dx.doi.org/10.1016/j.rasd.2009.09.009

Kendall, T., Megnin-Viggars, O., Gould, N., Taylor, C., Burt, L. R., & Baird, G., & the Guideline Development Group. (2013). Management of autism in children and young people: Summary of NICE and SCIE guidance. *BMJ, 347,* f4865. http://dx.doi.org/10.1136/bmj.f4865

Koegel, R. L., & Koegel, L. K. (2006). *Pivotal response treatments for autism: Communication, social, and academic development.* Baltimore, MD: Brookes.

Landa, R. J., Holman, K. C., & Garrett-Mayer, E. (2007). Social and communication development in toddlers with early and later diagnosis of autism spectrum disorders. *Archives of General Psychiatry, 64,* 853–864. http://dx.doi.org/10.1001/archpsyc.64.7.853

Lewis, V., & Boucher, J. (1995). Generativity in the play of young people with autism. *Journal of Autism and Developmental Disorders, 25,* 105–121. http://dx.doi.org/10.1007/BF02178499

Long, S. (2008). Computerized Profiling (Version 7.7.0) [Computer software]. Milwaukee, WI: Marquette.

MacWhinney, B. (2000). *The CHILDES project: Tools for analyzing talk* (3rd ed.). Mahwah, NJ: Erlbaum.

McIntosh, D. N., Reichmann-Decker, A., Winkielman, P., & Wilbarger, J. L. (2006). When the social mirror breaks: Deficits in automatic, but not voluntary, mimicry of emotional facial expressions in autism. *Developmental Science, 9,* 295–302. http://dx.doi.org/10.1111/j.1467-7687.2006.00492.x

Miller, J., & Chapman, R. (2008). *Systematic Analysis of Language Transcripts (SALT)* [Computer software]. Madison: University of Wisconsin–Madison, Waisman Center.

Mundy, P., & Crowson, M. (1997). Joint attention and early social communication: Implications for research on intervention with autism. *Journal of Autism and Developmental Disorders, 27,* 653–676. http://dx.doi.org/10.1023/A:1025802832021

Mundy, P., Delgado, C., Block, J., Venezia, M., Hogan, A., & Seibert, J. (2003). *Early Social Communication Scales (ESCS).* Coral Gables, FL: University of Miami.

Mundy, P., Sigman, M., & Kasari, C. (1990). A longitudinal study of joint attention and language development in autistic children. *Journal of Autism and Developmental Disorders, 20,* 115–128. http://dx.doi.org/10.1007/BF02206861

Mundy, P., Sigman, M., Ungerer, J., & Sherman, T. (1986). Defining the social deficits of autism: The contribution of non-verbal communication measures. *Journal of Child Psychology and Psychiatry, 27,* 657–669. http://dx.doi.org/ 10.1111/j.1469-7610.1986.tb00190.x

Myers, K., Vander Stoep, A., Zhou, C., McCarty, C. A., & Katon, W. (2015). Effectiveness of a telehealth service delivery model for treating attention-deficit/ hyperactivity disorder: A community-based randomized controlled trial. *Journal of the American Academy of Child & Adolescent Psychiatry, 54,* 263–274. http:// dx.doi.org/10.1016/j.jaac.2015.01.009

Nadel, J. (2014). *How imitation boosts development in infancy and autism spectrum disorder.* New York, NY: Oxford University Press.

O'Neill, D. (2009). *Language Use Inventory: An assessment of young children's pragmatic language development for 18- to 47-month-old children* [Manual]. Waterloo, Ontario, Canada: Knowledge in Development.

Oosterling, I., Visser, J., Swinkels, S., Rommelse, N., Donders, R., Woudenberg, T., . . . Buitelaar, J. (2010). Randomized controlled trial of the focus parent training for toddlers with autism: 1-year outcome. *Journal of Autism and Developmental Disorders, 40,* 1447–1458. http://dx.doi.org/10.1007/s10803-010-1004-0

Paul, R., Campbell, D., Gilbert, K., & Tsiouri, I. (2013). Comparing spoken language treatments for minimally verbal preschoolers with autism spectrum disorders. *Journal of Autism and Developmental Disorders, 43,* 418–431. http:// dx.doi.org/10.1007/s10803-012-1583-z

Paul, R., & Fahim, D. (2014). Assessing communication in autism spectrum disorders. In F. R. Volkmar, R. Paul, S. J. Rogers, & K. A. Pelphrey (Eds.), *Handbook of autism and pervasive developmental disorders* (4th ed., Vol. 2, pp. 673–694). New York, NY: Wiley.

Paul, R., & Norbury, C. (2012). *Language disorders from infancy through adolescence: Listening, speaking, reading, writing, and communicating* (4th ed.). St. Louis, MO: Mosby.

Pickles, A., Harris, V., Green, J., Aldred, C., McConachie, H., Slonims, V., . . . & the PACT Consortium. (2015). Treatment mechanism in the MRC preschool autism communication trial: Implications for study design and parent-focused therapy for children. *Journal of Child Psychology and Psychiatry, 56,* 162–170. http://dx.doi.org/10.1111/jcpp.12291

Prizant, B. M., & Wetherby, A. M. (2005). Critical issues in enhancing communication abilities for persons with autism spectrum disorders. In F. R. Volkmar, R. Paul, A. Klin, & D. Cohen (Eds.), *Handbook of autism and pervasive developmental disorders, Vol. 2: Assessment, interventions, and policy* (3rd ed., pp. 925–945). Hoboken, NJ: Plenum Press. http://dx.doi.org/10.1002/9780470939352.ch10

Rahman, A., Divan, G., Hamdani, S. U., Vajaratkar, V., Taylor, C., Leadbitter, K., . . . Green, J. (2016). Effectiveness of the parent-mediated intervention for children with autism spectrum disorder in south Asia in India and Pakistan (PASS):

A randomised controlled trial. *The Lancet. Psychiatry, 3,* 128–136. http://
dx.doi.org/10.1016/S2215-0366(15)00388-0

Reynell, J. K., & Gruber, C. P. (1990). *Reynell Developmental Language Scales.* Los
Angeles, CA: Western Psychological Services.

Rogers, S. J., Estes, A., Lord, C., Vismara, L., Winter, J., Fitzpatrick, A., . . .
Dawson, G. (2012). Effects of a brief early start Denver model (ESDM)-based
parent intervention on toddlers at risk for autism spectrum disorders: A randomized controlled trial. *Journal of the American Academy of Child & Adolescent
Psychiatry, 51,* 1052–1065. http://dx.doi.org/10.1016/j.jaac.2012.08.003

Rogers, S. J., Hepburn, S. L., Stackhouse, T., & Wehner, E. (2003). Imitation performance in toddlers with autism and those with other developmental disorders. *Journal of Child Psychology and Psychiatry, 44,* 763–781. http://dx.doi.org/
10.1111/1469-7610.00162

Saxena, S., Thornicroft, G., Knapp, M., & Whiteford, H. (2007). Resources for
mental health: Scarcity, inequity, and inefficiency. *The Lancet, 370,* 878–889.
http://dx.doi.org/10.1016/S0140-6736(07)61239-2

Schreibman, L., Dawson, G., Stahmer, A. C., Landa, R., Rogers, S. J., McGee,
G. G., . . . Halladay, A. (2015). Naturalistic developmental behavioral interventions: Empirically validated treatments for autism spectrum disorder. *Journal
of Autism and Developmental Disorders, 45,* 2411–2428. http://dx.doi.org/10.1007/
s10803-015-2407-8

Shire, S. Y., Goods, K., Shih, W., Distefano, C., Kaiser, A., Wright, C., . . . Kasari, C.
(2015). Parents' adoption of social communication intervention strategies:
Families including children with autism spectrum disorder who are minimally
verbal. *Journal of Autism and Developmental Disorders, 45,* 1712–1724. http://
dx.doi.org/10.1007/s10803-014-2329-x

Shire, S. Y., & Jones, N. (2015). Communication partners supporting children
with complex communication needs who use AAC: A systematic review.
Communication Disorders Quarterly, 37, 3–15. http://dx.doi.org/10.1177/
1525740114558254

Sigman, M., Mundy, P., Sherman, T., & Ungerer, J. (1986). Social interactions of
autistic, mentally retarded and normal children and their caregivers. *Journal of
Child Psychology and Psychiatry, 27,* 647–656.

Sigman, M., Ruskin, E., Arbelle, S., Corona, R., Dissanayake, C., Espinosa, M., . . .
Robinson, B. F. (1999). Continuity and change in the social competence of
children with autism, Down syndrome, and developmental delays. *Monographs
of the Society for Research in Child Development, 64,* 1–139. Retrieved from http://
www.jstor.org/stable/3181510

Smith, T. (2011). Applied behavior analysis and early intensive behavioral intervention. In D. G. Amaral, G. Dawson, & D. H. Geschwind (Eds.), *Autism spectrum
disorders* (pp. 1037–1055). New York, NY: Oxford University Press. http://dx.doi.org/
10.1093/med/9780195371826.003.0066

Smith, T., & Iadarola, S. (2015). Evidence base update for autism spectrum disorder. *Journal of Clinical Child and Adolescent Psychology, 44,* 897–922. http://dx.doi.org/10.1080/15374416.2015.1077448

Solomon, R., Van Egeren, L. A., Mahoney, G., Quon Huber, M. S., & Zimmerman, P. (2014). PLAY project home consultation intervention program for young children with autism spectrum disorders: A randomized controlled trial. *Journal of Developmental and Behavioral Pediatrics, 35,* 475–485. http://dx.doi.org/10.1097/DBP.0000000000000096

Sparrow, S. S., Cicchetti, D. V., & Saulnier, C. A. (2016). *Vineland Adaptive Behavior Scales* (3rd ed.). London, England: Pearson.

Stone, W. L., Ousley, O. Y., & Littleford, C. D. (1997). Motor imitation in young children with autism: What's the object? *Journal of Abnormal Child Psychology, 25,* 475–485. http://dx.doi.org/10.1023/A:1022685731726

Stone, W. L., & Yoder, P. J. (2001). Predicting spoken language level in children with autism spectrum disorders. *Autism, 5,* 341–361. http://dx.doi.org/10.1177/1362361301005004002

Sullivan, M., Finelli, J., Marvin, A., Garrett-Mayer, E., Bauman, M., & Landa, R. (2007). Response to joint attention in toddlers at risk for autism spectrum disorder: A prospective study. *Journal of Autism and Developmental Disorders, 37,* 37–48. http://dx.doi.org/10.1007/s10803-006-0335-3

Szatmari, P., Chawarska, K., Dawson, G., Georgiades, S., Landa, R., Lord, C., . . . Halladay, A. (2016). Prospective longitudinal studies of infant siblings of children with autism: Lessons learned and future directions. *Journal of the American Academy of Child & Adolescent Psychiatry, 55,* 179–187. http://dx.doi.org/10.1016/j.jaac.2015.12.014

Tager-Flusberg, H., & Kasari, C. (2013). Minimally verbal school-aged children with autism spectrum disorder: The neglected end of the spectrum. *Autism Research, 6,* 468–478. http://dx.doi.org/10.1002/aur.1329

Tager-Flusberg, H., Rogers, S., Cooper, J., Landa, R., Lord, C., Paul, R., . . . Yoder, P. (2009). Defining spoken language benchmarks and selecting measures of expressive language development for young children with autism spectrum disorders. *Journal of Speech, Language, and Hearing Research, 52,* 643–652. http://dx.doi.org/10.1044/1092-4388(2009/08-0136)

Tonge, B., Brereton, A., Kiomall, M., Mackinnon, A., & Rinehart, N. J. (2014). A randomised group comparison controlled trial of "preschoolers with autism": A parent education and skills training intervention for young children with autistic disorder. *Autism, 18,* 166–177. http://dx.doi.org/10.1177/1362361312458186

Ungerer, J. A., & Sigman, M. (1981). Symbolic play and language comprehension in autistic children. *Journal of the American Academy of Child Psychiatry, 20,* 318–337. http://dx.doi.org/10.1016/S0002-7138(09)60992-4

Wallace, K. S., & Rogers, S. J. (2010). Intervening in infancy: Implications for autism spectrum disorders. *Journal of Child Psychology and Psychiatry, 51,* 1300–1320. http://dx.doi.org/10.1111/j.1469-7610.2010.02308.x

Wetherby, A. M., Guthrie, W., Woods, J., Schatschneider, C., Holland, R. D., Morgan, L., & Lord, C. (2014). Parent-implemented social intervention for toddlers with autism: An RCT. *Pediatrics, 134,* 1084–1093. http://dx.doi.org/10.1542/peds.2014-0757

Wetherby, A. M., & Prizant, B. M. (2002a). *Communication and Symbolic Behavior Scales: Developmental profile.* Baltimore, MD: Brookes.

Wetherby, A. M., & Prizant, B. M. (2002b). *CSBS DP Infant-Toddler Checklist.* Retrieved from http://www.brookespublishing.com/resource-center/screening-and-assessment/csbs/csbs-dp/csbs-dp-itc/

Wetherby, A. M., Prizant, B. M., & Hutchinson, T. A. (1998). Communicative, social/affective, and symbolic profiles of young children with autism and pervasive developmental disorders. *American Journal of Speech-Language Pathology, 7,* 79–91. http://dx.doi.org/10.1044/1058-0360.0702.79

Wetherby, A. M., Watt, N., Morgan, L., & Shumway, S. (2007). Social communication profiles of children with autism spectrum disorders late in the second year of life. *Journal of Autism and Developmental Disorders, 37,* 960–975. http://dx.doi.org/10.1007/s10803-006-0237-4

Zimmerman, I. L., Steiner, V. G., & Pond, R. E. (2011). *Preschool Language Scales* (5th ed.). San Antonio, TX: Harcourt Assessment.

5

PARENT TRAINING FOR DISRUPTIVE BEHAVIOR IN AUTISM SPECTRUM DISORDER

KAREN BEARSS, LUC LECAVALIER, AND LAWRENCE SCAHILL

In addition to the core features of autism spectrum disorder (ASD), up to 50% of children exhibit high rates of disruptive behavior, such as tantrums, aggression, property destruction, and noncompliance (Hartley, Sikora, & McCoy, 2008; Mazurek, Kanne, & Wodka, 2013). In their own words, parents have described frequent "meltdowns," "outbursts," and other serious behavioral problems in the context of everyday life. These behaviors often present an extraordinary challenge to parents and are common reasons for seeking treatment. When behavioral problems reach levels of clinical significance, children may qualify for the *Diagnostic and Statistical Manual of Mental Disorders* (fifth ed.; DSM–5; American Psychiatric Association, 2013) or *The ICD–10 Classification of Mental and Behavioural Disorders* (ICD–10; World Health Organization, 1992) diagnoses of oppositional defiant disorder or conduct disorder. These two disorders fall under the category of disruptive behavior disorders (DBD) and are characterized by problems in behavioral and emotional self-control.

http://dx.doi.org/10.1037/0000111-006
Parent Training for Autism Spectrum Disorder: Improving the Quality of Life for Children and Their Families,
C. R. Johnson, E. M. Butter, and L. Scahill (Editors)

Although disruptive behavior is highly prevalent in children with ASD (Kaat & Lecavalier, 2013), it is not well understood whether these behavioral problems are specific signs of dysregulation in ASD or if they are due to the same impulse control and emotion regulation deficits in *DSM-* or ICD-defined psychiatric disorders (Lecavalier, Gadow, DeVincent, & Edwards, 2009). Leaving the diagnostic questions aside, tantrums and aggressive behavior in a child with ASD also could serve as a maladaptive method of communication.

CO-OCCURRENCE OF DISRUPTIVE BEHAVIOR AND ASD

The conceptual issues surrounding the nosology of psychiatric disorders in ASD have been hampered by fundamental problems of boundaries between DBD and ASD. Indeed, research on the phenomenology of DBD in ASD has focused on distinguishing between DBD and ASD, rather than examining their co-occurrence (Kaat & Lecavalier, 2013). For good reason, many studies have reported on the dimensional severity of disruptive behavior, rather than diagnostic categories. For example, using the parent-rated Nisonger Child Behavior Rating Form (NCBRF), Lecavalier (2006) reported that in a sample of 353 children with ASD in special education programs, approximately 25% were rated moderate or severe on items, such as "defiant" or "tantrums"; a little more than 20% were rated as "explosive." Two large-scale studies using well-characterized samples examined the frequency of aggression in youths with ASD (Kanne & Mazurek, 2011; Mazurek et al., 2013). In those studies, aggression was measured rather crudely: The Simons Simplex Collection (Kanne & Mazurek, 2011) used items from the Autism Diagnostic Interview–Revised (Rutter, Le Couteur, & Lord, 2003), and the Autism Treatment Network (Mazurek et al., 2013) used a single question from a parent survey. Nevertheless, data from both large-scale studies suggested that more than 50% of youths with ASD exhibited aggression toward others. As a whole, children with ASD in clinical populations have more severe aggressive behaviors than those with other developmental disabilities (Farmer & Aman, 2011), or non-ASD clinically ascertained samples, or children in the general population (Mayes et al., 2012). *Irritability*, a term that is intended to capture behaviors, such as tantrums, aggression, and self-injury, is common in youths with ASD and has been the focus of pharmacological and psychosocial treatment studies (Aman et al., 2009; Bearss et al., 2015; Research Units on Pediatric Psychopharmacology [RUPP] Autism Network, 2002; Research Units on Pediatric Psychopharmacology [RUPP] Autism Network, 2007). In those studies, the severity of this behavioral profile has been measured using the Aberrant Behavior Checklist (Aman, Singh, Stewart, & Field, 1985).

The prevalence of DBD in children with ASD is unclear; rates vary between 4% and 37% for oppositional defiant disorder, and 1% and 10%

for conduct disorder (Kaat & Lecavalier, 2013). The review by Kaat and Lecavalier (2013) suggests that as many as one in four children with an ASD meet diagnostic criteria for oppositional defiant disorder or conduct disorder. Based on this estimate, the rate of oppositional defiant disorder is higher than children in the general population and is roughly equal to the general population for conduct disorder. Findings also suggested that the presentation of DBD in ASD is not influenced by IQ or gender (Gadow, DeVincent, Pomeroy, & Azizian, 2004, 2005; Simonoff et al., 2008).

IMPACT OF DISRUPTIVE BEHAVIOR IN ASD

Disruptive behavior in children can interfere with academic progress, lead to further isolation from peers, and increase caregiver stress due to disruptions in daily activities (Brereton, Tonge, & Einfeld, 2006; Hartley et al., 2008; Herring et al., 2006; Scahill et al., 2012; Simonoff et al., 2008; Symon, 2005; Tonge et al., 2006). Disruptive behavior also can erode the family's quality of life (Hayes & Watson, 2013). Compared with parents of typically developing children, parents of children with ASD have reported a greater sense of helplessness and are more likely to avoid conflict when facing challenges of parenting (Iadarola et al., 2017; Pisula & Kossakowska, 2010). Disruptive behavior also poses additional barriers to the acquisition and regular performance of everyday living skills (Scahill et al., 2012; Scahill, Bearss, et al., 2016). Children with ASD and disruptive behavior who actively resist acquiring new skills or performing already acquired skills likely will fall behind in adaptive functioning.

CONTRIBUTORS TO DISRUPTIVE BEHAVIOR IN ASD

Communication difficulties are potential determinants of challenging behaviors in children with ASD. Many children with ASD have delays in communication skills and have not yet developed alternative strategies (e.g., the use of pictures, signs, or gestures) to compensate. In many cases, disruptive behavior, such as hitting or screaming, is an inappropriate but ironically effective way for the child to communicate needs. Thus, PT programs encourage parents to consider what the child may be trying to communicate through disruptive behavior. A tantrum could be saying, "This is too hard." Screaming could mean: "Leave me alone." Hitting could be communicating, "That's mine. Give it back."

Behavioral problems also may emerge when a parent holds unrealistic expectations about the child's skill level. For example, impaired receptive language could affect the child's understanding of verbal requests and predictably reduce compliance if commands are too complex. Conversely, parents may have lowered expectations about a child's abilities and refrain from placing appropriate demands on the child. Lower demands on the child may reduce noncompliance, but lower demands also may interfere with the acquisition of new skills.

PARENT TRAINING FOR DISRUPTIVE BEHAVIOR IN ASD

When disruptive behavior persists and impairs functioning at home, school, and in the community, intervention is warranted. In parent training (PT), parents are taught to implement specific procedures designed to improve parent–child interactions, decrease behavioral problems, and increase prosocial behaviors (Kazdin, 2005; Wierson & Forehand, 1994). With guidance from a therapist, parents learn to attend to the child's prosocial behaviors, ignore inappropriate behaviors, decrease the use of punitive and coercive discipline strategies, and increase the use of effective noncoercive child management strategies. These components are the centerpiece of PT for reducing behavioral problems (Kaminski, Valle, Filene, & Boyle, 2008). For children with ASD, PT also sets the stage for improved adaptive functioning.

Theoretical Foundations of Parent Training

The theoretical underpinnings of evidence-based PT programs for behavioral problems in children with ASD are based on operant conditioning and social learning theory. Operant conditioning and social learning theory are core components of applied behavior analysis. The organizing principle here is that behavior can be modified through the manipulation of its *antecedent* (i.e., the cue for the onset of a learned behavior) or its *consequence* (i.e., the event that immediately follows a behavior). Information about the events that precede a behavior is key to identifying the purpose or *function* of the behavior. Common functions of disruptive behavior include access to a tangible item (e.g., food, favorite toy), attention from others (i.e., positive reinforcement), escape or avoidance from a demand or an aversive stimuli (i.e., negative reinforcement), and sensory and other internal stimulation (i.e., automatic reinforcement; Iwata & Worsdell, 2005). Thus, analysis of behavior begins with the assertion that the child's disruptive behavior is not a random occurrence. The idea that the behavior is not a random occurrence runs counter to what parents may report in clinic. Parents can be eloquent about the actual behavior (i.e., the appearance, frequency, duration, intensity) but often describe meltdowns as unpredictable or coming "out of nowhere." They may be less able to describe the events and situations that increase the likelihood of the disruptive behavior. Faced with behavioral problems that they may not understand, parents may inadvertently respond in ways that reinforce the child's inappropriate behavior. By understanding the function of the behavioral problem, parents can learn to change their usual response and teach the child a more appropriate behavior (Bearss et al., 2018; Horner, Carr, Strain, Todd, & Reed, 2002).

PT uses the antecedent-behavior-consequence (A-B-C) model to break down the sequence to help parents identify the environmental circumstances that may provoke the behavior (i.e., antecedents) and the responses that maintain it (i.e., consequences). Identifying components of the A-B-C model, in turn, facilitates a better understanding of how to manipulate the environment by modifying the antecedents that trigger and the consequences that maintain a behavior. Parents are trained to recognize that behaviors are predictable and to identify how their response to a behavior may inadvertently promote their reoccurrence. For example, the parent who gives a toy to the child in response to a meltdown reinforces the behavior. In such a case, the parent would be instructed to not allow access to the toy in response to the behavioral problem, and to provide access to the toy as an appropriate reward when the child asks nicely. To monitor progress, parents are taught to record the child's response to intervention.

ASSESSMENT OF DISRUPTIVE BEHAVIOR IN ASD

As with any intervention, treatment should be initiated after completion of an assessment that provides an understanding of the child, family, and broader systems in which the child operates (for more information on clinical assessment, see Chapter 2, this volume). Multimodal (e.g., parent, teacher, other caregiver), multimethod (e.g., interview, observation, rating scales) assessment will provide the widest range of information that can be used in treatment planning (McMahon & Frick, 2005). Information gathered from multiple informants is preferred because perspectives between parents (i.e., mothers and fathers) and parents and teachers often are divergent (Stratis & Lecavalier, 2015). This information provides a foundation for guiding the family on the application of intervention strategies. For example, compliance with commands is tied to the child's receptive language. A receptive language threshold of about 18 months is required for the child to understand simple, one-step commands. Thus, if a child has receptive language delays, family expectations regarding the child's ability to understand and comply with commands will require adjustment.

Informant-Based Methods

Core features and associated deficits in children with ASD, such as language and cognitive delays, make self-reporting on historical events or internal states challenging. Therefore, clinicians often rely on caregiver-report to identify symptoms of psychiatric disorders. To supplement caregiver report, a number of instruments have been developed to measure disruptive behavior in children with ASD. Later, we briefly describe a few targeted areas to assess in the context of a caregiver interview and a few useful caregiver rating scales. We focus on caregiver-completed scales because they often are used to measure change in treatment.

Parenting Perspectives

Along with an assessment of parenting practices, as described in Chapter 2, focus on parenting perspectives is warranted. Some parents may be overly harsh (i.e., are oriented to the authoritarian parenting approach with an emphasis on punitive discipline strategies). Others may be permissive (i.e., provide appropriate warmth in the parent–child relationship but ineffective limit-setting and inadequate follow through with consequences). It may be informative to discuss parental understanding of what is "driving" the child's behavioral problems. This discussion may delve into parental perceptions on *locus of control*, which is the degree to which the parent feels he or she has the ability to influence the child's behavior and development. Parents with an *internal* locus of control acknowledge their impact on the child's behavior (e.g., "I know I don't follow through"). Conversely, parents with an *external* locus of control may attribute the child's behavior to environmental or biological factors, with the implication that the parents have little influence on the child's behavior. Available evidence has suggested that an internal locus of control is associated with higher maternal esteem, parental satisfaction, and fewer child behavioral problems (Hassall, Rose, & McDonald, 2005; Koeske & Koeske, 1992). Implementation of PT strategies may be especially challenging with parents who describe feeling like the child's behavior is due to external circumstances (e.g., "He was born that way," "It doesn't matter what I do; nothing works"). In contrast, parents who feel responsible but at a loss on how to manage their child's behavior may be more open and motivated to learn and apply PT techniques.

Topography of Target Behaviors

Identification of target behaviors and their functional properties can occur through informal discussion with the family, parent ratings, and behavioral observations. Initial discussion should include a description of the target behaviors that the parent hopes to modify in treatment. The parent should be guided to describe the problems in behavioral terms: specific behaviors, frequency of occurrence, duration, antecedents, consequences, and impact on the family (see Chapter 2). These descriptions of behaviors promote a common understanding of the child's target problems and provide useful information on severity. Parents may describe feeling on "pins and needles" in the immediate aftermath of a tantrum—apprehensive that the child may "go off again." Frequent and severe tantrums in a child may lead to reluctance to set limits in an effort to avoid future outbursts.

Discussion of the presence or absence of behaviors in specific settings can inform on how to approach PT. For example, a parent who reports that behavioral problems are present only at school may not feel that PT is warranted. In many cases, however, disruptive behavior is occurring both at school and at home. The parent may be underreporting due to tolerance and accommodation to the child's behavior. In such cases, parents may need help to recalibrate appropriate behavior and expectations before initiating PT. A positive indicator for PT is when a parent reports behavioral problems in the home that are less prominent at school. Such a report suggests that the child has some ability to regulate behavior at school and may prompt the parent to seek help in managing the child's behavior.

Parent-Report Checklists

Aberrant Behavior Checklist

The Aberrant Behavior Checklist (Aman et al., 1985) contains 58 items rated on a 4-point scale ranging from 0 (*not a problem*) to 3 (*the problem is severe*). Items are distributed on 5 subscales: Irritability (15 items), Social Withdrawal (16 items), Stereotypic Behavior (seven items), Hyperactivity/ Noncompliance (16 items), and Inappropriate Speech (four items). The original factor structure of the Aberrant Behavior Checklist recently was supported in a large sample of children with ASD (Kaat, Lecavalier, & Aman, 2014).

Home Situations Questionnaire-Autism Spectrum Disorder

The Home Situations Questionnaire-Autism Spectrum Disorder (HSQ-ASD) is a 24-item measure of noncompliance for children with ASD (Chowdhury et al., 2016). It is an adaptation of a 16-item scale developed to evaluate noncompliant behavior in children with DBD (Barkley & Edelbrock, 1987). Raters are asked whether a given situation poses a problem for a child. If the answer is "yes," severity is evaluated on a scale ranging from 1 (*mild severity*) to 9 (*significant severity*). Examples of situations are: when asked to leave the house, when in public places, or when parents are on the phone. The total severity score from all items endorsed "yes" is divided by 24 (the number of items) to derive a per-item mean. The HSQ-ASD contains two 12-item factors: Socially Inflexible and Demand Specific. The HSQ-ASD has been used in a number of multisite intervention studies in children with ASD (e.g., Aman et al., 2009; Bearss et al., 2015; Handen et al., 2015).

Nisonger Child Behavior Rating Form

The NCBRF (Aman, Tassé, Rojahn, & Hammer, 1996; Tassé, Aman, Hammer, & Rojahn, 1996) has a parent and teacher version with identical content and similar factor structures. Each version contains two sections: Social Competence and Problem Behaviors. The Social Competence contains 10 items rated on a 4-point scale ranging from 0 (*not true*) to 3 (*completely or always true*) and distributed on two subscales: Compliant/Calm and Adaptive/Social. Problem Behaviors contains 66 items, also rated on a 4-point scale ranging from 0 (*behavior did not occur or was not a problem*) to 3 (behavior occurred a lot or was a severe problem) and distributed on six subscales: Conduct Problem, Insecure/Anxious, Hyperactive, Self-Injury/Stereotypic, Self-Isolated/Ritualistic, and Overly Sensitive [parent]/Irritable [teacher]. Lecavalier, Aman, Hammer, Stoica, and Mathews (2004) showed that the original factor structure for the NCBRF held true for youngsters with ASD. Of particular relevance to DBD in ASD are the two social competence subscales, as well as the Conduct Problem and Hyperactive subscales. The NCBRF has not been used in large-scale treatment studies of children with ASD but has been as used as the primary outcome measure in large trials of children with DBD without ASD (Aman et al., 2002, 2014).

Children's Scale of Hostility and Aggression: Reactive/Proactive

The Children's Scale of Hostility and Aggression: Reactive/Proactive (C-SHARP; Farmer & Aman, 2010) is an informant checklist that includes five domains of aggression and hostile behavior. The C-SHARP was developed in a sample of children with intellectual and developmental disabilities, and has been shown to have adequate psychometric properties (Farmer & Aman, 2010). The factor structure was subsequently confirmed in a separate clinic-based sample, and the measurement invariance between children with ASD compared with children with other DD was upheld (Farmer et al., 2016). Reliability and validity for the C-SHARP have been established for assessment; it has not been used as an outcome measure in a treatment study.

Behavioral Observation

Functional assessments may use direct observations of the child in laboratory and naturalistic settings to identify the function of a behavior (Iwata & Worsdell, 2005; Reese, Richman, Belmont, & Morse, 2005). Understanding the function of a behavior informs intervention strategies designed to reduce it (Brosnan & Healy, 2011; Campbell, 2003; Horner et al., 2002).

There are three types of functional assessments: functional analysis, indirect functional assessment, and descriptive functional assessment (Tarbox et al., 2009). *Functional analysis* involves observation of the child where environmental events are deliberately manipulated during strictly controlled experimental conditions (Iwata, Dorsey, Slifer, Bauman, & Richman, 1994). Functional analysis has been researched extensively and often is recommended because it allows for a controlled test of factors that lead to disruptive behavior and then guide the development of successful interventions (Hanley, 2012). However, functional analysis requires specialized training, is time consuming, and involves setting up experimental conditions that may not be ecologically valid (Conroy, Fox, Crain, Jenkins, & Belcher, 1996; Sturmey, 1995). Although researchers have sought to address all of these limitations (Hanley, 2012; Iwata & Dozier, 2008), functional analysis frequently is not used in practice (Oliver, Pratt, & Normand, 2015).

Instead, providers may rely on indirect or descriptive functional assessment (Oliver et al., 2015). *Indirect functional assessment* involves interviewing parents or teachers to identify antecedents and consequences to a behavior. The therapist uses this information to develop hypotheses about the function of the behavior (Carr & Wilder, 2003; Durand & Crimmins, 1992; Matson & Vollmer, 1995). *Descriptive functional assessment* includes direct observation of antecedents and consequences surrounding the child's target behavior in the natural environment to identify the function of the behavioral problem (Carr & Wilder, 2003; Tarbox et al., 2009). Both indirect and descriptive functional assessments have the benefit of being more easily accomplished compared with functional assessment. Descriptive functional assessment is based on information about the child in the natural environment and has the additional benefit of focusing on prospective observational data collection instead of reliance on informant recall. These forms of functional assessment are limited, however, by the lack of control over extraneous environmental variables, such as attention provided by a sibling or unrestricted access to preferred items. In addition, systematic reviews have identified only a few studies on such assessments, and interventions based on these assessments have been less successful than those based on functional analysis (Herzinger & Campbell, 2007). Although functional analysis and descriptive functional assessment typically are conducted by professionals (e.g., board-certified behavior analysts, school personnel; Barton & Fettig, 2013), some research has suggested that with instruction from a clinician, parents can be taught to conduct a functional assessment to identify the purpose of behavioral problems that can be used to plan treatment (Frea & Hepburn, 1999; Lindgren et al., 2016; Suess, Wacker, Schwartz, Lustig, & Detrick, 2016; Wacker et al., 2013).

COMMON TECHNIQUES IN PARENT TRAINING FOR DISRUPTIVE BEHAVIOR

Common PT elements that follow the principles of applied behavior analysis include role playing, guided implementation with the child in session to support parental skill acquisition, homework so that parents can practice applying strategies in real life, and follow-up sessions to review and refine the behavioral techniques. Following education on the ABC model and functions of behavior, therapists may review with parents the following approaches: antecedent management strategies, consequence-based approaches, skill acquisition, and generalization and maintenance to promote stable change in the child and to enhance the parents' ability to apply skills learned in future situations and settings.

Antecedent Management Strategies

These preventive strategies are designed to avert the occurrence of behavioral problems by modifying the antecedents, that is, the triggers, of the behavior. Prevention strategies call on parents to think ahead to identify a predictable behavioral sequence (e.g., when told "no" [antecedent], the child has a tantrum). Once the pattern is identified, the parent can implement a strategy to eliminate or modify the antecedent of that behavior. Common antecedent management strategies follow.

Controlling the Environment

For safety concerns, a parent might place locks on drawers or cabinets that hold dangerous chemicals. To minimize property destruction, a parent can place breakable items out of reach. Valuable items may be put in a safe location. To prevent the onset of disruptive behavior, a parent might put certain items out of sight (e.g., cookies, a certain toy prone to cause fights between siblings). These environmental controls decrease the likelihood of the child's engaging in potentially harmful, dangerous, or disruptive behavior.

Creating Daily Structure and Routines

Increasing predictability in the child's daily routine (e.g., getting ready in the morning, bedtime routine) can avoid instances in which the child might protest in response to a new demand or transition from a preferred to nonpreferred activity.

Providing Choices

The provision of choices can be an effective replacement for saying "no" in everyday situations that trigger misbehavior in the child. Choices offer the child some control in the moment, but the parent defines the choices. For example, instead of telling a child, "No, you cannot have ice cream for breakfast," the parent can provide the choice "Would you like eggs or cereal for breakfast?"

Use of Visual and Auditory Cues

Visual cues include pictures, written lists, or timers that can serve as a reminder of a pending transition or a certain activity in the daily routine. The use of these cues can prevent behavioral problems and promote the child's independence and acquisition of daily living skills. For example, visual cues can help the child process information about the sequence of events by providing a sense of predictability, which may, in turn, promote the child's flexibility. Visual cues can be used to set up choices (e.g., a choice board), time passage and sequencing (e.g., timers to set up first this, then the next activity), and step-by-step presentation of daily routines (e.g., visual schedules, social stories). For example, developing a set of pictures showing the steps of the morning routine can remind the child what needs to be done before going to school, therefore avoiding confusion and promoting compliance. Setting a timer that signals the end of 20 minutes of computer time may be more effective than abruptly telling the child to turn off the computer.

Consequences

PT also includes several consequence-based techniques, including positive social attention, planned ignoring, time-out, differential reinforcement, behavioral contingencies, token economy systems, and compliance training.

Positive Social Attention

The goal of positive social attention is to reverse negative (and cyclical) parent–child interactions. Reversing negative interactions involves increasing parental awareness and acknowledgment of the child's appropriate behaviors. Specific positive social attention strategies include the use of praise and "catching the child being good." Praise involves overt verbal expression to the child following performance of positive behaviors. The use of praise can be especially powerful to highlight "positive opposite" situations. For example, for a child who frequently hits a sibling, praising moments when the child keeps his or her hands to himself or herself. Catching a child being good is an opportunity to praise the child for engaging in appropriate behavior. A parent may target specific times of the day (e.g., the morning routine) or certain situations (e.g., sharing toys with a sibling or prompt compliance to commands) that have been challenging.

Planned Ignoring

The "partner" to providing positive social attention is ignoring inappropriate behaviors. Common targets for planned ignoring are socially maintained (i.e., attention-seeking) behaviors, such as tantrums and whining. Planned ignoring requires complete disengagement (i.e., silently turning away, no eye contact or directed affect, no language directed toward the child) until the behavior subsides. When the behavior stops, the parent reengages with the child. Planned ignoring is best applied when the maladaptive behavior is not dangerous to the child, to others, or to property. Behaviors involving aggression, self-injury, or property destruction can be more challenging to ignore and may require the parent to intervene to reduce harm. A challenge with the application of planned ignoring is the potential for *extinction bursts* (i.e., an escalation of the behavior before it decreases). Parents often need guidance on how to handle situations in which the child engages in potentially dangerous or destructive behaviors. For example, if a child who is being ignored by parents begins to throw objects, the parent may be coached to continue the use of planned ignoring while physically redirecting the child to a different room. Otherwise, parental anxiety about the child's increasingly provocative behaviors may lead some parents to attend to the child and inadvertently reinforce the behavior.

Time-Out

Time-out is a form of planned ignoring in which the child is removed from all reinforcing stimuli. Time-out can be an effective approach for challenging and persistent target behaviors. Unfortunately, parents often make errors in the application of time-out that render the strategy ineffective. An important component to the effective use of time-out includes restricting its use to one or two target behaviors at a time to help promote predictability for the child regarding which behaviors will result in a time-out. Because time-out is more formally known as *time-out from reinforcement*, parents also must ensure that time-out is located in a safe, distraction-free area—not on the couch in front of the television or in the bedroom where the child has free access to toys. In addition, the parent deliberately ignores the child during the time-out, thus minimizing the amount of attention (positive or negative) that the child receives while in time-out. Parents should choose a predetermined minimum amount of time that the child is to stay in time-out. Once the child is seated quietly and the predetermined amount of time has passed, and the child is willing to complete the command, the time-out is over. This sequence avoids the problem of the child's "completing" the predetermined time (e.g., 5 minutes) while still very agitated and thus likely to reengage in the disruptive behavior. Another challenge involves situations in which the child is unwilling to stay in time-out. PT programs vary on how to address this issue, such as using a backup time-out room or removing a predetermined privilege if the child refuses to sit or stay in time-out.

Differential Reinforcement

This approach combines positive social reinforcement and planned ignoring to show that positive parental attention will be received only when the child engages in appropriate behavior. Negative behaviors will no longer receive attention (via the use of planned ignoring). For example, a child who requests a favorite toy or snack in a demanding manner is ignored by the parent until the child's negative behavior subsides. Only when the child asks for the item in an appropriate manner will the parent attend and respond to the child. To promote positive requesting, the parent also can praise instances in which the child spontaneously requests items in an appropriate way (e.g., "I like how you asked for the snack in a nice way. I'm happy to give it to you").

Behavioral Contingencies

Sometimes referred to as *behavioral contracts*, *behavioral contingencies* are designed to create clear expectations for the child, in advance, about a target behavior and its consequences. A common format for a behavioral contingency is the "If/First___, then___" statement. This statement involves a counterbalance of a parental demand with a reinforcer (e.g., "If you finish your dinner, then you can have ice cream"), natural positive consequence (e.g., "First you put your coat on, then you can go outside"), or punishment (e.g., "If you hit your sister, then you will go to time-out"). Strengths of behavioral contingencies and established rules are twofold. First, they provide a clear understanding to the child about what behavior is being targeted and the consequence for engaging in that behavior.

Second, they establish the rules ahead of time, which avoids bickering over what the child may perceive as arbitrary. This twofold approach sets up an opportunity for the child to consider whether to engage in a target behavior because, assuming the parent follows through, the child knows what the ramifications will be.

Token Economy System

A *token economy system* is an expanded version of behavioral contingency. In a token economy, the child earns points or stickers for engaging in targeted behaviors. The child can exchange accumulated points for preferred items (e.g., access to a favorite toy or preferred activity). Weekly allowance follows this principle in that a child is required to complete a set number of chores to earn a predetermined amount of money. Token economy systems provide an opportunity for collaboration between the parent and child to define the target behaviors and the desired rewards to be exchanged for the tokens. This collaborative effort promotes compromise between parent and child, and fosters engagement with the child.

Compliance Training

Teaching a child to comply with a command the first time it is given starts by teaching a parent how to deliver an effective command: one that is direct, simple, and given only once. The goal is to establish the importance of immediate compliance with a command to decrease occurrences of escape from the demand. These steps avoid common errors, such as repeating a command multiple times before having the child comply, providing a command that is too complex (e.g., multistep), and giving vague instructions or indicating that compliance is optional. Parents are taught to avoid statements such as, "Would you mind . . . ," "How about you . . . ," or "Let's do. . . ." Once they have given an effective command, parents are encouraged to follow through by using physical prompting or guidance to ensure that the child completes the demand. Parents are also coached to provide immediate praise as the child completes the command.

Skill Acquisition

Noncompliant and disruptive behavior interferes with regular performance of the child's current daily living skills and often derail parental efforts to introduce new skills. Reduction in disruptive behavior in PT opens the door to adaptive skills development (Scahill et al., 2012; Scahill, Bearss, et al., 2016). Thus, promoting daily living skills is an extension of teaching parents to manage behavioral problems in children with ASD.

Functional Communication Training

The premise behind functional communication training is that teaching the child a new appropriate mode of communication can be an effective replacement for communication through problematic behavior. In this model, the new behavior serves the same function as the maladaptive behavior, but is more appropriate and equally effective. For example, a child may whine or scream when asked to complete a routine task, such as zipping up his or her coat. The child's ensuing screaming communicates: "Zipping up my coat is too hard. . . . I don't want to"—but it is also inappropriate. The goal is to teach the child a more appropriate or functional way to make the request to obtain help with the zipper. Replacement communicative strategies can include the use of gestures, signs, or words. Parents are encouraged to respond quickly every time the child uses a more appropriate strategy. Doing so teaches the child that appropriate communication works better than disruptive and inappropriate requests to get needs met.

Generalization and Maintenance

Most PT programs conclude with teaching strategies that promote maintenance of treatment gains over time and generalization of appropriate behavior to other contexts not covered in the treatment program. Not surprisingly, parents may need preparation on how to apply PT strategies in new situations when conditions vary. For example, although a primary target of treatment may be to improve compliance at home, compliance in public places and at family events also is important.

Research Support for Parent Training for Disruptive Behavior

PT for disruptive behavior is among the strongest evidence-based treatments in child mental health (Dretzke et al., 2009; Michelson, Davenport, Dretzke, Barlow, & Day, 2013). Until recently, empirical support for PT strategies in children with ASD relied on a body of evidence from single-subject design studies and a collection of pilot trials (Bearss, Johnson, Handen, Smith, & Scahill, 2013; Campbell, 2003). To date, eight randomized controlled trials with sample sizes ranging from 26 to 180 have evaluated the efficacy of PT in children with ASD. In a meta-analysis of those studies that included a total of 653 children (ages 2–15), Postorino et al. (2017) showed that PT is an effective treatment (i.e., overall effect size of 0.58) for reducing disruptive behavior in young children with ASD. The two studies with the largest effect size had a wait-list control. Trials with the weakest effect size were relatively brief (i.e., 10 weeks or less). The meta-analysis provides solid support for PT programs with 10 to 12 sessions spread over 16 to 24 weeks. These results suggest that parents need time to apply behavioral management techniques and make use of coaching from the therapist to hone their skills.

The best studied PT intervention for reducing disruptive behavior and improving adaptive skills in children with ASD was developed by investigators from the RUPP and Research Units in Behavioral Intervention (RUBI) Autism Network. This body of work required building a treatment manual because there was no commercially available PT program for children with ASD and disruptive behavior (Johnson et al., 2007). This program consisted of 11 core sessions and up to two optional focal-problem sessions (e.g., toileting or sleep problems), as well as three telephone booster calls and two home visits delivered individually to the parent over the course of 24 weeks. The intervention is based on the principles and techniques of applied behavior analysis, but parents are the change agents. The program targets routine activities that often pose a daily struggle for parents of children with ASD, including getting dressed, getting ready for bed, or managing trips to the grocery store. With funding from the National Institute of Mental Health, the initial version of the RUPP manual was tested in a multisite feasibility trial with 17 children (RUPP Autism Network, 2007). This was followed by a 6-month, randomized trial comparing risperidone with risperidone plus PT in 124 school-age children (age 4–13 years) with ASD and serious behavioral problems. In that study, both treatments resulted in a substantial reduction of disruptive behavior; however, risperidone plus PT was superior to drug only (Aman et al., 2009). The study also showed that risperidone treatment can cause rapid weight gain and detrimental metabolic consequences (Scahill, Jeon, et al., 2016). The manual was revised for younger children with ASD and disruptive behavior under the simple assumption that a downward extension of the manual may prevent the emergence of more severe behaviors in school-age children and avert the need for medication. An open pilot trial of PT as a stand-alone treatment in 16 children between the ages of 3 and 7 years supported the feasibility and initial efficacy of the modified PT manual (Bearss et al., 2013, 2018).

The RUBI Autism Network conducted a National Institute of Mental Health-funded multisite trial (Bearss et al., 2015) in 180 children (age 3–7 years) with ASD and disruptive behavior. Subjects were randomly assigned to PT or a structured parent education program (PEP) for 6 months. PEP, which was created specifically for this randomized controlled trial, provided parents with up-to-date information on ASD (e.g., differential diagnosis, genetics, available treatments, educational placement). It also included strategies for parents to become effective advocates for their child with ASD. However, PEP did not include any information on child behavior management. As with PT, PEP was delivered individually to parents by trained therapists in 13 sessions over 24 weeks. This comparison condition was designed to control for time and attention (i.e., parental contact with the therapist). Outcomes were assessed by parent report and by independent evaluators who were blind to treatment assignment. Children also were followed for up to 24 weeks posttreatment.

In the RUBI trial, independent evaluators who were blind to treatment assignment classified 69% of children in PT with a positive response compared with 40% in the PEP group (Bearss et al., 2015). A key secondary outcome was change in adaptive skills as measured on the Vineland Adaptive Behavior Scales (Sparrow, Cicchetti, & Balla, 2005). Consistent with the model that reducing disruptive behavior sets the stage for improvements in adaptive skills, there was a significant improvement in Vineland Daily Living Skills in PT compared with no change in PEP (Scahill, Bearss, et al., 2016). Parents attended 92% of the core therapy sessions, and attrition was low at 11%. Therapist fidelity to the treatment was excellent, averaging 97%. These results provided strong evidence that the RUBI PT program significantly reduces disruptive behavior and improves daily living skills; in addition, parents are engaged in treatment and therapists can reliably deliver the intervention.

SPECIAL CONSIDERATIONS

Severe Behavioral Problems

PT is well suited for children with ASD who display moderate behavioral problems, and it is delivered to parents who have the ability to apply in-session didactic and interactive teaching materials into home and community settings. Children with severe behavioral problems (e.g., high frequency and intensity of aggression, self-injury, or both) may need more intensive treatment directed to the child. Although the RUPP/RUBI PT program (Aman et al., 2009; Bearss et al., 2015) was tested in children from 3 to 13 years of age, attempting an extinction procedure with an older child who is bigger and perhaps stronger than the parent may be better suited for trials conducted in well-controlled settings with a high level of support provided by the therapist. The RUPP study examined the combination of risperidone only to risperidone plus PT. The participants in that study were slightly older than the children in the RUBI study and had more severe behavioral problems at baseline (Aman et al., 2009). Thus, the combination of medication and PT may be an appropriate treatment plan for children with severe behavioral problems.

Child Cognitive Functioning

The RUPP and RUBI studies (Aman et al., 2009; Bearss et al., 2015) included children across a wide range of cognitive functioning. Children with receptive language skills below 18 months were excluded, however. To our knowledge, no other randomized trial of PT in very low-functioning children with ASD and co-occurring disruptive behavior has been conducted. Thus, efficacy of PT in this subpopulation of children is unknown. The basis of this exclusion criterion in the RUPP and RUBI trials was twofold. First, the differential diagnosis of an ASD from severe or profound intellectual disability is difficult. Second, although children were not required to be verbal, PT in its present form requires at least rudimentary receptive language (i.e., the ability to understand—and thus follow—simple one-step commands). Nonetheless, there is little doubt that children with receptive language below 18 months have disruptive behavior that diminishes the quality of life for the child and the family. As with revisions of the original PT program for school-age children (Bearss et al., 2013), modifications to the PT program also may be required to serve low-functioning, nonverbal children.

Co-Occurring Psychiatric Conditions

Other co-occurring conditions, such as attention-deficit/hyperactivity disorder (ADHD) and anxiety, may complicate the delivery of PT in children with ASD and disruptive behavior. Sofronoff, Leslie, and Brown (2004) included sessions on anxiety management in the PT program, which may have contributed to the observed efficacy in that study. Findings on the impact of PT on ADHD have been mixed. In the RUBI trial (Bearss et al., 2015), children with high ADHD and low ADHD symptom severity showed improvement in disruptive behavior in PT. In children with high levels of ADHD symptoms, however, there was no difference between PT and psychoeducation (PEP) on parent-rated disruptive behavior. For reasons that are unclear, within the PEP group, children in the high-severity ADHD group showed greater improvement that those with lower ADHD severity. That finding probably explains why there was no difference between PT and PEP in the high-severity ADHD group. In contrast, children with low ADHD symptoms showed statistically significant greater improvements in PT compared with PEP (Lecavalier et al., 2017).

A briefer PT intervention that was based on the RUBI program (Handen et al., 2015) compared atomoxetine alone with atomoxetine plus PT, pill placebo plus PT, and placebo alone in a sample of children with ASD and co-occurring ADHD. Although results supported the efficacy of the three active arms compared with placebo in reducing ADHD symptom severity, only atomoxetine and atomoxetine plus PT produced change in parent-ratings of noncompliant behavior (Handen et al., 2015). Those findings suggested that if medication management of ADHD is warranted, it may be advisable to initiate the medication before or concurrently with PT.

Disruptive and noncompliant behaviors may stem from anxiety in children with ASD (Bearss et al., 2016). The presence of anxiety may complicate the application of PT, although few studies have directly examined this question in children with ASD (Lecavalier et al., 2017; Sofronoff et al., 2004). In clinical populations other than ASD, there is evidence that children with low anxiety and disruptive behavior problems are responsive to interventions that focus on altering instrumental operant contingencies within the home (Beauchaine, Webster-Stratton, & Reid, 2005). In children with high anxiety, however, Pincus, Santucci, Ehrenreich, and Eyberg (2008) reported that parent–child interaction therapy without modifications is not effective as a stand-alone treatment to reduce childhood anxiety ($n = 10$; average age, 6 years). Investigating the application of PT in children with ASD plus prominent anxiety and disruptive behavior may be yet another subpopulation in which modifications are needed.

CASE EXAMPLE

Ben is a 5-year-old Caucasian boy who lives with his biological parents and 9-year-old sister. His history includes multiple co-occurring disorders and other developmental issues: premature birth, global developmental delays, ASD, apraxia, avoidant/restrictive food intake disorder, and strabismus. Ben is nonverbal and uses an augmentative and alternative communication device along with a handful of signs and gestures. Ben can undress himself independently but is not independent in dressing himself. He eats only foods with soft textures that require minimal chewing. Although occasionally successful with voiding in the toilet, he is not daytime or nighttime toilet trained. He is not taking any medications aside from vitamins and probiotics. Ben is in a self-contained life skills classroom that focuses on use of augmentative and alternative communication devices. In school, he is receiving 1 hour of speech and 1 hour of occupational therapy per week. Ben is in private speech therapy 35 minutes per week.

Ben was referred to the RUBI PT program due to parent-reported noncompliance, as well as mild physical aggression and self-injurious behaviors. His parents also expressed concern that Ben refuses to wear his eyeglasses at home or at school. He frequently is noncompliant with daily routines, such as getting dressed, feeding, and diaper changes. Mild physical aggression, such as light pushing of his mother or his sister, occurs a couple of times per week.

Biting episodes usually are brief and occur when parents ask him to stop playing on his tablet. His parents note that when they limit Ben's access to his tablet altogether, the frequency of biting decreases. Aside from two instances of biting another child last year, his parents have not received any reports of behavioral problems in the classroom or aggression toward peers.

Assessment Battery

Ben's IQ was derived from the Abbreviated Stanford–Binet Intelligence Scales-Fifth Edition (Roid, 2003). Although Ben was able to sit at the table and was cooperative throughout the testing, he was unable to engage in most testing items. Ben received a computed IQ score of 47, which places him in the moderately impaired range compared with other children his age. On the Adaptive Behavior Assessment System, Third Edition (Harrison & Oakland, 2015), Ben obtained a General Adaptive Composite score of 51. This summary score of performance across all skill areas places Ben in the moderately impaired range. On the parent-rated Social Responsiveness Scale, Second Edition (Constantino & Gruber, 2012), Ben received a t score of > 90 on the total score, indicating clinically significant deficits in reciprocal social behavior that are likely to interfere with everyday social interactions. Ben's parents reported significant disruptive behavior as measured by a score of 18 on the Aberrant Behavior Checklist-Irritability subscale and a mean severity score of 3.58 on the HSQ-ASD. These scores are consistent multiple types and topographies of disruptive behavior.

Based on the information provided by Ben's mother and father regarding his target behaviors and results from standardized testing, Ben and his family enrolled in the RUBI PT program.

Treatment

Ben's parents began the RUBI program and attended a total of 12 in-person sessions over the course of 15 weeks, followed by a 1-month in-person booster session. His parents initially collected ABC data to learn more about the function of Ben's tantrums and noncompliance (see Table 5.1). When reviewing those results with the therapist, common antecedents to Ben's target disruptive behaviors emerged, including demands during daily transitions (e.g., getting dressed, getting ready for bed, getting off the iPad) and when asked to stop an inappropriate behavior (e.g., "leave your sister's Kindle alone"). Ben's parents identified escape/avoidance and "getting what he wants" (i.e., tangible) as possible functions of his behavior. However, parents also noted that sometimes it was unclear whether he was engaging in the

TABLE 5.1
Antecedent-Behavior-Consequences: Data Examples

Antecedent	Behavior	Consequence	Function
Being told "no," he cannot have the phone	Pushes	I said, "No, thank you" (verbal reprimand)	To get what he wants
Told to put shirt on	Rolls away from his mother, falls back on the sofa	Mom took away the iPad	To escape (getting dressed)
Told "it's time for bed"	Shuts the door on his parents (he was playing with the iPad)	Mom reopened the door, touched the iPad, and told him to put it away (which he then complied with)	Escape (bedtime); to get what he wants (more iPad time)

behavior to "get what he wants" (e.g., more time on the iPad) or to "escape" (e.g., from starting his bedtime routine).

See Table 5.2 for a detailed account of treatment activities and generated strategies. Initial prevention strategies focused on aiding Ben with transitions (e.g., using a timer to provide warnings), as well as a change in the afternoon snack routine to reduce whining before dinner and to reduce Ben's demands for inappropriate snacks (e.g., cookies). A visual schedule was introduced at the third session to promote understanding and compliance with the daily routine. The schedule was readily accepted by Ben and even prompted his engagement in tasks that he previously had refused to do (e.g., brush his teeth). Putting eyeglasses on was added to the schedule to indicate when he needed to put them on, and Ben readily accepted this addition. A separate visual for wearing eyeglasses eventually was created and involved a two-sided card (i.e., green = glasses on; red = glasses off).

Reinforcement strategies targeted naturalistic opportunities to tie Ben's requests for a preferred item to completion a specific demand (e.g., if Ben requested his father's phone, his father would prompt him first to put his dish in the sink, then he could have the phone). For the functional communication session, the therapist learned that different methods were being used at home, school, and speech therapy. This information led to a discussion about the importance of using a consistent communication system. The teaching skills sessions targeted coaching Ben on how to put on his eyeglasses independently. The supplemental toileting session focused on timed, prompted trips to the bathroom as a way for Ben to earn access to his favorite video. The RUBI program emphasized the importance of applying strategies in a

TABLE 5.2
Summary of Strategies

Target behaviors	Prevention strategy	Reinforcement strategy	Consequence strategy	Functional communication	Skill training
Noncompliance	Use timer to provide warning for transition to bedtime routine Use timer to support Ben's practice with wearing his glasses Use visual schedule to support the evening routine and to show Ben when he needs to wear his glasses To address possible setting event of hunger, present snack first on returning home from school, then free play	Look for opportunities to use natural reinforcers (e.g., if Ben is asking for dad's phone, first give him a small chore to complete before he can have access to the phone)	Use compliance training steps (i.e., get Ben's attention, give the command one time, use physical prompting, praise) to target compliance with putting a dish in the sink and sitting in the chair If Ben takes another person's Wii remote, then he will lose his turn in the game		

| Adaptive skills | Set up a structured play time on the weekend in which mom or dad will play with Ben for 5 minutes (e.g., using trains, cars) with the goal of promoting and expanding imaginative play themes | Promote use of Ben's AAC device; if he uses another strategy (e.g., sign, hand over hand), prompt him to use his device instead to request | Conduct a task analysis of putting on glasses; determine what one step will be the focus of teaching and what prompts can be used to support the learning process; once Ben has mastered the one step, move onto the next step (via forward or backward chaining) |
| Toileting | Increase liquids after school and do timed trips every 60 minutes, have a bucket of fun activities to entertain Ben while he sits on the toilet for up to 3 minutes; a specific reward (e.g., the Wii) will be given if Ben successfully voids; a visual will be placed across from the toilet showing what Ben earns (e.g., the Wii) for going pee. | | |

Note. Strategies using functional communication and skill training were not developed specifically for noncompliance. Toileting relied on a variety of strategies, such as prevention, reinforcement, and guided compliance. ACC = augmentative and alternative communication.

TABLE 5.3
Parent-Report Outcome Measures

	ABC-I	HSQ-ASD mean severity
Baseline	18	3.58
Midtreatment	12	2.63
Endpoint	7	1.21
1-month follow-up	5	1.04

Note. ABC-I = Aberrant Behavior Checklist-Irritability subscale; HSQ-ASD = Home Situations Questionnaire-Autism Spectrum Disorder.

manner that promoted consistency and predictability in Ben's daily routine. His parents understood this principle and successfully implemented effective parenting techniques. At a 1-month follow up visit, Ben's parents reported substantial decrease in noncompliance on the HSQ-ASD, as well as tantrums, aggression, and self-injury as measured on the ABC-Irritability subscale (see Table 5.3).

REFERENCES

Aman, M. G., Bukstein, O. G., Gadow, K. D., Arnold, L. E., Molina, B. S. G., McNamara, N. K., . . . Findling, R. L. (2014). What does risperidone add to parent training and stimulant for severe aggression in child attention-deficit/hyperactivity disorder? *Journal of the American Academy of Child & Adolescent Psychiatry, 53*, 47–60.e1. http://dx.doi.org/10.1016/j.jaac.2013.09.022

Aman, M. G., De Smedt, G., Derivan, A., Lyons, B., Findling, R. L., & Risperidone Disruptive Behavior Study Group. (2002). Double-blind, placebo-controlled study of risperidone for the treatment of disruptive behaviors in children with subaverage intelligence. *American Journal of Psychiatry, 159*, 1337–1346. http://dx.doi.org/10.1176/appi.ajp.159.8.1337

Aman, M. G., McDougle, C. J., Scahill, L., Handen, B., Arnold, L. E., Johnson, C., . . . & Wagner, A. (2009). Medication and parent training in children with pervasive developmental disorders and serious behavior problems: Results from a randomized clinical trial. *Journal of the American Academy of Child & Adolescent Psychiatry, 48*, 1143–1154. http://dx.doi.org/10.1097/CHI.0b013e3181bfd669

Aman, M. G., Singh, N. N., Stewart, A. W., & Field, C. J. (1985). The Aberrant Behavior Checklist: A behavior rating scale for the assessment of treatment effects. *American Journal of Mental Deficiency, 89*, 485–491.

Aman, M. G., Tassé, M. J., Rojahn, J., & Hammer, D. (1996). The Nisonger CBRF: A child behavior rating form for children with developmental disabilities.

Research in Developmental Disabilities, *17*, 41–57. http://dx.doi.org/10.1016/0891-4222(95)00039-9

American Psychiatric Association. (2013). *Diagnostic and statistical manual of mental disorders* (5th ed.). Arlington, VA: Author.

Barkley, R. A., & Edelbrock, C. (1987). Assessing situational variation in children's problem behaviors: The Home and School Situations Questionnaires. In R. Prinz (Ed.), *Advances in behavioral assessment of children and families* (pp. 157–176). Greenwich, CT: JAI Press.

Barton, E. E., & Fettig, A. (2013). Parent-implemented interventions for young children with disabilities: A review of fidelity features. *Journal of Early Intervention*, *35*, 194–219. http://dx.doi.org/10.1177/1053815113504625

Bearss, K., Johnson, C., Handen, B., Butter, E., Lecavalier, L., Smith, T., & Scahill, L. (2018). *Parent training for disruptive behaviors*. New York, NY: Oxford University Press.

Bearss, K., Johnson, C., Handen, B., Smith, T., & Scahill, L. (2013). A pilot study of parent training in young children with autism spectrum disorders and disruptive behavior. *Journal of Autism and Developmental Disorders*, *43*, 829–840. http://dx.doi.org/10.1007/s10803-012-1624-7

Bearss, K., Johnson, C., Smith, T., Lecavalier, L., Swiezy, N., Aman, M., . . . Scahill, L. (2015). Effect of parent training vs parent education on behavioral problems in children with autism spectrum disorder: A randomized clinical trial. *JAMA*, *313*, 1524–1533. http://dx.doi.org/10.1001/jama.2015.3150

Bearss, K., Taylor, C. A., Aman, M. G., Whittemore, R., Lecavalier, L., Miller, J., . . . Scahill, L. (2016). Using qualitative methods to guide scale development for anxiety in youth with autism spectrum disorder. *Autism*, *20*, 663–672. http://dx.doi.org/10.1177/1362361315601012

Beauchaine, T. P., Webster-Stratton, C., & Reid, M. J. (2005). Mediators, moderators, and predictors of 1-year outcomes among children treated for early-onset conduct problems: A latent growth curve analysis. *Journal of Consulting and Clinical Psychology*, *73*, 371–388. http://dx.doi.org/10.1037/0022-006X.73.3.371

Brereton, A. V., Tonge, B. J., & Einfeld, S. L. (2006). Psychopathology in children and adolescents with autism compared to young people with intellectual disability. *Journal of Autism and Developmental Disorders*, *36*, 863–870. http://dx.doi.org/10.1007/s10803-006-0125-y

Brosnan, J., & Healy, O. (2011). A review of behavioral interventions for the treatment of aggression in individuals with developmental disabilities. *Research in Developmental Disabilities*, *32*, 437–446. http://dx.doi.org/10.1016/j.ridd.2010.12.023

Campbell, J. M. (2003). Efficacy of behavioral interventions for reducing problem behavior in persons with autism: A quantitative synthesis of single-subject research. *Research in Developmental Disabilities*, *24*, 120–138. http://dx.doi.org/10.1016/S0891-4222(03)00014-3

Carr, J. E., & Wilder, D. A. (2003). *Functional assessment and intervention: A Guide to understanding problem behavior* (2nd ed.). Homewood, IL: High Tide Press.

Chowdhury, M., Aman, M. G., Lecavalier, L., Smith, T., Johnson, C., Swiezy, N., . . . Scahill, L. (2016). Factor structure and psychometric properties of the revised Home Situations Questionnaire for autism spectrum disorder: The Home Situations Questionnaire-Autism Spectrum Disorder. *Autism, 20,* 528–537. http://dx.doi.org/10.1177/1362361315593941

Conroy, M., Fox, J., Crain, L., Jenkins, A., & Belcher, K. (1996). Evaluating the social and ecological validity of analog assessment procedures for challenging behaviors in young children. *Education and Treatment of Children, 19,* 233–256.

Constantino, J. N., & Gruber, C. P. (2012). *The Social Responsiveness Scale Manual, Second Edition (SRS-2).* Los Angeles, CA: Western Psychological Services.

Dretzke, J., Davenport, C., Frew, E., Barlow, J., Stewart-Brown, S., Bayliss, S., . . . Hyde, C. (2009). The clinical effectiveness of different parenting programmes for children with conduct problems: A systematic review of randomised controlled trials. *Child and Adolescent Psychiatry and Mental Health, 3,* 7. http://dx.doi.org/10.1186/1753-2000-3-7

Durand, V. M., & Crimmins, D. B. (1992). *The Motivation Assessment Scale (MAS) administration guide.* Topeka, KS: Monaco.

Farmer, C. A., & Aman, M. G. (2010). Psychometric properties of the Children's Scale of Hostility and Aggression: Reactive/Proactive (C-SHARP). *Research in Developmental Disabilities, 31,* 270–280. http://dx.doi.org/10.1016/j.ridd.2009.09.014

Farmer, C. A., & Aman, M. G. (2011). Aggressive behavior in a sample of children with autism spectrum disorders. *Research in Autism Spectrum Disorders, 5,* 317–323. http://dx.doi.org/10.1016/j.rasd.2010.04.014

Farmer, C. A., Kaat, A. J., Mazurek, M., Lainhart, J., Dewitt, M., Cook, E., . . . Aman, M. G. (2016). Confirmation of the factor structure and measurement invariance of the Children's Scale of Hostility and Aggression: Reactive/Proactive in clinic-referred children with and without autism spectrum disorder. *Journal of Child and Adolescent Psychopharmacology, 26,* 10–18. http://dx.doi.org/10.1089/cap.2015.0098

Frea, W. D., & Hepburn, S. L. (1999). Teaching parents of children with autism to perform functional assessments to plan interventions for extremely disruptive behaviors. *Journal of Positive Behavior Interventions, 1,* 112–122. http://dx.doi.org/10.1177/109830079900100205

Gadow, K. D., DeVincent, C. J., Pomeroy, J., & Azizian, A. (2004). Psychiatric symptoms in preschool children with PDD and clinic and comparison samples. *Journal of Autism and Developmental Disorders, 34,* 379–393. http://dx.doi.org/10.1023/B:JADD.0000037415.21458.93

Gadow, K. D., DeVincent, C. J., Pomeroy, J., & Azizian, A. (2005). Comparison of *DSM–IV* symptoms in elementary school-age children with PDD versus clinic and community samples. *Autism, 9,* 392–415. http://dx.doi.org/10.1177/1362361305056079

Handen, B. L., Aman, M. G., Arnold, L. E., Hyman, S. L., Tumuluru, R. V., Lecavalier, L., . . . Smith, T. (2015). Atomoxetine, parent training, and their combination in children with autism spectrum disorder and attention-deficit/ hyperactivity disorder. *Journal of the American Academy of Child & Adolescent Psychiatry, 54,* 905–915. http://dx.doi.org/10.1016/j.jaac.2015.08.013

Hanley, G. P. (2012). Functional assessment of problem behavior: Dispelling myths, overcoming implementation obstacles, and developing new lore. *Behavior Analysis in Practice, 5,* 54–72. http://dx.doi.org/10.1007/BF03391818

Harrison, P., & Oakland, T. (2015). *Adaptive Behavior Assessment System, Third Edition.* Torrance, CA: Western Psychological Services.

Hartley, S. L., Sikora, D. M., & McCoy, R. (2008). Prevalence and risk factors of maladaptive behaviour in young children with autistic disorder. *Journal of Intellectual Disability Research, 52,* 819–829. http://dx.doi.org/10.1111/ j.1365-2788.2008.01065.x

Hassall, R., Rose, J., & McDonald, J. (2005). Parenting stress in mothers of children with an intellectual disability: The effects of parental cognitions in relation to child characteristics and family support. *Journal of Intellectual Disability Research, 49,* 405–418. http://dx.doi.org/10.1111/j.1365-2788.2005.00673.x

Hayes, S. A., & Watson, S. L. (2013). The impact of parenting stress: A meta-analysis of studies comparing the experience of parenting stress in parents of children with and without autism spectrum disorder. *Journal of Autism and Developmental Disorders, 43,* 629–642. http://dx.doi.org/10.1007/s10803-012-1604-y

Herring, S., Gray, K., Taffe, J., Tonge, B., Sweeney, D., & Einfeld, S. (2006). Behaviour and emotional problems in toddlers with pervasive developmental disorders and developmental delay: Associations with parental mental health and family functioning. *Journal of Intellectual Disability Research, 50,* 874–882. http://dx.doi.org/10.1111/j.1365-2788.2006.00904.x

Herzinger, C. V., & Campbell, J. M. (2007). Comparing functional assessment methodologies: A quantitative synthesis. *Journal of Autism and Developmental Disorders, 37,* 1430–1445. http://dx.doi.org/10.1007/s10803-006-0219-6

Horner, R. H., Carr, E. G., Strain, P. S., Todd, A. W., & Reed, H. K. (2002). Problem behavior interventions for young children with autism: A research synthesis. *Journal of Autism and Developmental Disorders, 32,* 423–446. http:// dx.doi.org/10.1023/A:1020593922901

Iadarola, S., Levato, L., Harrison, B., Smith, T., Lecavalier, L., Johnson, C., . . . Scahill, L. (2017). Teaching parents behavioral strategies for ASD: Effects on stress, strain, and competence. *Journal of Autism and Developmental Disorders, 48,* 1031–1040. http://dx.doi.org/10.1007/s10803-017-3339-2

Iwata, B. A., Dorsey, M. F., Slifer, K. J., Bauman, K. E., & Richman, G. S. (1994). Toward a functional analysis of self-injury. *Journal of Applied Behavior Analysis, 27,* 197–209. http://dx.doi.org/10.1901/jaba.1994.27-197

Iwata, B. A., & Dozier, C. L. (2008). Clinical application of functional analysis methodology. *Behavior Analysis in Practice, 1*, 3–9. http://dx.doi.org/10.1007/BF03391714

Iwata, B. A., & Worsdell, A. S. (2005). Implications of functional analysis methodology for the design of intervention programs. *Exceptionality, 13*, 25–34. http://dx.doi.org/10.1207/s15327035ex1301_4

Johnson, C. R., Handen, B. L., Butter, E., Wagner, A., Mulick, J., Sukhodolsky, D. G., . . . Smith, T. (2007). Development of a parent training program for children with pervasive developmental disorders. *Behavioral Interventions, 22*, 201–221. http://dx.doi.org/10.1002/bin.237

Kaat, A. J., & Lecavalier, L. (2013). Disruptive behavior disorders in children and adolescents with autism spectrum disorders: A review of the prevalence, presentation, and treatment. *Research in Autism Spectrum Disorders, 7*, 1579–1594. http://dx.doi.org/10.1016/j.rasd.2013.08.012

Kaat, A. J., Lecavalier, L., & Aman, M. G. (2014). Validity of the aberrant behavior checklist in children with autism spectrum disorder. *Journal of Autism and Developmental Disorders, 44*, 1103–1116. http://dx.doi.org/10.1007/s10803-013-1970-0

Kaminski, J. W., Valle, L. A., Filene, J. H., & Boyle, C. L. (2008). A meta-analytic review of components associated with parent training program effectiveness. *Journal of Abnormal Child Psychology, 36*, 567–589. http://dx.doi.org/10.1007/s10802-007-9201-9

Kanne, S. M., & Mazurek, M. O. (2011). Aggression in children and adolescents with ASD: Prevalence and risk factors. *Journal of Autism and Developmental Disorders, 41*, 926–937. http://dx.doi.org/10.1007/s10803-010-1118-4

Kazdin, A. E. (2005). *Parent management training: Treatment for oppositional, aggressive, and antisocial behavior in children and adolescents.* New York, NY: Oxford University Press.

Koeske, G. F., & Koeske, R. D. (1992). Parenting locus of control: Measurement, construct validation, and a proposed conceptual model. *Social Work Research & Abstracts, 28*, 37–46. http://dx.doi.org/10.1093/swra/28.3.37

Lecavalier, L. (2006). Behavioral and emotional problems in young people with pervasive developmental disorders: Relative prevalence, effects of subject characteristics, and empirical classification. *Journal of Autism and Developmental Disorders, 36*, 1101–1114. http://dx.doi.org/10.1007/s10803-006-0147-5

Lecavalier, L., Aman, M. G., Hammer, D., Stoica, W., & Mathews, G. L. (2004). Factor analysis of the Nisonger Child Behavior Rating Form in children with autism spectrum disorders. *Journal of Autism and Developmental Disorders, 34*, 709–721. http://dx.doi.org/10.1007/s10803-004-5291-1

Lecavalier, L., Gadow, K. D., DeVincent, C. J., & Edwards, M. C. (2009). Validation of *DSM–IV* model of psychiatric syndromes in children with autism spectrum disorders. *Journal of Autism and Developmental Disorders, 39*, 278–289. http://dx.doi.org/10.1007/s10803-008-0622-2

Lecavalier, L., Smith, T., Johnson, C., Bearss, K., Swiezy, N., Aman, M. G., . . . Scahill, L. (2017). Moderators of parent training for disruptive behaviors in young children with autism spectrum disorder. *Journal of Abnormal Child Psychology*, *45*, 1235–1245. http://dx.doi.org/10.1007/s10802-016-0233-x

Lindgren, S., Wacker, D., Suess, A., Schieltz, K., Pelzel, K., Kopelman, T., . . . Waldron, D. (2016). Telehealth and autism: Treating challenging behavior at lower cost. *Pediatrics*, *137*(Suppl. 2), S167–S175. http://dx.doi.org/10.1542/peds.2015-2851O

Matson, J. L., & Vollmer, T. R. (1995). *The questions about behavior functions (QABF) user's guide*. Baton Rouge, LA: Scientific Publishers.

Mayes, S. D., Calhoun, S. L., Aggarwal, R., Baker, C., Mathapati, S., Anderson, R., & Petersen, C. (2012). Explosive, oppositional, and aggressive behavior in children with autism compared to other clinical disorders and typical children. *Research in Autism Spectrum Disorders*, *6*, 1–10. http://dx.doi.org/10.1016/j.rasd.2011.08.001

Mazurek, M. O., Kanne, S. M., & Wodka, E. L. (2013). Physical aggression in children and adolescents with autism spectrum disorders. *Research in Autism Spectrum Disorders*, *7*, 455–465. http://dx.doi.org/10.1016/j.rasd.2012.11.004

McMahon, R. J., & Frick, P. J. (2005). Evidence-based assessment of conduct problems in children and adolescents. *Journal of Clinical Child and Adolescent Psychology*, *34*, 477–505. http://dx.doi.org/10.1207/s15374424jccp3403_6

Michelson, D., Davenport, C., Dretzke, J., Barlow, J., & Day, C. (2013). Do evidence-based interventions work when tested in the "real world?" A systematic review and meta-analysis of parent management training for the treatment of child disruptive behavior. *Clinical Child and Family Psychology Review*, *16*, 18–34. http://dx.doi.org/10.1007/s10567-013-0128-0

Oliver, A. C., Pratt, L. A., & Normand, M. P. (2015). A survey of functional behavior assessment methods used by behavior analysts in practice. *Journal of Applied Behavior Analysis*, *48*, 817–829. http://dx.doi.org/10.1002/jaba.256

Pincus, D. B., Santucci, L. C., Ehrenreich, J. T., & Eyberg, S. M. (2008). The implementation of modified parent–child interaction therapy for youth with separation anxiety disorder. *Cognitive and Behavioral Practice*, *15*, 118–125. http://dx.doi.org/10.1016/j.cbpra.2007.08.002

Pisula, E., & Kossakowska, Z. (2010). Sense of coherence and coping with stress among mothers and fathers of children with autism. *Journal of Autism and Developmental Disorders*, *40*, 1485–1494. http://dx.doi.org/10.1007/s10803-010-1001-3

Postorino, V., Sharp, W. G., McCracken, C. E., Bearss, K., Burrell, T. L., Evans, A. N., & Scahill, L. (2017). A systematic review and meta-analysis of parent training for disruptive behavior in children with autism spectrum disorder. *Clinical Child and Family Psychology Review*, *20*, 391–402. http://dx.doi.org/10.1007/s10567-017-0237-2

Reese, R. M., Richman, D. M., Belmont, J. M., & Morse, P. (2005). Functional characteristics of disruptive behavior in developmentally disabled children with and without autism. *Journal of Autism and Developmental Disorders, 35,* 419–428. http://dx.doi.org/10.1007/s10803-005-5032-0

Research Units on Pediatric Psychopharmacology (RUPP) Autism Network. (2002). Risperidone in children with autism for serious behavioral problems. *New England Journal of Medicine, 347,* 314–321.

Research Units on Pediatric Psychopharmacology (RUPP) Autism Network. (2007). Parent training for children with pervasive developmental disorders: A multi-site feasibility trial. *Behavioral Interventions, 22,* 179–199. http://dx.doi.org/10.1002/bin.236

Roid, G. H. (2003). *Stanford–Binet Intelligence scales* (5th ed.). Itasca, IL: Riverside.

Rutter, M., Le Couteur, A., & Lord, C. (2003). *Autism Diagnostic Interview–Revised.* Los Angeles, CA: Western Psychological Services.

Scahill, L., Bearss, K., Lecavalier, L., Smith, T., Swiezy, N., Aman, M. G., . . . Johnson, C. (2016). Effect of parent training on adaptive behavior in children with autism spectrum disorder and disruptive behavior: Results of a random-ized trial. *Journal of the American Academy of Child & Adolescent Psychiatry, 55,* 602–609.e3. http://dx.doi.org/10.1016/j.jaac.2016.05.001

Scahill, L., Jeon, S., Boorin, S. G., McDougle, C. J., Aman, M. G., Dziura, J., . . . Vitiello, B. (2016). Weight and metabolic consequences of risperidone in young children with autism spectrum disorder. *Journal of the American Acad-emy of Child & Adolescent Psychiatry, 55,* 415–423. http://dx.doi.org/10.1016/j.jaac.2016.02.016

Scahill, L., McDougle, C. J., Aman, M. G., Johnson, C., Handen, B., Bearss, K., . . . Vitiello, B. (2012). Effects of risperidone and parent training on adaptive functioning in children with pervasive developmental disorders and serious behavioral problems. *Journal of the American Academy of Child & Adolescent Psychiatry, 51,* 136–146. http://dx.doi.org/10.1016/j.jaac.2011.11.010

Simonoff, E., Pickles, A., Charman, T., Chandler, S., Loucas, T., & Baird, G. (2008). Psychiatric disorders in children with autism spectrum disorders: Prevalence, comorbidity, and associated factors in a population-derived sample. *Journal of the American Academy of Child & Adolescent Psychiatry, 47,* 921–929. http://dx.doi.org/10.1097/CHI.0b013e318179964f

Sofronoff, K., Leslie, A., & Brown, W. (2004). Parent management training and Asperger syndrome: A randomized controlled trial to evaluate a parent based intervention. *Autism, 8,* 301–317. http://dx.doi.org/10.1177/1362361304045215

Sparrow, S. S., Cicchetti, D., & Balla, D. A. (2005). *Vineland Adaptive Behavior Scales–2nd Edition: Manual.* Minneapolis, MN: NCS Pearson.

Stratis, E. A., & Lecavalier, L. (2015). Informant agreement for youth with autism spectrum disorder or intellectual disability: A meta-analysis. *Journal of Autism and Developmental Disorders, 45,* 1026–1041. http://dx.doi.org/10.1007/s10803-014-2258-8

Sturmey, P. (1995). Analog baselines: A critical review of the methodology. *Research in Developmental Disabilities, 16,* 269–284. http://dx.doi.org/10.1016/0891-4222(95)00014-E

Suess, A. N., Wacker, D. P., Schwartz, J. E., Lustig, N., & Detrick, J. (2016). Preliminary evidence on the use of telehealth in an outpatient behavior clinic. *Journal of Applied Behavioral Analysis, 49*, 686–692. http://dx.doi.org/10.1002/jaba.305

Symon, J. B. (2005). Expanding interventions for children with autism: Parents as trainers. *Journal of Positive Behavior Interventions, 7*, 159–173. http://dx.doi.org/10.1177/10983007050070030501

Tarbox, J., Wilke, A., Najdowski, E., Findel-Pyles, A., Balasanyan, C., Caveney, R., . . . Tia, D. (2009). Comparing indirect, descriptive, and experimental functional assessments of challenging behavior in children with autism. *Journal of Developmental and Physical Disabilities, 21*, 493–514. http://dx.doi.org/10.1007/s10882-009-9154-8

Tassé, M. J., Aman, M. G., Hammer, D., & Rojahn, J. (1996). The Nisonger Child Behavior Rating Form: Age and gender effects and norms. *Research in Developmental Disabilities, 17*, 59–75. http://dx.doi.org/10.1016/0891-4222(95)00037-2

Tonge, B., Brereton, A., Kiomall, M., Mackinnon, A., King, N., & Rinehart, N. (2006). Effects on parental mental health of an education and skills training program for parents of young children with autism: A randomized controlled trial. *Journal of the American Academy of Child & Adolescent Psychiatry, 45*, 561–569. http://dx.doi.org/10.1097/01.chi.0000205701.48324.26

Wacker, D. P., Lee, J. F., Padilla Dalmau, Y. C., Kopelman, T. G., Lindgren, S. D., Kuhle, J., . . . Waldron, D. B. (2013). Conducting functional communication training via telehealth to reduce the problem behavior of young children with autism. *Journal of Developmental and Physical Disabilities, 25*, 35–48. http://dx.doi.org/10.1007/s10882-012-9314-0

Wierson, M., & Forehand, R. (1994). Parent behavioral training for child noncompliance: Rationale, concepts, and effectiveness. *Current Directions in Psychological Science, 3*, 146–150. http://dx.doi.org/10.1111/1467-8721.ep10770643

World Health Organization. (1992). *The ICD–10 classification of mental and behavioural disorders: Clinical descriptions and diagnostic guidelines.* Geneva, Switzerland: Author.

6

PARENT TRAINING FOR SLEEP DISTURBANCES IN AUTISM SPECTRUM DISORDER

CYNTHIA R. JOHNSON AND BETH A. MALOW

In addition to the core features discussed in more detail in earlier chapters (i.e., deficits in social interactions, communication, and repetitive and restrictive patterns of behavior), children with autism spectrum disorder (ASD) present with a host of associated behavioral issues. One notable area of difficulty is that individuals with ASD often experience poorly regulated sleep patterns and habits, which add to the family's burden, including poor sleep quality for family members and adverse impacts on the child's functioning in several areas.

SLEEP PROBLEMS IN AUTISM SPECTRUM DISORDER

The sleep patterns commonly seen in individuals with ASD fall in the dysomnias, which includes sleep onset delay, night wakings, and early morning waking (Deliens, Leproult, Schmitz, Destrebecqz, & Peigneux, 2015;

http://dx.doi.org/10.1037/0000111-007
Parent Training for Autism Spectrum Disorder: Improving the Quality of Life for Children and Their Families,
C. R. Johnson, E. M. Butter, and L. Scahill (Editors)

Reynolds & Malow, 2011). These dysregulated sleep patterns result in fragmented and inadequate total sleep time based on chronological age. Children with ASD also commonly have sleep association difficulties in which sleep is under erroneous stimulus control (e.g., only able to fall asleep in a specific chair, able to settle for sleep only if a parent is present, need a parent's hair to twirl to settle for sleep). Children who are prone to wake after sleep onset but who depend on an adult to fall asleep may remain awake for extended periods unless the sleep association is again introduced (e.g., having the hair of a parent to twirl). Furthermore, parents of children with ASD often report noncompliance and bedtime struggles even before settling in a sleeping space. Bedtime resistance has been reported as the most frequently reported sleep disturbance (Johnson, Turner, Foldes, Brooks, Kronk, & Wiggs, 2013). It is also more often than not that children with ASD experience more than one of these behavioral sleep problems. For example, a child may be distressed with the bedtime routine, become overly aroused, which interferes with the ability to settle for sleep and thus results in delayed sleep onset. Then once asleep, the child is highly likely to wake at some point during the night and not be able to self-sooth to reinitiate sleep. Moreover, children with ASD are reported to wake early in the morning (Wiggs & Stores, 2004).

There is also a small, incomplete body of literature suggesting that individuals with ASD may have more medically based sleep disturbances, including sleep-related breathing disorders and movement disorders, parasomnias, and circadian rhythm sleep disorder. The prevalence of sleep-disordered breathing (SDB) in ASD does not appear to be higher than in typically developing children (Goldman, Richdale, Clemons, & Malow, 2012). Nonetheless, addressing SDB is very much warranted. For example, for the one child with SDB in one study, an adenotonsillectomy resulted in improvements in ASD symptoms and attention (Malow, McGrew, Harvey, Henderson, & Stone, 2006).

Movement disorders in sleep include rhythmic movement disorder, Ekbom's syndrome (i.e., restless-legs syndrome [RLS]), and periodic limb movements in sleep (PLMS). *Rhythmic movement disorder* involves repetitive movements during the wake-to-sleep transition that involve the legs, arms, trunk, or head. *RLS* is experienced as an uncomfortable sensation in the legs, which is more likely at night and when supine with movement improvement. *PLMS* is repetitive leg movements during sleep. These movements in individuals with ASD may be mistaken for stereotypical behaviors. Although these sleep-related movement disorders are not known to occur with any more frequency in ASD than in typically developing children, accurate diagnosis is challenging, given communication difficulties in children with ASD, even if parents report observation of behaviors suggestive of a movement disorder.

Parasomnias include both non–rapid eye movement (non-REM)–associated sleep abnormalities and rapid eye movement (REM)–associated sleep abnormalities. Non-REM disorders occur in the first half of the night and include night terrors in which the child is only partially aroused, sleepwalking, confusional arousals, and bruxism (i.e., teeth grinding). There have been some reports of an increase of parasomnias in children with ASD (Goldman et al., 2011). However, those reports primarily have been based on parent report and have not been confirmed with objective data from polysomnography (PSG; Malow, McGrew, et al., 2006). REM abnormalities were reported in one study (Buckley et al., 2010) but not in another (Malow, Marzec, et al., 2006).

Although adolescence is associated with a change in *circadian rhythm*, which is the internal clock steering the sleep–wake cycle, limited evidence has suggested that this circadian rhythm may be altered in ASD (Glickman, 2010). This change could result in a child's sleep schedule's being at odds with the rest of the family's. The setting of the circadian rhythm is driven by both biological and environmental factors, including social cues. Hence, for children with ASD who may not understand social cues, they may be susceptible to these sleep–wake cycle alterations.

Although the array of sleep disturbances are discussed to increase their awareness among clinicians who provide care to children with ASD and their parents, it is the dysomnias coupled with bedtime resistance that are most commonly observed and that are problematic for families of children with ASD. In a later section in this chapter, assessment practices to differentially determine the type of sleep disturbances present is discussed.

PREVALENCE AND IMPACT OF SLEEP DISTURBANCES IN CHILDREN WITH AUTISM SPECTRUM DISORDER

The literature suggests that up to 80% of children with ASD experience some type of sleep disturbance (Johnson, Turner, Foldes, Malow, & Wiggs, 2012; Park et al., 2012; Sivertsen, Posserud, Gillberg, Lundervold, & Hysing, 2012). This percentage is considerably higher than the approximate 25% within the general population of children who have sleep disturbances (Owens, 2007). Although previously believed that sleep disturbances seen in ASD were associated with developmental levels, more recent works have indicated a high rate of sleep disturbances in ASD, regardless of intellectual/cognitive levels (Allik, Larsson, & Smedje, 2006a; Sivertsen et al., 2012). Hence, the common occurring sleep disturbances appear to be more related to ASD than intellectual disability.

The importance of sleep in children increasingly has been recognized, particularly with regard to brain maturation in early years (Kurth et al., 2010).

Decades of research have demonstrated the deleterious impact of inadequate sleep on a range of domains. In addition to the restorative function sleep plays (Dahl, 1996), inadequate sleep is known to negatively impact cognition, attention, memory consolidation, and daytime behavioral adjustment, in general (Gruber et al., 2011; Owens, 2009; Sadeh, 2007; Vriend et al., 2012). In addition, some limited work has suggested that sleep consolidation is a predictor of language learning in young children (Dionne et al., 2011). Moreover, there is a link between inadequate sleep and development of obesity (Magee & Hale, 2012). In children with ASD, sleep disturbances may exacerbate both core ASD symptoms and challenging behavioral and emotional problems (Allik, Larsson, & Smedje, 2006b; Goldman et al., 2011; Malow, Marzec, et al., 2006; Mazurek & Sohl, 2016).

Furthermore, the impact of sleep disturbances in children on their families can be quite substantial. Heightened parental stress, anxiety, and depression have been documented in parents who care for children with ASD and sleep disturbances (Doo & Wing, 2006; Hollway & Aman, 2011). Not surprisingly, parents' own sleep is adversely impacted (Couturier et al., 2005).

WHY DO CHILDREN WITH AUTISM SPECTRUM DISORDER COMMONLY HAVE SLEEP DISTURBANCES?

Johnson (1996) long ago proposed that the core social and communication deficits of ASD and often co-occurring cognitive deficits interfere with the child's ability for self-soothing. Consequently, children with ASD may be less able to promote sleep onset independently or return to sleep on waking after sleep onset. Children with ASD also may have difficulty understanding social and environmental cues that are part of the bedtime routine. Some children with ASD develop idiosyncratic bedtime routines that hinder sleep, such as insisting on toys being arranged just so (Henderson, Barry, Bader, & Jordan, 2011). Moreover, children with ASD have hypersensitivities that likely influence sleep, such as being overly sensitive to sound and light (Leekam, Nieto, Libby, Wing, & Gould, 2007; Mazurek & Petroski, 2015).

Children with ASD also commonly have medical issues that may negatively impact sleep. These issues include gastrointestinal problems, seizures, co-occurring anxiety, depression, and attention-deficit/hyperactivity disorder, and medication side effects (e.g., stimulants, serotonin reuptake inhibitors; Ibrahim, Voigt, Katusic, Weaver, & Barbaresi, 2009; Liu, Hubbard, Fabes, & Adam, 2006; Mazurek & Petroski, 2015; Reynolds & Malow, 2011; Valicenti-McDermott et al., 2006; Veatch, Maxwell-Horn, & Malow, 2015).

Several neurotransmitters with important roles in the neurobiological systems underlying the sleep–wake cycle have been implicated in ASD. Alteration in melatonin secretion patterns in children with ASD may contribute to sleep disturbance. There are reports in the literature that have noted lower mean plasma melatonin levels and lower urinary excretion of melatonin sulfate in ASD compared with typically developing controls (Rossignol & Frye, 2011; Tordjman et al., 2012). Melatonin is synthesized from the neurotransmitter serotonin, and the serotonin system in ASD may be altered, as well (Reynolds & Malow, 2011). However, the finding of lower levels of melatonin has been equivocal with a recent report of normal overnight melatonin profiles (Goldman et al., 2014). Furthermore, dysregulation of the diurnal cortisol rhythm, with lower than the expected fall in cortisol, have been observed in children with ASD (Corbett, Schupp, Levine, & Mendoza, 2009). This stress hormone plays a role in circadian rhythms and may play a role in sleep patterns in ASD.

Overall, disruptive behavior, elaborate bedtime routines, difficulties with self-soothing, understanding of environmental cues, known or unknown medical problems, and neurochemical alterations may interfere with developing a stable sleep–wake cycle in children with ASD.

SPECIFIC ASSESSMENT PROCEDURES

In view of the high rates of sleep disturbances in children with ASD, it is imperative that sleep disturbances be screened as part of routine practice in the evaluation process. For example, during an initial evaluation when a question of ASD is being determined, the presence of sleep disturbances should systematically be assessed by asking parents about typical sleep patterns for their child. Questions would include the total amount slept per night (i.e., typical bedtime, duration to sleep onset, and typical wake time) and nap habits; presence of disruptive behaviors around bedtime; an account of where the child falls asleep; what is needed for sleep onset with respect to parent intervention; and accounts of snoring, restlessness, night wakings, possible night terrors, sleep walking, any atypical body movements, bruxism, and signs of daytime sleepiness. To be further queried are medical comorbidities that may negatively impact sleep, including gastrointestinal symptoms, such as reflux, constipation, and abdominal pain, and any signs of seizures. Sources of possible pain also should be considered to ensure sleep disturbance is not secondary to untreated pain or irritation. Furthermore, an assessment of the child's nutrition and food intake should be taken to rule out hunger as interfering with sleep.

Sleep Questionnaires

If parents report positive accounts of one or more of these issues, administering a standard pediatric sleep questionnaire is recommended. There is a plethora of sleep questionnaires available but only a handful have adequate psychometric properties (Spruyt & Gozal, 2011). One pediatric sleep question-naire, the Children's Sleep Habits Questionnaire (CSHQ; Owens, Spirito, & McGuinn, 2000) has been used widely in ASD in recent years. The CSHQ originally was developed to screen for sleep disorders for 4- to 10-year-olds based on the pediatric International Classification of Sleep Disorders (Thorpy, 1990). The 33-item scale consists of eight subscales: (a) Bedtime Resistance, (b) Sleep Onset Delay, (c) Sleep Duration, (d) Sleep Anxiety, (e) Night Wakings, (f) Parasomnias, (g) Sleep Disordered Breathing, and (h) Daytime Sleepiness. These subscales range in length from 1 item (Sleep Onset Delay) to 8 items (Daytime Sleepiness). The initial publication on this measure described some psychometric properties that were adequate. Results of a receiver-operating characteristic curve analysis (Owens et al., 2000) suggested that a total score of 41 was optimal as the clinical cutoff for sleep problems. A later study showed that the CSHQ discriminated between good and poor sleepers in preschoolers down to 2 years of age (Goodlin-Jones, Sitnick, Tang, Liu, & Anders, 2008). Subsequent studies examining the factor structure of the CSHQ failed to replicate the eight subscales in general pediatric populations (Li et al., 2007; Waumans et al., 2010; Schlarb, Schwerdtle, & Hautzinger, 2010). In a relatively large sample of children with ASD, the factor structure also did not replicate, and suggestions were made for a modified version of the CSHQ for use in children with ASD (Johnson et al., 2016) This modified version includes the following components or subscales: Sleep Dysregulation, Insufficient Sleep, Sleep-Onset Association Problems, Medical Sleep Disorders, and Sleep Anxiety.

Another questionnaire, the Modified Simonds and Parraga Sleep Ques-tionnaire (MSPSQ; Simonds & Parraga, 1982; Wiggs & Stores, 1998), has been used in a couple of studies in the treatment of sleep disturbances in chil-dren with ASD and other developmental disabilities (Johnson et al., 2013; Wiggs & Stores, 1998). The Composite Sleep Index, a severity score of six items from the full MSPSQ, was used as an outcome in both the Johnson et al. (2013) and Wiggs and Stores (1998) studies. The full 36 items tap into common sleep problem categories to include bedtime resistance/struggles, sleep onset delay, parasomnias, SDB, sleep anxiety, and daytime sleepiness. The measure ends with a few additional questions aimed at gathering further measures about previous treatment for sleep disturbance and about how it impacts other family members' sleep. Wiggs and Stores (1996) reported the test–retest reliabilities for a 2-week period to be .83 to 1.0. In a larger study of individuals with intellectual disability, Maas et al. (2011) found the internal consistency of the items of the MSPSQ to be good. The MSPSQ has been reported to be acceptable to parents (Wiggs & Stores, 1996).

Another useful measure is the Family Inventory of Sleep Habits (Malow et al., 2009). This instrument provides useful information about the bedtime routine, sleep environment, and parent–child interactions at bedtime. The original measure was 22-items, but a shorter 12-item version has been validated (Malow et al., 2014).

Sleep Diary Recordings and Bedtime Information

In addition to sleep questionnaires, sleep diary recordings are commonly collected as part of a finer level of sleep evaluation. Information collected nightly includes when the child goes to bed, when he or she falls asleep, when the child wakes at night, and when he or she wakes in the morning. Sleep diary recordings often are completed before and during an intervention to monitor change in sleep. For children with concomitant behavioral issues, information about the antecedents and consequences of problematic behaviors around bedtime and throughout the night also might be collected. An example of such a record is provided in Figure 6.1. A drawback of keeping a sleep diary is that a parent may be unaware of when a child falls asleep or wakes at night. Sleep diaries also are labor intensive. However, they can be invaluable when consistently and accurately collected in determining sleep patterns to develop individualized intervention plans.

Detailed information about the current bedtime routine, if there is one, also is important in making recommendations to improve bedtime problems. Collectively, this information can inform what recommendations to make and what sleep problems are most interfering and should be targeted first. The shortcomings of these measures are they are subjective and not always accurate if a third party is recording; caregivers may be aware only when the child is disruptive and wakes them.

Actigraphy

Actigraphs are watchlike devices that measure gross movement as a proxy for sleep and increasingly are used as an objective measure of sleep–wake cycle. Using computer software–specialized algorithms based on age, estimates of sleep parameters may be measured to include timing of sleep, sleep continuity, and sleep duration. Software packages can generate a number of sleep variables to include (a) total sleep time (a primary aim outcome), (b) sleep onset time, (c) morning waking time, (d) frequency of night wakings, (e) longest sleep period, and (f) sleep efficiency (i.e., percentage of time spent sleeping while in bed and lights off). Actigraphy data show modest correlation with parent report, suggesting that actigraphy can be complementary with parent reports (Goodlin-Jones, Tang, Liu, & Anders, 2008; Moon, Corkum, & Smith, 2011; Wiggs & Stores, 2004). The specificity for detecting night wakings in children has been called into question with incomplete agreement on optimal placement (Meltzer, Montgomery-Downs, Insana,

(Complete for your child's previous night of sleep)

Name: _____

Date: _____

Child's daytime naps (record times and durations):		Child went to bed last night at ____time	Child stayed awake 30 minutes or longer after bedtime	Child fell asleep alone in own bed	Child woke up during the night (record times and durations):		Child moved to someone else's bed during the night	Child got out of bed this morning at ____time	Child had difficulty waking for the day:
Time	Duration	Was this time: regular, earlier, or later	Yes___ / No___	Yes___ / No___	Time	Duration	Yes___ / No___	Was this time: regular, earlier, or later	Yes___ / No___

Sleep Antecedent-Behavior-Consequence Log

Time	Antecedent *What was happening before, at the time the behavior began?*	Behavior *Description of problem*	Consequence *What did you do/how was the behavior handled?*

Figure 6.1. Sleep diary. From *Are Children With Fragile X Syndrome Losing Their Zzzz's . . . and Y?* (Doctoral dissertation, University of Pittsburgh), by R. Kronk, 2008. Retrieved from http://d-scholarship.pitt.edu/6894/1/KronkDissertationPittApril2008. pdf. Copyright 2008 by Rebecca Kronk. Adapted with permission.

& Walsh, 2012). There also is the potential for malfunction. Nonetheless, actigraphy is used and accepted widely as a low-cost, objective measure to augment other assessment methods (Holley, Hill, & Stevenson, 2010). Actigraphy has been used to measure treatment response in a few studies of children with ASD and sleep disturbances (Cortesi, Giannotti, Sebastiani, Panunzi, & Valente, 2012; Johnson et al., 2013; Malow et al., 2014).

Polysomnography

The PSG sleep study is held as the gold standard in the assessment of sleep problems and is warranted in some incidences. Unlike actigraphy, PSG measures sleep structure. PSG monitors many aspects of physiological functioning during sleep to include electroencephalogram, electromyogram (i.e., skeletal muscle activation), eye movement (i.e., electrooculography), heart rhythm (i.e., electrocardiogram), airflow and nasal pressure, and oxygen saturation. This diagnostic, multicomponent test of physiological parameters is necessary in evaluating for sleep-related breathing disorder, RLS, periodic limb movement disorder, narcolepsy, seizures, and other unexplained arousal problems (e.g., unexplained daytime sleepiness). Limitations include cost and intrusiveness. Children with ASD may not tolerate being in the unfamiliar environment of the sleep laboratory or having electrodes placed on them, particularly if they have sensory sensitivities.

Other Behavior Questionnaires

Obtaining parent-completed questionnaires about daytime behaviors is recommended when providing parent training (PT) targeting sleep for children with ASD. Such behavioral questionnaires are important to both screen for other coexisting behavioral health issues that may adversely impact sleep such as hyperactivity and anxiety. These health issues are discussed in the earlier assessment chapter of this book (see Chapter 2).

SPECIFIC PARENT TRAINING STRATEGIES

Parents tackle the daily struggles in caring for a child with ASD. However, during the day, other supports may be in place, such as intensive therapies and educational programming. It is in the evening when parents are most likely to be solo in caring for their child. Hence, addressing sleep disturbances through a PT modality is uniquely fitting. Teaching parents in the use of specific behavioral interventions targeting sleep problems for typically developing children is widely regarded as effective (Meltzer & Mindell, 2014; Mindell, Kuhn, et al., 2006). Teaching parents in behavioral techniques is considered standard care in pediatrics broadly and much preferred over sleep-enhancing medications in pediatrics, many of which have adverse effects (Mindell, Kuhn, et al., 2006). Many of the behavioral-based interventions developed for children with typical development have been used with children with ASD, with some modifications and additional components. Although the limited research is promising, there are far fewer empirical studies in ASD compared with the literature for children with typical development. Most of the studies conducted thus far have been either case studies or single subject in research design. To date, there have been only a handful of randomized controlled trials (RCTs). The PT techniques described as follows are categorized as antecedent/prevention techniques, consequence approaches, and multicomponent PT procedures.

Antecedent/Prevention Interventions

Sleep Education/Hygiene and Positive Bedtime Routine

Under this category is what would be considered *sleep hygiene*. This term is borrowed from the adult insomnia literature in which the first line of intervention is on the education of the importance of sleep and healthy sleep habits, such as limiting exercise close to bedtime but getting adequate exercise during the day, avoiding caffeine and alcoholic drinks near bedtime, reserving the bed/bedroom for sleep, and avoiding screen time around bedtime. For children with ASD, gathering detailed information about a typical day from waking through the bedtime can assist with schedule changes that may improve bedtime and sleep behaviors. In addition to these guidelines, establishing a positive bedtime routine as at least one component in working with parents is recommended. Such a routine would include not only adhering to sleep hygiene guidelines but introducing a routine that results in positive parent–child interactions and avoids activities that may be conflictual (e.g., asking the child to do a nonpreferred task) or overstimulating (e.g., playing tickle games with siblings). For children with ASD, this routine may be particularly important but also more challenging to implement. For example, a child needs to brush his or her teeth before bedtime but may find this routine distressing. Hence, toothbrushing may need to be earlier in the evening, and compliance with toothbrushing may need to be addressed earlier in the day. Likewise, children with ASD may have few or restricted interests, so identifying activities that are compatible with settling for sleep may be challenging and require discussion with the parents.

Bedtime Fading

Bedtime fading is a procedure often used to target delayed sleep onset, whereby a bedtime is set closer to the actual time a child is currently falling asleep. This bedtime is followed until the child is regularly falling asleep within 20 minutes of the bedtime, then the bedtime is "faded" to an earlier time in small increments (e.g., 10 p.m., then 9:45, then 9:30). Bedtime fading has been used in conjunction with *response cost*, in which the child is removed from the bed if he or she does not fall asleep within 20 minutes and is kept up for approximately 60 minutes (Piazza, Fisher, & Sherer, 1997). This Piazza et al. (1997) study was conducted on an inpatient unit, and parents were then instructed in the procedure close to time of discharge. Since the initial report of this procedure, it has been used in other small studies and an RCT multicomponent program (Johnson et al., 2013). This adjunct of removing the child from the bed may not be acceptable to parents. However, for children who do not respond to other approaches to decrease sleep onset latency, this procedure may be a consideration, and close discussion with parents may be necessary to determine acceptability of this technique.

Sleep Restriction

With *sleep restriction*, a child's total sleep is determined usually using sleep diaries collected for a week or two. Parents then are instructed to temporarily reduce the child's sleep to 90% of the duration that the child is currently sleeping. Once the child is sleeping during this period, the duration is increased. Although bedtime fading has been used primarily to target sleep onset delay, sleep restriction has been used to reduce night wakings and bedtime resistances.

Scheduled Waking

Scheduled waking is a procedure whereby parents are taught to wake their child around 15 minutes before the event they wish to change, such as a night waking or night terror. Once the child is awake, parents are taught to respond to their child either as they typically would had the child woken spontaneously or in a neutral fashion. Once the targeted sleep behavior shows improvements, the scheduled wakings are systematically faded and eventually eliminated. This approach has been recommended in the pediatric literature but has been reported in the literature once in recent years in ASD (Durand, 2002). Similar to bedtime fading with response cost, these procedures may prove challenging for parents to implement when other alternatives still are available for exploration. However, Durand (2002) reported that parents were satisfied with the result from this procedure in this small, single-subject study.

Visual Cues, Visual Schedules, Social Stories, and Bedtime Pass

Although not studied as a stand-alone procedure, *visual cues* and *visual schedules* have been used for children with ASD (Schneider & Goldstein, 2010). The use of visual schedules is broadly accepted as being helpful for children with ASD; visual cues and visual schedules, included in two of the multicomponent programs to specifically target sleep, are discussed more later in this section. *Social stories*, developed by Carol Gray (http://carolgraysocialstories.com) have been popular to teach children with ASD social skills and improve daytime behaviors (Ozdemir, 2008), and also have been used to improved bedtime and sleep behaviors (Johnson et al., 2013; P. Moore, 2004). Another approach with limited data so far that can be conceptualized as an antecedent approach is the use of a *bedtime pass*. In this approach, parents provide the child with a "pass" that may be in the form of a physical card or token to use for one shout-out at bedtime. This procedure as originally described was used with children with typical development and involves a level of understanding on the part of the child (B. A. Moore, Friman, Fruzzetti, & MacAleese, 2007).

Consequence Interventions

A commonly used consequence approach used for typically developing children to address sleep disturbances is extinction, also called standard extinction when referring to its use specifically to sleep. *Extinction* is a common behavioral procedure by which reinforcement previously provided is withheld following an unwanted behavior. Usually it is social attention that is withheld. This approach also is referred to as "planned ignoring" (see Chapter 5). With standard extinction, a child who is crying, complaining, or repeatedly asking questions to gain a parent's return to the bedroom is ignored by the adult. A drawback of using extinction to decrease behavior is the phenomenon of an *extinction burst*, which is a sometimes extreme increase in the targeted behavior. Parents can be taught how to implement extinction for bedtime and sleep problems, but an extinction burst may result in a child's crying louder and longer, making it stressful for a parent to ignore. For parents of children with ASD, an inability to ignore an extinction burst may be more likely because the parents have more worries about their child's well-being and safety.

An alternative is *graduated extinction*, a procedure whereby parents are taught to enter their child's bedroom based on a set schedule to briefly check on the child, give a quick reassurance, and perhaps indicate what is expected (e.g., "time to go to bed"). The schedule can be every 5 minutes, increasing gradually over time (e.g., 10 minutes, then 20 minutes). Graduated extinction has been used to target bedtime resistance, settling/sleep onset delay, night wakings, and early morning waking. This version of extinction likely is far more acceptable to parents. Quick improvements have been shown to ensue with this approach (Montgomery, Stores, & Wiggs, 2004). Several studies (Moon et al., 2011; Moore, 2004) have instructed parents in the identification of reinforcers and the use of reinforcement for positive bedtime and sleep behaviors, such as compliance with the bedtime routine and staying in the bedroom.

Multicomponent Interventions

Multicomponent PT programs have been used to target an array of sleep disturbances. These programs have been delivered either individually or in group format as a package (Cortesi et al., 2012; Johnson et al., 2013; Malow et al., 2014; Moss, Gordon, & O'Connell, 2014; Wiggs & Stores, 1998). These packaged programs have included the interventions as described earlier, but at least two have included video vignettes to enhance parent learning (Johnson et al., 2013; Malow et al., 2014) and have included other components tailored for individuals with ASD. For example, the use of visual supports and visual schedules were used because that approach is widely accepted with children with ASD to promote following routines throughout the day (Hodgdon, 1995; Waters, Lerman, & Hovanetz, 2009). In the Johnson et al. (2013) program, visual schedules and supports were discussed in a session on preventive/antecedent approaches after a session on the basics of behavioral principles. Attention to sensory strategies and communication strategies were included in the Moss et al. study (2014). Although, collectively, these multicomponent PT programs provide promise for behavioral PT in the amelioration of sleep disturbances in ASD, the "active ingredients" cannot be identified. However, most of these programs allowed for individualization.

SPECIAL CONSIDERATIONS

Children with ASD often present with other risky behaviors that impact addressing sleep disturbances, including risk of elopement and other unsafe behaviors. Hence, PT should include a review of the safety of the sleeping environment. Johnson et al. (2013) made a home visit at the beginning of the PT program to assess these issues and the sleep environment for any needed changes to be introduced into the PT program. If a home visit is not viable, obtaining photos or videos of the child's sleep environment in the context of other rooms (e.g., distance from bathroom, caregivers' room, external door) could be useful, or the use of technologies like FaceTime, VSee, or Skype to virtually visit the home could be highly valuable in providing PT to target sleep disturbances. In a larger context, consideration of the neighborhood is important when providing parents with recommendations. For example, as part of sleep hygiene and antecedent interventions, it might be recommended that the child get more outside physical activity during the day. However, is this a reasonable expectation given the living situation? Another important consideration in working with parents with ASD is to understand the child's cognitive abilities and weaknesses, and receptive language level. Parents may overestimate their child's skills, and some strategies, such as the bedtime pass and social stories, may be ineffective for children with limited receptive language skills and lower cognitive skills.

Use of melatonin as an adjunct to PT is another consideration. Although melatonin does not address behavioral bedtime resistance, teach self-soothing to promote sleep, or help with night wakings, melatonin is safe and inexpensive, and has shown promise as a treatment for sleep onset delay in children with ASD (Malow et al., 2012; Rossignol & Frye, 2011).

CASE EXAMPLES

Case 1: Kevin

Description and Assessment

Kevin[1] is a 6-year-old boy who meets diagnostic criteria for ASD based on clinical evaluation and corroborated by the administration of the Autism Diagnostic Observation Schedule and the Autism Diagnostic Interview–Revised (Lord et al., 2012; Lord, Rutter, & Le Couteur, 1994). Cognitive assessment suggests delays in all areas assessed, including nonverbal reasoning, fine motor skills, receptive language, and expressive language. Although 6 years of age, Kevin has the skills of a 4-year-old. He recently was successfully toilet trained for both day and night. Parents report a number of sleep issues. Kevin is very challenging around his evening routine. His parents report that bath time seems to "rev him up." He very much enjoys bath time. He splashes and laughs, and engages in a number of repetitive, stereotypical behaviors. He becomes distressed when made to get out of the bathtub. He then fights having his teeth brushed. After this battle, his parents attempt to read a book to him, but he shows little interest, so they allow him to use an iPad for a few minutes in the hope of him calming down. Typically, the bedtime routine starts with the bath around 7:00 p.m. with the goal of having lights off at 8:00 p.m. However, it usually is the case that lights are not off until 9:00 p.m. Kevin usually leaves his room three to five times to wander around the house before finally falling to sleep close to 11:00 p.m. He often falls asleep on a large dog bed. He usually is up by 5:30 a.m. and wanders through the house opening cabinets in search of his iPad. Although Kevin does not have a regular nap, sleep diary data showed that he sometimes falls asleep around 5 p.m. while his parents are preparing dinner. His parents completed the Composite Sleep Index on which a score of 9 was obtained, suggesting significant sleep issues. His parents completed a sleep diary record, which showed that he slept on average less than 6 hours per night and usually awoke around 1:30 a.m. or 2 a.m. It usually takes him around 60 minutes to fall back to sleep.

---

[1]Clinical material has been disguised to protect client confidentiality.

Sleep Parent Training Intervention

Kevin's parents were first educated about the nature of sleep, including the importance of sleep, developmental changes in sleep as children age, and the basics of sleep hygiene. An explanation of the antecedent-behavior-consequence model of learning theory was provided with examples of how antecedents and consequences influence sleep and bedtime behaviors. Kevin's parents had already removed all electronics from the room. They had placed a low night-light in case he needed to get to the bathroom, which was close to his bedroom. In a second session, the parent and parent trainer discussed Kevin's daily schedule in detail. This discussion led to recommendations to set Kevin's bedtime much later than 8:00 p.m. because he was not falling asleep until nearly 11:00 p.m. The start of his bedtime routine then would be considerably later so that it would be associated with bedtime and sleep. A visual schedule of the bedtime routine was developed because Kevin had responded to visual schedules in his classroom at school. These changes would target both the significantly long sleep latency and his wandering. Other schedule changes included moving his bath to the morning and increasing his physical activity by going to the nearby park either before dinner or after dinner, given that, temporarily, his bedtime would be later. In lieu of the iPad at bedtime, his parents identified a few soothing activities that the occupational therapist had suggested as alternatives. Parents were instructed further to not allow a late afternoon nap; rather, Kevin could be outside engaging in physical activity. So, the initial new bedtime set was 10:30 p.m., with a bedtime routine starting at 10:00 p.m. After a week of falling asleep by 10:40 p.m., the bedtime was moved up by 15 minutes to 10:15 p.m. Parents were instructed to only move the bedtime up after Kevin had fallen asleep within 10 minutes of the bedtime for 7 consecutive nights. After several weeks, Kevin was successfully falling asleep by 9 p.m. and sleeping through the night until 5:30 a.m. He also continued to sleep on the dog bed. To work with the parents on helping with the early morning waking, a couple of quiet activities were identified for a "morning box" that would occupy Kevin until other family members arose for the day. As a first step toward getting Kevin to sleep in his bed, the dog bed was systematically moved closer to his bed and eventually placed on top of his bed. The dog bed was to be faded out slowly, but the parents chose to remain at this step.

Case 2: Hector

Description and Assessment

Hector is a 3-year-old boy with ASD. Developmental testing indicates only mild delay in expressive language and fine motor skills. Receptive language and cognitive skills are at age expectancy. Hector's sleep disturbances include sleep onset delay, sleep onset problems, inadequate total sleep, and night wakings. Hector is a very active child throughout the day, as was confirmed by a high score on the Hyperactivity subscale on the Aberrant Behavior Checklist (Aman, 2005). Sleep diary and actigraphy data show that Hector sleeps less than 7 hours per night and only rarely takes a daytime nap. He takes nearly an hour to fall asleep in the bed with his mother, brother, and two dogs. His mother, a single parent, admits she is anxious about having her two boys sleep in their own bedrooms without her. After Hector finally falls asleep, he almost always has at least one night waking per night. When he awakes, he wakes his mother and requests that she brew coffee. Although Hector does not like the coffee, he likes the flavored cream that goes into the coffee. He and his grandmother started this ritual at her house. Once awake, he is up for an hour or more. Hector has other rituals that interfere with bedtime and sleep. He perseverates on wearing wrestling attire handed down from his brother, but his mother puts pajamas on him after a bath, which results in a tantrum. Hector and his brother watch wrestling on TV after dinner while his mother cleans up. Dinner is after bath time, so Hector watches wrestling up to bedtime. Bedtime is 9:30 p.m. to accommodate everyone. Hector is compliant about getting into bed but has to be close to his mother and have the two dogs in just the right position. If the dogs move, this distresses Hector, and he needs to get them back where he wishes them to be. Hector's mother has to get everyone up by 6:00 a.m.

Sleep Parent Training Intervention

For this family, PT started with education about sleep hygiene, with particular attention paid to so much screen time close to bedtime. A close look at the entire daily schedule with his mother indicated that Hector spent early morning to late afternoon with his grandmother while his mother worked. It was learned that he was indeed getting small amounts of coffee with large amounts of flavored nondairy coffee creamer throughout the day. He also was allowed to watch wrestling during the day as he was in the evening. Schedule changes were made to include getting outdoors in good weather and not watching wrestling when he was with his grandmother. Coffee was replaced with orange juice. In the afternoon, his mother would take a walk with Hector in a wooded area he liked. The order of the evening was changed so that dinner was before bath time because Hector found bath time relaxing. Hector also was allowed to wear a wrestling singlet as pajamas because it seemed the material was more comfortable to him. Instead of watching wrestling, his mother and brother read books about wrestling to him as he cuddled with his dogs. Bedtime with lights out was set at 10:00 p.m. Initially,

PT included no changes regarding where Hector slept because this was sure to be a stressful change for his mother.

The changes in the bedtime routine proved to be successful in making a more positive evening for everyone. Once Hector was falling asleep within 20 minutes of bedtime, the bedtime was pushed back to 9:45 p.m. and then to 9:30 p.m. For night wakings, his mother was taught to use a modified graduated extinction, whereby she would acknowledge he was awake, give him some brief physical comfort, and then ignore. She did this every 7 minutes until he fell back asleep. Using this modified graduate extinction procedure, night wakings quickly decreased.

Around the third PT session, the goal of getting Hector to sleep in his bedroom was discussed. In view of the mother's anxiety about his not being in the room with her, there was first discussion about her fear of what might happen. His room was close to his mother's, furnished with a small toddler bed, and absent of other distracting items. There was a small nightlight in the room but, otherwise, the room was conducive for sleep. A photographic picture schedule was developed for the new routine of his going to his bedroom to sleep. His mother was instructed how to use this schedule. To make the room even more appealing, his mother bought sheets and a pillowcase with a wrestling theme. On the first night of this new schedule, it was decided that his mother would sit close to Hector and comfort him until he fell asleep. Once he was falling asleep in his own bed with his mother by his side, she was taught to slowly, systematically move herself farther away from the bed. A photo of his mother sitting farther away was added to the picture schedule to enhance Hector's understanding of what to expect. The visual schedule showed Hector that the dogs were allowed to stay in his room on the floor next to him. After 6 weeks, his mother was able to leave the room on most nights without Hector's becoming distressed. If he did become distressed, his mother used graduated extinction, whereby where she came into his bedroom every 7 minutes to reassure him and remind him with visual cues that he was to go to sleep. Hector's mother attended five PT sessions, and the clinician made two home visits and FaceTime coaching on two occasions. His mother was satisfied with the changes and reported enjoying her time to herself and getting a better night's sleep.

REFERENCES

Allik, H., Larsson, J. O., & Smedje, H. (2006a). Insomnia in school-age children with Asperger syndrome or high-functioning autism. *BMC Psychiatry, 6*, 18–29. http://dx.doi.org/10.1186/1471-244X-6-18

Allik, H., Larsson, J. O., & Smedje, H. (2006b). Sleep patterns of school-age children with Asperger syndrome or high-functioning autism. *Journal of Autism and Developmental Disorders, 36*, 585–595. http://dx.doi.org/10.1007/s10803-006-0099-9

Aman, M. G. (2005). *Annotated bibliography on the Aberrant Behavior Checklist (ABC)* Unpublished manuscript, Department of Psychiatry, The Ohio State University, Columbus, OH. Retrieved from https://psychmed.osu.edu/wp-content/uploads/2017/02/ABC_Annotated_Bibliography_08-28-2015.pdf

Buckley, A. W., Rodriguez, A. J., Jennison, K., Buckley, J., Thurm, A., Sato, S., & Swedo, S. (2010). Rapid eye movement sleep percentage in children with autism compared with children with developmental delay and typical development. *Archives of Pediatrics & Adolescent Medicine, 164*, 1032–1037. http://dx.doi.org/10.1001/archpediatrics.2010.202

Corbett, B. A., Schupp, C. W., Levine, S., & Mendoza, S. (2009). Comparing cortisol, stress, and sensory sensitivity in children with autism. *Autism Research, 2*, 39–49. http://dx.doi.org/10.1002/aur.64

Cortesi, F., Giannotti, F., Sebastiani, T., Panunzi, S., & Valente, D. (2012). Controlled-release melatonin, singly and combined with cognitive behavioural therapy, for persistent insomnia in children with autism spectrum disorders: A randomized placebo-controlled trial. *Journal of Sleep Research, 21*, 700–709. http://dx.doi.org/10.1111/j.1365-2869.2012.01021.x

Couturier, J. L., Speechley, K. N., Steele, M., Norman, R., Stringer, B., & Nicolson, R. (2005). Parental perception of sleep problems in children of normal intelligence with pervasive developmental disorders: Prevalence, severity, and pattern. *Journal of the American Academy of Child & Adolescent Psychiatry, 44*, 815–822. http://dx.doi.org/10.1097/01.chi.0000166377.22651.87

Dahl, R. E. (1996). The impact of inadequate sleep on children's daytime cognitive function. *Seminars in Pediatric Neurology, 3*, 44–50. http://dx.doi.org/10.1016/S1071-9091(96)80028-3

Deliens, G., Leproult, R., Schmitz, R., Destrebecqz, A., & Peigneux, P. (2015). Sleep disturbances in autism spectrum disorders. *Review Journal of Autism and Developmental Disorders, 2*, 343–356. http://dx.doi.org/10.1007/s40489-015-0057-6

Dionne, G., Touchette, E., Forget-Dubois, N., Petit, D., Tremblay, R. E., Montplaisir, J. Y., & Boivin, M. (2011). Associations between sleep-wake consolidation and language development in early childhood: A longitudinal twin study. *Sleep, 34*, 987–995. http://dx.doi.org/10.5665/SLEEP.1148

Doo, S., & Wing, Y. K. (2006). Sleep problems of children with pervasive developmental disorders: Correlation with parental stress. *Developmental Medicine and Child Neurology, 48*, 650–655. http://dx.doi.org/10.1017/S001216220600137X

Durand, V. M. (2002). Treating sleep terrors in children with autism. *Journal of Positive Behavior Interventions, 4*, 66–72. http://dx.doi.org/10.1177/109830070200400201

Glickman, G. (2010). Circadian rhythms and sleep in children with autism. *Neuroscience and Biobehavioral Reviews, 34*, 755–768. http://dx.doi.org/10.1016/j.neubiorev.2009.11.017

Goldman, S. E., Adkins, K. W., Calcutt, M. W., Carter, M. D., Goodpaster, R. L., Wang, L., . . . Malow, B. A. (2014). Melatonin in children with autism spectrum disorders: Endogenous and pharmacokinetic profiles in relation to sleep. *Journal of Autism and Developmental Disorders, 44*, 2525–2535. http://dx.doi.org/10.1007/s10803-014-2123-9

Goldman, S. E., McGrew, S., Johnson, K., Richdale, A., Clemons, T., & Malow, B. (2011). Sleep is associated with problem behaviors in children and adolescents with autism spectrum disorders. *Research in Autism Spectrum Disorders, 5*, 1223–1229. http://dx.doi.org/10.1016/j.rasd.2011.01.010

Goldman, S. E., Richdale, A. L., Clemons, T., & Malow, B. A. (2012). Parental sleep concerns in autism spectrum disorders: Variations from childhood to adolescence. *Journal of Autism and Developmental Disorders, 42*, 531–538. http://dx.doi.org/10.1007/s10803-011-1270-5

Goodlin-Jones, B. L., Sitnick, S. L., Tang, K., Liu, J., & Anders, T. F. (2008). The Children's Sleep Habits Questionnaire in toddlers and preschool children. *Journal of Developmental and Behavioral Pediatrics, 29*, 82–88. http://dx.doi.org/10.1097/DBP.0b013e318163c39a

Goodlin-Jones, B. L., Tang, K., Liu, J., & Anders, T. F. (2008). Sleep patterns in preschool-age children with autism, developmental delay, and typical development. *Journal of the American Academy of Child & Adolescent Psychiatry, 47*, 930–938. http://dx.doi.org/10.1097/CHI.0b013e3181799f7c

Gruber, R., Wiebe, S., Montecalvo, L., Brunetti, B., Amsel, R., & Carrier, J. (2011). Impact of sleep restriction on neurobehavioral functioning of children with attention deficit hyperactivity disorder. *Sleep, 34*, 315–323. http://dx.doi.org/10.1093/sleep/34.3.315

Henderson, J. A., Barry, T. D., Bader, S. H., & Jordan, S. S. (2011). The relation among sleep, routines, and externalizing behavior in children with an autism spectrum disorder. *Research in Autism Spectrum Disorders, 5*, 758–767. http://dx.doi.org/10.1016/j.rasd.2010.09.003

Hodgdon, L. A. (1995). *Visual strategies for improving communication: Vol. 1. Practical supports for school and home*. Troy, MI: QuirkRoberts.

Holley, S., Hill, C. M., & Stevenson, J. (2010). A comparison of actigraphy and parental report of sleep habits in typically developing children aged 6 to 11 years. *Behavioral Sleep Medicine, 8*, 16–27. http://dx.doi.org/10.1080/15402000903425462

Hollway, J. A., & Aman, M. G. (2011). Sleep correlates of pervasive developmental disorders: A review of the literature. *Research in Developmental Disabilities, 32*, 1399–1421. http://dx.doi.org/10.1016/j.ridd.2011.04.001

Ibrahim, S. H., Voigt, R. G., Katusic, S. K., Weaver, A. L., & Barbaresi, W. J. (2009). Incidence of gastrointestinal symptoms in children with autism: A population-based study. *Pediatrics, 124*, 680–686. http://dx.doi.org/10.1542/peds.2008-2933

Johnson, C. R. (1996). Sleep problems in children with mental retardation and autism. *Child and Adolescent Psychiatric Clinics of North America, 5,* 673–683.

Johnson, C. R., DeMand, A., Lecavalier, L., Smith, T., Aman, M., Foldes, E., & Scahill, L. (2016). Psychometric properties of the Children's Sleep Habits Questionnaire in children with autism spectrum disorder. *Sleep Medicine, 20,* 5–11. http://dx.doi.org/10.1016/j.sleep.2015.12.005

Johnson, C. R., Turner, K. S., Foldes, E., Brooks, M. M., Kronk, R., & Wiggs, L. (2013). Behavioral parent training to address sleep disturbances in young children with autism spectrum disorder: A pilot trial. *Sleep Medicine, 14,* 995–1004. http://dx.doi.org/10.1016/j.sleep.2013.05.013

Johnson, C. R., Turner, K. S., Foldes, E. L., Malow, B. A., & Wiggs, L. (2012). Comparison of sleep questionnaires in the assessment of sleep disturbances in children with autism spectrum disorders. *Sleep Medicine, 13,* 795–801. http://dx.doi.org/10.1016/j.sleep.2012.03.005

Kronk, R. (2008). *Are children with Fragile X syndrome losing their zzzz's . . . and y?* (Doctoral dissertation, University of Pittsburgh). Retrieved from http://d-scholarship.pitt.edu/6894/1/KronkDissertationPittApril2008.pdf

Kurth, S., Ringli, M., Geiger, A., LeBourgeois, M., Jenni, O. G., & Huber, R. (2010). Mapping of cortical activity in the first two decades of life: A high-density sleep electroencephalogram study. *Journal of Neuroscience, 30,* 13211–13219. http://dx.doi.org/10.1523/JNEUROSCI.2532-10.2010

Leekam, S. R., Nieto, C., Libby, S. J., Wing, L., & Gould, J. (2007). Describing the sensory abnormalities of children and adults with autism. *Journal of Autism and Developmental Disorders, 37,* 894–910. http://dx.doi.org/10.1007/s10803-006-0218-7

Li, S. H., Jin, X. M., Shen, X. M., Wu, S. H., Jiang, F., Yan, C. H., . . . Qiu, Y. L. (2007). Development and psychometric properties of the Chinese version of Children's Sleep Habits Questionnaire. *Zhonghua Er Ke Za Zhi, 45,* 176–180.

Liu, X., Hubbard, J. A., Fabes, R. A., & Adam, J. B. (2006). Sleep disturbances and correlates of children with autism spectrum disorders. *Child Psychiatry and Human Development, 37,* 179–191. http://dx.doi.org/10.1007/s10578-006-0028-3

Lord, C., Rutter, M., & Le Couteur, A. (1994). Autism Diagnostic Interview-Revised: A revised version of a diagnostic interview for caregivers of individuals with possible pervasive developmental disorders. *Journal of Autism and Developmental Disorders, 24,* 659–685. http://dx.doi.org/10.1007/BF02172145

Lord, C., Rutter, M. L., DiLavore, P. C., Risi, S., Gotham, K., & Bishop, S. (2012). *Autism Diagnostic Observation Schedule, Second Edition (ADOS-2) manual (Part I): Modules 1–4.* Torrance, CA: Western Psychological Services.

Maas, A. P., Didden, R., Korzilius, H., Braam, W., Collin, P., Smits, M. G., & Curfs, L. M. (2011). Psychometric properties of a sleep questionnaire for use in individuals with intellectual disabilities. *Research in Developmental Disabilities*, *32*, 2467–2479. http://dx.doi.org/10.1016/j.ridd.2011.07.013

Magee, L., & Hale, L. (2012). Longitudinal associations between sleep duration and subsequent weight gain: A systematic review. *Sleep Medicine Reviews*, *16*, 231–241. http://dx.doi.org/10.1016/j.smrv.2011.05.005

Malow, B., Adkins, K. W., McGrew, S. G., Wang, L., Goldman, S. E., Fawkes, D., & Burnette, C. (2012). Melatonin for sleep in children with autism: A controlled trial examining dose, tolerability, and outcomes. *Journal of Autism and Developmental Disorders*, *42*, 1729–1737. http://dx.doi.org/10.1007/s10803-011-1418-3

Malow, B. A., Adkins, K. W., Reynolds, A., Weiss, S. K., Loh, A., Fawkes, D., . . . Clemons, T. (2014). Parent-based sleep education for children with autism spectrum disorders. *Journal of Autism and Developmental Disorders*, *44*, 216–228. http://dx.doi.org/10.1007/s10803-013-1866-z

Malow, B. A., Crowe, C., Henderson, L., McGrew, S. G., Wang, L., Song, Y., & Stone, W. L. (2009). A sleep habits questionnaire for children with autism spectrum disorders. *Journal of Child Neurology*, *24*, 19–24. http://dx.doi.org/10.1177/0883073808321044

Malow, B. A., Marzec, M. L., McGrew, S. G., Wang, L., Henderson, L. M., & Stone, W. L. (2006). Characterizing sleep in children with autism spectrum disorders: A multidimensional approach. *Sleep*, *29*, 1563–1571. http://dx.doi.org/10.1093/sleep/29.12.1563

Malow, B. A., McGrew, S. G., Harvey, M., Henderson, L. M., & Stone, W. L. (2006). Impact of treating sleep apnea in a child with autism spectrum disorder. *Pediatric Neurology*, *34*, 325–328. http://dx.doi.org/10.1016/j.pediatrneurol.2005.08.021

Mazurek, M. O., & Petroski, G. F. (2015). Sleep problems in children with autism spectrum disorder: Examining the contributions of sensory over-responsivity and anxiety. *Sleep Medicine*, *16*, 270–279. http://dx.doi.org/10.1016/j.sleep.2014.11.006

Mazurek, M. O., & Sohl, K. (2016). Sleep and behavioral problems in children with autism spectrum disorder. *Journal of Autism and Developmental Disorders*, *46*, 1906–1915. http://dx.doi.org/10.1007/s10803-016-2723-7

Meltzer, L. J., & Mindell, J. A. (2014). Systematic review and meta-analysis of behavioral interventions for pediatric insomnia. *Journal of Pediatric Psychology*, *39*, 932–948. http://dx.doi.org/10.1093/jpepsy/jsu041

Meltzer, L. J., Montgomery-Downs, H. E., Insana, S. P., & Walsh, C. M. (2012). Use of actigraphy for assessment in pediatric sleep research. *Sleep Medicine Reviews*, *16*, 463–475. http://dx.doi.org/10.1016/j.smrv.2011.10.002

Mindell, J. A., Kuhn, B., Lewin, D. S., Meltzer, L. J., Sadeh, A., & the American Academy of Sleep Medicine. (2006). Behavioral treatment of bedtime problems and night wakings in infants and young children. *Sleep*, *29*, 1263–1276.

Montgomery, P., Stores, G., & Wiggs, L. (2004). The relative efficacy of two brief treatments for sleep problems in young learning disabled (mentally retarded) children: A randomised controlled trial. *Archives of Disease in Childhood, 89*, 125–130. http://dx.doi.org/10.1136/adc.2002.017202

Moon, E. C., Corkum, P., & Smith, I. M. (2011). Case study: A case-series evaluation of a behavioral sleep intervention for three children with autism and primary insomnia. *Journal of Pediatric Psychology, 36*, 47–54. http://dx.doi.org/10.1093/jpepsy/jsq057

Moore, B. A., Friman, P. C., Fruzzetti, A. E., & MacAleese, K. (2007). Brief report: Evaluating the Bedtime Pass Program for child resistance to bedtime—A randomized, controlled trial. *Journal of Pediatric Psychology, 32*, 283–287. http://dx.doi.org/10.1093/jpepsy/jsl025

Moore, P. (2004). The use of social stories in a psychology service for children with learning disabilities: A case study of a sleep problem. *British Journal of Learning Disabilities, 32*, 133–138. http://dx.doi.org/10.1111/j.1468-3156.2004.00278.x

Moss, A. H., Gordon, J. E., & O'Connell, A. (2014). Impact of Sleepwise: An intervention for youth with developmental disabilities and sleep disturbance. *Journal of Autism and Developmental Disorders, 44*, 1695–1707. http://dx.doi.org/10.1007/s10803-014-2040-y

Owens, J. A. (2007). Classification and epidemiology of childhood sleep disorders. *Sleep Medicine Clinics, 2*, 353–361. http://dx.doi.org/10.1016/j.jsmc.2007.05.009

Owens, J. A. (2009). Neurocognitive and behavioral impact of sleep disordered breathing in children. *Pediatric Pulmonology, 44*, 417–422. http://dx.doi.org/10.1002/ppul.20981

Owens, J. A., Spirito, A., & McGuinn, M. (2000). The Children's Sleep Habits Questionnaire (CSHQ): Psychometric properties of a survey instrument for school-aged children. *Sleep, 23*, 1–9. http://dx.doi.org/10.1093/sleep/23.8.1d

Ozdemir, S. (2008). The effectiveness of social stories on decreasing disruptive behaviors of children with autism: Three case studies. *Journal of Autism and Developmental Disorders, 38*, 1689–1696. http://dx.doi.org/10.1007/s10803-008-0551-0

Park, S., Cho, S., Cho, I. H., Kim, B., Kim, J., Shin, M., . . . Yoo, H. J. (2012). Sleep problems and their correlates and comorbid psychopathology of children with autism spectrum disorders. *Research in Autism Spectrum Disorders, 6*, 1068–1072. http://dx.doi.org/10.1016/j.rasd.2012.02.004

Piazza, C. C., Fisher, W. W., & Sherer, M. (1997). Treatment of multiple sleep problems in children with developmental disabilities: Faded bedtime with response cost versus bedtime scheduling. *Developmental Medicine & Child Neurology, 39*, 414–418.

Reynolds, A. M., & Malow, B. A. (2011). Sleep and autism spectrum disorders. *Pediatric Clinics of North America, 58*, 685–698. http://dx.doi.org/10.1016/j.pcl.2011.03.009

Rossignol, D. A., & Frye, R. E. (2011). Melatonin in autism spectrum disorders: A systematic review and meta-analysis. *Developmental Medicine & Child Neurology, 53*, 783–792. http://dx.doi.org/10.1111/j.1469-8749.2011.03980.x

Sadeh, A. (2007). Consequences of sleep loss or sleep disruption in children. *Sleep Medicine Clinics, 2*, 513–520. http://dx.doi.org/10.1016/j.jsmc.2007.05.012

Schlarb, A. A., Schwerdtle, B., & Hautzinger, M. (2010). Normierung und psychometrische Eigenschaften der deutschen Version des Children's Sleep Habits Questionnaire (CSHQ-DE). [Validation and psychometric properties of the German version of the Children's Sleep Habits Questionnaire (CSHQ-DE)]. *Somnologie: Schlafforschung und Schlafmedizin, 14*, 260–266. http://dx.doi.org/10.1007/s11818-010-0495-4

Schneider, N., & Goldstein, H. (2010). Using social stories and visual schedules to improve socially appropriate behaviors in children with autism. *Journal of Positive Behavior Interventions, 12*, 149–160. http://dx.doi.org/10.1177/1098300709334198

Simonds, J. F., & Parraga, H. (1982). Prevalence of sleep disorders and sleep behaviors in children and adolescents. *Journal of the American Academy of Child & Adolescent Psychiatry, 21*, 383–388. http://dx.doi.org/10.1016/S0002-7138(09)60942-0

Sivertsen, B., Posserud, M. B., Gillberg, C., Lundervold, A. J., & Hysing, M. (2012). Sleep problems in children with autism spectrum problems: A longitudinal population-based study. *Autism, 16*, 139–150. http://dx.doi.org/10.1177/1362361311404255

Spruyt, K., & Gozal, D. (2011). Development of pediatric sleep questionnaires as diagnostic or epidemiological tools: A brief review of dos and don'ts. *Sleep Medicine Reviews, 15*, 7–17. http://dx.doi.org/10.1016/j.smrv.2010.06.003

Thorpy, M. J. (Chair). (1990). *International Classification of Sleep Disorders: Diagnostic and coding manual.* Rochester, MN: American Sleep Disorders Association.

Tordjman, S., Anderson, G. M., Bellissant, E., Botbol, M., Charbuy, H., Camus, F., . . . Touitou, Y. (2012). Day and nighttime excretion of 6-sulphatoxymelatonin in adolescents and young adults with autistic disorder. *Psychoneuroendocrinology, 37*, 1990–1997. http://dx.doi.org/10.1016/j.psyneuen.2012.04.013

Valicenti-McDermott, M., McVicar, K., Rapin, I., Wershil, B. K., Cohen, H., & Shinnar, S. (2006). Frequency of gastrointestinal symptoms in children with autistic spectrum disorders and association with family history of autoimmune disease. *Journal of Developmental and Behavioral Pediatrics, 27*(Suppl. 2), S128–S136. http://dx.doi.org/10.1097/00004703-200604002-00011

Veatch, O. J., Maxwell-Horn, A. C., & Malow, B. A. (2015). Sleep in autism spectrum disorders. *Current Sleep Medicine Reports, 1*, 131–140. http://dx.doi.org/10.1007/s40675-015-0012-1

Vriend, J. L., Davidson, F. D., Corkum, P. V., Rusak, B., McLaughlin, E. N., & Chambers, C. T. (2012). Sleep quantity and quality in relation to daytime functioning in children. *Children's Health Care, 41*, 204–222. http://dx.doi.org/10.1080/02739615.2012.685039

Waters, M. B., Lerman, D. C., & Hovanetz, A. N. (2009). Separate and combined effects of visual schedules and extinction plus differential reinforcement on problem behavior occasioned by transitions. *Journal of Applied Behavior Analysis, 42*, 309–313. http://dx.doi.org/10.1901/jaba.2009.42-309

Waumans, R. C., Terwee, C. B., Van den Berg, G., Knol, D. L., Van Litsenburg, R. R., & Gemke, R. J. (2010). Sleep and sleep disturbance in children: Reliability and validity of the Dutch version of the Child Sleep Habits Questionnaire. *Sleep, 33*, 841–845. http://dx.doi.org/10.1093/sleep/33.6.841

Wiggs, L., & Stores, G. (1996). Severe sleep disturbance and daytime challenging behaviour in children with severe learning disabilities. *Journal of Intellectual Disability Research, 40*, 518–528.

Wiggs, L., & Stores, G. (1998). Behavioural treatment for sleep problems in children with severe learning disabilities and challenging daytime behaviour: Effect on sleep patterns of mother and child. *Journal of Sleep Research, 7*, 119–126. http://dx.doi.org/10.1046/j.1365-2869.1998.00107.x

Wiggs, L., & Stores, G. (2004). Sleep patterns and sleep disorders in children with autistic spectrum disorders: Insights using parent report and actigraphy. *Developmental Medicine and Child Neurology, 46*, 372–380. http://dx.doi.org/10.1017/S0012162204000611

7

PARENT TRAINING FOR FOOD SELECTIVITY IN AUTISM SPECTRUM DISORDER

T. LINDSEY BURRELL, WILLIAM SHARP, CRISTINA WHITEHOUSE, AND CYNTHIA R. JOHNSON

OVERVIEW OF FOOD SELECTIVITY IN CHILDREN WITH AUTISM SPECTRUM DISORDER

Behavioral and medical problems commonly are observed in children with autism spectrum disorder (ASD). One of these problems includes a five-fold increase in the odds of developing a feeding problem—most often in the form of severe food selectivity—compared with peers, (Sharp, Berry, et al., 2013). Poor dietary diversity in ASD is associated with vitamin and mineral deficiencies, poor bone growth, and constipation (Hediger et al., 2008; Sharp, Berry, McElhanon, & Jaquess, 2014). Children with ASD also are more likely to experience gastrointestinal (GI) complaints. A recent meta-analysis concluded that children with ASD were 4 times more likely to experience general GI complaints, were more than 3 times more prone to experience constipation and diarrhea, and were twice as likely to experience abdominal

http://dx.doi.org/10.1037/0000111-008
Parent Training for Autism Spectrum Disorder: Improving the Quality of Life for Children and Their Families,
C. R. Johnson, E. M. Butter, and L. Scahill (Editors)

pain when compared with peers (McElhanon, McCracken, Karpen, & Sharp, 2014). Feeding difficulties and related health concerns also increase the stress and challenges of raising a child with ASD and decrease overall quality of life for families (Khanna et al., 2011).

Given the detrimental impact of food selectivity on both child health and parent well-being, it is imperative that treatment seeks to improve meal-time behaviors and expand dietary intake while concurrently maximizing parental functioning. One way is through parent training (PT). Increased evidence has indicated that PT can be used to address a variety of common challenges for children with ASD, including feeding problems (Johnson, Foldes, DeMand, & Brooks, 2015; Sharp, Jaquess, Morton, & Miles, 2011). Past reports, however, have varied in the manner in which parents are involved. In general, feeding interventions involve trained clinicians who provide direct intervention before generalizing individualized protocols to parents (Laud, Girolami, Boscoe, & Gulotta, 2009; Sharp et al., 2011). Far less common are examples of parents who serve as the primary interventionists to target food selectivity in children with ASD (Johnson et al., 2015; Sharp, Burrell, & Jaquess, 2013). This gap in the research literature is unfortunate, given that parents are in the unique position of spending the most time with their children to be able to potentially implement frequent intervention surrounding mealtime behavior.

The purpose of this chapter is to provide an overview of feeding problems in children with ASD; describe the medical, nutritional, and social consequences of food selectivity; and review common assessment and treatment approaches to expand the variety of foods consumed. We begin with a general description of feeding problems in ASD, including the pattern, prevalence, impact, and possible etiology of food selectivity in this population. Then, we review assessment procedures for evaluating feeding problems and specific intervention strategies often incorporated into PT to treat feeding problems in children with ASD. The chapter concludes with special considerations in treatment and a detailed case study of children with ASD and food selectivity.

TYPES OF FEEDING PROBLEMS IN ASD

Food selectivity is the most frequently documented and well-researched feeding problem associated with ASD. It most often involves strong prefer-ences for starches and snack foods coinciding with a bias against fruits and vegetables. Associated mealtime difficulties include disruptive mealtime behavior (e.g., tantrums, crying), rigidity surrounding eating (e.g., only eat-ing in a specific location; requiring certain utensils), and avoidance of certain food items based on the sensory characteristic (e.g., texture). Less frequent are descriptions of children with ASD who require supplemental formula (e.g., bottle or a feeding tube dependence) due to inadequate oral intake, which more commonly is observed in children with complex medical histories that may include gastroesophageal reflux, gastroenteritis, and food allergies (Brown et al., 2014; Silverman et al., 2013). Available research also has suggested that children with ASD and food selectivity may not be at increased risk for medical comorbidities (Ledford & Gast, 2006).

Severe food selectivity in ASD most often involves deficits in dietary variety, not volume, and children with ASD typically consume enough food to meet gross energy needs (Sharp, Berry, et al., 2013; Sharp et al., 2014). Because children with ASD typically consume an adequate volume of food, this may explain why, historically, feeding concerns in ASD have been overlooked in relation to other areas of clinical concern. The clinical picture, however, for food selectivity in ASD is more complicated from a nutritional and medical standpoint, and requires looking beyond anthropometrics to determine overall impact of atypical patterns of intake, including enhanced risk for underlying dietary insufficiencies and associated poor health outcomes (e.g., obesity).

PREVALENCE AND IMPACT OF FEEDING PROBLEMS IN ASD

Prevalence estimates of feeding problems in ASD have ranged from 46% to 89% (Cermak, Curtin, & Bandini, 2010; Ledford & Gast, 2006), with the wide range largely attributed to differences in sample source and assessment methods (see Table 7.1). Understanding of feeding problems in ASD requires first differentiating severe food selectivity from mild feeding problems often observed during childhood. Up to 40% of healthy toddlers and early school-age children without ASD experience some form of mealtime difficulty (Mayes & Volkmar, 1993). Common issues include fluctuating hunger and picky eating patterns, which may occur in as many as 50% of children at some point in time (Carruth, Ziegler, Gordon, & Barr, 2004). *Picky eating*, which includes consuming a limited variety of foods, an unwillingness to try new foods (i.e., food neophobia), and/or displaying strong food preferences, is observed in nearly 30% of children under 5 but only 13% of 6-year-old children (Cardona Cano et al., 2015). Vegetables and fruits, particularly those with a bitter taste, tend to be the most rejected foods (Dovey, Staples, Gibson, & Halford, 2008). Although picky eating is a common childhood problem and can be stressful for caregivers, research has suggested that picky eating most often is a fluctuating, temporary problem that is part of typical development.

In contrast, children with ASD and severe food selectivity often display persistent feeding problems that extend into adolescence and adulthood. For

TABLE 7.1

Variations in Definitions and Prevalence Estimates of Food Selectivity Within and Across Studies

Study	ASD sample size	Definition/proxy for food selectivity	Prevalence
Collins et al. (2003)	107	Always eating the normal (usual) family diet	20%–40%
		Refuses food for no obvious reason	59%–96%
		Obsessive eating habits	33%–59%
Dominick, David, Lainhart, Tager-Flusberg, and Folstein (2007)	54	Atypical eating behavior	76%
		Restricted range of foods	63%
		Preference for a particular food	58%
Emond, Emmett, Steer, and Golding (2010)	79	Very choosy	38%
Lockner, Crowe, and Skipper (2008)	20	Resists trying new foods	95%
		Picky eater	79%
		Has favorite food texture	68%
		Eats a variety of foods	16%
Matson, Fodstad, and Dempsey (2009)	112	Will eat only certain foods	79%
		Prefers food of a certain texture or smell	76%
Nadon et al. (2011)	48	Doesn't try new foods	77%
		Refuses food eaten before	77%
		Is selective for textures	63%
		Cannot tolerate new food on plate	63%
		Experiences "phases" of wanting the same food for prolonged period	60%
		Always/often needs a different meal from the rest of the family	52%
		Does not eat at day care, school, or restaurant	38%
		Diet includes less than 20 different foods	38%
		Is fixated on recipes	35%

Study	N		%
Provost et al. (2010)	24	Has food preferences	95%
		Is a picky eater	74%
		Has favorite food textures	71%
		Has no eating problems	37%
		Eats a variety of foods	12%
		Has eating difficulty at restaurants	54%
		Has eating difficulty at school	25%
Raiten and Massaro (1986)	40	Dislikes certain foods and won't eat them	60%
		Has food cravings	53%
		Accepts/prefers a variety of foods	55%
		Prefers carbohydrate foods	45%
		Is unwilling to try new foods	40%
		Prefers food to be prepared/served in a certain way	35%
		Prefers the same food	28%
		Insists on ritual at table	25%
		Refuses foods that require a lot of chewing	18%
Schmitt et al. (2008)	20	Avoids mushy foods	100%
		Chooses food based on texture	70%
		Prefers crispy or crunchy foods	63%
		Is a picky eater	60%
		Eats a variety of foods	40%
Schreck et al. (2004)	138	Eats a narrow range of foods	72%

Note. ASD = autism spectrum disorder.

example, Kuschner et al. (2015) noted that approximately 35% of adolescents and young adults with ASD reported being afraid of eating new or unfamiliar foods, whereas fewer than 20% of typically developing peers reported similar signs of food neophobia. A longitudinal study by Suarez, Nelson, and Curtis (2014) indicated no change in food selectivity in 52 children with ASD over a 20-month period. Food selectivity in ASD often coincides with disruptive behavior that exceeds mild concerns observed with picky eating. For example, children with ASD are more likely to exhibit strong refusal behaviors (e.g., crying, throwing objects, aggression) when presented with seemingly benign or novel feeding demands, such as the sight or smell of nonpreferred foods (Sharp, Jaquess, & Lukens, 2013). As a result, children may refuse to sit at the family dinner table and/or display problem behaviors when family members prepare or consume nonpreferred foods (Ausderau & Juarez, 2013).

Health Impact

Poor dietary diversity in ASD is associated with vitamin and mineral deficiencies (Sharp, Berry, et al., 2013), and, in extreme cases, may result in diet-related diseases not frequently observed in pediatric populations, such as scurvy, rickets, xerophthalmia, and vision loss (Clark, Rhoden, & Turner, 1993; Ma, Thompson, & Weston, 2016; Uyanik, Dogangun, Kayaalp, Korkmaz, & Dervent, 2006). Johnson et al. (2014) demonstrated that as parent rating of feeding problems increased, nutritional status decreased. Clearly, not all children with ASD are at risk for this level of malnutrition; however, these studies highlight the potential detrimental impact of food selectivity and the need for interventions to improve dietary diversity.

There also is emerging evidence that children with ASD are at increased risk for obesity compared with non-ASD peers. Hill, Zuckerman, and Fombonne (2015) identified 14 studies documenting this trend, with the estimated prevalence for obesity ranging from 10% to 42.6%. However, two studies that included large samples of children with ASD demonstrated strikingly similar results. Hill et al. (2015) compared the weight status of 5,053 children (age 2–17 years) with ASD with a representative cross-sectional sample of the general U.S. population. Among children with ASD, 33.6% were overweight and 18% were obese. De Vinck-Baroody et al. (2015) also found 33.9% and 18.2% of children with ASD fell in the obese and overweight range, respectively. Differences between the general population and the sample of children with ASD were evident as early as age 2 (Hill et al., 2015). High rates of obesity in this population correspond with patterns of food selectivity involving energy-dense yet nutritionally void foods.

Parental Stress and Family Functioning Impact

Chronic feeding issues in ASD can negatively impact caregivers and decrease overall quality of life for families. Curtin et al. (2015) reported that compared with parents of children without ASD, parents of children with ASD were significantly more likely to report that their child's behavior at mealtimes negatively impacted their spouse/partner and represented a source of stress in their relationship. Suarez, Atchison, and Lagerwey (2014) reported that caregivers experienced deep dissatisfaction surrounding meals, describing family mealtime as stressful, chaotic, and energy depleting. Marquenie, Rodger, Mangohig, and Cronin (2011) reported a similar pattern of eroded family interactions associated with food selectivity, with meals lacking positive interactions. Caregivers further reported that their child's food selectivity limited other family members' mealtime food choices. Unlike meals for families of children without ASD, mealtimes for families of children with ASD appear less likely to serve as a means to strengthen the family unit by providing time together to communicate and develop shared family rituals and routines (Fulkerson, Story, Neumark-Sztainer, & Rydell, 2008).

WHY DO CHILDREN WITH ASD COMMONLY EXPERIENCE FEEDING PROBLEMS?

Medical Factors

Organic factors associated with painful or difficult eating, such as gastroesophageal reflux, gastroenteritis, and food allergies, often precipitate or play a role in the development of chronic feeding concerns in other pediatric populations. Therefore, it is important to first evaluate whether children with ASD are experiencing GI dysfunction or other associated medical conditions that may contribute to the pattern of food selectivity. A recent meta-analysis concluded that children with ASD were four times more likely to experience general GI complaints, more than three times more prone to experience constipation and diarrhea, and were twice as likely to experience abdominal pain when compared with peers (McElhanon et al., 2014). Unfortunately, lack of data prohibited analysis of GI symptoms, such as gastroesophageal reflux or food allergies, that often precipitate feeding concerns in other pediatric populations. As a result, McElhanon et al. (2014) emphasized that the most logical conclusion, based on expert consensus (Buie et al., 2010), was to assume that rates of other GI pathophysiology in ASD occur at levels similar to those observed in the general population. Furthermore, most available research has suggested that children with ASD seeking intervention for food selectivity do not present with an underlying GI etiology or organic pathology (Ledford & Gast, 2006). For example, Sharp, Jaquess, Morton, and Herzinger (2010) reported that only 22% of children with ASD seeking intervention for food selectivity presented with a documented medical concern, whereas 98% of children without ASD presenting with food refusal and feeding tube dependence had one or more medical concerns.

Behavioral Rigidity and Sensory Sensitivity

It has been posited that food selectivity may represent an additional manifestation of repetitive behavior and restricted interests. Rigidity often is reflected in the pattern of food selectivity (i.e., strong preference for snacks and processed foods) typically observed in children with ASD and may influence other aspects of mealtimes, such as preference for using the same utensils and/or particular food presentations (Ahearn, Castine, Nault, & Green, 2001; Schreck, Williams, & Smith, 2004). For example, Provost, Crowe, Osbourn, McClain, and Skipper (2010) reported that children with ASD were significantly more likely to consume foods in a repetitive manner, limit foods to a certain texture, and have more difficulty eating outside the home setting (e.g., schools, restaurants). Nadon, Feldman, Dunn, and Gisel (2011) reported that food preference differed based on the mealtime environment, such as not eating the same food at day care and at home. Hyper- and hyporeactivity to sensory input are common among individuals with ASD, which also may influence food choice among children with ASD (American Psychiatric Association, 2013), including restricting dietary intake based on the sensory characteristics of food such as the color, taste, small, and/or temperature (Nadon et al., 2011; Tomchek & Dunn, 2007).

Disrupted Parent–Child Interaction

A prominent feature of food selectivity in ASD is persistent, disruptive mealtime behaviors in response to the presentation of nonpreferred foods (Sharp, Jaquess, et al., 2013). Problem behaviors during meals often function as a means to escape or avoid aversive feeding experiences (Piazza et al., 2003). In response to these behaviors, caregivers understandably remove food and end the meal (Piazza, 2008). Consequently, the child escapes the feeding demand, and these behaviors are inadvertently reinforced, shaped, and strengthened over time. Parents also learn that food removal leads to a rapid cessation in the child's challenging behavior, providing escape from unpleasant mealtime interactions. As a result, caregivers may be more likely to end meals prematurely in response to problem behaviors. Faced with repeated lack of success introducing new foods, caregivers may cease presenting nonpreferred foods and resort to preparing multiple menus at each meal: one for the child with ASD and one reflecting the more varied diet of the family (Marquenie et al., 2011). The child subsequently has little or no exposure to food outside his or her limited dietary repertoire and contributes to the continued food selectivity over time.

ASSESSMENT OF FEEDING PROBLEMS IN ASD

A multidisciplinary approach to assessment before treatment usually is recommended for children with chronic feeding concerns (Lukens & Silverman, 2014). This approach is particularly salient when working with children with ASD and food selectivity, given possible increased risk of comorbid GI concerns and nutritional deficiencies. Comprehensive feeding evaluations often include a behavioral psychologist, dietitian, physician, speech-language pathologist (SLP), and occupational therapist (OT; see Table 7.2 for a description of provider roles). The involvement of these specialty areas provides important

TABLE 7.2
Recommended Areas of Assessment by Discipline

Specialty area	Primary assessment focus	Description
Medicine	Possible organic pathology	Screens for common organic issues that may cause or exacerbate discomfort or dysfunction along the gastrointestinal tract (e.g., aspiration, GERD, food allergy, constipation)
Nutrition	Dietary status	Evaluates intake of food and nutrients, and growth patterns/ anthropometrics, including a detailed analysis of micronutrient and macronutrient intake
Psychology	Mealtime behaviors/ family functioning	Determines patterns of behavior that disrupt meals and help maintain food selectivity, as well as the overall impact of food selectivity on the family unit
Speech language pathology/ occupational therapy	Oral-motor skills	Assesses the use, coordination, movement, strength, and endurance of the lips, cheeks, tongue, and jaw as they pertain to consuming various textures of foods and overall swallow safety

Note. GERD = gastroesophageal reflux disease.

guidance and safeguards when assessing, developing, and implementing inter-ventions with consideration to behavioral, dietary, medical, and oral-motor concerns, respectively, observed in pediatric feeding disorders (Sharp et al., 2010). The timing and role of each provider may be determined by the nature and severity of the presenting problem (e.g., lack of success advancing food texture or further narrowing of dietary diversity). An important first step when working with any child with a feeding disorder involves ruling out the potential contribution of organic factors (e.g., gastroesophageal reflux, food allergy) that may cause pain or discomfort along the GI tract. This step may require adopting a lower threshold for obtaining subspecialty consultation (e.g., pediatric gastro-enterologist, allergist) and increased reliance on objective testing to recognize pathology and facilitate a diagnosis, given limitations in communication often observed in ASD (Buie et al., 2010).

Once organic pathology is ruled out or food selectivity persists despite medical intervention, the assessment process should shift to evaluating the severity of food selectivity and identifying what other factors may be main-taining a child's restricted diet. An SLP or OT with expertise in pediatric feeding disorders should evaluate oral-motor skills when underlying oral dysfunction is suspected (e.g., muscle weakness). A dietician should evalu-ate dietary needs/omissions to help identify key food items/groups to target during intervention that address nutritional deficiencies that may impede growth and development. A psychologist, in turn, identifies the pattern, intensity, and function of the problem behaviors, as well as the impact that food selectivity has on the family's overall quality of life. This information may be obtained through structured clinical interview, caregiver questionnaires, and direct mealtime observation.

Clinical Interview

A clinical interview focusing on food selectivity in ASD should seek to collect information regarding preferred and nonpreferred food items, the family's approach to structuring meals, and current and past strategies for addressing disruptive mealtime behavior. To identify patterns of food selec-tivity, questions should focus on specific food items within a child's dietary repertoire (i.e., fruit, vegetable, meat/beans, dairy, grains) and/or preference for certain sensory characteristics (e.g., texture, color, temperature) of pre-ferred foods. Identifying previously accepted or "dropped" foods from a child's diet also will provide important insights into the trajectory of food selectivity over time, as well as inform intervention planning.

A functional assessment should be part of the clinical interview to sys-tematically assess events that precede a target behavior (i.e., antecedents) and the environmental factors (i.e., consequences) that may be maintaining problem behaviors (Iwata & Worsdell, 2005; Reese, Richman, Belmont, & Morse, 2005). This information can be obtained through structured questions and/or observation of the behavior (see Table 7.3). Antecedents relevant to mealtime structure include the timing and location of meals, the variety of foods presented, typical bite volume and portion size, and consumption of preferred food items between meals (i.e., "grazing"). This information provides important insights into the demands being placed on a child during a meal, as well as the potential resources (e.g., an established meal schedule) and barriers (i.e., difficulty limiting access to food between meals) to consider

TABLE 7.3
Recommended Lines of Inquiry Regarding Meal Structure, Feeding Behaviors, and Strategies for Managing Mealtime Difficulties

Antecedents	Initial question (Additional probes, if needed)
Meal location	Where do meals take place? (At the kitchen table? On the couch? In front of the TV?)
Schedule	How often do meals occur? (Do you have a schedule? What time does each meal occur)?
Food	How many foods typically are presented during meals? (Do meals only involve preferred foods? When do you present nonpreferred foods?)
People	Who is present during meals? (Are other caregivers or siblings present? Do you eat together as a family?)
Format	How does your child eat during meals? (Does he or she eat independently? Using utensils or finger feeding?)
Portion size	How much food do you present at meals? (Do you fill up the plate or bowl? Is the presentation different with nonpreferred foods?)
Bite volume	How large are the bites that your child accepts? (Does the bite size differ across foods? If so, which foods involve larger and smaller bites?)
Grazing	Does your child have access to foods in between meals? (Are there any limits placed on access to these foods? How often does he or she eat these foods?)

Behaviors	
Acceptance	Has your child recently accepted any new or nonpreferred food? (How often does this occur? What was different about this meal/situation?)
Swallowing	Will he or she swallow the food once accepted? (Was chewing involved? Any expulsion/spitting? What about holding or pocketing the food?)
Disruptions	What other problem behaviors occur when nonpreferred food is presented during meals? (Pushing away the food/plate? Tantrums? Crying?)

(*continues*)

TABLE 7.3
Recommended Lines of Inquiry Regarding Meal Structure, Feeding
Behaviors, and Strategies for Managing Mealtime Difficulties   (*Continued*)

Behaviors	Initial question (Additional probes, if needed)
Elopement	Does he or she remain at the table throughout the meal? (What happens if you try to bring him or her back? What happens if you remove the food?)
Aggression	Has aggression ever occurred in response to nonpreferred foods? (Was this directed at caregivers/sibling? How often does this occur?)
Other	Does your child display any other problem behaviors during meals? (Negative statements? Refusal to come to the table? Self-injury?)

Consequences	
General strategies	How have you responded to problem behaviors in the past? (How did you come up with these strategies? Have you found anything that helps?)
Current state	Are you currently trying to introduce new foods? (When was the last time you tried to present nonpreferred foods? Why did you stop?)
Food removal	How do meals end? (Do you remove the nonpreferred food? What happens after the food is removed?)
Items	Are there certain items or activities that he or she has access to during meals? (Does he or she watch TV? Play games? Have access to toys during meals?)
Attention	Are there certain things you say when trying to get him or her to try new foods? (Do you ever try and talk him or her into trying the food? Reprimand when he or she refuses?)

when designing intervention. It also is critical to determine specific behaviors interfering with the introduction of new foods and/or disrupting meals. In the feeding situation, children may engage in disruptive behavior, including turning their heads, pushing the spoon away, leaving the table, crying, and/or aggression. It also may be the case that in some instances, the child willingly accepts and swallows small bites of new or nonpreferred foods. Thus, determining the topography and intensity of refusal behaviors, and summarizing a child's general reaction to the presentation of nonpreferred foods, can help determine the appropriate starting point for treatment. Current and past strategies for managing feeding concerns provide important insights into factors that may have shaped and/or currently maintain food selectivity (e.g., removing nonpreferred food). In many cases, caregivers may no longer attempt to introduce new foods into their child's diet, given the intensity and persistence of refusal behaviors. In such cases, the interview process may require focusing on historical patterns of interactions when nonpreferred foods were presented during meals.

Parent-Report Questionnaires and Inventories

Parent questionnaires often are a useful way to obtain information about feeding behaviors. Questionnaires are easy to administer, do not require extensive training, and can lead to the identification of feeding patterns and treatment options (Seiverling, Williams, & Sturmey, 2010). However, to date, only one questionnaire has been developed and revised that specifically assesses mealtime behavior problems in the ASD population. The Brief Autism Mealtime Behavior Inventory (BAMBI), developed by Lukens and Linscheid (2008), is an 18-item questionnaire that examines feeding problems across three domains: (a) Limited Variety, which examines the child's willingness to try new foods; (b) Food Refusal, which measures disruptive behavior present when foods are rejected by a child; and (c) Features of Autism, which specifically assesses behaviors common in ASD (e.g., self-injury; rigid, repetitive behavior). A later study by DeMand, Johnson, and Foldes (2015) described a revised BAMBI with 15 questions and a four-factor structure (i.e., Food Selectivity, Disruptive Mealtime Behaviors, Food Refusal, Mealtime Rigidity). Both the BAMBI and revised BAMBI offer a brief, standardized parent questionnaire that is useful in identifying the frequency and severity of often idiosyncratic mealtime behavior problems specific to children with ASD.

Although not specifically designed to assess mealtime concerns in ASD, a variety of other parent-completed questionnaires are available for use with pediatric populations. For example, the Children's Eating Behavior Inventory (CEBI; Archer, Rosenbaum, & Streiner, 1991) is a measure that includes items assessing food preferences, motor skills, and the impact of feeding on family dynamics and interactions. The CEBI has been used to evaluate treatment outcomes for children with ASD receiving treatment for feeding problems (Laud et al., 2009). Similarly, the Behavioral Pediatric Feeding Assessment Scale (Crist & Napier-Phillips, 2001) and the Screening Tool of Feeding Problems (Matson & Kuhn, 2001) are two other general feeding assessments used in past research to assess the presence of feeding problems among children with ASD.

Completion of a food diary or record is another common approach to assessing food selectivity, as well as dietary adequacy (Bandini et al., 2010). Food records are obtained by asking a parent to record the volume of foods, supplements, and drinks consumed by the child over a 3-day period. Nutrition professionals can analyze these food records using specialized software that provides a detailed summary of nutritional insufficiencies or excesses. Food diaries are more time consuming for the parents, may be susceptible to estimate and omission errors, and require nutrition professionals to analyze content. However, the food records can provide important data to inform treatment.

Mealtime Observation

Direct observation of a meal or a simulated meal allows for further evaluation of the function or reason why the child is engaging in problem behavior during meals, as well as for confirms the presence and severity of dietary restrictions. For example, Levin and Carr (2001) and Najdowski, Wallace, Doney, and Ghezzi (2003) conducted functional analyses of problem behavior during meals in children with ASD, evaluating behavior in four conditions: attention, escape, no interactions, and a control play condition. Their findings indicated that problem behaviors were highest in the escape conditions, suggesting that disruptive behavior likely functioned as a means to escape contact with aversive or nonpreferred foods. Direct observation also can be used to determine the extent to which children refuse novel foods and can provide additional insight into the patterns and severity of food selectivity (Ahearn et al., 2001; Sharp, Jaquess, et al., 2013). Understanding the function of a child's behavior and response to novel feeding demands combined with information regarding general patterns of parent–child and other family interactions during meals can be valuable to informing treatment planning and identifying initial goals for intervention (Brosnan & Healy, 2011; Ellingson, Miltenberger, Stricker, Galensky, & Garlinghouse, 2000).

Clinicians should consider the strengths, weaknesses, and availability of measures used to assess feeding problems in children with ASD. Compared with interviews and questionnaires, direct assessments are more time consuming but are considered the gold standard assessment method by some (e.g., Piazza et al., 2003) because they provide objective and quantitative data regarding acceptance or rejection of foods. However, there are drawbacks to the direct assessment method. In addition to the time required to conduct formal meal observations, introducing an observer at a meal may alter a child's response to the presentation of food and, thus, not provide an accurate depiction of a "typical meal" during the initial assessment process. With this in mind, formal data collection during intervention represents a valuable tool for clinicians to track progress, particularly when caregivers are conducting meals in the home setting. Data collection also is a critical step in evaluating successful implementation of a feeding intervention. Caregivers should take data on both appropriate (e.g., accepting and swallowing bites) and inappropriate (e.g., pushing spoon away, crying) mealtime behaviors. Frequent and consistent data collection allow caregivers and clinicians to closely monitor a child's response to treatment and guide decisions regarding the introduction of new feeding demands. Awareness of the advantages and disadvantages of each assessment method can assist in assessment decisions, including determination of other disciplines that should be involved in the child's clinical evaluation.

The clinical interview can provide guidance in identifying assessments and disciplines needed for further evaluation of the feeding problem. For example, if the reported concern obtained through the interview is limited dietary intake of a wide range of food textures, assessment should include evaluation from a behavioral clinician (psychologist, behavior analyst) and dietitian. The involvement of the dietitian should focus on potential nutritional gaps in a child's diet associated with food selectivity that should be targeted during intervention. The clinician should consider the use of self-report measures, such as the BAMBI (Lukens & Linscheid, 2008), and a meal observation to provide insight into the factors affecting feeding behavior. The dietitian likely would need to assess the child's nutritional intake through the use of a food diary or dietary recall. However, if a child is only eating naturally smooth or pureed foods and/or having difficulty advancing to higher texture requiring chewing, the assessment team should expand to include an SLP or OT, who likely would need to be involved in the assessment. The SLP or OT would need to evaluate the child's oral-motor abilities to determine if the child has the oral-motor skills in place necessary to consume higher textured foods (e.g., chopped or natural texture). The timing and role of each provider may be determined by the nature and severity of the presenting problem—keeping in mind that a multidisciplinary team involving medical, behavioral, oral-motor, and nutritional evaluation is recommended among patients with more complex feeding concerns.

SPECIFIC PARENT TRAINING STRATEGIES

Behaviorally based intervention is the most researched and well-supported treatment for chronic feeding issues, including treatment of food selectivity in ASD (Ledford & Gast, 2006). Among past reports, there is variability in the ways parents are involved in the treatment process. Feeding interventions typically have involved trained clinicians who provide direct intervention before generalizing individualized behavioral treatments to parents (Laud et al., 2009; Sharp et al., 2011). A growing body of research, however, has suggested that PT can be used to address feeding problems in children with ASD, with parents serving as the primary interventionists at the onset of intervention (Cosbey & Muldoon, 2016; Johnson et al., 2015; Sharp, Burrell, et al., 2013; see Table 7.4 for an overview of these programs). These three structured treatment programs

TABLE 7.4

Comparison of Parent Training Programs to Expand Dietary
Diversity in Children With ASD

Treatment detail	Autism MEAL plan	PT-F	EAT-UP
Delivery format	Group-based	Individual sessions	Individual sessions
Session location	Clinic	Clinic	Home
Child involvement in sessions	No	No	Yes
Manual-based curriculum	Yes	Yes	No[a]
Fixed duration (length)	Yes (8 sessions)	Yes (9 sessions)	No (9–21 sessions)

Note. ASD = autism spectrum disorder; Autism MEAL Plan = Autism Manage Eating Aversions and Low Intake Plan; PT-F = Parent Training for Feeding Problems in ASD; EAT-UP = Easing Anxiety Together With Understanding and Perseverance.
[a]The authors note shared components across families but do not describe use of a treatment manual to guide intervention.

share common goals: to expand dietary diversity and decrease challenging behaviors during meals. Sharp, Burrell, et al. (2013) developed a structured, eight-session program called the Autism Manage Eating Aversions and Low Intake (MEAL) Plan, and Johnson et al. (2015) developed a nine-session curriculum called the Parent Training for Feeding Problems in ASD (PT-F) program. Cosbey and Muldoon (2016) developed the Easing Anxiety Together With Understanding and Perseverance (EAT-UP) program that involves a tailored time line (range: 9–21 sessions), depending on progression through the treatment hierarchy. Although there are noticeable differences in the delivery of program content (see Table 7.4 for a summary), all three share core components across programs: (a) considering nutritional counseling and dietary variety; (b) implementing antecedent-based manipulations, such as structured meals and use of visual supports; (c) enhancing communication, commands, and prompting during meals; and (d) teaching consequence-based strategies to manage problem behaviors in the meal.

Nutritional Counseling and Dietary Considerations

Treatment of food selectivity in ASD involves expanding dietary diversity and increasing flexibility with feeding demands, which necessitates intentional selection of target foods for intervention. The *Dietary Guidelines for Americans, 2010* (U.S. Department of Agriculture & U.S. Department of Health and Human Services, 2010) provides general guidance for ensuring ideal dietary intake; it emphasizes the importance of consuming a variety of foods across all food groups. With this in mind, nutrition counseling during

PT focuses on identifying frequently rejected food types and/or groups that may represent gaps or concerns for growth and development. A review of a child's current pattern of intake—supported through the use of a diet record—can help guide caregivers in selecting target foods (Johnson et al., 2015). The Autism MEAL Plan (Sharp, Burrell, et al., 2013) includes activities to help families identify nutritional gaps (e.g., fruits, vegetables) in the child's diet to emphasize the importance of dietary diversity and to encourage presentation of fewer highly-processed foods. PT also may involve collaboration with a dietitian, as implemented by Cosbey and Muldoon (2016), to determine if current dietary patterns place a child at risk for micronutrient and macronutrient deficiencies—a particularly salient concern in cases involving extreme food selectivity (e.g., rejecting one of more food groups). Guidance for monitoring and interpreting a child's anthropometric parameters (i.e., height, weight, body-mass index [BMI]) can help with intervention planning and the establishment of treatment goals, including identifying whether the primary feeding concern involves restriction in the volume versus variety of food consumed during meals. Reviewing growth charts and established standards—including underweight (BMI-for-age, < 5th percentile), normal weight (BMI-for-age, 5th–84th percentile), overweight (BMI-for-age, 85th–94th percentile), or obese (BMI-for-age > 95th percentile)—will allow caregivers to identify where a child falls within these categories (Kuczmarski et al., 2002). Food selectivity usually does not coincide with compromised growth in children with ASD (Sharp, Berry, et al., 2013); however, obesity is a prominent concern.

Antecedent Manipulations

Antecedents, or the events that precede a behavior, are common components in most behavioral feeding interventions (Sharp et al., 2010). Increased reliance on antecedent manipulations when targeting food selectivity in ASD has been emphasized in the treatment literature due to the unique cognitive and behavioral profile often observed in this population (e.g., resistance to change, heightened sensory defensiveness; Sharp et al., 2011; Sharp, Burrell, et al., 2013). Antecedent management strategies may include modifying the mealtime routine and structure (e.g., establishing a regular meal schedule, reducing grazing), bite demand (i.e., bite size, texture, type), and feeder format (i.e., self- or non–self-feeder); allowing the child to make choices (i.e., cherry or strawberry yogurt); and/or using visual and auditory cues (e.g., timers, visual rules). The use of these strategies is particularly salient in PT. Antecedent manipulations provide structure while concurrently providing a means to reduce feeding demands so that a child is more likely to be successful during meals and caregivers are more likely to persist with intervention.

Mealtime Routine and Structure

A foundational aspect of PT for food selectivity in ASD involves revising the daily schedule and establishing a regular mealtime routine. Establishing a regular routine in which food is available only at certain times and at the same location (i.e., the dinner table) provides clarity of the behavioral expectations during meals. Increasing the structure surrounding meals also should eliminate a child's free access to food between meals and reduce grazing, which may influence hunger and hinder consumption during regularly scheduled meals. One method used to standardize the mealtime routine is a visual schedule that indicates when mealtimes will occur and what foods will be presented within each meal (Cosbey & Muldoon, 2016; Johnson et al., 2015). Additionally, caregivers can use timers to indicate mealtime duration, time to next meal, and time between bites within a meal. Mealtime structure also refers to using appropriate seating (e.g., high chair, booster seat), modifying the physical environment to minimize distractions, implementing a consistent pace in the meal, and assuring that caregivers remain present at the table and actively involved in the intervention process. Each of these methods helps promote predictability and establish behavioral expectations. Furthermore, the structure of the meal should include a regular cadence, with breaks between bites (e.g., 30 seconds) to allow adequate time to chew and swallow (Sharp et al., 2010). Breaks also briefly remove the feeding demand while providing the opportunity for high-quality interactions between the child and parent.

Antecedent Strategies to Introduce Foods

Antecedent strategies include reducing the bite volume/portion size of nonpreferred food presented during meals. Research has suggested larger bite volumes increase response effort during meals, thus resulting in lower rates of acceptance and increased problem behaviors among children with feeding difficulties (Kerwin, Ahearn, Eicher, & Burd, 1995). A simple modification, such as reducing the bite volume (e.g., the size of a green pea or kernel of corn) of new or nonpreferred foods, may improve a child's response to an intervention and decrease the likelihood of food refusal. With this in mind, treatment planning, at a minimum, should assess whether age-appropriate portions and/or larger bites may overwhelm a child with food selectivity and ASD, thus decreasing the likelihood that a meal will end on a positive note. Similarly, it is important to consider the duration of the meal, including the number or bites and/or the length of the meal. In general, shorter meal durations are recommended at the onset of intervention, with target food presented for a predetermined length (e.g., five bites or 5 minutes—whichever comes first) or demand level (e.g., touching the food item one time to the lips).

Antecedent strategies for introducing food also refer to the variety of nonpreferred foods presented during meals and the order that new foods are introduced. Responses to presentation of nonpreferred foods may range from mild to severe (Sharp, Jaquess, et al., 2013). Some children with ASD may not tolerate the sight or smell of nonpreferred foods, whereas others may be willing to touch and even take a small bite. Assisting caregivers with identifying the first few food items to target during intervention is critical to gaining momentum for expanding the diet. Intervention may involve either initially targeting a previously consumed or dropped food or first working on foods that are similar to those that the child already consumes. For example, many children with ASD and food selectivity consume foods similar in taste (e.g., primarily starches) and texture (e.g., crunchy snack foods). Expanding variety within a food group may permit a parent to subsequently build on this early success and gradually introduce new sensory experiences during the meal (e.g., tastes, textures). The involvement of preferred foods also should be considered. Interspersing bites of less preferred food with bites of preferred food may increase the likelihood of compliance and decrease the aversive quality of the meal. Presenting a lower ratio of high demand/low probability items (i.e., nonpreferred foods) compared with low demand/high probability (i.e., preferred foods) within the meal, such as 80% preferred to 20% non-preferred bites, can increase bite acceptance. Over time, this ratio can be shifted as the child acclimates and becomes accustomed to the new food item. This design also may produce behavioral momentum, thus increasing the likelihood that the child will accept bites of nonpreferred foods if preceded by consumption of preferred foods (Patel et al., 2006).

Stimulus fading procedures often guide advancement in mealtime demands, including increasing the bite volume, meal duration, and variety of foods presenting during a meal (Sharp et al., 2011). When designing an intervention, it is important to determine the appropriate entry point for introducing new foods—which can be outlined using a feeding demand hierarchy. In doing so, the overall goal is to identify a demand with the highest likelihood of success—that is, the child's making contact with new food and the parent's following through with the mealtime demand. Steps may include beginning with a single rice-sized bite of nonpreferred food interspersed with bites of highly preferred foods. Subsequent steps may involve increasing the number of bites of the target food, increasing the bite volume, or adding a second nonpreferred food. For example, EAT-UP involves a visual hierarchy aimed at gradually increasing tolerance of less preferred foods, which also includes steps before consumption of food (e.g., tolerates on plate, touches with hand, spits out bite). Progression in the hierarchy should be guided by decision rules informed by formalized data collected on the child's behavior during meals. A terminal goal for expanding dietary diversity would involve a child's consuming a variety of foods at age-appropriate portions (e.g., one quarter cup of corn with dinner). To increase success with achieving this goal, antecedent management strategies should combine clear commands and consequence-based strategies to address disruptive behavior and promote contact with new foods.

Enhancement of Communication, Commands, and Prompting

Teaching parents strategies for improving communication, such as guidelines for effective commands and parental requests, frequently are incorporated into well-established PT curricula that target disruptive behavior and noncompliance in children without ASD (Baker, 2008; Kazdin, 2005; McNeil & Hembree-Kigin, 2011) and with ASD (Bearss et al., 2015). It is not surprising, therefore, that PT targeting food selectivity in ASD incorporates these same strategies, with adaptations for use during meals. General PT guidelines for effective commands involve ensuring that commands are direct, specific, and positively stated while concurrently avoiding questions, vague requests, and/or excessive prompting or coaxing. In the context of a meal, examples of commands include "take a bite," "sit in your chair," and "pick up your spoon." Commands given during meals should be reasonable for the child to complete. In the case of food selectivity in ASD, feeding commands may involve initially targeting exploration, increasing tolerance, or taking a small bite of a new or nonpreferred food items versus consuming age appropriate portions.

Consequence-Based Strategies to Modify Feeding Problems

A *consequence*, or what follows a behavior, helps shape and maintain behaviors (Carr & Wilder, 2003). The results of research studies that have evaluated the reason children engage in disruptive behavior during meals have suggested that consequences that increase appropriate behavior and eliminate escape from mealtime demands represent important treatment elements (Levin & Carr, 2001; Najdowski et al., 2003). Positive and negative reinforcement procedures (e.g., providing access to a preferred item or activity and/or removing an aversive stimulus) commonly are included in behavioral treatment packages to increase exploration, acceptance, and swallowing of novel foods (Ledford & Gast, 2006; Sharp et al., 2011; Williams, Field, & Seiverling, 2010). Consequence-based procedures also may include removing attention (i.e., ignoring) and persisting with feeding demands, despite the occurrence of problem behavior during meals.

To increase appropriate mealtime behavior, intervention planning must first identify items that a child is motivated to earn, that is, potential reinforcers. This process can be facilitated through the use of a structured preference assessment, observation, or parent ranking (Williams et al.,

2010). All three PT programs involve positive reinforcement either in the form of social attention by parents (e.g., specific praise) or access to preferred items following completion of the desired behavior (e.g., swallowing bite of nonpreferred food; Cosbey & Muldoon, 2016; Johnson et al., 2015; Sharp, Burrell, et al., 2013). To ensure that the child has the opportunity to contact reinforcement contingencies; intervention also should involve some level of persistence or method for placing refusal behaviors on extinction. Persistence may include keeping the spoon at the child's lips until acceptance occurs, a procedure referred to as "nonremoval of the spoon" (Sharp, Burrell, et al., 2013); guided compliance (Johnson et al., 2015); and follow-through with stated expectations (Cosbey & Muldoon, 2016). Past reports also have included the use of a "nonremoval of the plate," a procedure that involves ignoring disruptive behavior, redirecting a child back to the table in response to leaving, and continuing the presentation of food on a plate for a prespecified amount of time (Sharp et al., 2010).

The Autism MEAL Plan, PT-F, and EAT-UP each incorporate strategies to address noncompliance (e.g., refusal to complete mealtime demands) to promote contingency contacting and/or promotion of new skill acquisition. The Autism MEAL Plan includes a four-step prompting procedure to encourage self-feeding, which involves a parent's proceeding through a series of increasingly supportive prompts. These prompts include a visual presentation of the food (e.g., placing the food in front of the child), verbal instruction (e.g., "take a bite"), modeling the behavior using a separate utensil combined with verbal instruction, and physical, hand-over-hand guidance to complete the bite. The Autism MEAL Plan and PT-F also include the use of chaining procedures as a means to promote self-feeding by which the child is systematically taught and reinforced for mastering individual steps in the behavior chain. EAT-UP describes the use of a two-verbal prompt limit before assisting the child to complete the step to meet the hierarchy target and promote exposure to food. PT-F uses a number of strategies that include high-probability request sequencing and guided compliance to address noncompliance. These strategies can be challenging for parents and should be considered when planning intervention. Given that some level of problem behavior can be anticipated when introducing new foods, the application of these procedures should be approached with caution and usually after a parent has been trained successfully in antecedent-based approaches.

SPECIAL CONSIDERATIONS

Several variables warrant consideration when designing PT for feeding problems in children with ASD. First, treatment should be viewed as a dynamic process involving multicomponent packages to provide comprehensive treatment. The three PT programs described in this chapter recognize the importance of a multimethod approach and do not involve implementing strategies in isolation (Cosbey & Muldoon, 2016; Johnson et al., 2015; Sharp, Burrell, et al., 2013). Second, assessment and treatment of food selectivity in children with ASD often necessitate a multidisciplinary approach to care (Sharp et al., 2010). At a minimum, children involved in PT should be followed by a primary care physician, and the therapist should review potential organic factors (e.g., reflux) associated with feeding disorders in other pediatric populations before beginning intervention. Additional referrals to supporting disciplines, such as nutrition, SLP, OT, and gastroenterology also may be warranted depending on the child's presenting problem (e.g., omission of complete food groups) and possible etiology (e.g., constipation, oral-motor deficits) of the feeding problem. Treatment of children with ASD and feeding problems should be individualized to meet the goals of the child and the family. Parents of children with ASD often experience high levels of stress associated with comorbid medical and behavioral challenges commonly found with children with ASD (Lecavalier, Leone, & Wiltz, 2006). Thus, designing an intervention that limits the demands on the caregivers and is consistent with their family routines and beliefs is an important part in developing a successful intervention.

CASE EXAMPLE

Diego[1] is a 6-and-a-half-year-old child who meets diagnostic criteria for ASD. He lives at home with his parents and older sister. Diego had obtained an IQ score of 88 on a standardized intelligence test with nonverbal skills in the average range and verbal skills in the low average range. Diego's parents report concerns about their son's eating habits—due to his limited dietary variety—over a period of at least 3 years. At the time of the evaluation, Diego's diet predominately consisted of crunchy foods, such as pretzels, potato chips, and animal crackers. He drank one brand of a fortified chocolate drink and a strawberry yogurt smoothie. Caregivers allowed Diego to graze on foods throughout the day to ensure he received enough calories. Diego's mother prepared his lunch for school each day because he refused foods presented in that setting. Although his parents prepared an evening meal, Diego briefly came to the table but did not consume any foods. When nonpreferred foods were presented to Diego at home, he turned away from the feeding demand but otherwise was not disruptive. Due to these feeding concerns and lack of progress with prior occupational therapy that targeted feeding, caregivers

---

[1]Clinical material has been disguised to protect client confidentiality.

sought behavioral feeding treatment. Caregivers reported that they did not persist with feeding demands due to the concern that Diego would drop or stop accepting all foods. Although his weight was in the normal range and he was growing appropriately, Diego's parents indicated significant concern about his nutrition. At the beginning of PT, his parents jointly completed the BAMBI (Lukens & Linscheid, 2008). A score of 55 was obtained, which suggests significant feeding/mealtime behavioral concerns.

Before intervention, a 3-day diet record was obtained to evaluate Diego's daily intake. A dietitian reviewed this information to determine if Diego's nutritional needs were being met. Once it was determined that Diego did not have nutritional deficiencies, likely due to the fortified drink he consumed, the PT therapist worked with the caregivers to increase the overall structure and limit grazing to manipulate hunger and increase motivation to try new foods. A visual schedule was made to support the change in Diego's routine, which provided a visual cue regarding when food would be available and specified the behavioral expectation that he remain seated at the table during meals. Parents then were instructed to identify Diego's preferred items and activities that could be used to increase appropriate mealtime behavior. Reinforcers included iPad apps, iTunes cards, money, and small toy bugs. A reinforcement plan was developed specifically to increase Diego's acceptance of yogurt. He participated in the treatment by selecting the type of yogurts he would eat to earn access to an iPad app. This strategy was successful in expanding Diego's acceptance of a number of different favors and brands of yogurts. Following success with expanding Diego's diet to include yogurt, the family identified acceptance of fruits as the next treatment goal. Applesauce was chosen due to its similar texture to the newly accepted food, yogurt. A highly preferred activity (i.e., purchasing and using new applications on his tablet) was used to increase acceptance of applesauce, and consumption of yogurt was reinforced by social attention (e.g., "great job eating your yogurt!"). Slowly, the parents were instructed to fade in higher texture apples by placing small pieces of apple chunks into the applesauce until Diego eventually was consuming slices of apples without the applesauce. With the success of introducing yogurt, applesauce, and apple slices, his parents identified green beans as the next target food because Diego did not consume any vegetables and green beans were a commonly served vegetable in the home. The parents expressed concern that vegetables would be more challenging for Diego; therefore, the demand hierarchy began with a green bean being placed on Diego's plate, without prompting or requiring consumption. Once Diego tolerated the green bean on his plate, the demand hierarchy increased to include smelling it, kissing it, licking it, and then eventually accepting a bite. Diego's parents were taught how to use escape extinction (see Chapter 9 for a more detailed description of escape). This approach was used to increase his consumption of cheese, a food Diego occasionally would request and consume. His parents placed cheese on his plate and used a timer to indicate the time Diego had to complete the feeding demand to earn extra playtime with his father. If he did not consume the cheese before the time elapsed, he still was required to sit until he ate the cheese. The parents were taught how to systematically ignore any inappropriate mealtime behavior (e.g., saying "no," pushing the plate away). The combination of antecedent management and consequence-based strategies (e.g., reinforcement, planned ignoring, escape extinction) were successful in expanding the variety of foods Diego consumed. Although Diego's diet still was limited, his parents were much less concerned about his nutrition now that he was consuming at least one food item from each food group. His parents also expressed that they had learned strategies that would permit the family to continue to expand Diego's dietary variety.

REFERENCES

Ahearn, W. H., Castine, T., Nault, K., & Green, G. (2001). An assessment of food acceptance in children with autism or pervasive developmental disorder-not otherwise specified. *Journal of Autism and Developmental Disorders, 31*, 505–511. http://dx.doi.org/10.1023/A:1012221026124

American Psychiatric Association. (2013). *Diagnostic and statistical manual of mental disorders* (5th ed.). Arlington, VA: Author.

Archer, L. A., Rosenbaum, P. L., & Streiner, D. L. (1991). The Children's Eating Behavior Inventory: Reliability and validity results. *Journal of Pediatric Psychology, 16*, 629–642. http://dx.doi.org/10.1093/jpepsy/16.5.629

Ausderau, K., & Juarez, M. (2013). The impact of autism spectrum disorders and eating challenges on family mealtimes. *ICAN: Infant, Child, & Adolescent Nutrition, 5*, 315–323. http://dx.doi.org/10.1177/1941406413502808

Baker, J. (2008). *No more meltdowns: Positive strategies for managing and preventing out-of-control behaviors*. Arlington, TX: Future Horizons.

Bandini, L. G., Anderson, S. E., Curtin, C., Cermak, S., Evans, E. W., Scampini, R., . . . Must, A. (2010). Food selectivity in children with autism spectrum disorders and typically developing children. *Journal of Pediatrics, 157*, 259–264. http://dx.doi.org/10.1016/j.jpeds.2010.02.013

Bearss, K., Johnson, C., Smith, T., Lecavalier, L., Swiezy, N., Aman, M., . . . Scahill, L. (2015). Effect of parent training vs parent education on behavioral problems in children with autism spectrum disorder: A randomized clinical trial. *JAMA, 313*, 1524–1533. http://dx.doi.org/10.1001/jama.2015.3150

Brosnan, J., & Healy, O. (2011). A review of behavioral interventions for the treatment of aggression in individuals with developmental disabilities.

Research in Developmental Disabilities, 32, 437–446. http://dx.doi.org/10.1016/j.ridd.2010.12.023

Brown, J., Kim, C., Lim, A., Brown, S., Desai, H., Volker, L., & Katz, M. (2014). Successful gastrostomy tube weaning program using an intensive multidisciplinary team approach. *Journal of Pediatric Gastroenterology and Nutrition, 58,* 743–749.

Buie, T., Campbell, D. B., Fuchs, G. J. I. I. I., III, Furuta, G. T., Levy, J., Vandewater, J., . . . Winter, H. (2010). Evaluation, diagnosis, and treatment of gastrointestinal disorders in individuals with ASDs: A consensus report. *Pediatrics, 125* (Suppl. 1), S1–S18. http://dx.doi.org/10.1542/peds.2009-1878C

Cardona Cano, S., Tiemeier, H., Van Hoeken, D., Tharner, A., Jaddoe, V. W., Hofman, A., . . . Hoek, H. W. (2015). Trajectories of picky eating during childhood: A general population study. *International Journal of Eating Disorders, 48,* 570–579. http://dx.doi.org/10.1002/eat.22384

Carr, J. E., & Wilder, D. A. (2003). *Functional assessment and intervention: A guide to understanding problem behavior* (2nd ed.). Homewood, IL: High Tide Press.

Carruth, B. R., Ziegler, P. J., Gordon, A., & Barr, S. I. (2004). Prevalence of picky eaters among infants and toddlers and their caregivers' decisions about offering a new food. *Journal of the American Dietetic Association, 104*(Suppl. 1), s57–s64. http://dx.doi.org/10.1016/j.jada.2003.10.024

Cermak, S. A., Curtin, C., & Bandini, L. G. (2010). Food selectivity and sensory sensitivity in children with autism spectrum disorders. *Journal of the American Dietetic Association, 110,* 238–246. http://dx.doi.org/10.1016/j.jada.2009.10.032

Clark, J. H., Rhoden, D. K., & Turner, D. S. (1993). Symptomatic vitamin A and D deficiencies in an eight-year-old with autism. *Journal of Parenteral and Enteral Nutrition, 17,* 284–286. http://dx.doi.org/10.1177/0148607193017003284

Collins, M. R., Kyle, R., Smith, S., Laverty, A., Roberts, S., & Eaton-Evans, J. (2003). Coping with the usual family diet: Eating behavior and food choices of children with Down's syndrome, autistic spectrum disorders or Cri du Chat syndrome and comparison groups of siblings. *Journal of Learning Disabilities, 7,* 137–155. http://dx.doi.org/10.1177/1469004703007002004

Cosbey, J., & Muldoon, D. (2016). EAT-UP™ family-centered feeding intervention to promote food acceptance and decrease challenging behaviors: A single-case experimental design replicated across three families of children with autism spectrum disorder. *Journal of Autism and Developmental Disorders, 47,* 564–578. http://dx.doi.org/10.1007/s10803-016-2977-0

Crist, W., & Napier-Phillips, A. (2001). Mealtime behaviors of young children: A comparison of normative and clinical data. *Journal of Developmental and Behavioral Pediatrics, 22,* 279–286. http://dx.doi.org/10.1097/00004703-200110000-00001

Curtin, C., Hubbard, K., Anderson, S. E., Mick, E., Must, A., & Bandini, L. G. (2015). Food selectivity, mealtime behavior problems, spousal stress, and family food choices in children with and without autism spectrum disorder. *Journal of Autism and Developmental Disorders, 45,* 3308–3315. http://dx.doi.org/10.1007/s10803-015-2490-x

DeMand, A., Johnson, C., & Foldes, E. (2015). Psychometric properties of the brief autism mealtime behaviors inventory. *Journal of Autism and Developmental Disorders, 45*, 2667–2673. http://dx.doi.org/10.1007/s10803-015-2435-4

de Vinck-Baroody, O., Shui, A., Macklin, E. A., Hyman, S. L., Leventhal, J. M., & Weitzman, C. (2015). Overweight and obesity in a sample of children with autism spectrum disorder. *Academic Pediatrics, 15*, 396–404. http://dx.doi.org/10.1016/j.acap.2015.03.008

Dominick, K. C., David, N. O., Lainhart, J., Tager-Flusberg, H., & Folstein, S. (2007). Atypical behaviors in children with autism and children with a history of language impairment. *Research in Developmental Disabilities, 28*, 145–162. http://dx.doi.org/10.1016/j.ridd.2006.02.003

Dovey, T. M., Staples, P. A., Gibson, E. L., & Halford, J. C. (2008). Food neophobia and "picky/fussy" eating in children: A review. *Appetite, 50*, 181–193. http://dx.doi.org/10.1016/j.appet.2007.09.009

Ellingson, S. A., Miltenberger, R. G., Stricker, J., Galensky, T. L., & Garlinghouse, M. (2000). Functional assessment and intervention for challenging behaviors in the classroom by general classroom teachers. *Journal of Positive Behavior Interventions, 2*, 85–97. http://dx.doi.org/10.1177/109830070000200202

Emond, A., Emmett, P., Steer, C., & Golding, J. (2010). Feeding symptoms, dietary patterns, and growth in young children with autism spectrum disorders. *Pediatrics, 126*, 337–342. http://dx.doi.org/10.1542/peds.2009-2391

Fulkerson, J. A., Story, M., Neumark-Sztainer, D., & Rydell, S. (2008). Family meals: Perceptions of benefits and challenges among parents of 8- to 10-year-old children. *Journal of the American Dietetic Association, 108*, 706–709. http://dx.doi.org/10.1016/j.jada.2008.01.005

Hediger, M. L., England, L. J., Molloy, C. A., Yu, K. F., Manning-Courtney, P., & Mills, J. L. (2008). Reduced bone cortical thickness in boys with autism or autism spectrum disorder. *Journal of Autism and Developmental Disorders, 38*, 848–856. http://dx.doi.org/10.1007/s10803-007-0453-6

Hill, A. P., Zuckerman, K. E., & Fombonne, E. (2015). Obesity and autism. *Pediatrics, 136*, 1051–1061. http://dx.doi.org/10.1542/peds.2015-1437

Iwata, B., & Worsdell, A. S. (2005). Implications of functional analysis methodology for the design of intervention programs. *Exceptionality, 13*, 25–34. http://dx.doi.org/10.1207/s15327035ex1301_4

Johnson, C. R., Foldes, E., DeMand, A., & Brooks, M. M. (2015). Behavioral parent training to address feeding problems in children with autism spectrum disorder: A pilot trial. *Journal of Developmental and Physical Disabilities, 27*, 591–607. http://dx.doi.org/10.1007/s10882-015-9437-1

Johnson, C. R., Turner, K., Stewart, P. A., Schmidt, B., Shui, A., Macklin, E., . . . Hyman, S. L. (2014). Relationships between feeding problems, behavioral characteristics and nutritional quality in children with ASD. *Journal of Autism and Developmental Disorders, 44*, 2175–2184. http://dx.doi.org/10.1007/s10803-014-2095-9

Kazdin, A. E. (2005). Child, parent, and family-based treatment of aggressive and antisocial child behavior. In E. Hibbs & P. Jensen (Eds.), *Psychosocial treatments for child and adolescent disorders* (2nd ed., pp. 445–476). Washington, DC: American Psychological Association.

Kerwin, M. E., Ahearn, W. H., Eicher, P. S., & Burd, D. M. (1995). The costs of eating: A behavioral economic analysis of food refusal. *Journal of Applied Behavior Analysis, 28,* 245–260. http://dx.doi.org/10.1901/jaba.1995.28-245

Khanna, R., Madhavan, S. S., Smith, M. J., Patrick, J. H., Tworek, C., & Becker-Cottrill, B. (2011). Assessment of health-related quality of life among primary caregivers of children with autism spectrum disorders. *Journal of Autism and Developmental Disorders, 41,* 1214–1227. http://dx.doi.org/10.1007/s10803-010-1140-6

Kuczmarski, R. J., Ogden, C. L., Guo, S. S., Grummer-Strawn, L. M., Flegal, K. M., Mei, Z., . . . Johnson, C. L. (2002). 2000 CDC growth charts for the United States: Methods and development. *Vital and Health Statistics: Series 11, Data from the National Health Survey* (pp. 1–190).

Kuschner, E. S., Eisenberg, I. W., Orionzi, B., Simmons, W. K., Kenworthy, L., Martin, A., & Wallace, G. L. (2015). A preliminary study of self-reported food selectivity in adolescents and young adults with autism spectrum disorder. *Research in Autism Spectrum Disorders, 15–16,* 53–59. http://dx.doi.org/10.1016/j.rasd.2015.04.005

Laud, R. B., Girolami, P. A., Boscoe, J. H., & Gulotta, C. S. (2009). Treatment outcomes for severe feeding problems in children with autism spectrum disorder. *Behavior Modification, 33,* 520–536. http://dx.doi.org/10.1177/0145445509346729

Lecavalier, L., Leone, S., & Wiltz, J. (2006). The impact of behaviour problems on caregiver stress in young people with autism spectrum disorders. *Journal of Intellectual Disability Research, 50,* 172–183. http://dx.doi.org/10.1111/j.1365-2788.2005.00732.x

Ledford, J. R., & Gast, D. L. (2006). Feeding problems in children with autism spectrum disorders: A review. *Focus on Autism and Other Developmental Disabilities, 21,* 153–166. http://dx.doi.org/10.1177/10883576060210030401

Levin, L., & Carr, E. G. (2001). Food selectivity and problem behavior in children with developmental disabilities: Analysis and intervention. *Behavior Modification, 25,* 443–470. http://dx.doi.org/10.1177/0145445501253004

Lockner, D. W., Crowe, T. K., & Skipper, B. J. (2008). Dietary intake and parents' perception of mealtime behaviors in preschool-age children with autism spectrum disorder and in typically developing children. *Journal of the American Dietetic Association, 108,* 1360–1363. http://dx.doi.org/10.1016/j.jada.2008.05.003

Lukens, C. T., & Linscheid, T. R. (2008). Development and validation of an inventory to assess mealtime behavior problems in children with autism. *Journal of Autism and Developmental Disorders, 38,* 342–352. http://dx.doi.org/10.1007/s10803-007-0401-5

Lukens, C. T., & Silverman, A. H. (2014). Systematic review of psychological interventions for pediatric feeding problems. *Journal of Pediatric Psychology, 39,* 903–917. http://dx.doi.org/10.1093/jpepsy/jsu040

Ma, N. S., Thompson, C., & Weston, S. (2016). Brief report: Scurvy as a manifestation of food selectivity in children with autism. *Journal of Autism and Developmental Disorders, 46,* 1464–1470. http://dx.doi.org/10.1007/s10803-015-2660-x

Marquenie, K., Rodger, S., Mangohig, K., & Cronin, A. (2011). Dinnertime and bedtime routines and rituals in families with a young child with an autism spectrum disorder. *Australian Occupational Therapy Journal, 58,* 145–154. http://dx.doi.org/10.1111/j.1440-1630.2010.00896.x

Matson, J. L., Fodstad, J. C., & Dempsey, T. (2009). The relationship of children's feeding problems to core symptoms of autism and PDD-NOS. *Research in Autism Spectrum Disorders, 3,* 759–766. http://dx.doi.org/10.1016/j.rasd.2009.02.005

Matson, J. L., & Kuhn, D. E. (2001). Identifying feeding problems in mentally retarded persons: Development and reliability of the screening tool of feeding problems (STEP). *Research in Developmental Disabilities, 22,* 165–172. http://dx.doi.org/10.1016/S0891-4222(01)00065-8

Mayes, L., & Volkmar, F. (1993). Nosology of eating and growth disorders in early childhood. *Child and Adolescent Psychiatric Clinics of North America, 2,* 15–25.

McElhanon, B. O., McCracken, C., Karpen, S., & Sharp, W. G. (2014). Gastrointestinal symptoms in autism spectrum disorder: A meta-analysis. *Pediatrics, 133,* 872–883. http://dx.doi.org/10.1542/peds.2013-3995

McNeil, C. B., & Hembree-Kigin, T. L. (2011). *Parent–child interaction therapy* (2nd ed.). New York, NY: Springer.

Nadon, G., Feldman, D. E., Dunn, W., & Gisel, E. (2011). Mealtime problems in children with autism spectrum disorder and their typically developing siblings: A comparison study. *Autism, 15,* 98–113. http://dx.doi.org/10.1177/1362361309348943

Najdowski, A. C., Wallace, M. D., Doney, J. K., & Ghezzi, P. M. (2003). Parental assessment and treatment of food selectivity in natural settings. *Journal of Applied Behavior Analysis, 36,* 383–386. http://dx.doi.org/10.1901/jaba.2003.36-383

Patel, M. R., Reed, G. K., Piazza, C. C., Bachmeyer, M. H., Layer, S. A., & Pabico, R. S. (2006). An evaluation of a high-probability instructional sequence to increase acceptance of food and decrease inappropriate behavior in children with pediatric feeding disorders. *Research in Developmental Disabilities, 27,* 430–442. http://dx.doi.org/10.1016/j.ridd.2005.05.005

Piazza, C. C. (2008). Feeding disorders and behavior: What have we learned? *Developmental Disabilities Research Reviews, 14,* 174–181. http://dx.doi.org/10.1002/ddrr.22

Piazza, C. C., Fisher, W. W., Brown, K. A., Shore, B. A., Patel, M. R., Katz, R. M., . . . Blakely-Smith, A. (2003). Functional analysis of inappropriate mealtime behaviors. *Journal of Applied Behavior Analysis, 36,* 187–204. http://dx.doi.org/10.1901/jaba.2003.36-187

Provost, B., Crowe, T. K., Osbourn, P. L., McClain, C., & Skipper, B. J. (2010). Mealtime behaviors of preschool children: Comparison of children with autism spectrum disorder and children with typical development. *Physical & Occupational Therapy in Pediatrics, 30*, 220–233. http://dx.doi.org/10.3109/01942631003757669

Raiten, D. J., & Massaro, T. (1986). Perspectives on the nutritional ecology of autistic children. *Journal of Autism and Developmental Disorders, 16*, 133–143. http://dx.doi.org/10.1007/BF01531725

Reese, R. M., Richman, D. M., Belmont, J. M., & Morse, P. (2005). Functional characteristics of disruptive behavior in developmentally disabled children with and without autism. *Journal of Autism and Developmental Disorders, 35*, 419–428. http://dx.doi.org/10.1007/s10803-005-5032-0

Schmitt, L., Heiss, C. J., & Campbell, E. E. (2008). A comparison of nutrient intake and eating behaviors of boys with and without autism. *Topics in Clinical Nutrition, 23*, 23–31. http://dx.doi.org/10.1097/01.TIN.0000312077.45953.6c

Schreck, K. A., Williams, K., & Smith, A. F. (2004). A comparison of eating behaviors between children with and without autism. *Journal of Autism and Developmental Disorders, 34*, 433–438. http://dx.doi.org/10.1023/B:JADD.0000037419.78531.86

Seiverling, L., Williams, K., & Sturmey, P. (2010). Assessment of feeding problems in children with autism spectrum disorder. *Journal of Developmental and Physical Disabilities, 22*, 401–413. http://dx.doi.org/10.1007/s10882-010-9206-0

Sharp, W. G., Berry, R. C., McCracken, C., Nuhu, N. N., Marvel, E., Saulnier, C. A., . . . Jaquess, D. L. (2013). Feeding problems and nutrient intake in children with autism spectrum disorders: A meta-analysis and comprehensive review of the literature. *Journal of Autism and Developmental Disorders, 43*, 2159–2173. http://dx.doi.org/10.1007/s10803-013-1771-5

Sharp, W. G., Berry, R. C., McElhanon, C. O., & Jaquess, D. (2014). Dietary diversity in children with autism. In V. B. Patel, V. R. Preedy, & C. R. Martin (Eds.), *Comprehensive guide to autism* (pp. 2077–2097). New York, NY: Springer. http://dx.doi.org/10.1007/978-1-4614-4788-7_127

Sharp, W. G., Burrell, T. L., & Jaquess, D. L. (2013). The Autism MEAL Plan: A parent-training curriculum to manage eating aversions and low intake among children with autism. *Autism, 18*, 712–722. http://dx.doi.org/10.1177/1362361313489190

Sharp, W. G., Jaquess, D. L., & Lukens, C. T. (2013). Multi-method assessment of feeding problems among children with autism spectrum disorders. *Research in Autism Spectrum Disorders, 7*, 56–65. http://dx.doi.org/10.1016/j.rasd.2012.07.001

Sharp, W. G., Jaquess, D. L., Morton, J. F., & Herzinger, C. V. (2010). Pediatric feeding disorders: A quantitative synthesis of treatment outcomes. *Clinical Child and Family Psychology Review, 13*, 348–365. http://dx.doi.org/10.1007/s10567-010-0079-7

Sharp, W. G., Jaquess, D. L., Morton, J. F., & Miles, A. G. (2011). A retrospective chart review of dietary diversity and feeding behavior of children with autism spectrum disorder before and after admission to a day treatment program. *Focus on Autism and Other Developmental Disabilities, 26,* 37–48. http://dx.doi.org/10.1177/1088357609349245

Silverman, A. H., Kirby, M., Clifford, L. M., Fischer, E., Berlin, K. S., Rudolph, C. D., & Noel, R. J. (2013). Nutritional and psychosocial outcomes of gastrostomy tube-dependent children completing an intensive inpatient behavioral treatment program. *Journal of Pediatric Gastroenterology and Nutrition, 57,* 668–672. http://dx.doi.org/10.1097/MPG.0b013e3182a027a3

Suarez, M. A., Atchison, B. J., & Lagerwey, M. (2014). Phenomenological examination of the mealtime experience for mothers of children with autism and food selectivity. *American Journal of Occupational Therapy, 68,* 102–107. http://dx.doi.org/10.5014/ajot.2014.008748

Suarez, M. A., Nelson, N. W., & Curtis, A. B. (2014). Longitudinal follow-up of factors associated with food selectivity in children with autism spectrum disorders. *Autism, 18,* 924–932. http://dx.doi.org/10.1177/1362361313499457

Tomchek, S. D., & Dunn, W. (2007). Sensory processing in children with and without autism: A comparative study using the short sensory profile. *American Journal of Occupational Therapy, 61,* 190–200. http://dx.doi.org/10.5014/ajot.61.2.190

U.S. Department of Agriculture and U.S. Department of Health and Human Services. (2010, December). *Dietary guidelines for Americans, 2010* (7th ed.). Washington, DC: U.S. Government Printing Office.

Uyanik, O., Dogangun, B., Kayaalp, L., Korkmaz, B., & Dervent, A. (2006). Food faddism causing vision loss in an autistic child. *Child: Care, Health and Development, 32,* 601–602. http://dx.doi.org/10.1111/j.1365-2214.2006.00586.x

Williams, K. E., Field, D. G., & Seiverling, L. (2010). Food refusal in children: A review of the literature. *Research in Developmental Disabilities, 31,* 625–633. http://dx.doi.org/10.1016/j.ridd.2010.01.001

8

PARENT TRAINING FOR TOILETING IN AUTISM SPECTRUM DISORDER

DANIEL W. MRUZEK, BENJAMIN L. HANDEN, COURTNEY A. APONTE, TRISTRAM SMITH, AND RICHARD M. FOXX

Many parents and other caregivers find it difficult to teach their child with autism spectrum disorder (ASD) how to use the toilet for bladder and bowel elimination. It may take weeks and even months of concerted training to establish successful toilet use, and, for some children, success may be partial, short lived, or altogether absent. Comprehensive toilet training requires not only using the toilet when taken to the bathroom by others (i.e., being "habit trained," described later in this chapter), but self-initiation of trips to the toilet and independent completion of related skills, including unfastening and fastening clothing, wiping self with toilet paper, and washing hands. Additional instructional goals include maintenance of toileting skills across time and generalization to novel settings, such as public restrooms. On a positive note, toilet training provides a ready-made "laboratory" for parents to practice several key principles of instruction, including

The authors gratefully acknowledge the assistance of Tanya L. Petti in the development of some of the figures used in this chapter.

http://dx.doi.org/10.1037/0000111-009
Parent Training for Autism Spectrum Disorder: Improving the Quality of Life for Children and Their Families,
C. R. Johnson, E. M. Butter, and L. Scahill (Editors)

consideration of antecedent events, use of positive reinforcement, shaping behavior, prompting and prompt-fading, functional communication training, and data monitoring. Parents can apply each of these principles to a broad range of instructional goals as their child ages.

PREVALENCE AND IMPACT
OF TOILETING PROBLEMS IN ASD

In the general population of children ages 4 to 17 years, the prevalence rate is 10.5% for incontinence (3.3% daytime only, 1.8% daytime and nighttime, and 5.4% nighttime) and 4.4% for encopresis (Loening-Baucke, 2007). In individuals with ASD, *enuresis* (i.e., incontinence of urine) and *encopresis* (i.e., incontinence of feces) are recognized as much more prevalent, although limited epidemiological data are available. In one study of 183 children with ASD, ages 2 to 17 years, approximately 60% had not established daytime urinary continence by 4 years of age (Stanberry-Beal et al., 2014). Although this percentage dropped to about 15% by age 6 years, intellectual disability and lower levels of overall adaptive functioning were associated with enuresis well into the school-age years.

Negative consequences of urine and bowel incontinence include physical discomfort, compromised hygiene, and decreased privacy. Other threats to quality of life include reduced personal autonomy (e.g., depending on others for help with clothing changes or initiation of bathroom trips), rejection and teasing by peers, and reduced opportunities for inclusion (e.g., acceptance into some day care, general education, and employment settings is dependent on being continent). For students, urine accidents necessitate clothing changes during the school day, disrupting schedules and reducing instructional time. Parents, teaching staff, and other caregivers are burdened with tasks associated with the individual's care, including regularly changing wet or soiled clothing, interrupting family activities (e.g., accidents while at stores or restaurants), and paying for costly diapers and pull-ups (Macias, Roberts, Saylor, & Fussell, 2006).

WHY DO CHILDREN WITH ASD
COMMONLY HAVE TOILETING PROBLEMS?

Four overlapping features of ASD may impede toilet training.

Slow Rate of Learning

More than 30% of children with ASD have intellectual disability (Christensen et al., 2016), and many also have expressive and receptive language deficits that interfere with instruction and establishment of expectations. Also, because they are less attuned to social norms as same-aged peers, these children may not respond to the encouragement of adults to use the toilet or may not be embarrassed by bowel or bladder accidents. Fine and gross motor delays also may hinder aspects of toileting routines, such as lowering and raising clothing. Although these are not well understood, some individuals with ASD demonstrate sensory sensitivities that may complicate training, as well (e.g., distress from loud toilet flushes), potentially deterring them from relaxing the muscles required for bowel and bladder elimination (Dalrymple & Ruble, 1992). Some conditions commonly associated with ASD, such as attention-deficit/hyperactivity disorder and sleep difficulties, can pose additional challenges (von Gontard & Equit, 2015). Further complicating matters is this: Unlike many adaptive skills that can be practiced repeatedly in a single training session (e.g., handwashing, shoe tying), opportunities for productive toilet use typically occur only a few times per day, often at unexpected moments (Belva, Matson, Barker, Shoemaker, & Mahan, 2011).

Competing Learning History

With the delay in learning toileting skills, children with ASD may establish idiosyncratic, inflexible routines for daily bowel and bladder elimination. Most notably, over time, urinating or defecating while wearing the diaper or pull-up may become so habitual that the child is unlikely to do so in its absence (Luiselli, 1996). As a result, elimination routines may have no association with the toilet. Furthermore, because of the "convenient" ongoing presence of the diaper or pull-up, elimination routines may become so automatic that the child does not demonstrate obvious behaviors that signal imminent voiding, such as increased motor movements or distinct posturing. These behaviors alert caregivers and provide them with a chance to take the child to the toilet. Because many individuals with ASD prefer routine, these patterns of behavior may be difficult to interrupt and replace with new routines for bowel and bladder elimination.

Possible Gastrointestinal Complications

Some children with ASD have restricted diets that can contribute to constipation and/or diarrhea (Fulceri et al., 2016; see also Chapter 7 in this book for more information on food selectivity). As a result, the individual child may have a disrupted bowel schedule and abdominal pain associated with bowel movements (BMs). Trips to the toilet may be associated with this discomfort, resulting in an aversion to bathroom trips that are part of a toilet training program (Blum, Taubman, & Nemeth, 2004).

Anxiety

All of the foregoing factors make some individuals with ASD anxious and impatient to escape or avoid systematic efforts at toilet training. Other factors, such as expectations to sit on a potentially uncomfortable toilet for minutes at a time, well-intentioned cajoling by caregivers, disruption of preferred activities, and the potential ambiguity of the *how* and *what* of the task also can raise anxiety. This increased anxiety hinders toileting success, thus creating long-standing frustration for the child and family.

SPECIFIC ASSESSMENT PROCEDURES

Three areas of assessment are important to complete before initiating toilet training.

Physical Examination

Before initiating daytime toilet training, consultation with a qualified medical professional, such as the child's pediatrician, will ensure that there are no physical/medical impediments to achieving toileting success, such as physical abnormalities of the genitals, a urinary tract infection, or endocrine or neurologic disorder (Iorember, 2017). This is particularly important when prior, systematic toilet training attempts have not been successful, if the child demonstrates signs of discomfort or pain when attempting to void, or when there is unresolved, chronic constipation.

Child's Training Readiness

Before toilet training, it is important to determine if the child is developmentally ready. Doing so shortens the process and reduces stress for both parent and child, making success more likely. Some signs in typically developing children that also are relevant to children with ASD include an ability to imitate others, a desire to please caregivers, an expression of interest in toilet training (e.g., watching siblings, comments about toileting), and an ability to pull clothes up and down, sit on the toilet, remain dry for at least 2 hours, recognize when wet and dry, indicate a need to void, and follow simple directions (Polaha, Warzak, & Dittmer-McMahon, 2002). Additional signs of readiness in some children with ASD include an increase in vocalizations (i.e., verbal or nonverbal) when desiring an object or when frustrated, and an increase or decrease in motor activity before voiding. Other signs of possible readiness include moving to a particular location (e.g., a bedroom) before voiding or a daily voiding pattern or routine (e.g., on getting off the bus from school).

It is not a prerequisite that a child demonstrate all of the aforementioned signs of readiness before the initiation of toilet training (Wheeler, 2007). This is especially true for children who are school-age or older and have significant developmental delays. For these older children, incontinence becomes an increasing barrier to inclusion and a greater burden for caregivers, making toilet training a greater priority. Importantly, individuals with severe intellectual disability can participate in instruction and learn at least some toileting skills, provided they can participate in instruction with minimal challenging behavior. It is most important that they (a) usually follow simple instructions, (b) can sit calmly on the toilet for at least 2 to 3 minutes, and (c) are not severely resistant to the toileting tasks or physically aggressive toward others or self during the toileting routine (Mruzek, McAleavey, Engel, & Smith, 2016).

For these older children who are not yet toilet trained, habit training may be a reasonable goal (Dunlap, Koegel, & Koegel, 1984). *Habit training* involves teaching a child to comply with scheduled bathroom trips and to urinate or defecate in the toilet; it does not require the child to initiate trips to the toilet on his or her own or to take care of all related tasks (e.g., pulling clothing up and down, wiping, washing hands) independently. During intensive toilet training, habit training frequently is the first toilet training program initiated. Many children succeed with habit training without clearly demonstrating a need to go or without even recognizable precursor behaviors. Habit training is discussed further in the Special Considerations section of this chapter.

Readiness of the Family

The availability of the family to focus on implementing the training program is important to consider. If, for example, a family is experiencing an unexpected job loss, serious illness, or move into a new home, it may be best to postpone toilet training their child. Prematurely suspending toilet training once initiated risks "teaching" the child that resisting toilet use long enough will result in an end of the new expectations and a return to the child's old routine (e.g., voiding in a diaper with cleanup by parents). As a result, future training attempts typically become more difficult. Therefore, careful planning with families and timing of the toilet training program are critical.

SPECIFIC PARENT TRAINING STRATEGIES

Most strategies for toilet training individuals with ASD are based on the principles of behavior analysis and are variants of the methods articulated by Azrin and Foxx (1971) in a series of classic articles and books. In some cases, a *rapid approach* is used in which the caregivers set aside a day or a few consecutive days, such as particular weekend or vacation, to focus intensely on toilet training (Cicero & Pfadt, 2002; Kroeger & Sorensen, 2010; LeBlanc, Carr, Crossett, Bennett, & Detweiler, 2005). During that time, many day-to-day family routines are temporarily suspended or modified. A key advantage of this approach is that progress may be realized quickly; however, this approach is not without its potential difficulties. For example, some families may be unable to set aside a block of time for intensive training due to the demands of their busy calendars or the need to care for multiple children or other family members. Also, the intense schedule may result in strife between the parent and child. In those cases, families may prefer a more gradual training routine in which they set aside blocks of time for toilet training, as their schedule allows. In both cases, training often involves taking the child to the bathroom on a set schedule.

Irrespective of the specific approach, the target skill in the early stages of toilet training involves three essential, co-occurring components: (a) the individual experiences bladder or bowel pressure while (b) sitting or standing on or at the toilet, while (c) maintaining a relaxed physiological state. For training purposes, one additional variable is vital: immediate, salient, and powerful reinforcement of toileting behavior, such as a parent's praise combined with a tangible reward (e.g., access to a favorite electronic device). Later, we embed these skills in the broader set of skills related to initiation of toilet use, communication of the need to use the toilet, self-care with clothing and handwashing, and generalization across settings (Mruzek, Silverman, & Varghese, 2012).

Structure and Format of Professional Consultation

Although many parents successfully plan and train their child with ASD on their own, others benefit from consultation with an expert in instructing children with ASD (e.g., psychologist or behavior analyst with input from a pediatrician). Consulting with an expert is particularly beneficial if the child demonstrates an especially slow rate of learning, is nonverbal, engages in persistent challenging behaviors that interfere with training, or has attempted and failed toilet training previously. Although the specific schedule of consultation will depend on a number of variables, an initial consultation with parents followed by a series of three to five briefer "booster" sessions over about a 3-month period often is an effective model. During the initial consultation, the individualized plan is developed with the parents. Because so many questions arise during the first few days of program implementation, the first booster session is scheduled for about one week after the initiation of the toilet training program by the parents, allowing for early modifications of the program based on review of data and parent observations. Subsequent booster sessions are scheduled out in 2- to 3-week intervals to review status, troubleshoot difficulties, and plan next steps. We have found that the initial consultation may take about 2 hours, whereas booster sessions typically are more brief (Mruzek, McAleavey, & Smith, 2014).

Initial Consultation

As in all good instruction, a solid training plan recognizes the child's developmental strengths and weaknesses, as well as his or her individual preferences for the specifics of the routine and reinforcement of target behavior. The toilet training planning guide in Table 8.1 offers a semistructured way of completing this planning process through step-by-step review of key program considerations. These considerations are discussed next.

TABLE 8.1
Toilet Training Parent Training Planning Guide

Area	Considerations
Goal of program	• Bowel, bladder, both? • Habit training or independence training?
Consideration of potential barriers	• ASD-related deficits (e.g., communication)? • Absence of precursor behaviors? • Aversion to cloth underwear? • Limited number of potential reinforcers? • Caregiver buy-in? • Limitations or concerns with physical environment or family schedule?
Identification of relevant supports	• Modified seat and/or footstool? • Functional communication supports? • Visual supports and reminders?
Data-keeping	• Form captures relevant information? • Review content, purpose and schedule with parents
Reinforcement	• Develop menu of potential reinforcers • Reinforcers available contingent on target behaviors • Specific target behaviors and schedule reviewed
Underwear vs. diapers	• Rationale for cloth underwear reviewed • Plan for eliminating diapers needed?
Precursor behaviors	• Review importance of identifying precursor behaviors and encourage vigilance
Training schedule	• Establish a training schedule based on child's daily voiding patterns and parents' availability
Coordination with others	• Identify training settings and plan for coordination across settings

Note. ASD = autism spectrum disorder.

Goals of the Program

For most children with ASD, independent use of the toilet for urination and defecation is the ultimate goal; however, for some children, particularly for younger children and individuals with severe intellectual disability, the goal may be that they void when taken to the toilet by others. On the other hand, some children with ASD will already use the toilet when initiated by caregivers at time of referral, but the parent may be having difficulty teaching the child to initiate toilet use on his or her own. In these cases, independent initiation of toileting is the goal. Some children will be continent for urine but not bowel, or vice versa, meaning that one or the other skill is the key target of instruction.

Identification of Potential Barriers to Effective Training

There are many potential barriers to carrying out a consistent toilet training program. With regard to the child, these barriers may include communication deficits, oppositional or otherwise off-task behaviors (e.g., intense preoccupations or stereotypies), absence of precursor behaviors indicating an impending void, aversion to cloth underwear or toilet, limited reinforcement options, or resistance to change in routine. During initial planning, a thorough conversation with parents and other caregivers who know the child well usually reveal potential training challenges that are important to take into account in the child's training program.

There also are potential barriers related to the training environment. Has everyone involved with the child "bought in" to the effort? If not, then the initial toilet training may need to focus on times when the child is under the care of an adult who is willing to implement the program (e.g., the teacher but not grandmother). Moreover, there may be specific settings where toilet training cannot take place (e.g., during a long bus ride to school). There may be new furniture or carpets in the home that could be ruined if the child had an accident. In such cases, the items need to be covered, removed, or blocked off to prevent the child from using that area of the home. Other potential barriers need to be identified, such as not having enough time or a parent's having other responsibilities (e.g., caring for other children) that might interfere with toilet training. Although it might be ideal to implement a toilet training program for 8 hours per day, starting with 2 hours might be the only way to implement the program consistently. Parents and teachers should develop a list of these and other potential barriers before implementing a toileting program to address them up front and better ensure program success.

Adaptive and Instructional Supports

Adaptive supports are devices that help with tasks related to toileting, such as a modified toilet seat for comfort, handrails to improve balance for a child with motor difficulties, or a footstool to use while sitting on the toilet. The most beneficial adaptive supports are items that promote a relaxed physiological and behavioral state by helping the child sit upright on the toilet with feet comfortably planted on the floor or footstool.

Instructional supports are materials for teaching the component skills of toileting, from initiating the routine through washing hands when done. The most common are visual supports, such as icons to prompt a trip to the bathroom or remind a child to sit calmly once on the toilet. A social story or similar picture-based presentation can be used to prime toileting instruction and can be reviewed with the child at the start of a training session. As a child progresses, a task list that includes pictures to represent each step in the toileting routine may increase independence (Smith, 2012).

Data-Keeping

Keeping data on a child's toileting successes and accidents (as well as "dry" periods) is the only way to accurately determine if progress is being made. Figure 8.1 illustrates a scatter plot data form that captures most of the relevant information. For program monitoring and planning, the chart must indicate exactly when accidents or successes occurred. In addition, it should contain space to note when the child has been "dry." A code for bowel movement (i.e., BM) can be added, as well. Other codes to indicate self-initiation (i.e., I), spontaneously requested (i.e., R), or prompted (i.e., P) can be added if self-initiation or requesting is a goal. The chart also can be used to remind the parent or teacher when to take the child to the toilet. Some parents may record data daily. Others may not have the time or wherewithal to do so but can collect data on a more limited schedule, such as 3 days before a consultation visit (Mruzek et al., 2017).

Reinforcement

A critical component of any training program is reinforcement of target behavior, including voiding in the toilet, as well as compliant behavior during the toileting routine (Autism Treatment Network, Autism Speaks, 2012). The most effective *reinforcers* are items or activities that can be delivered immediately after the child has urinated or defecated into the toilet. These reinforcers might include a favorite cartoon, song, or game on an electronic device; an attractive toy; or a sip of a favorite drink or bite of a favorite food. Developing a short list of rewards usually helps prevent the child from becoming bored with one item or activity used repeatedly. Also, it is important that parents hold these items and activities in abeyance until the child has used the toilet or met an associated training goal. A child may be

Name: _____ Dates: _____

Place an "X" in the box that corresponds to time/day of urination.
Place a "+" in the box that corresponds to time/day of defecation.
Circle the "X" or the "+" if child successfully urinated or defecated in the toilet.
Place a "D" in the box that corresponds to when child was "dry."

TIME	Sunday	Monday	Tuesday	Wednesday	Thursday	Friday	Saturday
7:00 a.m.–7:30 a.m.							
7:30 a.m.–8:00 a.m.							
8:00 a.m.–8:30 a.m.							
8:30 a.m.–9:00 a.m.							
9:00 a.m.–9:30 a.m.							
9:30 a.m.–10:00 a.m.							
10:00 a.m.–10:30 a.m.							
10:30 a.m.–11:00 a.m.							
11:00 a.m.–11:30 a.m.							
11:30 a.m.–12:00 p.m.							
12:00 p.m.–12:30 p.m.							
12:30 p.m.–1:00 p.m.							
1:00 p.m.–1:30 p.m.							
1:30 p.m.–2:00 p.m.							
2:00 p.m.–2:30 p.m.							
2:30 p.m.–3:00 p.m.							
3:00 p.m.–3:30 p.m.							
3:30 p.m.–4:00 p.m.							
4:00 p.m.–4:30 p.m.							
4:30 p.m.–5:00 p.m.							
5:00 p.m.–5:30 p.m.							
5:30 p.m.–6:00 p.m.							
6:00 p.m.–6:30 p.m.							
6:30 p.m.–7:00 p.m.							
7:00 p.m.–7:30 p.m.							
7:30 p.m.–8:00 p.m.							
8:00 p.m.–8:30 p.m.							

Figure 8.1. Scatter plot data form.

terrifically motivated by a favorite electronic game; however, if he or she has open access to that game throughout the day, it probably will not be an effective reinforcer for toileting.

Underwear Versus Diapers

It is often more difficult to toilet train a child who remains in diapers or pull-ups (Simon & Thompson, 2006). Using diapers conveys the message to the child that it is acceptable to urinate, irrespective of location. Also, disposable diapers are designed to absorb moisture, wicking it away from the child's skin; therefore, the child experiences little or no discomfort when wet or soiled. In addition, a child may learn to urinate and/or defecate only when wearing a diaper (a habit that may be difficult to unlearn), and caregivers will be unaware of the exact moment when an accident has occurred. Therefore, when toilet training begins, the child should be wearing cloth underwear.

When switching from diapers to cloth underwear, some parents will report that their child does not appear bothered or uncomfortable when wet or soiled, which may be because of the novelty of the experience. In those cases, encourage parents to continue with the use of cloth underwear for at least several days. The child may develop an aversion to being wet/soiled following repeated contrasts with being clean and dry. For children who are resistant to using cloth underwear, purchasing "special" underwear that depicts the child's favorite characters or objects may be helpful. Also, using the term *big boy* or *big girl* pants also may provide motivation, especially if there are older siblings in the home who are toilet trained (Azrin & Foxx, 1971). Stains to furniture and carpet from leaking underwear can be mitigated through the use of plastic training pants that cover the cloth underwear.

Precursor Behaviors

Precursor behaviors are behavioral signs that a child might be ready to urinate or have a BM. Although each child is unique, a number of behaviors are common. Some children with diaper rituals go off to a private part of the house to have a BM. Other children show facial signs of pushing when preparing to have a BM. Children who need to urinate may cross their legs, engage in a kind of dance, become more active, or vocalize more. Many parents already know the signs for their child. Attending to such signs and immediately prompting the child to use the toilet will further enhance the child's progress. Some children with ASD do not demonstrate any noticeable precursor behaviors at the onset of training, but as training progresses, begin to do so. This is progress! Encourage parents to be aware of the child's behavior during training, watch for precursor behaviors, and, when observed, initiate a bathroom trip.

Training Schedule

Due to the busy routine of family life, parents need to identify specific times when they will conduct toilet training with their child. The training schedule should be based on (a) the child's daily patterns of urination and/or defecation and (b) opportunities for parents to train the child in the context of their busy schedules. The scatter plot in Figure 8.1 can show when the child is most likely to urinate and defecate. For example, a child may tend to urinate right after dinner or have a BM before bedtime. These times are prime opportunities to implement toilet training. Parents may be able to reserve portions of the day or week for intervals of toilet training (e.g., before their child's bath, as part of the bedtime routine, Saturdays). These training intervals can be specified on a weekly calendar that is placed in a convenient spot in the home (e.g., bathroom mirror). Although programmatic fidelity may be less than perfect, parents should be encouraged to adhere to the schedule. As with most types of skills instruction, more training will usually net faster acquisition of skill.

Once the weekly training schedule has been determined, there is a question regarding how often the child should be prompted to go to the toilet to try to void. About every 15 or 20 minutes often is a good rate. However, if the child demonstrates signs of impending urination or BM, he or she should be taken to the toilet immediately.

Coordination With Others

Planning should include consideration of how parents will coordinate with other caregivers, such as day care, school staff, or extended family who regularly care for the child (e.g., grandparents). Their participation in implementing the training program can accelerate progress and prevent parent burnout. It is important to keep the program consistent across environments, meaning that parents and others need to talk with each other, share data, and ensure that supplies and supports are available in all settings (e.g., extra underwear at school). The same prompting strategies and consequences for accidents need to be used across environments (although the available reinforcers might differ somewhat).

On some occasions, caregivers in one setting will not agree to take on the demands of the toilet training program, and parents may worry that the program will fail without everyone's participation. This is not the case. Involvement of all caregivers could overwhelm some children (as well as parents and teachers). Some families start the process at home and then move the program to school once the child has been successful (or vice versa). Once the child has made substantial progress with toileting in one setting, other caregivers can focus on generalizing skills to these other settings, a task that now may be more doable for them.

Additional Considerations for Training Days

After planning and preparation are completed, it is time to get started with the actual toilet training. Key considerations for toilet training implementation include the following.

Increasing Fluid Intake

Unless they have a physical condition, individuals who are not toilet trained may urinate at low rates during the day. Accordingly, to increase the rate of urination (and, hence, opportunity for successful toilet use), make extra fluids available. Usually, this can be accomplished by encouraging sips of water and, perhaps, a favorite juice (if the child's weight and nutrition are not a concern) in the minutes before and during training intervals. If juice is being used, take note of its fiber content, concentration, and the volume being consumed. Large volumes of some juices, such as apple juice, may result in gastrointestinal upset, which will likely adversely impact toilet training efforts.

Initiating Trips to the Bathroom

During training, the goal is that the child will stop what he or she is doing, walk to the bathroom, lower his or her clothing, and sit on (or stand at) the toilet. In practice, the child probably will need the parent's prompting, assistance, and encouragement to complete these steps, at least in the early stages. To promote success, the parent should signal the onset of a transition to the bathroom with a clear, succinct direction using a positive tone (e.g., "Time to go potty!").

If helpful, a visual support, such as a picture symbol of a toilet, may be paired with—or even replace—this verbal direction to promote the child's comprehension. Remind parents that if the child does not initiate the trip to the bathroom, it is best to avoid pleading, cajoling, rationalizing, teasing, or engaging in similar behaviors that may do little more than reinforce the child's avoidance. Rather, encourage parents to immediately and gently physically guide the child to the bathroom. Once at the bathroom and, again, when the child is on or at the toilet, praise his or her participation in the routine (e.g., "I love how you're using the potty!" "What a big boy!" "You're doing great!").

Maintaining a Relaxing Training Environment

The goal is to maintain a calm, quiet, supportive environment so that the child relaxes and has the greatest opportunity to void successfully. Simply put, an individual cannot urinate or defecate if he or she is overly aroused, because it is physically impossible to do so (Foxx & Azrin, 1973). Besides ensuring the child's comfort (as described earlier in the Adaptive and Instructional Supports section of this chapter), the parent may find it advantageous to sit directly across from the child on a small stool (almost knee to knee). It is best if the parent does not talk at all; however, he or she may need to offer occasional, calm, positive, soothing words of encouragement and reassurance. Ongoing conversation with the child or with others (immediately present or on a telephone), as well as teasing, boisterous game playing, cajoling, or, of course, threats should be avoided. It is best if the child does not have any objects while on the toilet; however, some children do not sit still, may tinker with their surroundings, or are prone to engaging in counterproductive stereotypy. These behaviors can be overcome by giving them items that maintain their interest, such as favorite picture books; soft, calming music; or toys. Items that may be too arousing and thus counterproductive include many electronic games and cause-and-effect toys.

Invoking the 5-Minute Rule

Limit the time that the child sits on the toilet to about 5 minutes or until he or she voids, so that the toileting attempts do not become unduly burdensome or boring for the child. This limit will help prevent escape-related behavior or off-task leisure behavior (e.g., attempting to flush the toilet, playing with the water). If a child is going to successfully void in the toilet, he or she will usually do so within about the first 5 minutes of his or her time there. For some children, it is helpful to use a timer while they are on the toilet, if doing so provides reassurance or reminder of expectations.

Responding When the Child Is Unsuccessful While on the Toilet

In the early stages of training, if the child does not urinate or defecate while on the toilet, he or she can still be praised and receive other types of reinforcement for sitting and cooperating with the toileting routine. Typically, these reinforcers are not as powerful as the ones given for a successful void. However, once those skills are attained, reinforcement typically is reserved for a successful urination or BM. In cases in which 5 minutes have passed and the child has not been successful, simply end the session in a neutral manner (e.g., "OK. We're all done. You can go back outside, and we'll try again later"). At no point should the parent scold or criticize the child for not using the toilet; doing so risks making future bathroom trips more difficult.

Doing Dry Pants Checks

For many children with ASD, dry pants checks during training can be a powerful way of using reinforcement to promote avoiding accidents and using the toilet (Foxx & Azrin, 1973). These checks entail the parent's intermittently checking the child's pants and underwear, and delivering reinforcement if the clothing has remained clean and dry (e.g., offering praise and a small tangible reinforcer, such as a sticker). Often, it is helpful for parents to set a timer for a fixed interval (e.g., every 15 minutes) to prompt their initiation of these checks. This procedure can be faded as the child progresses with his or her training program.

Responding When the Child Has an Accident

There are different schools of thought regarding how to handle accidents (Kroeger & Sorensen-Burnworth, 2009). Some recommend immediately changing the child in a neutral manner, meaning providing limited social interactions or attention. A second option, especially for children who have the ability to do so, is to require the child to do much of the cleaning up. This means that the child must clean himself or herself, change his or her clothing, place soiled items in the washing machine, and clean the surrounding area, if needed. A third option is to then have the child practice appropriate toileting a number of times (e.g., walking to the bathroom and sitting on the toilet for a few seconds, returning to the location where accident occurred, and then walking back to the bathroom again multiple times; Kroeger & Sorensen-Burnworth, 2009). This approach may not be advisable in schools or other public settings because it may compromise the student's personal dignity to repeatedly return to the bathroom.

Our general advice is to start with a more neutral approach to accidents and then to increase the child's participation if minimal progress is being made. However, older, more capable children can appropriately be required to participate in the cleanup from the beginning. A word of caution: We do not want cleaning up and/or practicing appropriate toileting to lead to resistance and noncompliance, which only creates additional problems and moves the focus from the goal of toilet training. If this is the case, it is probably best to deemphasize this aspect of the toilet training program and, instead, focus efforts on reinforcement of participation in the toileting routine and suspension of reinforcement when accidents occur.

Scheduling Booster Consultation Sessions

A booster session discussion guide is presented in Table 8.2 that offers a semistructured way of monitoring progress, troubleshooting difficulties, and planning next steps in the toilet training plan. Key components of this guide include gathering the parent's impressions regarding overall progress, reviewing data, assessing parent adherence to the training program, identifying difficulties in implementing the toileting routine, and troubleshooting barriers to progress.

Reviewing data with parents, especially data plotted for visual inspection, can be valuable for pointing out subtle signs of progress and troubleshooting stalled programs in a timely manner (Figure 8.2). Of course, an increase in the

TABLE 8.2
Booster Consultation Sessions: Discussion Guide

Area	Considerations
Parent's impressions of:	
Overall progress	• Does parent report progress, regression, or no change?
	• Is parent feeling positive about status of the training program?
Review of data	• Done a visual inspection of data with parent to assess trend, variability, level of data (e.g., accidents, toilet use)?
	• Are the data consistent with parent impressions?
Review of training routine	• Is parent implementing program with fidelity?
	• Is training schedule being maintained?
	• Are data being collected?
Barriers or challenges	• Are instructional and adaptive supports helpful?
	• Are there any new barriers or challenges to progress?
Determine next-step plans	• Identify current goals and related instructional strategies
	• Ensure that supports and strategies have been reviewed adequately with parent
	• Monitor for parent burnout, especially in early stages of training

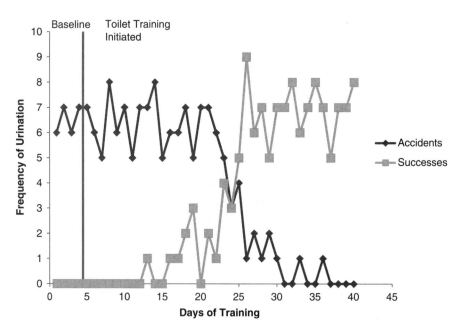

Figure 8.2. Toileting data plotted for visual inspection.

rate of toileting success and a decrease in the rate of accidents are signs of progress, but there are other, more subtle signs of progress, particularly in the early stages of training, that are important to point out to parents. For example, a child may exhibit a noticeable increase or decrease in the rate of accidents as he or she adjusts to the new expectations. The emergence of new precursor behaviors, such as an increase in vocalizations before the onset of voiding, suggests that a child is becoming increasingly sensitive to body cues. In the early stages of training, dribbling or short bursts of urine into the toilet bowl may well be an indication of progress, and are behaviors that can be reinforced and shaped into more productive urination. A specimen collection pan (an inexpensive, plastic toilet bowl insert) can be positioned to take the guesswork out of efforts to determine if the child is demonstrating these early signs of progress.

In addition to analyzing progress and making technical decisions about the training program, these booster sessions are an important opportunity to support and encourage parents, particularly during the days before the establishment of regular toilet use by their child. For many parents, the scheduled bathroom trips are time consuming, disruptive to daily routine, and isolating. The child may protest, tantrum, or purposely withhold his or her urine or bowel elimination until no longer on the toilet. Other children may suddenly have many more accidents as they adjust to the new expectations regarding toilet use, requiring additional effort for parents. Parents may perceive this increase as a sign that the training is "not working" or making their child's elimination habits worse. Therefore, it is essential to partner with parents by focusing not only on developing a technically sound, individualized training program for the child but also on providing reassurance and encouragement throughout the training process. Often parents benefit from being reminded that progress often is gradual and variable. Parents should be aware that there may be days of minimal or no apparent progress and, even after an interval of successful toileting, a return to baseline that may persist for a day or more. This variability in performance is typical of human behavior, especially in the early stages of learning a new skill.

It is important to watch for circumstances that can develop in which the child becomes comfortable with a new arrangement for bowel and bladder elimination that does *not* include toileting. For example, a child training at home and school may get into the habit of having urine accidents on the school bus in the morning and afternoon. When these kinds of "comfortable" arrangements have been identified, strategies must be used to address them to encourage the child's eventual use of the toilet. For example, with regard to the bus and similar transportation arrangements, the child might be encouraged to void immediately before getting on the bus and given a "reward card" to hold onto while on the bus that can be redeemed for a prize on arrival at school or home, contingent on remaining dry.

Teaching the Entire Bathroom Routine

As the child becomes increasingly successful in toileting, attention should be turned to the broader sequence of skills related to bathroom use, including initiating bathroom trips, indicating the need for the toilet, and engaging in self-care skills, including pulling down and pulling up clothing, wiping with toilet paper, flushing the toilet, and washing hands. In the early stages of training, the child is usually, by necessity, directed to the toilet through the verbal and physical guidance of the parent. To promote greater independence in initiating toileting, parents may systematically fade the intensity of their guidance through use of a *prompt hierarchy strategy* (Mruzek et al., 2012). For example, they may gradually decrease physical guidance until only verbal directions and prompting are used, and then reduce verbal directions to a brief phrase (e.g., "Use the potty, then we'll get going"). For older children who we want to become completely independent, prompts from parents may consist solely of simple visual supports when they suspect their child has a full bladder. These can be faded as the child begins to initiate toilet use on his or her own. In all cases, parents should reinforce increasingly independent initiation of toileting through praise and, as necessary, tangible or token reinforcement.

To teach fluency across all of the steps that compose the bathroom routine, a picture-based task board can be used to represent each step. The most effective way of organizing this task board is through a process of task analysis, in which each of the key steps of bathroom use are identified and "chained" together as a multistep activity, in which the conclusion of one step sets the occasion for the initiation of the next one (Mruzek et al., 2012; see Figure 8.3). Each step can be taught through prompt fading and reinforcement of correct responding.

Figure 8.3. A task board for toileting. The Picture Communication Symbols ©1981–2011 by Mayer-Johnson LLC. All Rights Reserved Worldwide. Used with permission. Boardmaker® is a trademark of Mayer-Johnson LLC.

Communicating the Need to Use the Toilet

Communicating the need or intention to use the toilet is another important skill that often must be taught systematically by parents and other caregivers. In many cases, this skill may require functional communication training in which the child with ASD is prompted to indicate that he or she needs to use the toilet as part of the broader toileting routine. For children with limited spoken language skills, visual supports such as those used in the Picture Exchange Communication System (Bondy & Frost, 2002) or an electronic augmentative system may be used to support this instruction. For example, depending on the typical communication strategy used with the child, a parent may physically prompt a child to hold up, hand, or point to a bathroom picture posted at eye level on a wall and say, "Potty, please" or "Need to use the potty" (see Figure 8.4). Parents should be encouraged to reinforce this communicative behavior through immediate, positive responding (e.g., "Thanks for telling me!") and fade or decrease their prompting as the child gradually demonstrates greater independence.

Figure 8.4. Picture symbol for indicating need for bathroom. The Picture Communication Symbols ©1981–2011 by Mayer-Johnson LLC. All Rights Reserved Worldwide. Used with permission. Boardmaker® is a trademark of Mayer-Johnson LLC.

Maintenance and Generalization of Toileting Skill

Once the child is using the toilet reliably, training focus should shift to maintenance and generalization. *Maintenance* refers to the continuation of the child's toileting over time, when the structured training program has ended. *Generalization* refers to the child's use of this skill in settings other than the training environment, including school, stores, restaurants, and places of worship. Once children with ASD have established toileting habits, many maintain the routine with little difficulty. For others, enuresis and encopresis may be chronic conditions that intermittently reappear for days or weeks throughout the year. These setbacks may occur during physical illness (e.g., cold or ear infection), disruptions in routines (e.g., start of the school year, vacations), or other significant life events (e.g., moving to a new house). Some children, perhaps especially those who only recently have begun using the toilet, may drop out of their toileting routine following the conclusion of training and resume having regular accidents. In those cases, it is critical that the clinician remind the parent that this is not wholly unanticipated and that there are strategies for getting the child's consistent use of the toilet back on track. Also, parents may be reassured to know that recovery of skill usually is not as time or labor intensive as original training. Parents can again use the supports and strategies that they used to originally train their child, including regular scheduling of trips and powerful, immediate reinforcement for using the toilet.

Some children with ASD use a toilet in a familiar setting, such as at their home, but not in other settings (e.g., school, home of extended family), resulting in accidents. A key instructional strategy to promote generalization of toilet use across settings is *transfer of stimulus control*, a strategy in which we gradually fade stimuli in or out so that new stimuli evoke the desired behavior. Planning community outings, such as to libraries and restaurants, for the purpose of teaching generalization of toileting skills often is helpful. During these trips, the child may be given extra fluids to drink to promote opportunities for success. Salient materials used in the original training setting are used in these training environments, thereby promoting generalization of skill. These materials may include visual supports (e.g., a "Time for Potty" card like the one presented in Figure 8.4), spoken directions, communication supports, token boards, and task boards.

Stimulus transfer procedures even can be used to promote generalization across trainers (Rincover & Koegel, 1975). For example, for a child who uses the bathroom at home under the direction of his or her mother, the mother may visit the child at school during the hour after lunch because teachers have noted that this is when the child often has urine accidents. During this hour, the child is supplied with extra fluids, and the mother might play a fun board game with him or her at a table adjacent to the bathroom. When the mother notices signs that the child has a full bladder, she initiates their standard "home" routine. When implementing these types of stimulus transfer procedures, it is important that the adults in the "new" setting are physically close to the original trainer during implementation of the routine, gradually assume the trainer role, and deliver powerful reinforcement for toilet use. Through this type of pairing, the "new" caregivers acquire stimulus control over the child's behavior of toilet use.

SPECIAL CONSIDERATIONS

Some problems, which may be especially common in ASD, need to be addressed before a traditional training can be initiated.

Aversion to Elements of the Bathroom Setting or Training Routine

Some children have aversions to the bathroom, often related to anxiety or fear. Many children react anxiously to sounds, such as the flushing of a toilet, especially a public toilet. Many public toilets also flush automatically, which can startle a child. Other children simply refuse to sit on the toilet. There are a number of different approaches to address these aversions. If the problem is primarily distress due to the sound of the toilet flushing, the parent can prevent flushing (e.g., placing a note over the electronic sensor on the toilet), direct the child to wear headphones, or use other strategies to mute the sound. Alternatively, the child initially could be toilet trained on a potty chair that is located outside of the bathroom.

A shaping procedure also can gradually help a child get used to spending time in the bathroom and/or on the toilet (Ricciardi, Luiselli, & Camare, 2006). *Shaping* involves developing a number of small steps toward the target behavior. For example, the first step might involve simply walking into and out of the bathroom. This behavior then would immediately be reinforced. After a number of successful walks to the bathroom, the next step might be to walk into the bathroom and touch the toilet. Subsequent steps might involve sitting on the toilet briefly with the seat up and, eventually, sitting for 5 minutes. A set of steps for the shaping procedure (which also can be referred to as systematic desensitization) might include:

- walk in and out of bathroom;
- walk into bathroom and touch toilet;

- walk into bathroom and sit on toilet with top closed (gradually increase this step to 5 minutes);
- walk into bathroom, pull down pants, and sit on toilet with top closed for 5 minutes; and
- walk into bathroom, pull down pants, and sit on toilet with top open for 1 minute (gradually increase to 5 minutes).

Training Individuals With Severe Intellectual Disability

A child with more limited cognitive abilities often is capable of being habit trained using similar steps described earlier to teach the child to urinate or defecate in the toilet when seated there by a caregiver. Once the child can reliably do that, the caregivers can place the child on the toilet at regular intervals (e.g., every 2 hours). Another option is to make toileting part of the child's routine so that he or she can attain a greater level of independence. For example, the child could be taught to use the toilet in his or her morning routine, evening routine, before meals, before leaving for school, immediately after returning home from school, and so on. As the child progresses over time, fully independent toileting (i.e., having the child initiate when needed) can be addressed.

Enuresis Alarms for Daytime Training

Enuresis alarms consist of a sensor placed in the child's underwear that activates an audible tone alerting caregivers at the onset of urination; they then can direct the child to the toilet and encourage him or her to complete voiding. Alarms have the potential to be a useful adjunct to a multicomponent daytime toilet training protocol for children with ASD; however, limited research is available to draw conclusions regarding their effectiveness (Levato et al., 2016).

Urine alarms may be particularly helpful when the child shows few obvious indications of the onset of urination, when standard toilet training strategies have yielded limited progress, or when regularly scheduled trips to the toilet are inadvisable (e.g., when the child persistently protests during trips). Most children with ASD tolerate the disposable sensor in their underwear and, with proper training by the clinician, most parents implement the device with their child with little difficulty (Mruzek et al., 2017). When using the alarm, parents should be advised to monitor for new precursor behaviors that may manifest through the repeated pairing of the onset of accidents with the alarm. Also, at the onset of alarm, they should immediately and forthrightly direct the child to the bathroom to use the toilet (e.g., "Hold it! Time to go potty!").

CASE EXAMPLES

Despite our careful planning and best efforts at implementation, ongoing problem solving is a critical ingredient of successful toilet training programs for children with ASD. Some common problems and related considerations follow.

Antonio: "Progress Is Sooooo Slow!"

Background

Antonio[1] is an 8-year-old boy with ASD and concurrent intellectual disability. His parents recently have initiated a toilet training program developed in consultation with the school psychologist at their son's school. After 9 days of concerted effort, he has not yet used the toilet once, and both parents are wondering if they are on the right track.

Considerations

Learning a new skill like toileting can be a slow process. It may take a number of days of concerted effort before the child demonstrates noticeable progress, even dribbling a small amount of urine into the toilet. Antonio's parents need to take time to shape relaxed behavior while he is on the toilet by reinforcing his efforts. They should carefully monitor the quality of reinforcement that is available for him. Have they identified items that really motivate Antonio? If not, they could add some new rewards to his menu! His parents may consider keeping extra liquids available for Antonio during training intervals to provide more opportunities for practice. If possible, his parents could consider having more than one adult initiating training each day so that one person does not get burned out from being the sole provider.

Jennifer: "She Goes Before I Can Get Her to the Toilet!"

Background

Jennifer is a 5-year-old girl with ASD who completely soaks her underwear at the onset of urination. Furthermore, she provides no signs of impending urination. Jennifer's father reports that as a result, she has no opportunity to urinate in the toilet. He asks, "How is she ever going to learn to use the toilet when her accidents are so fast I can't get her into the bathroom?"

---

[1]Clinical material is fictional.

Considerations

This is a common problem, especially in the beginning stages of training. First, her father needs to be sure she is in cloth underwear, not diapers or pull-ups. During some training intervals, he should spend time with Jennifer at a location immediately adjacent to the bathroom, perhaps with some toys at a table positioned in a hallway or adjacent bedroom. As soon as he detects that she has begun to urinate, he should immediately say in a loud voice, "Stop! Time for the bathroom." Here is an important distinction: The parent's voice should be startling but not harsh or scary. Jennifer's father should immediately take her to the toilet and reinforce any urination into the toilet, even dribbles. He probably will need to repeat this procedure several times over several days; however, he may find that Jennifer (a) will begin to show signs of impending urination (e.g., crossing her legs, increased motor activity) and (b) be more likely to urinate at least a little into the toilet—a behavior that can be shaped across subsequent training days. If this procedure fails after several days, Jennifer may be a good candidate for the addition of a urine alarm in her training plan.

Jimmy: "He Likes to Go in His Diaper—Not the Toilet!"

Background

Jimmy is a 5-year-old with ASD. He has near-age-appropriate language skills and can dress himself. However, his family has been unable to toilet train him. Jimmy appears to like to defecate in his diaper. When his parents remove his diaper and place him in underwear, he holds his BM back until he is given a diaper. He will often request a diaper so that "he can go"; but, on the toilet, Jimmy will refuse to defecate.

Considerations

Jimmy clearly has the ability to control his BMs for long periods. That he requests a diaper suggests that he is even aware of an impending BM; therefore, troubleshooting in this case centers on nudging him to transfer defecation from the diaper to the toilet (Luiselli, 1996). First, his parents should double check to ensure that they have identified powerful reinforcers for Jimmy (e.g., a favorite DVD), to which they should limit access except for voiding in the toilet. Next, they might use these reinforcers to gradually shape toileting. For example, they might place Jimmy in underwear but provide a diaper when he asks. However, they should require that Jimmy then go into the bathroom (but not sit on the toilet) to defecate. Once he defecates in the diaper, they should give him access to his favorite DVD for 10 minutes. Once Jimmy is requesting a diaper and defecating in it regularly in the bathroom, his parents should require that he sit on the toilet, wearing a diaper while he defecates. The toilet seat can be up, but an in-between step with the toilet seat down might be needed. Once Jimmy is consistently defecating in his diaper while sitting on the toilet, his parents should begin to either cut a hole in the diaper or fold it back so that Jimmy actually defecates in the toilet (and will continue to use access to the favorite DVD as a reinforcer). Jimmy's parents then should continue to cut the diaper or fold it back until the diaper is no longer necessary.

Anthony: "He Was Doing Great, But Now He's Back to a Lot of Accidents Again!"

Background

When Anthony was 8 years old, his parents used a structured toilet training program. After several weeks of diligent effort, Anthony learned to use the toilet and had no accidents for weeks at a time. Despite that progress, Anthony, now age 10, still has occasional periods of regression characterized by several consecutive days with multiple accidents. These periods tend to occur when the family travels, when he is ill, or when his routine changes. What should they do?

Considerations

For some individuals, enuresis and/or encopresis may have a chronic quality, with long periods of remission followed by occasional flare-ups, especially during periods of stress, disruption in routine, or physical illness. It is helpful to identify these episodes as temporary setbacks, not as total losses of skill. To prevent flare-ups, when Anthony's parents anticipate a disruption to his routine, they can reintroduce some of the supports and strategies from the original training, especially scheduled trips, reminders, and rewards for successful toilet use. They should avoid reintroducing diapers/pull-ups, if at all possible, because this may increase the probability of accidents and delay a return to regular toilet use.

If novel or public bathrooms are a challenge for Anthony (e.g., those encountered while on family vacation), his parents should consider practice trips to local public restrooms during periods when he is doing well with toilet use and warmly compliment his success. Despite best efforts, when Anthony does have an accident, his parents need to react with as little fanfare as possible. They should encourage a prompt changing of clothes in a matter-of-fact tone and provide a brief reminder of expectations going forward. If a period of regression in toileting skills persists for more than a few days, Anthony's parents should consult with his pediatrician to ensure that there is no undiagnosed medical complication.

REFERENCES

Autism Treatment Network, Autism Speaks. (2012). *ATN/AIR-P parent's guide to toilet training in autism.* Retrieved from https://www.autismspeaks.org/science/resources-programs/autism-treatment-network/atn-air-p-toilet-training

Azrin, N. H., & Foxx, R. M. (1971). A rapid method of toilet training the institutionalized retarded. *Journal of Applied Behavior Analysis, 4,* 89–99. http://dx.doi.org/10.1901/jaba.1971.4-89

Belva, B., Matson, J. L., Barker, A., Shoemaker, M. E., & Mahan, S. (2011). The relationship between adaptive behavior and specific toileting problems according to the Profile on Toileting Issues (POTI). *Journal of Developmental and Physical Disabilities, 23,* 535–542. http://dx.doi.org/10.1007/s10882-011-9245-1

Blum, N. J., Taubman, B., & Nemeth, N. (2004). Why is toilet training occurring at older ages? A study of factors associated with later training. *Journal of Pediatrics, 145,* 107–111. http://dx.doi.org/10.1016/j.jpeds.2004.02.022

Bondy, A., & Frost, L. (2002). *The picture exchange communication system.* Newark, DE: Pyramid Educational Products.

Christensen, D. L., Bilder, D. A., Zahorodny, W., Pettygrove, S., Durkin, M. S., Fitzgerald, R. T., . . . Yeargin-Allsopp, M. (2016). Prevalence and characteristics of autism spectrum disorder among 4-year-old children in the autism and developmental disabilities monitoring network. *Journal of Developmental and Behavioral Pediatrics, 37,* 1–8. http://dx.doi.org/10.1097/DBP.0000000000000235

Cicero, F. R., & Pfadt, A. (2002). Investigation of a reinforcement-based toilet training procedure for children with autism. *Research in Developmental Disabilities, 23,* 319–331. http://dx.doi.org/10.1016/S0891-4222(02)00136-1

Dalrymple, N. J., & Ruble, L. A. (1992). Toilet training and behaviors of people with autism: Parent views. *Journal of Autism and Developmental Disorders, 22,* 265–275. http://dx.doi.org/10.1007/BF01058155

Dunlap, G., Koegel, R. L., & Koegel, L. K. (1984). *Toilet training for children with severe handicaps: A field manual for coordinating training procedures across multiple community settings.* Huntington, WV: Marshall University.

Foxx, R. M., & Azrin, N. H. (1973). Dry pants: A rapid method of toilet training children. *Behaviour Research and Therapy, 11,* 435–442. http://dx.doi.org/10.1016/0005-7967(73)90102-2

Fulceri, F., Morelli, M., Santocchi, E., Cena, H., Del Bianco, T., Narzisi, A., . . . Muratori, F. (2016). Gastrointestinal symptoms and behavioral problems in preschoolers with autism spectrum disorder. *Digestive and Liver Disease, 48,* 248–254. http://dx.doi.org/10.1016/j.dld.2015.11.026

Iorember, F. M. (2017). Enuresis. In T. K. McInerney, H. M. Adam, D. E. Campbell, T. G., DeWitt, J. M. Foy, & D. M. Kamat (Eds.), *American Academy of Pediatrics textbook of pediatric care* (2nd ed., pp. 2005–2010). Elk Grove Village, IL: American Academy of Pediatrics.

Kroeger, K., & Sorensen, R. (2010). A parent training model for toilet training children with autism. *Journal of Intellectual Disability Research, 54,* 556–567. http://dx.doi.org/10.1111/j.1365-2788.2010.01286.x

Kroeger, K. A., & Sorensen-Burnworth, R. (2009). Toilet training individuals with autism and other developmental disabilities: A critical review. *Research in Autism Spectrum Disorders, 3,* 607–618. http://dx.doi.org/10.1016/j.rasd.2009.01.005

LeBlanc, L. A., Carr, J. E., Crossett, S. E., Bennett, C. M., & Detweiler, D. D. (2005). Intensive outpatient behavioral treatment of primary urinary incontinence of children with autism. *Focus on Autism and Other Developmental Disabilities, 20,* 98–105. http://dx.doi.org/10.1177/10883576050200020601

Levato, L. E., Aponte, C. A., Wilkins, J., Travis, R., Aiello, R., Zanibbi, K., . . . Mruzek, D. W. (2016). Use of urine alarms in toilet training children with intellectual and developmental disabilities: A review. *Research in Developmental Disabilities, 53–54,* 232–241. http://dx.doi.org/10.1016/j.ridd.2016.02.007

Loening-Baucke, V. (2007). Prevalence rates for constipation and faecal and urinary incontinence. *Archives of Disease in Childhood, 92,* 486–489. http://dx.doi.org/10.1136/adc.2006.098335

Luiselli, J. K. (1996). A transfer of stimulus control procedure applicable to toilet training programs for children with developmental disabilities. *Child & Family Behavior Therapy, 18,* 29–34. http://dx.doi.org/10.1300/J019v18n02_04

Macias, M. M., Roberts, K. M., Saylor, C. F., & Fussell, J. J. (2006). Toileting concerns, parenting stress, and behavior problems in children with special health care needs. *Clinical Pediatrics, 45,* 415–422. http://dx.doi.org/10.1177/0009922806289616

Mruzek, D. W., McAleavey, S., Engel, S., & Smith, T. (2016). A novel enuresis alarm for toilet training students with intellectual disability: An initial evaluation in a school setting. *Journal of Special Education Technology, 31,* 217–227. http://dx.doi.org/10.1177/0162643416673915

Mruzek, D. W., McAleavey, S., Loring, W. A., Butter, E., Smith, T., McDonnell, E., . . . Zanibbi, K. (2017). A pilot investigation of an iOS-based app for toilet training children with autism spectrum disorder. *Autism.* Advance online publication. http://dx.doi.org/10.1177/1362361317741741

Mruzek, D. W., McAleavey, S., & Smith, T. (2014). *Teaching toileting skills to children with autism using a moisture pager: Clinician's manual.* Rochester, NY: University of Rochester.

Mruzek, D. W., Silverman, L., & Varghese, B. (2012). Individual instruction, part 1: Teaching approaches. In T. Smith (Ed.), *Making inclusion work for students with autism spectrum disorders: An evidence-based guide* (pp. 198–224). New York, NY: Guilford Press.

Polaha, J., Warzak, W. J., & Dittmer-McMahon, K. (2002). Toilet training in primary care: Current practice and recommendations from behavioral pediatrics. *Journal of Developmental and Behavioral Pediatrics, 23,* 424–429. http://dx.doi.org/10.1097/00004703-200212000-00005

Ricciardi, J. N., Luiselli, J. K., & Camare, M. (2006). Shaping approach responses as intervention for specific phobia in a child with autism. *Journal of Applied Behavior Analysis, 39,* 445–448. http://dx.doi.org/10.1901/jaba.2006.158-05

Rincover, A., & Koegel, R. L. (1975). Setting generality and stimulus control in autistic children. *Journal of Applied Behavior Analysis, 8,* 235–246. http://dx.doi.org/10.1901/jaba.1975.8-235

Simon, J. L., & Thompson, R. H. (2006). The effects of undergarment type on the urinary continence of toddlers. *Journal of Applied Behavior Analysis, 39,* 363–368. http://dx.doi.org/10.1901/jaba.2006.124-05

Smith, T. (2012). Adapting the daily routine. In T. Smith (Ed.), *Making inclusion work for students with autism spectrum disorders: An evidence-based guide* (pp. 123–165). New York, NY: Guilford Press.

Stanberry-Beal, J., Redla, V., Vogler-Elias, D., Baltus Hebert, E., Yingling, J., & Mruzek, D. W. (2014, June). *Toileting independence in autism spectrum disorder.* Poster session presented at the meeting of the American Association on Intellectual Disability, Orlando, FL.

von Gontard, A., & Equit, M. (2015). Comorbidity of ADHD and incontinence in children. *European Child & Adolescent Psychiatry, 24,* 127–140. http://dx.doi.org/10.1007/s00787-014-0577-0

Wheeler, M. (2007). *Toilet training for individuals with autism or other developmental issues.* Arlington, TX: Future Horizons.

9

PARENT TRAINING FOR ELOPEMENT IN AUTISM SPECTRUM DISORDER

NATHAN A. CALL, MINDY SCHEITHAUER,
JOANNA LOMAS MEVERS, AND COLIN MUETHING

Having a child go missing or run away is one of the most frightening events a parent can experience. This highly stressful event is more likely for parents of children with autism spectrum disorder (ASD) than for parents of typically developing children. Several terms have been used in the literature to describe a child's leaving a caregiver or designated area without permission, which may be an indication that the specific form and circumstances of this behavior can differ dramatically for individual children (Solomon & Lawlor, 2013). For example, some have used the term *wandering* to describe this behavior (Murphy et al., 2005), suggesting aimlessness. Conversely, others have used the term *bolting* (Burgoyne et al., 2014), which connotes a child running to (or away from) a specific location or activity. Some children with ASD engage in an opportunistic form of this behavior by waiting until a parent's attention is diverted elsewhere, likely contributing to it sometimes

http://dx.doi.org/10.1037/0000111-010
Parent Training for Autism Spectrum Disorder: Improving the Quality of Life for Children and Their Families,
C. R. Johnson, E. M. Butter, and L. Scahill (Editors)

being referred to as *absconding* (Lowe et al., 2007). Some children with ASD persist in their attempts to run away, even when a parent is trying to physically restrain them. In contrast, parents of other children can easily prevent or redirect them from running or wandering.

Such variability in how this class of behavior is manifest across children with ASD illustrates the complexities of categorizing and treating it. However, regardless of the name used, all forms of this behavior share the fact that they put children with ASD at serious risk of harm. Because the treatment literature seems to have settled on the term *elopement* (Bodfish, 1992), we use that term throughout the remainder of this chapter to refer to any instance of a child's leaving supervision without permission, regardless of the specific characteristics of the child's behavior. However, such specifics, as well as others described in this chapter, often are the critical determinants of how a clinician might best train parents in the practices and skills necessary to successfully address this dangerous behavior.

DESCRIPTION OF ELOPEMENT AS PROBLEM BEHAVIOR IN ASD AND ASSOCIATED NEGATIVE CONSEQUENCES

The risk associated with elopement is significant, even compared with many other forms of problem behavior. Unlike behaviors such as aggression, or even most forms of self-injury, a single instance of elopement has the potential to be fatal. The specific risks encountered by a child who elopes are myriad but include abduction and a range of accidents. In perhaps the most comprehensive study on the prevalence and consequences of elopement, Anderson et al. (2012) surveyed 1,218 parents of children with ASD. Of those whose child exhibited elopement, the average duration of an elopement event exceeded 40 minutes, more than enough time for harm to befall a child with ASD. Furthermore, 65% of elopement events involved a close call with traffic injury and 24% involved a risk of drowning. Elopement contributes to accidents, which are one of the leading causes of premature death for individuals with ASD, a statistic that is especially concerning, given that the mortality rate for children with developmental delays is twice the rate of typically developing peers (Shavelle, Strauss, & Pickett, 2001). In addition, the core symptoms of ASD can make elopement even more dangerous than for typically developing children. For example, a child with ASD may not respond to instructions or rules related to remaining safe, understand social cues related to danger, or be able to provide the critical information necessary to reunite them with parents.

In addition to the danger it poses for children with ASD, elopement also creates significant challenges for the families of these individuals. It is a major source of stress for parents, with 43% reporting that their concerns about elopement disrupts their sleep, and a majority (62%) reporting that it prevents them from leaving their home or attending community events (Anderson et al., 2012). Such restrictions lead families of these children to become isolated at precisely the moment when they are most in need of assistance. Thus, it is not surprising that 56% of these parents have reported that elopement is the most stressful child behavior that they deal with and that it has had a profound negative effect on family functioning (Anderson et al., 2012). Furthermore, 50% of parents of children with ASD who elope have reported receiving no guidance on preventing or addressing their child's elopement (Anderson et al., 2012), potentially exacerbating their anxiety and frustration. Such findings are particularly concerning because family functioning has been shown to correlate with the prognosis of a child with ASD (K. Davis & Gavidia-Payne, 2009). Combined, the tremendous impact of elopement on the family and the life-threatening consequences for the child have prompted the Interagency Autism Coordinating Committee (2011) to establish the development of effective treatments for this behavior as a major priority.

PREVALENCE OF ELOPEMENT IN CHILDREN WITH AUTISM SPECTRUM DISORDER

Estimates of the prevalence of elopement in children with ASD suggest that it is a widespread problem. For example, Murphy et al. (2005) sampled 166 parents of children with severe intellectual disabilities and/or autism, and found that 39% reported at least some problems with elopement, with 23% indicating that it was a severe problem. Similarly, in a study of 62 adults with ASD living in residential facilities, staff reported that elopement was a problem for 34% of the residents (Matson & Rivet, 2008).

Although those studies focused on individuals with severe intellectual disabilities and/or who lived in residential facilities, similarly high prevalence rates of elopement have been found in samples that have focused more specifically on children with ASD. Anderson et al. (2012) found that an alarming 49% of the 1,218 parents of a child with ASD surveyed reported that their child had eloped at least once after the age of 4. Of those who reported a history of elopement for their child, approximately half indicated that their child had been missing long enough to cause concern. Furthermore, many children with a history of elopement reportedly did so frequently, with 29% of parents indicating multiple elopement attempts per day, and another 35% reporting at least weekly elopement attempts. To establish a comparison with typically developing children, the authors also asked about elopement by siblings of those children; they found that only 13% had eloped after age 4. Thus, even though some elopement appears to be developmentally normative, those with ASD elope more often and are more likely to continue to do so as they age.

Although elopement may be distinctive in terms of the danger it poses, it is similar to several other forms of challenging behavior exhibited by individuals with ASD in that it tends to be correlated with the presence and degree of intellectual disability (Borthwick-Duffy, 1994; Kiernan & Kiernan, 1994; Kiernan & Qureshi, 1993; McClintock, Hall, & Oliver, 2003; Oliver, Murphy, & Corbett, 1987). That is, elopement is more common in children with ASD with lower intellectual and developmental levels (Anderson et al., 2012; Murphy et al., 2005). However, although elopement does occur in other populations with cognitive impairments, such as those with other developmental disabilities (Jacobson, 1982) and dementia (Lai & Arthur, 2003), it does seem to be more prevalent in individuals with ASD. For example, Matson and Rivet (2008) found that individuals with autism were significantly more likely to engage in elopement than residents of the same developmental centers who had an intellectual disability only. Thus, there seems to be some feature(s) specific to the ASD phenotype that makes these individuals more susceptible to elopement.

The reason individuals with ASD elope more frequently than individuals with other developmental or intellectual disabilities may have to do with the unique characteristics of ASD. For example, diminished awareness of other people and the dangers inherent in leaving their supervision may increase the risk that a child with ASD will elope. Furthermore, certain social situations may be aversive for children with ASD and therefore cause them to elope from social contexts. In addition, intense interests in specific items/ activities could motivate elopement to a greater degree than is observed in individuals with other developmental or intellectual disabilities. For example, our clinic treated a child with ASD who had a significant history of eloping to access balloons. His interest in balloons was so profound that he attempted to elope nearly constantly, requiring his mother to enlist the assistance of another adult to help her physically restrain him from running away whenever they left their home. On the day of his first appointment at our center, he exited the car before it was stopped and was struck by an automobile while running toward a balloon display across the street. That was his second such traffic accident. Fortunately, his injuries were not serious. However, this case illustrates how ASD symptomatology, specifically intense interests combined with diminished tendency to perceive or follow socially constructed rules, such as the importance of remaining near a parent and being aware of danger, contributed to this child's elopement.

REASONS FOR ELOPEMENT IN CHILDREN WITH ASD

As previously described, the characteristics of an individual child's elopement, such as the rapidity, covertness, and resistance to attempts to prevent it, differ significantly among individual children with ASD. However, the manner of characterizing a particular child's elopement that has the most significant implications for parent training (PT)–based interventions is the purpose the elopement serves for that child. The reason the child elopes is referred to as the *function* of the elopement.

Studies have shown that elopement can serve a variety of functions for different children with ASD (Call, Alvarez, Simmons, Lomas Mevers, & Scheithauer, 2017). For example, there are published cases of individuals eloping because doing so has resulted in access to preferred items or activities in the past (R. S. Tarbox, Wallace, & Williams, 2003). The previous example of the child who eloped toward balloons represents this type of function, referred to as a *tangible function*. Another common example of this type of elopement is a child who runs away from a parent while at the store toward the toy aisle because he or she has learned that doing so results in being able to play with new toys briefly before the child is retrieved.

The elopement of other children with ASD serves an *escape function* because it may allow them to avoid or escape from an activity that is nonpreferred, such as completing homework, brushing teeth, or being in loud or chaotic environments. For example, a child may run away from a parent and even attempt to leave the building during dentist appointments if the procedure is aversive. Another common example is when a child attempts to leave a classroom when academic work is presented or leave a loud party or other environment that includes potentially aversive stimuli.

The elopement of some children serves an *attention function* because it has resulted in attention from parents or other caregivers (Kodak, Grow, & Northup, 2004; R. S. Tarbox et al., 2003). Research has shown that caregiver attention is nearly ubiquitous as a result of problem behavior generally (St. Peter et al., 2005), and elopement is particularly likely to result in attention from caregivers because they either must prevent elopement or retrieve the child. The form of attention delivered by caregivers when a child elopes may be especially likely to be reinforcing for some children with ASD. For example, physical interaction, such as holding the child's hand or a parent's chasing a child in an attempt to retrieve him or her, may be sufficiently reinforcing to produce attention-maintained elopement.

What elopement maintained by attention, tangible items/activities, or escape from nonpreferred activities or events share is that the behavior is maintained by consequences that are mediated by another person (i.e., *social functions*). However, for other children with ASD, elopement may directly produce consequences that are sufficiently reinforcing to maintain the behavior (Carr, 1977). The maintaining relationship between elopement and this type of consequence is referred to as an *automatic function* because the consequences are produced by the behavior itself. The distinction between automatic and socially maintained elopement is one with profound implications for treatment, in part because parents are far more likely to be able to exert control over social but not automatic consequences.

The literature indicates that elopement can occur for any of the aforementioned reasons and that for some children, elopement even is maintained by multiple functions (Call, Pabico, Findley, & Valentino, 2011; T. N. Davis et al., 2013; Lang et al., 2009; Perrin, Perrin, Hill, & DiNovi, 2008; Piazza et al., 1997). Thus, there is no predominant function of elopement for children with ASD. To illustrate this point, parents of children with ASD who had a history of elopement reported roughly equivalent probability of their child's elopement occurring for most of the reasons presented: 36% indicated that their child eloped to "reach a place he or she enjoys," 34% indicated that their child eloped to "escape an anxious situation," 30% responded that their child eloped to "escape uncomfortable sensory stimuli," and another 30% reported that their child eloped to "[pursue] his or her special topic" (Anderson et al., 2012). Notably, these percentages sum to greater than 100%, again indicating that it appears to be common for elopement to serve more than one function for a given child with ASD. Similarly, a consecutive controlled case series analysis of outcomes from an intensive clinical program that frequently treats elopement exhibited by children with ASD found that elopement served more than one function for 36% of participants (Call et al., 2017).

In the Anderson et al. (2012) survey, 53% of parents reported that their child with ASD eloped because he or she enjoyed running and/or exploring, suggesting that the child's elopement may have served an automatic function. However, Call et al. (2017) found that elopement was maintained by automatic reinforcement for only 18% of individuals with whom they conducted systematic analyses of function. The method by which function was identified in those two studies may account for such a discrepancy in observed prevalence of elopement maintained by automatic consequences. Call et al. conducted systematic assessments of function, called *functional analyses*, in which the child was directly observed under a variety of tightly controlled conditions. Functional analysis is widely considered to be the most thorough methodology for identifying the function of an individual's problem behavior (Beavers, Iwata, & Lerman, 2013). In contrast, Anderson et al. relied on caregiver report to determine function. Past research regarding the prevalence of various functions maintaining problem behavior has suggested that parents frequently draw mistaken conclusions about the function of their child's problem behavior (J. Tarbox et al., 2009; Thompson & Iwata, 2007). That is, parents frequently struggle to identify the function of their child's problem behavior based solely on their observations of their child in the natural environment because those settings generally include many confounding variables. For example, a parent may conclude that their child's elopement occurs randomly because of the sheer number of variables that precede or follow elopement (e.g., time of day, presence of preferred items, attention from others, noise level). This complexity inherent in the natural environment makes it challenging to discern an accurate pattern that is correlated with elopement. Thus, parents may conclude that their child simply likes to explore or runs because he or she enjoys it. In contrast, functional analyses can evaluate these variables in a highly controlled manner to detect a social function that otherwise might appear to be random or exploratory. Thus, the lower prevalence of elopement that serves an automatic function for children with ASD is to be expected when function is identified via functional analyses compared with caregiver report.

The function of a child's elopement is a key to PT-based interventions because commonly recommended behavioral techniques actually can exacerbate elopement when not selected based on function. For example, holding a child's hand after he or she attempts to run away could increase elopement if physical interactions are reinforcing for that child. Similarly, placing a child in time-out in a quiet corner after he or she tries to leave the house may be reinforcing if the function of the child's elopement is to escape from loud siblings. In both examples, a clinician who has identified the function of the child's elopement can avoid contraindicated treatment components in lieu of others that take the function of the child's elopement into account.

ASSESSING THE FUNCTION OF ELOPEMENT

Within a function analysis, the influence of specific environmental variables is systematically evaluated within separate conditions, each of which serves as an analog to a situation in the natural environment that is hypothesized to evoke elopement. The function of the child's elopement is determined by observing elevated rates of elopement across repeated sessions of a particular condition compared with a control condition in which the variables hypothesized to maintain elopement are absent. For example, a condition designed to evaluate whether a child's elopement is maintained by access to tangible items or activities may create an analog to a real-world scenario that would evoke elopement by having a clinician restrict the child's access to his or her favorite toy. If the child eloped, the clinician would then give the item back. Similarly, to evaluate whether elopement is maintained by escape from nonpreferred demands, the clinician might present a homework task followed by a break from those demands, should elopement occur. In an attention condition, the therapist may divert his or her attention by appearing busy and then provide the child with attention contingent on elopement. Elevated rates of elopement in any of these conditions relative to a condition that includes no demands, free access to tangible items, and/or free access to attention suggest that the consequence in that condition is responsible for maintaining the child's elopement.

However, some unique aspects of elopement create challenges for commonly used functional analysis methods (e.g., Iwata et al., 1982/1994). For example, results from typical functional analyses may be complicated by the fact that retrieving a child who has eloped always includes at least some attention, even in test conditions that are not designed to evaluate the influence of attention on elopement. Furthermore, for children who elope rapidly or do so exclusively in settings with potential hazards (e.g., busy parking lots), functional analyses may be too dangerous to conduct in naturalistic settings. It is sometimes impossible to isolate certain key variables in naturalistic settings. For example, it can be difficult to control the reaction of onlookers.

Fortunately, functional analysis procedures have been modified to specifically address these aspects of elopement (e.g., Kodak et al., 2004; Lang et al., 2009). In one method, elopement is assessed using an arrangement in which the child can elope from one room to another (Piazza et al., 1997). An example of a test condition using this two-room arrangement involves having one empty room—either completely empty, which would eliminate potential confounding variables but may not be realistic, or simply devoid of the child's preferred items—and one room containing highly preferred items or activities. The child is shown the room with the preferred items and then guided to the empty room. If the child elopes from the empty room to the room with the preferred items, he or she is allowed a brief period of access to the preferred items before being guided back to the empty room. Data are collected on the number of times the individual elopes from the empty room to the room with the preferred items/activities. Test conditions for other functions have been similarly adapted for the purpose of assessing elopement using this two-room arrangement.

Given what is known about the importance of function in the treatment of problem behaviors generally and the apparent variability in the function of elopement across individuals, best practices for treating elopement include conducting a functional assessment (Lang et al., 2009). However, functional analyses of elopement require expertise and, in some cases, specialized facilities that may not always be available. Fortunately, other forms of functional assessment have been developed that, although less thorough, may constitute an adequate assessment of the function of elopement for many individuals.

Unlike functional analyses, which require direct observation of elopement, indirect assessments instead rely on information gathered from other sources (J. Tarbox et al., 2009), such as record reviews, structured and semistructured interviews, informal surveys, and rating scales. Although often considered less thorough, such indirect assessments of function still can produce important information that can suggest the likely function of a child's elopement and/or assist in the creation of hypotheses to be evaluated using more thorough methods of functional assessment (Floyd, Phaneuf, & Wilczynski, 2005). For example, information from indirect assessments that indicate that a child consistently elopes to the same place (e.g., a neighbor's swimming pool) may be a sufficiently strong indicator that the child's elopement serves a tangible function (i.e., gaining access to water), such that more intensive functional assessments may not be necessary unless treatments are unsuccessful. Similarly, information from indirect assessments that there is a consistent context from which the child elopes (e.g., math class) may be a sufficiently strong indicator that the elopement is maintained by escape from the academic demands or other features present during math class (e.g., the math teacher), and that additional assessment is superfluous unless treatment is unsuccessful.

Of the different types of indirect assessments, interviews are likely the simplest and most flexible for gathering information, including the frequency of elopement, common antecedents and consequences, chronicity, and which treatment approaches have been attempted previously. Several structured interviews have been developed for this purpose, such as the Functional Assessment Interview (O'Neill et al., 1997). Even when there are plans to conduct a more thorough form of functional assessment, it is advisable to first conduct an interview (structured or unstructured) to gather important information that can inform the design and implementation of a more comprehensive assessment.

In addition to interviews, a number of rating scales have been developed to identify function, including the Motivation Assessment Scale (MAS; Durand & Crimmins, 1988), Functional Assessment Screening Tool (FAST; Iwata et al., 2013), Problem Behavior Questionnaire (Lewis, Scott, & Sugai, 1994), and Questions About Behavioral Function (QABF; Paclawskyj, Matson, Rush, Smalls, & Vollmer, 2001). Advantages of these measures include that they require little time to administer and less clinical experience to interpret. However, there has been little systematic evaluation of these rating scales, and what psychometric data have been collected generally have been modestly supportive. For example, the interrater reliability of most of these measures has been found to be low to moderate: 71.5% for the FAST, 52% for the MAS, and 57% for the QABF (Iwata et al., 2013; C. M. Smith, Smith, Dracobly, & Pace, 2012), whereas the interrater reliability of the Problem Behavior Questionnaire has not been evaluated. In addition, comparisons with results from a functional analysis have yielded only moderate agreement: 68.3% for the FAST, 56.3% for the QABF, and 43.8% for the MAS (Iwata et al., 2013; Paclawskyj et al., 2001). Furthermore, none of these indirect assessments has been evaluated specifically for elopement. Thus, results from these measures should be interpreted with caution, with the most appropriate application being as a single source of information in a multimethod assessment of function.

Descriptive methods also are a viable alternative when a functional analysis of elopement is not feasible. These methods are similar to functional analyses in that the child is directly observed and elopement events are recorded. However, unlike functional analyses, antecedent and consequence variables are not systematically manipulated, but, rather, are allowed to occur naturally in the environment. Thus, descriptive methods can provide information about the relationship or correlation between elopement and naturally occurring environmental events (Bijou, Peterson, & Ault, 1968) but cannot identify conclusive causal relationships. One example of a descriptive method that can show the correlation between elopement and environmental events is antecedent-behavior-consequence data collection (Lanovaz, Argumedes, Roy, Duquette, & Watkins, 2013). This method consists of observing the child and recording environmental events that precede and follow an elopement event. Because parents can be trained to collect antecedent-behavior-consequence data, this approach can be an especially helpful tool when a therapist cannot reliably observe elopement due to either reactivity to a therapist's presence or because elopement only occurs infrequently.

PARENT TRAINING STRATEGIES

There is a relatively well-developed literature on training parents to implement interventions for their children (Bearss, Burrell, Stewart, & Scahill, 2015). Various combinations of didactic, role, play, and in vivo training have been shown to effectively establish the skills necessary for parents to address a range of problem behaviors exhibited by their children (Kaminski, Valle, Filene, & Boyle, 2008). Similarly, there has been some research on building a therapeutic alliance, addressing parent concerns, and ensuring treatment adherence by parents (Allen & Warzak, 2000; Schmidt, Chomycz, Houlding, Kruse, & Franks, 2014). Rather than describing effective PT methods that may be common to parent-mediated interventions for a range of child issues, this section focuses on the specific practices and skills necessary for parents to address elopement, and how existing best practices for PT may need to be adapted for this behavior.

Although many forms of child problem behavior can be significantly concerning to parents, those with children with ASD who elope are likely to experience particular distress due to the gravity of the problem and its inherent risks. For instance, the caregiver of a child we treated who frequently eloped in the middle of the night (and was able to successfully elude lock and alarm systems installed to prevent his elopement) reported that she frequently slept very little at night out of fear of her child's leaving the home. The caregiver's frequent exhaustion made it difficult to work through treatment strategies during our appointments; she often slept during the times we had asked her to collect data.

In addition to the stress parents experience due to their child's elopement, a host of additional issues can disrupt parents' ability to implement caregiver-mediated treatments effectively. For example, parents have reported fearing the stigma of being viewed as neglectful when their children elope (Solomon & Lawlor, 2013) and, as a result, may be less willing to practice treatment procedures in public places. Similarly, that some parents of children with ASD who elope avoid going into the community could diminish social supports needed to incorporate PT-based interventions.

Clinicians may need to be particularly adaptable when training parents of children with ASD in the use of strategies to reduce elopement. For example, some types of functional assessments and treatments may require one to travel to locations where a child is most likely to elope. Anderson et al. (2012) found that 74% of parents indicated that their children with ASD were most likely to elope from their own home, followed by stores (40%) and school settings (29%). Thus, children with ASD may be unlikely to exhibit elopement in clinic settings, limiting opportunities to observe it during the assessment process (see the description earlier about the disadvantages of certain functional assessment methods) or to conduct in vivo training with parents. That is, if a child never elopes, it may be hard to observe parents implementing treatment strategies so that a clinician can gauge fidelity and provide feedback. In our own clinical experience, we have found it necessary to conduct assessments of elopement and treatment sessions in a variety of settings, including parks, day care facilities, malls, post offices, and restaurants.

PT-based interventions for elopement are most effective when the treatment is individualized and function based (Lang et al., 2009). Individualized intervention packages should take into account the results of a functional assessment, the child's size and level of cognitive functioning, parent resources, and the setting(s) in which elopement occurs (Call et al., 2017). The goals of individualized treatment packages are twofold: (a) to reduce the probability of the child's elopement and (b) to reduce risk of harm if the child does elope.

In addition to selecting individual treatment components that are most likely to reduce a child's elopement, the intervention also must be individualized to maximize social and ecological validity. That is, it is equally important to consider how the treatment must be adapted to the unique aspects of a family's circumstances and resources. For example, a single parent with multiple children is likely to find some potential treatment components, such as vigilant monitoring, to be unfeasible. Conversely, families with multiple caregivers and a single child who elopes may find such intensive monitoring more manageable but have their own set of barriers to treatment success. Such barriers include the potential for inconsistent implementation across caregivers or differences of opinion regarding treatment acceptability and resulting discrepancies in buy-in. Similarly, locks and other physical modifications, such as baby gates, can aid in the prevention of elopement but can be prohibitively expensive for families of limited financial means. A variety of other barriers, such as caregiver's mental health, work schedules, and extended family's willingness to implement interventions, also can create barriers to consistent treatment implementation and therefore treatment success.

The individual components of PT-based interventions for elopement comprise two major categories: (a) antecedent strategies that are implemented before elopement occurs and (b) consequence manipulation strategies that are used following an incident of elopement. *Antecedent strategies* frequently are preventative in nature and may be used to either reduce the likelihood of elopement or reduce the impact of an elopement event if it does occur. In contrast, *consequence manipulation strategies* involve using reinforcement and extinction to teach the child that eloping has less preferred outcomes than remaining near supervision. In most cases, the best outcome is achieved when a combination of antecedent and consequence strategies is used.

Antecedent Strategies

Antecedent strategies can be divided into those that are preventative and those that are focused on risk mitigation. With respect to preventative strategies, there are many commonly recommended modifications to the environment that make elopement impossible or at least significantly more effortful for the child. These modifications include putting locks and alarms on doors and windows of one's home, activating child locks in the car, consistently holding hands in public places, and bringing additional caregivers on outings to large or crowded places to assist with supervision. Caregivers often can benefit from a therapist's conducting a home evaluation and observation in settings where elopement is common to help identify these strategies at the outset of PT.

Some parents may have adopted maladaptive antecedent strategies that will need to be addressed, such as avoiding outings or areas where elopement is likely. For example, a parent of a child who consistently attempts to elope when on community outings may discontinue such outings with his or her child unless absolutely necessary. Although this practice may prevent elopement temporarily, it is not an effective long-term strategy because it does not decrease the probability of elopement occurring the next time the child must be taken into the community. When parents have adopted these strategies to avoid elopement, it is the role of the clinician to educate them about how these practices may not be helpful in the long run and to provide alternative approaches. In the preceding example, a more adaptive strategy would be establishing some antecedent techniques that will increase the likelihood of successful trips into the community, such as keeping outings brief and maintaining vigilant supervision, so that the trip is likely to end following appropriate behavior as opposed to elopement. After the child experiences success with short and highly supervised trips, these components can be gradually decreased.

Social stories can be another helpful tool for proactively addressing problem behavior (e.g., Kuttler, Myles, & Carlson, 1998; Swaggart et al., 1995), especially for children with higher cognitive levels. Social stories can be used to teach the child where it is safe for him or her to go and where it is not, as well as the associated dangers of leaving safe areas. Parents are likely to require assistance from a clinician in developing appropriate social stories, as well as coaching to ensure that those stories are used with other reinforcement-based strategies. For children who may not benefit from social stories due to intellectual impairments, boundaries can be established by physically walking around the area in which the child is expected to remain (e.g., walking around the edges of a playground or around the backyard). Parents also can use physical markings, such as rope, tape, or temporary barriers, to more clearly indicate boundaries. Over time and with successful pairing with instructions and reinforcement, it may be possible to gradually eliminate these physical barriers using fading techniques.

Another common preventative strategy involves diminishing the child's motivation to elope by providing the functional reinforcer before elopement occurs. For example, the parent of a child who frequently elopes to the toy aisle of a store can be coached to bring a few preferred toys from home that the child can hold while at that store. Similarly, if a child elopes to escape from a particular type of task or to get attention, the parent can provide frequent breaks on a set schedule or high-quality attention (e.g., enthusiastic praise) during activities when elopement is likely. However, sometimes the functional reinforcer cannot be delivered easily, or the natural consequences accessed by eloping are more reinforcing than those that can be delivered by a parent. For example, a child's own toys may not compete effectively with the novel toys available in the toy aisle. However, providing alternative reinforcers still can decrease elopement in this scenario because they are accessible with no effort from the child. The value of competing items also can be enhanced by restricting access to them when they are not being used as part of an elopement prevention protocol (Roane, Call, & Falcomata, 2005). It is important to consider that parents initially may forget to provide access to competing items but remember when the child attempts to elope. Unfortunately, belated delivery of competing items (i.e., after an elopement attempt) is likely to reinforce elopement rather than prevent it. Thus, clinicians should emphasize the importance of providing access to competing items on an antecedent basis only.

Because a single occurrence of elopement is potentially life threatening, interventions successful in reducing but not eliminating elopement are not likely to be considered completely successful (Lang et al., 2009). However, no treatment can guarantee complete elimination. Therefore, establishing a formal plan for mitigating the risks associated with elopement, should it occur, is a critical element of PT-based interventions. As described earlier, a key purpose of antecedent strategies is to minimize the negative impact of elopement should the child succeed in leaving supervision. Several sources have developed parent toolkits that can provide guidance to parents (National Autism Association, 2012) A major task for a clinician who is conducting PT is to guide parents as they develop an elopement emergency plan to ensure that the parents are prepared to respond to an elopement event. At a minimum, the plan should include having the parents gather important information and documents, such as how to rapidly notify local emergency responders, and keep recent photographs of their child easily accessible. Such planning allows information and documents to be shared quickly with those who may be recruited to help search for a missing child. Parents should identify family members and friends who live nearby and recruit a search team comprising those who agree to be contacted and assist in searching assigned areas for the child during an elopement event. Parents also should be guided to identify nearby hazards, such as busy streets or bodies of water, and areas where their child is likely to elope. They should plan to check those locations first during an elopement event, even if their child does not show a propensity for seeking them out because they pose particular risk of serious harm.

Antecedent strategies focused on minimizing risk of harm also can include having the child wear jewelry, tags, or clothing labels that provide the child's name and emergency contact information. Similarly, tracking devices that the child can wear have tremendous potential to decrease the time required to retrieve a child who has eloped. Although these devices are becoming increasingly available, some require collaboration with local emergency response or law enforcement agencies. Thus, if parents' local agencies do not support these systems, parents may require support from a clinician as they lobby and educate local officials in an effort to adopt the use of such devices.

Teaching key skills to the child can be crucial in decreasing the risk of harm from elopement. For example, teaching a child to safely cross a street decreases the chances that the child will be struck by an automobile after eloping. Similarly, ensuring that the child is able to swim can prevent drowning accidents, and teaching the child to provide personal information (e.g., parent's name, address) increases the chances that a child who is found by others can be reunited with caregivers. Parents are likely to need support from clinicians on how to most effectively teach these skills (Rogers, Hemmeter, & Wolery, 2010; T. Smith, 2001).

Behavior Plan: Consequence-Based Strategies

As discussed previously, consequence-based strategies involve procedures implemented by a parent following either an instance of elopement to decrease the probability that it will happen again or following alternative and appropriate behaviors to increase the likelihood that it will occur in the future. Implementing these strategies can be challenging, and it may be helpful for parents to practice them under controlled circumstances before routine use. Thus, early in treatment, the parent may need to be coached to conduct the treatment during practice shopping trips without actually purchasing food so that they can focus on implementing the treatment.

It also is important to ensure success of early treatment attempts so that the child's alternative behavior is reinforced. Thus, criteria for reinforcement may need to be modest. Therefore, initial implementation may not meet parents' expectations for treatment success. For example, for a child who elopes during grocery shopping, practice trips to the store initially may need to be brief (e.g., only a few minutes) so that the child can earn reinforcement for staying in close proximity to the parent. Although there may be plans to eventually increase requirements for the child to more acceptable levels, it frequently is important to manage the parent's expectations regarding what is possible at the outset of treatment.

In addition, it is important that consequence-based strategies be implemented consistently. Inconsistency across caregivers is especially likely if they are using different definitions of elopement. For example, one parent may feel uncomfortable in the grocery store unless the child is standing immediately next to the cart. In contrast, another may find it acceptable for the child to wander some distance away so long as he or she is in sight. Under those circumstances, the child is likely to have a different experience with the two parents, even if both implement exactly the same intervention but do so based on differing definitions of elopement. As a result, the treatment may be less effective for one parent or may be ineffective altogether. Thus, one of the first goals of PT is to establish a consistent definition of elopement to be used by all caregivers. It is crucial that the definition be as specific as possible and rely on observable behaviors, rather than on inferences about the child's intent. Examples include "moving more than 5 feet away from a parent when outside of the home without asking for and receiving permission," "moving past the boundaries of the side and back of the house when playing in the backyard," "touching a doorknob of a door that leads to the outside when in the home," or "leaving the mulched area of the playground."

Extinction

Extinction is likely the most common and, whenever possible, the most critical treatment component incorporated into PT-based interventions for elopement. That is, there is some evidence that treatments for elopement may not be successful without extinction (Call et al., 2011). As most commonly implemented, *extinction* involves ensuring that the reinforcer that maintains elopement is no longer provided when elopement occurs. In practice, the specifics of how extinction is implemented can differ, depending on the function of the child's elopement. Therefore, the ability to determine the specific form of extinction to be implemented with a particular child is one of the major reasons for conducting a functional assessment of the child's elopement (see the description of functional assessment of elopement earlier in this chapter).

For elopement that serves an escape function, extinction involves ensuring that the child is not allowed to escape or avoid nonpreferred activities by eloping. For example, if a child elopes to avoid doing homework, the parent should prevent elopement and continue to prompt the child to complete the homework until the child complies. Similarly, a child whose elopement serves as an escape from loud noises likely will run away from a noisy birthday party. Extinction for this child would involve ensuring that the child remains at the birthday party for some time following the elopement attempt (McCord, Iwata, Galensky, Ellingson, & Thomson, 2001).

How the parent implements the extinction procedure to prevent escape largely depends on the size of the child and the parent. Ideally, the parent will be able to safely keep the child at the birthday party with no more than minimal physical guidance or gentle hand-over-hand prompting to complete the homework. However, for large or persistent children, it may be physically impossible for a parent to implement the extinction procedure to prevent escape. Under such circumstances, it is sometimes possible to bring the task or stimulus to the child, rather than keep the child in proximity to the task or stimulus. This approach minimizes both the reinforcement following elopement and the need to physically move or restrain the child. When the aversive stimulus is not portable, it may be possible to instead ensure that some other nonpreferred stimulus remains present until the child returns to the situation that evoked the escape-maintained elopement, such as repeated prompting by the parent (i.e., "nagging"). Although this approach may not be true extinction in that access to the functional reinforcer is not prevented, it may be sufficiently similar that it still can result in the child's learning that elopement will not produce complete escape from nonpreferred stimuli.

For problem behavior maintained by access to preferred items or activities, extinction involves preventing the child from accessing those items or activities through elopement (Call et al., 2011). For example, if a child elopes to see a train, his or her parent should block the child's sight of the train or guide the child back to an area where the train is not visible. Similar to implementing extinction for escape-maintained elopement, other strategies may need to be used if the child is too large for the parent to move or otherwise prevent from accessing the functional reinforcer. A parent may need to stand between the child and a preferred item to block his or her view, unplug or turn off an electronic device, or otherwise prevent the child from playing with an item, even if it the parent cannot immediately remove the item from the child's grasp.

If a child's elopement is maintained by attention, the parent should be coached to refrain from providing anything more than the minimum possible amount and quality of attention following instances of elopement (Sansbury, Sanchez, & Jones, 2009). Implementing extinction for elopement that serves this function often is the most problematic because the act of elopement generally requires some degree of attention to maintain safety. Frequently, the type of attention the child most enjoys following elopement is being chased by a caregiver. Looking back at the parent—sometimes accompanied by laughing or smiling as the parent attempts to stop the child from eloping—is an indicator that this is the case. In this situation, it often takes substantial coaching and troubleshooting by a clinician to overcome the parent's natural tendency to chase his or her child who has eloped. Instead, the clinician and parent must work together to find an appropriate balance between ensuring the child's safety and minimizing attention. Sometimes such a balance involves walking briskly (as opposed to running) and physically retrieving the child without speaking. Other times, finding this balance involves beginning treatment in a context in which the risk of harm from elopement is minimized (e.g., a contained space with a single exit and with the a therapist strategically placed at that exit), so that no chasing, retrieval, or vocal attending is necessary. After elopement has ceased in this setting, the procedures can be gradually generalized to other settings.

Differential Reinforcement

Some parents of children with ASD, especially those of children with language delays, may have concerns with implementing extinction because they consider elopement to be an indicator of their child's desires. For example, a parent may view elopement by the child at a loud party as the child's requesting to leave. Clinicians working with parents of children who elope can ease this concern by stressing that the functional reinforcer still should be available but not contingent on elopement. In each of the preceding examples, it is appropriate for children to access the functional reinforcers (e.g., playing with toys, looking at trains, getting a break from a loud party, accessing caregiver attention), at least occasionally. That is, the reinforcer is not problematic so much as the child's use of elopement to access it. Thus, it is crucial that the child learns to use appropriate behavior to access the functional reinforcer rather than elopement.

Differential Reinforcement of Alternative Behavior. Sometimes a specific appropriate alternative behavior will be readily apparent, such as requesting a preferred item or completing a task, rather than eloping toward or away from it, respectively. In that case, *differential reinforcement of alternative behavior* (DRA) is appropriate (Falcomata, Roane, Feeney, & Stephenson, 2010). When training parents to implement DRA, it first is important to ensure that the child has the requisite skill in his or her repertoire. If not, it will be necessary to teach it or help the parent to do so. Once the child has the required skill, parents can be trained to deliver the functional reinforcer (if possible) or a reinforcer that is as similar as possible whenever the child exhibits the alternative behavior. Initially, parents should reinforce every instance of the alternative behavior until the rate of elopement has decreased. Once the alternative behavior is well established, parents can use a variety of approaches to teach the child to wait for the preferred items (Fisher, Thompson, Hagopian, Bowman, & Krug, 2000; Hagopian, Boelter, & Jarmolowicz, 2011), increase the variety of alternative behaviors (Lee, McComas, & Jawor, 2002), or emit only the alternative behavior when the functional reinforcer is available (Hanley, Iwata, & Thompson, 2001).

Differential Reinforcement of Other Behavior. *Differential reinforcement of other behavior* (DRO) involves delivering reinforcement following a period without elopement (Call et al., 2011). There is some evidence that selecting the duration of the initial DRO interval can be guided by the rate of the problem behavior under baseline conditions (e.g., Thompson, Iwata, Hanley,

Dozier, & Samaha, 2003). For example, a child who elopes after working on homework for an average of 10 minutes is likely to be successful with a longer DRO interval than a child who elopes the moment homework is presented. However, as with DRA, reinforcement initially should be delivered more often. Thus, in the preceding example, beginning with a DRO interval of 8 minutes is more likely to ensure that the child receives reinforcement and is successful. Many parents implement DRO more consistently when they are encouraged to use a timer to keep track of the targeted interval. Similarly, parents can use visual timers to indicate to the child how much longer he or she will have to wait for the reinforcer. After the child consistently experiences success (i.e., refrains from eloping long enough to access reinforcement), parents can gradually increase the DRO interval.

As with DRA, it usually is best for the reinforcer used in the DRO to match the reinforcer shown to maintain elopement in the functional assessment. However, there are circumstances under which a reinforcer other than the functional reinforcer should be used. Such situations include (a) when the functional reinforcer cannot be identified reliably through functional assessment, (b) results of the functional assessment indicate that elopement is maintained by automatic reinforcement, or (c) the functional reinforcer cannot be delivered reliably (e.g., the functional reinforcer is going swimming). Nonfunctional reinforcers work best if they are sufficiently potent to override the value of the reinforcers naturally produced by elopement (Mace, 1994). Thus, it is considered best practice to conduct a preference assessment to determine which items are most likely to serve as reinforcers (see Hagopian, Long, & Rush, 2004, for a detailed description of preference assessments).

TOPICS FOR FUTURE RESEARCH

As described earlier, the prevalence of elopement by children with ASD appears to be higher than for children with other developmental disabilities. Although this chapter has proposed some potential explanations for this finding, such as the role of communication deficits, repetitive interests, and deficits in interpreting social situations, further research is necessary to definitively confirm the role of these factors in elopement. Studying this issue is important because it may provide guidance to clinicians about specific treatments that may be uniquely effective (or ineffective) for children with ASD.

To date, the literature on the treatment of elopement consists almost exclusively of case studies or relatively small samples using single-subject research methods (see Call et al., 2017, for an exception). Thus, there is a tremendous need for clinical trials that can establish the efficacy and effectiveness of PT-based interventions for elopement in children with ASD. In particular, the treatments presented in the literature generally have consisted of individualized, and frequently very intensive or laborious treatment packages. Thus, developing PT-based interventions that can be delivered by a range of clinicians and in a number of settings is critical to increasing access to effective treatments for elopement.

Future research also should focus on identifying the child or behavioral characteristics that determine which specific strategies are most effective in the treatment of a child's elopement. The literature on the treatment of elopement has tended to focus on relatively high-frequency elopement and elopement that serves a clear function. In contrast, the literature on the treatment of infrequent elopement, for which the function may be more difficult to assess, is less well developed. Unfortunately, elopement that meets this description seems to be relatively common and remains exceedingly dangerous. For example, the first time a patient of ours eloped, he had wandered more than a mile from home before he was found. When asked why he left, he responded that his birthday was next week and he wanted to "invite the whole world," so he began walking in the direction of the airport. This example illustrates both the danger posed even by infrequent elopement and how the motivation for elopement may be sporadic and inconsistent. That is, although this boy was unlikely to elope again for this particular reason, his parents were exceedingly frightened that they could not predict what might motivate future elopement attempts.

As described at the beginning of this chapter, there are a variety of ways in which elopement differs in terms of frequency, covertness, rapidity, function, and so on, leading to a wide range of terms for this behavior. Each of these characteristics can present unique challenges for parents and clinicians. Unfortunately, the literature generally does not distinguish among types of elopement based on such variables. There have been some attempts to develop a typology of elopement or wandering in the literature on patients with dementia (Algase, Antonakos, Beattie, Beel-Bates, & Yao, 2009), and some of this work could guide future research in children with ASD. Such a typology could be helpful in identifying variables that mediate the effectiveness of various treatments. Regardless of the individual characteristics, the need for effective and individualized PT-based treatments for elopement is clear.

CASE EXAMPLE

Darrell[1] is a 15-year-old boy who was admitted to an outpatient program for the treatment of elopement. He communicates rudimentary wants and needs using sign language, and can follow simple verbal instructions. He

---

[1]Clinical material has been disguised to protect client confidentiality.

exhibits severe symptoms of ASD (86th percentile), based on results of the Childhood Autism Rating Scale (second edition; Schopler, Van Bourgondien, Wellman, & Love, 2010). Darrell's mother describes the elopement as bolting and reports that it occurs both at home and in the community an average of 10 times per day. Darrell's mother is unable to identify a consistent reason for his elopement. However, she reports that it often occurs in wide-open spaces, such as parking lots and parks. Darrell also has a history of eloping from his home, prompting his parents to install locks on all of the doors and windows. Due to his elopement and history of leaving the house unsupervised, his parents monitor him at all times and avoid trips into the community with Darrell.

At the commencement of treatment, we helped Darrell's mother develop and implement an elopement emergency plan. This plan included (a) preventative measures, such as installing additional locks or door or window alarms; (b) steps to expedite the parents' response to an elopement emergency, such as identifying individuals close by who could be called on to search for Darrell and placing emergency responder contact information in accessible locations; and (c) guidelines on how to respond in the event of that Darrell went missing (e.g., identifying dangerous locations nearby where people should search first).

An initial interview with Darrell's mother failed to clarify the function of his elopement. Thus, we conducted a functional analysis that rotated between a control condition and different test conditions designed to determine whether elopement was maintained by escape from demands, access to preferred items, access to attention, or automatic reinforcement, respectively. These conditions were conducted following the previously described procedure of using two rooms. During test conditions, Darrell always began in one of the rooms that had been set up to contain the potential reinforcer being evaluated in that condition. In the attention and tangible conditions, this meant that the he received social attention from a therapist or access to an item identified as highly preferred (i.e., an iPad), respectively. When sessions from the attention condition began, the therapist guided Darrell to the other room, where the therapist restricted his attention. Similarly, when sessions from the tangible condition began, the therapist left the iPad in the first room and guided him to the second room that did not contain any preferred items. For the escape condition, Darrell did not receive attention or the iPad in the first room, which instead was kept empty. However, when he moved to the second room and the session began, the therapist prompted him to engage in a nonpreferred task (i.e., tracing his name, matching items by color). In each of these conditions, Darrell could elope to the first room and access attention, the iPad, or a break from the demands, depending on the condition. After 30 seconds of the relevant consequence, the therapist always guided him back to the second room and resumed restricting attention and access to the iPad, or presenting demands as appropriate for that condition. The functional analysis also included an "alone" condition to ascertain whether elopement was automatically reinforcing. In this condition, Darrell was left alone in the second room and allowed to freely elope from room to room without consequence (therapists observed continuously using a camera system). We compared results of these test conditions with those from a control condition in which Darrell was able to maintain access to therapist attention and the iPad, without any demands.

During this functional analysis, Darrell intermittently eloped from the second room across all conditions, including the control condition. Undifferentiated results such as these raise the possibility that an individual's elopement is not sensitive to any of the social consequences embedded within the attention, escape, or tangible conditions, suggesting that it is maintained automatic reinforcement. To confirm this hypothesis, we conducted a series of sessions from the alone condition without interspersing sessions from any of the other conditions. If Darrell's elopement had served a social function, it would be expected to decrease across these successive sessions because the absence of any programmed consequences would constitute extinction. However, persistence of elopement across these sessions, which were designed specifically to exclude any programmed consequences, generally is considered confirmation that the reinforcers maintaining elopement are instead produced automatically by the elopement itself (Vollmer, Marcus, Ringdahl, & Roane, 1995). In Darrell's case, he continued to elope during these sessions in the absence of any programmed consequences, leading us to conclude that his elopement served an automatic function.

Concluding that Darrell's elopement was maintained by automatic reinforcement meant that we did not have control over the reinforcers that maintained it. Thus, it was necessary to develop a treatment that included arbitrary consequences that could override the naturally occurring ones automatically produced by elopement. For Darrell, this treatment consisted of differentially providing a highly preferred item contingent on remaining in close proximity to a caregiver. We evaluated this treatment during short walks with Darrell around the treatment unit. Initially, walks were extremely brief (i.e., 5–10 feet). If he successfully walked to the designated destination without eloping (i.e., he remained in close proximity to the therapist), he received a very small portion of a preferred snack. Elopement also was placed on extinction, meaning that if Darrell began to elope, the therapist attempted to physically block him from leaving the area and gently guided him to the designated destination instead. If Darrell successfully eloped, the therapist retrieved him, guided him back to the area from which he had eloped, and then to the designated destination. Darrell did not receive the preferred item if the therapist had to guide him in this way.

Once we consistently observed significantly reduced rates of elopement during these early treatment sessions, the duration of these walks began to systematically increase. This process continued until Darrell was able to walk with the therapist for 5 minutes without eloping. At this point, we generalized the treatment to new locations and destinations. For example, Darrell walked with the therapist to the playground outside of the treatment facility.

Next, we trained Darrell's mother to implement all of the components of the treatment using a behavioral skills training model (i.e., didactics, then role play, followed by in vivo practice with feedback). A therapist also accompanied her as she implemented the treatment in the home and community, including a grocery store and nearby park. Once Darrell's mother demonstrated that she could implement all of the treatment components independently with high fidelity, she began to implement treatment in the home without therapists while collecting data that she returned to the treatment team each day. Finally, the therapist trained personnel at Darrell's school to implement the treatment to ensure consistency across caregivers and settings. His caregivers continued to systematically increase the duration of walks in consultation with the treatment team. Darrell's mother reported that treatment remained successful at reducing elopement in all settings. She even reported that the family took a 5-day vacation to Walt Disney World—something that they previously would not have contemplated doing—and that Darrell did not elope at all during their trip.

REFERENCES

Algase, D. L., Antonakos, C., Beattie, E. R. A., Beel-Bates, C. A., & Yao, L. (2009). Empirical derivation and validation of a wandering typology. *Journal of the American Geriatrics Society, 57*, 2037–2045. http://dx.doi.org/10.1111/j.1532-5415.2009.02491.x

Allen, K. D., & Warzak, W. J. (2000). The problem of parental nonadherence in clinical behavior analysis: Effective treatment is not enough. *Journal of Applied Behavior Analysis, 33*, 373–391. http://dx.doi.org/10.1901/jaba.2000.33-373

Anderson, C., Law, J. K., Daniels, A., Rice, C., Mandell, D. S., Hagopian, L., & Law, P. A. (2012). Occurrence and family impact of elopement in children with autism spectrum disorders. *Pediatrics, 130*, 870–877. http://dx.doi.org/10.1542/peds.2012-0762

Bearss, K., Burrell, T. L., Stewart, L., & Scahill, L. (2015). Parent training in autism spectrum disorder: What's in a name? *Clinical Child and Family Psychology*

Review, *18*, 170–182. http://dx.doi.org/10.1007/s10567-015-0179-5 (Erratum published 2015, *Clinical Child and Family Psychology Review*, *18*, p. 183. http://dx.doi.org/10.1007/s10567-015-0183-9)

Beavers, G. A., Iwata, B. A., & Lerman, D. C. (2013). Thirty years of research on the functional analysis of problem behavior. *Journal of Applied Behavior Analysis*, *46*, 1–21. http://dx.doi.org/10.1002/jaba.30

Bijou, S. W., Peterson, R. F., & Ault, M. H. (1968). A method to integrate descriptive and experimental field studies at the level of data and empirical concepts. *Journal of Applied Behavior Analysis*, *1*, 175–191. http://dx.doi.org/10.1901/jaba.1968.1-175

Bodfish, J. W. (1992). AWOL behavior. In E. A. Konarski, J. E. Favell, & J. E. Favell (Eds.), *Manual for the assessment and treatment of the behavior disorders of people with mental retardation* (Tab BD17, pp. 1–8). Morganton, NC: Western Carolina Center Foundation.

Borthwick-Duffy, S. A. (1994). Epidemiology and prevalence of psychopathology in people with mental retardation. *Journal of Consulting and Clinical Psychology*, *62*, 17–27. http://dx.doi.org/10.1037/0022-006X.62.1.17

Burgoyne, L., Dowling, L., Fitzgerald, A., Connolly, M., P Browne, J., & Perry, I. J. (2014). Parents' perspectives on the value of assistance dogs for children with autism spectrum disorder: A cross-sectional study. *BMJ Open*, *4*, e004786. http://dx.doi.org/10.1136/bmjopen-2014-004786

Call, N. A., Alvarez, J. P., Simmons, C. A., Lomas Mevers, J. E., & Scheithauer, M. C. (2017). Clinical outcomes of behavioral treatments for elopement in individuals with autism spectrum disorder and other developmental disabilities. *Autism*, *21*, 375–379.

Call, N. A., Pabico, R. S., Findley, A. J., & Valentino, A. L. (2011). Differential reinforcement with and without blocking as treatment for elopement. *Journal of Applied Behavior Analysis*, *44*, 903–907. http://dx.doi.org/10.1901/jaba.2011.44-903

Carr, E. G. (1977). The motivation of self-injurious behavior: A review of some hypotheses. *Psychological Bulletin*, *84*, 800–816. http://dx.doi.org/10.1037/0033-2909.84.4.800

Davis, K., & Gavidia-Payne, S. (2009). The impact of child, family, and professional support characteristics on the quality of life in families of young children with disabilities. *Journal of Intellectual and Developmental Disability*, *34*, 153–162. http://dx.doi.org/10.1080/13668250902874608

Davis, T. N., Durand, S., Bankhead, J., Strickland, E., Blenden, K., & Dacus, S., . . . Machalicek, W. (2013). Brief report: Latency functional analysis of elopement. *Behavioral Interventions*, *28*, 251–259. http://dx.doi.org/10.1002/bin.1363

Durand, V. M., & Crimmins, D. B. (1988). Identifying the variables maintaining self-injurious behavior. *Journal of Autism and Developmental Disorders*, *18*, 99–117. http://dx.doi.org/10.1007/BF02211821

Falcomata, T. S., Roane, H. S., Feeney, B. J., & Stephenson, K. M. (2010). Assessment and treatment of elopement maintained by access to stereotypy. *Journal of Applied Behavior Analysis, 43,* 513–517. http://dx.doi.org/10.1901/jaba.2010.43-513

Fisher, W. W., Thompson, R. H., Hagopian, L. P., Bowman, L. G., & Krug, A. (2000). Facilitating tolerance of delayed reinforcement during functional communication training. *Behavior Modification, 24,* 3–29. http://dx.doi.org/10.1177/0145445500241001

Floyd, R. G., Phaneuf, R. L., & Wilczynski, S. M. (2005). Measurement properties of indirect assessment methods for functional behavioral assessment: A review of research. *School Psychology Review, 34,* 58–73.

Hagopian, L. P., Boelter, E. W., & Jarmolowicz, D. P. (2011). Reinforcement schedule thinning following functional communication training: Review and recommendations. *Behavior Analysis in Practice, 4,* 4–16. http://dx.doi.org/10.1007/BF03391770

Hagopian, L. P., Long, E. S., & Rush, K. S. (2004). Preference assessment procedures for individuals with developmental disabilities. *Behavior Modification, 28,* 668–677. http://dx.doi.org/10.1177/0145445503259836

Hanley, G. P., Iwata, B. A., & Thompson, R. H. (2001). Reinforcement schedule thinning following treatment with functional communication training. *Journal of Applied Behavior Analysis, 34,* 17–38. http://dx.doi.org/10.1901/jaba.2001.34-17

Interagency Autism Coordinating Committee. (2011, February 9). [Letter to Secretary of U.S. Department of Health and Human Services Kathleen Sebelius]. Interagency Autism Coordinating Committee, Washington, DC. Retrieved from https://iacc.hhs.gov/publications/general/2011/letter_safety_sebelius_031611.pdf

Iwata, B. A., DeLeon, I. G., & Roscoe, E. M. (2013). Reliability and validity of the functional analysis screening tool. *Journal of Applied Behavior Analysis, 46,* 271–284. http://dx.doi.org/10.1002/jaba.31

Iwata, B. A., Dorsey, M. F., Slifer, K. J., Bauman, K. E., & Richman, G. S. (1994). Toward a functional analysis of self-injury. *Journal of Applied Behavior Analysis, 27,* 197–209. (Reprinted from *Analysis and Intervention in Developmental Disabilities, 2,* 3–20, 1982). http://dx.doi.org/10.1901/jaba.1994.27-197

Jacobson, J. W. (1982). Problem behavior and psychiatric impairment within a developmentally disabled population. II: Behavior severity. *Applied Research in Mental Retardation, 3,* 369–381. http://dx.doi.org/10.1016/S0270-3092(82)80004-0

Kaminski, J. W., Valle, L. A., Filene, J. H., & Boyle, C. L. (2008). A meta-analytic review of components associated with parent training program effectiveness. *Journal of Abnormal Child Psychology, 36,* 567–589. http://dx.doi.org/10.1007/s10802-007-9201-9

Kiernan, C., & Kiernan, D. (1994). Challenging behaviour in school for pupils with severe learning difficulties. *Mental Handicap Research, 7,* 177–201. http://dx.doi.org/10.1111/j.1468-3148.1994.tb00126.x

Kiernan, C., & Qureshi, H. (1993). Challenging behaviour. In C. Kiernan (Ed.), *Research to practice: Implications of research on the challenging behaviour of people with learning disability* (pp. 53–65). Kidderminster, England: British Institute of Learning Disabilities.

Kodak, T., Grow, L., & Northup, J. (2004). Functional analysis and treatment of elopement for a child with attention deficit hyperactivity disorder. *Journal of Applied Behavior Analysis, 37,* 229–232. http://dx.doi.org/10.1901/jaba.2004.37-229

Kuttler, S., Myles, B. S., & Carlson, J. K. (1998). The use of social stories to reduce precursors to tantrum behavior in a student with autism. *Focus on Autism and Other Developmental Disabilities, 13,* 176–182. http://dx.doi.org/10.1177/108835769801300306

Lai, C. K. Y., & Arthur, D. G. (2003). Wandering behaviour in people with dementia. *Journal of Advanced Nursing, 44,* 173–182. http://dx.doi.org/10.1046/j.1365-2648.2003.02781.x

Lang, R., Rispoli, M., Machalicek, W., White, P. J., Kang, S., Pierce, N., . . . Lancioni, G. (2009). Treatment of elopement in individuals with developmental disabilities: A systematic review. *Research in Developmental Disabilities, 30,* 670–681. http://dx.doi.org/10.1016/j.ridd.2008.11.003

Lanovaz, M. J., Argumedes, M., Roy, D., Duquette, J. R., & Watkins, N. (2013). Using ABC narrative recording to identify the function of problem behavior: A pilot study. *Research in Developmental Disabilities, 34,* 2734–2742. http://dx.doi.org/10.1016/j.ridd.2013.05.038

Lee, R., McComas, J. J., & Jawor, J. (2002). The effects of differential and lag reinforcement schedules on varied verbal responding by individuals with autism. *Journal of Applied Behavior Analysis, 35,* 391–402. http://dx.doi.org/10.1901/jaba.2002.35-391

Lewis, T. J., Scott, T. M., & Sugai, G. (1994). The problem behavior questionnaire: A teacher-based instrument to develop functional hypotheses of problem behavior in general education classrooms. *Assessment for Effective Intervention, 19*(2–3), 103–115.

Lowe, K., Allen, D., Jones, E., Brophy, S., Moore, K., & James, W. (2007). Challenging behaviours: Prevalence and topographies. *Journal of Intellectual Disability Research, 51,* 625–636. http://dx.doi.org/10.1111/j.1365-2788.2006.00948.x

Mace, F. C. (1994). The significance and future of functional analysis methodologies. *Journal of Applied Behavior Analysis, 27,* 385–392. http://dx.doi.org/10.1901/jaba.1994.27-385

Matson, J. L., & Rivet, T. T. (2008). Characteristics of challenging behaviours in adults with autistic disorder, PDD-NOS, and intellectual disability. *Jour-*

nal of Intellectual and Developmental Disability, 33, 323–329. http://dx.doi.org/
10.1080/13668250802492600

McClintock, K., Hall, S., & Oliver, C. (2003). Risk markers associated with challenging behaviours in people with intellectual disabilities: A meta-analytic study. Journal of Intellectual Disability Research, 47, 405–416. http://dx.doi.org/
10.1046/j.1365-2788.2003.00517.x

McCord, B. E., Iwata, B. A., Galensky, T. L., Ellingson, S. A., & Thomson, R. J. (2001). Functional analysis and treatment of problem behavior evoked by noise. Journal of Applied Behavior Analysis, 34, 447–462. http://dx.doi.org/10.1901/
jaba.2001.34-447

Murphy, G. H., Beadle-Brown, J., Wing, L., Gould, J., Shah, A., & Holmes, N. (2005). Chronicity of challenging behaviours in people with severe intellectual disabilities and/or autism: A total population sample. Journal of Autism and Developmental Disorders, 35, 405–418. http://dx.doi.org/10.1007/
s10803-005-5030-2

National Autism Association. (2012). Big red safety toolkit. Retrieved from http://
nationalautismassociation.org/docs/BigRedSafetyToolkit.pdf

Oliver, C., Murphy, G. H., & Corbett, J. A. (1987). Self-injurious behaviour in people with mental handicap: A total population study. Journal of Intellectual Disability Research, 31, 147–162. http://dx.doi.org/10.1111/
j.1365-2788.1987.tb01351.x

O'Neill, R. E., Horner, R. H., Albin, R. W., Storey, K., Sprague, J. R., & Newton, J. S. (1997). Functional assessment of problem behavior: A practical assessment guide. Pacific Grove, CA: Brooks/Cole.

Paclawskyj, T. R., Matson, J. L., Rush, K. S., Smalls, Y., & Vollmer, T. R. (2001). Assessment of the convergent validity of the Questions About Behavioral Function scale with analogue functional analysis and the Motivation Assessment Scale. Journal of Intellectual Disability Research, 45, 484–494. http://
dx.doi.org/10.1046/j.1365-2788.2001.00364.x

Perrin, C. J., Perrin, S. H., Hill, E. A., & DiNovi, K. (2008). Brief functional analysis and treatment of elopement in preschoolers with autism. Behavioral Interventions, 23, 87–95. http://dx.doi.org/10.1002/bin.256

Piazza, C. C., Hanley, G. P., Bowman, L. G., Ruyter, J. M., Lindauer, S. E., & Saiontz, D. M. (1997). Functional analysis and treatment of elopement. Journal of Applied Behavior Analysis, 30, 653–672. http://dx.doi.org/10.1901/jaba.1997.30-653

Roane, H. S., Call, N. A., & Falcomata, T. S. (2005). A preliminary analysis of adaptive responding under open and closed economies. Journal of Applied Behavior Analysis, 38, 335–348. http://dx.doi.org/10.1901/jaba.2005.85-04

Rogers, L., Hemmeter, M. L., & Wolery, M. (2010). Using a constant time delay procedure to teach foundational swimming skills to children with autism. Topics in Early Childhood Special Education, 30, 102–111. http://dx.doi.org/
10.1177/0271121410369708

Sansbury, T., Sanchez, A., & Jones, P. (2009). Functional analysis and treatment of attention-maintained elopement in children with autism and downs syndrome using discriminative stimuli. *Proceedings of UHCL Student Research Project, 1,* 1–7.

Schmidt, F., Chomycz, S., Houlding, C., Kruse, A., & Franks, J. (2014). The association between therapeutic alliance and treatment outcomes in a group triple P intervention. *Journal of Child and Family Studies, 23,* 1337–1350. http://dx.doi.org/10.1007/s10826-013-9792-4

Schopler, E., Van Bourgondien, M. E., Wellman, G. J., & Love, S. R. (2010). *Childhood Autism Rating Scale, (CARS2).* Torrance, CA: Western Psychological Services.

Shavelle, R. M., Strauss, D. J., & Pickett, J. (2001). Causes of death in autism. *Journal of Autism and Developmental Disorders, 31,* 569–576. http://dx.doi.org/10.1023/A:1013247011483

Smith, C. M., Smith, R. G., Dracobly, J. D., & Pace, A. P. (2012). Multiple-respondent anecdotal assessments: an analysis of interrater agreement and correspondence with analogue assessment outcomes. *Journal of Applied Behavior Analysis, 45,* 779–795. http://dx.doi.org/10.1901/jaba.2012.45-779

Smith, T. (2001). Discrete trial training in the treatment of autism. *Focus on Autism and Other Developmental Disabilities, 16,* 86–92. http://dx.doi.org/10.1177/108835760101600204

Solomon, O., & Lawlor, M. C. (2013). "And I look down and he is gone": Narrating autism, elopement and wandering in Los Angeles. *Social Science & Medicine, 94,* 106–114. http://dx.doi.org/10.1016/j.socscimed.2013.06.034

St. Peter, C. C., Vollmer, T. R., Bourret, J. C., Borrero, C. S., Sloman, K. N., & Rapp, J. T. (2005). On the role of attention in naturally occurring matching relations. *Journal of Applied Behavior Analysis, 38,* 429–443. http://dx.doi.org/10.1901/jaba.2005.172-04

Swaggart, B. L., Gagnon, E., Bock, S. J., Earles, T. L., Quinn, C., Myles, B. S., & Simpson, R. L. (1995). Using social stories to teach social and behavioral skills to children with autism. *Focus on Autistic Behavior, 10,* 1–16. http://dx.doi.org/10.1177/108835769501000101

Tarbox, J., Wilke, A. E., Najdowski, A. C., Findel-Pyles, R. S., Balasanyan, S., Caveney, A. C., . . . Tia, B. (2009). Comparing indirect, descriptive, and experimental functional assessments of challenging behavior in children with autism. *Journal of Developmental and Physical Disabilities, 21,* 493–514. http://dx.doi.org/10.1007/s10882-009-9154-8

Tarbox, R. S. E., Wallace, M. D., & Williams, L. (2003). Assessment and treatment of elopement: A replication and extension. *Journal of Applied Behavior Analysis, 36,* 239–244. http://dx.doi.org/10.1901/jaba.2003.36-239

Thompson, R. H., & Iwata, B. A. (2007). A comparison of outcomes from descriptive and functional analyses of problem behavior. *Journal of Applied Behavior Analysis, 40*, 333–338. http://dx.doi.org/10.1901/jaba.2007.56-06

Thompson, R. H., Iwata, B. A., Hanley, G. P., Dozier, C. L., & Samaha, A. L. (2003). The effects of extinction, noncontingent reinforcement and differential reinforcement of other behavior as control procedures. *Journal of Applied Behavior Analysis, 36*, 221–238. http://dx.doi.org/10.1901/jaba.2003.36-221

Vollmer, T. R., Marcus, B. A., Ringdahl, J. E., & Roane, H. S. (1995). Progressing from brief assessments to extended experimental analyses in the evaluation of aberrant behavior. *Journal of Applied Behavior Analysis, 28*, 561–576. http://dx.doi.org/10.1901/jaba.1995.28-561

10

CONCLUSIONS AND FUTURE DIRECTIONS

LAWRENCE SCAHILL AND ERIC M. BUTTER

The body of scientific knowledge on parent training (PT) for children with autism spectrum disorder (ASD) reviewed in this book reflects the best available research evidence. In this volume, our authors have plumbed this large body of evidence across multiple behavioral targets and a wide range of subgroups of children with ASD. This accumulated evidence has emerged from meta-analyses (Nevill, Lecavalier, & Stratis, 2018; Postorino et al., 2017), randomized clinical trials with solid effect sizes (Bearss et al., 2015; Scahill et al., 2016), and an array of other scientific reports, such as quasiexperimental studies, single-subject designs, and case series (Bearss et al., 2013).

The gap between science and practice in child mental health generally is a recognized and persistent problem (Aarons, Hurlburt, & Horwitz, 2011). The emerging body of empirical support for various types of PT in children with ASD is an important development. But it also is a call to action for the field to identify and surmount barriers to the actual translation

http://dx.doi.org/10.1037/0000111-011
Parent Training for Autism Spectrum Disorder: Improving the Quality of Life for Children and Their Families,
C. R. Johnson, E. M. Butter, and L. Scahill (Editors)

of evidenced-based treatments in practice settings. Although randomized controlled trials (RCTs) often are regarded as the foundation of the evidence base, there are important differences between efficacy studies of psychosocial interventions and the application of empirically supported clinical practice (Weisz et al., 2013). RCTs often are conducted in academic centers with well-trained therapists and selected participants. In RCTs, training and supervision of therapists reduce variability in the delivery of the intervention. Carefully constructed entry criteria enhance internal validity. These structural and design features are intended to test the intervention under optimal conditions. However, children seeking treatment in community settings may present with different clinical characteristics. Because of these differences, clinicians in community settings may not be convinced that the trial participants and families described in the study are the same as the children and families that seek treatment in their clinical settings. In addition to differences in study samples and children in real-world settings, community clinicians may view treatment manuals as rigid, unnecessarily complicated, or both. Clinicians also may be concerned that manual-guided PT training programs obstruct the therapeutic alliance with parents (Weisz et al., 2013). Based on the reviews of PT interventions in this book, we are confident that these interventions can be flexibly applied by a range of clinicians in community settings. Although several PT interventions described in this book are ready for export into clinical settings, there are several challenges ahead. The transfer of evidence-based interventions falls under the rubrics of dissemination and implementation (Brownson, Colditz, & Proctor, 2018). *Dissemination* refers to the transmission of information about evidence-based interventions, as well as information on how to deliver those interventions. *Implementation* is a set of actions designed to promote actual adoption of an evidence-based intervention.

Dissemination (i.e., getting the word out) is necessary but not sufficient to bring about community uptake of PT. Effective dissemination involves efforts to communicate the supportive evidence and the content of specific PT programs. Such efforts may involve offering publications and making presentations to professional and community groups. Effective dissemination, however, also requires listening. For example, clinicians from community practice settings participating in a workshop may accept that PT for disruptive behavior is empirically supported, but they may feel that it is not a good fit in their clinical setting. In presentations to parent support groups, some parents may bristle at the unintended implication that they are somehow to blame for the child's disruptive behavior. Parental preferences, constraints in the clinical environment, or both may affect the acceptance of evidence-based treatment. For example, some parents may prefer group treatment rather than one-on-one treatment with a parent; others may prefer one-on-one treatment. Clinics in rural areas may require the use of telehealth as the mode of treatment delivery (Bearss, Burrell, et al., 2018). Some parents may express concern about the burden of weekly visits. Sociocultural considerations also may affect how the message of PT comes across to some parents (Lau, 2006). Drawing out these concerns and frank discussion to address them may enhance the acceptability of the specific PT program. Conversely, failure to explore and address these concerns likely will impede acceptance and adoption of the PT intervention.

Implementation is, or ought to be, the goal of intervention research. Narrowing the gap between demonstrating the efficacy of a given PT program and adopting it in clinical practice will require concerted action. The term *implementation science* has entered the lexicon over the past 10 to 15 years (Brownson et al., 2018). This relatively new scientific pursuit begins with the premise that time and dissemination are unlikely to produce efficient and effective changes in practice. In addition to the previously described barriers confronting dissemination, implementation efforts also may face institutional and policy impediments. A clinic administrator may express concern about the cost of training clinicians in a PT program—especially if the training pulls the clinician away from providing billable services. Despite the evidence supporting a specific PT program, administrators and clinicians may require assurance that the new treatment is cost effective compared with treatment as usual and that third-party payers will cover the new treatment (Castelnuovo, Pietrabissa, Cattivelli, Manzoni, & Molinari, 2016; Weisz et al., 2013). The PT programs that are flexible (although still reliably delivered), do not require extensive clinician training, and are time limited are more likely to be adopted in clinical settings (Brownson et al., 2018).

CLINICAL EXPERTISE

Meta-analyses of PT interventions in children with disruptive behavior without ASD noted that promoting positive parent–child interactions; teaching specific techniques, such as time out; and urging parents to practice new skills with their children were more likely to improve disruptive behavior in children (Kaminski, Valle, Filene, & Boyle, 2008; Postorino et al., 2017). This review and the PT interventions cited in this book, however, do not fully describe the necessary clinical competencies for effective delivery of PT. These competencies can be fostered through specific training on one or more PT programs. Clinical acumen also is enhanced by experience that enables the clinician to integrate evidence-based intervention with idiographic child characteristics. No treatment manual will cover the wide range of clinical situations that may occur during the course of delivering a PT program. The challenge for the clinician is to maintain a parent–therapist alliance, attend to the immediate concern, and then return to the intervention.

Several clinical competencies appear to support effective implementation of PT. For example, empathy is central to building and maintaining a therapeutic relationship for any psychotherapeutic intervention (Norcross & Wampold, 2011). It also is central to effective delivery of PT in children with ASD. Although regarded as necessary, the importance of empathy may not be explicitly described in technique-oriented PT manuals. Careful attention to pacing the delivery of PT also is warranted. Clinicians who march through the material in a given session may miss signals about parental readiness to embrace a specific technique.

Evidence-based PT manuals are best placed in the hands of clinicians who are familiar with applied behavior analysis. Equally important, however, is the recognition that the parent is the center of treatment—not the therapist (Burrell & Borrego, 2012). The goal of PT is to promote parental self-efficacy and empower the parent to be the agent of change (Iadarola et al., 2018). Clinicians who draw on experience and training to deliver PT in a fluid and flexible manner likely will have more success with PT interventions. Thus, evidence-based practice not only requires clinicians who are well-trained in the PT intervention but flexibility in the delivery of PT (Bearss, Johnson, et al., 2018).

In summary, the next phase of research in PT for children with ASD will involve continued dissemination and will need to break ground in implementation. New methods of training therapists that are cost effective and yet remain attentive to clinical competencies that support effective translation of evidence-based PT programs into community settings are current research priorities. Identification of barriers to implementation of PT in community settings will require dialogue with practitioners, parents, and policymakers. Failure to engage in these discussions will hinder the adoption of PT in these settings. In contrast, frank discussions on barriers may point the way toward solutions. Although fidelity to the content of an empirically supported PT program is a prerequisite for successful treatment, attention to the therapeutic relationship and flexible pacing of the intervention also are essential. Thus, effective implementation of PT for children with ASD will be called on to integrate training on how to deliver strategies and techniques to parents, with attention to parental engagement and the therapeutic relationship.

REFERENCES

Aarons, G. A., Hurlburt, M., & Horwitz, S. M. (2011). Advancing a conceptual model of evidence-based practice implementation in public service sectors. *Administration and Policy in Mental Health and Mental Health Services Research*, 38, 4–23. http://dx.doi.org/10.1007/s10488-010-0327-7

Bearss, K., Burrell, T. L., Challa, S. A. Postorino, V., Gillespie, S. E., Crooks, C., & Scahill, L. (2018). Feasibility of parent training via telehealth for children with autism spectrum disorder and disruptive behavior: A demonstration pilot. *Journal of Autism Developmental Disorders, 48,* 1020–1030. http://dx.doi.org/10.1007/s10803-017-3363-2

Bearss, K., Johnson, C., Handen, B., Butter, E., Lecavalier, L., Smith, T., & Scahill, L. (2018). *Parent training for disruptive behaviors.* New York, NY: Oxford University Press.

Bearss, K., Johnson, C., Smith, T., Lecavalier, L., Swiezy, N., Aman, M., . . . Scahill, L. (2015). Effect of parent training vs parent education on behavioral problems in children with autism spectrum disorder: A randomized clinical trial. *JAMA, 313,* 1524–1533. http://dx.doi.org/10.1001/jama.2015.3150

Bearss, K., Lecavalier, L., Minshawi, N., Johnson, C., Smith, T., Handen, B., . . . Scahill, L. (2013). Toward an exportable parent training program for disruptive behaviors in autism spectrum disorders. *Neuropsychiatry, 3,* 169–180. http://dx.doi.org/10.2217/npy.13.14

Brownson, R. C., Colditz, G. A., & Proctor, E. K. (2018). *Dissemination and implementation research in health: Translating science and practice.* New York, NY: Oxford University Press.

Burrell, T. L., & Borrego, J., Jr. (2012). Parents' involvement in ASD treatment: What is their role? *Cognitive and Behavioral Practice, 19,* 423–432. http://dx.doi.org/10.1016/j.cbpra.2011.04.003

Castelnuovo, G., Pietrabissa, G., Cattivelli, R., Manzoni, G. M., & Molinari, E. (2016). Not only clinical efficacy in psychological treatments: Clinical psychology must promote cost-benefit, cost-effectiveness, and cost-utility analysis. *Frontiers in Psychology, 7,* 563. http://dx.doi.org/10.3389/fpsyg.2016.00563

Iadarola, S., Levato, L., Harrison, B., Smith, T., Lecavalier, L., Johnson, C., . . . Scahill, L. (2018). Teaching parents behavioral strategies for autism spectrum disorder (ASD): Effects on stress, strain, and competence. *Journal of Autism and Developmental Disorders, 48,* 1031–1040. http://dx.doi.org/10.1007/s10803-017-3339-2

Kaminski, J. W., Valle, L. A., Filene, J. H., & Boyle, C. L. (2008). A meta-analytic review of components associated with parent training program effectiveness. *Journal of Abnormal Child Psychology, 36,* 567–589. http://dx.doi.org/10.1007/s10802-007-9201-9

Lau, A. S. (2006). Making the case for selective and directed cultural adaptations of evidence-based treatments: Examples from parent training. *Clinical Psychology: Science and Practice, 13,* 295–310. http://dx.doi.org/10.1111/j.1468-2850.2006.00042.x

Nevill, R. E., Lecavalier, L., & Stratis, E. A. (2018). Meta-analysis of parent-mediated interventions for young children with autism spectrum disorder. *Autism, 22,* 84–98. http://dx.doi.org/10.1177/1362361316677838

Norcross, J. C., & Wampold, B. E. (2011). Evidence-based therapy relationships: Research conclusions and clinical practices. *Psychotherapy, 48,* 98–102. http://dx.doi.org/10.1037/a0022161

Postorino, V., Sharp, W. G., McCracken, C. E., Bearss, K., Burrell, T. L., Evans, A. N., & Scahill, L. (2017). A systematic review and meta-analysis of parent training for disruptive behavior in children with autism spectrum disorder. *Clinical Child and Family Psychology Review, 20,* 391–402. http://dx.doi.org/10.1007/s10567-017-0237-2

Scahill, L., Bearss, K., Lecavalier, L., Smith, T., Swiezy, N., Aman, M. G., . . . Johnson, C. (2016). Effect of parent training on adaptive behavior in children with autism spectrum disorder and disruptive behavior: Results of a randomized trial. *Journal of the American Academy of Child & Adolescent Psychiatry, 55,* 602–609.e3. http://dx.doi.org/10.1016/j.jaac.2016.05.001

Weisz, J. R., Kuppens, S., Eckshtain, D., Ugueto, A. M., Hawley, K. M., & Jensen-Doss, A. (2013). Performance of evidence-based youth psychotherapies compared with usual clinical care: A multilevel meta-analysis. *JAMA Psychiatry, 70,* 750–761. http://dx.doi.org/10.1001/jamapsychiatry.2013.1176

INDEX

Confusional arousals, 151
Consequences
    in parent training for disruptive
        behavior, 120, 125, 127–130
    in parent training for elopement,
        245–249
    in parent training for food selectivity,
        192–193
    in parent training for sleep
        disturbances, 160
Constipation, 173, 205
Coparenting, 73–74
Cortisol, 153
Creative play, 87
Cronin, A., 179
Crowe, T. K., 180
CSBS (Communication and Symbolic
    Behavior Scales), 94, 102
CSBS DP (Communication and
    Symbolic Behavior Scale
    Developmental Profile)
    Infant-Toddler Checklist, 95
C-SHARP (Children's Scale of
    Hostility and Aggression:
    Reactive/Proactive), 124
Cultural competence, 17, 65
Curtin, C., 179
Curtis, A. B., 178

Daily living skills
    and clinical assessment, 39
    clinical assessment of, 46
    promotion of, 130
Data-keeping, 211
Daytime sleepiness, 154
DBDs (disruptive behavior disorders),
    117–119, 123
Deafness, 41
Defiant Children program, 11
DeMand, A., 185
Dementia, 250
Depression
    and parent training for sleep
        disturbances, 152
    as symptom of autism spectrum
        disorder, 5
Descriptive assessment, 49
Descriptive functional assessment,
    125–126
Descriptive methods, 240

Developmental social-pragmatic (DSP)
    models, 88, 93–94, 97
De Vinck-Baroody, O., 178
*Diagnostic and Statistical Manual of
    Mental Disorders (DSM–5)*,
    45, 117
Diarrhea, 205
Didactic training, 240
Dietary Guidelines for Americans (U.S.
    Department of Agriculture &
    U.S. Department of Health and
    Human Services), 188
Dietitians, 181
Differential reinforcement (applied
    behavioral analysis)
    and naturalistic developmental
        behavioral interventions, 24
    and parent training for disruptive
        behavior, 129
    in parent training for elopement,
        248–249
Differential reinforcement of alternative
    behavior (DRA), 248
Differential reinforcement of other
    behavior (DRO), 248–249
Direct instruction, 39
Direct observation. *See* Behavioral
    observation
Disability, 63
Discrete trial training (DTT)
    in applied behavioral analysis, 5
    and parent training for social
        communication, 88
Disruptive behavior disorders (DBDs),
    117–119, 123
Disruptive behaviors
    clinical assessment of, 39, 40,
        121–126
    as common symptom of autism
        spectrum disorder, 5
    development of parent training for
        treatment of, 11
    and parent engagement, 62
    parent-mediated interventions
        for, 26
    parent training for. *See* Parent
        training for disruptive
        behavior
    and parent training for elopement,
        247

Family systems interventions, 66
Fear, 223
Feeding problems. *See also* Food
    selectivity
    causes of, 179–181
    clinical assessment of, 50, 181–187
    impact of, 178–179
    and parent engagement, 62
    as symptom of autism spectrum
        disorder, 5
Feldman, D. E., 180
Focal concerns, 20
Foldes, E., 185
Fombonne, E., 178
Food allergies, 175, 179
Food diaries, 185–186
Food refusal, 20
Food selectivity
    assessment of, 181–187
    and parent target problems, 51
    parent training for. *See* Parent
        training for food selectivity
Foxx, R. M., 207
Functional analysis
    in case example, 251–252
    and clinical assessment, 49
    and parent training for disruptive
        behavior, 125–126
    in parent training for elopement,
        236–240
Functional Assessment Interview, 239
Functional assessments
    of food selectivity, 182–183
    and parent training for disruptive
        behavior, 125–126
Functional communication training
    in parent training for disruptive
        behavior, 131
    in parent training for toileting
        difficulties, 221
Functions (applied behavioral analysis)
    determination of, 23–24
    of elopement, 235–240
    in parent training for disruptive
        behavior, 120

Gastroenteritis, 175, 179
Gastroenterologists, 194
Gastroesophageal reflux, 175, 179
Gastrointestinal problems

and parent training for food
    selectivity, 173, 182
and parent training for sleep
    disturbances, 152
and parent training for toileting
    difficulties, 205
Gender, 119
Generalization
    in parent training for disruptive
        behavior, 131
    in parent training for toileting
        difficulties, 222
Genetics, 41
Ghezzi, P. M., 186
Gisel, E., 180
Gonzales, J., 66
Graduated extinction, 160
Gray, Carol, 159
Group programs, 17–18, 262
Gulsrud, A. C., 97

Habit training, 207
Health, 178
Helplessness, 119
Help-seeking behaviors, 64
Herzinger, C. V., 180
High-intensity parent training
    programs, 15
Hill, A. P., 178
Home Situations Questionnaire-Autism
    Spectrum Disorder (HSQ-ASD)
    in case example, 136, 140
    overview, 49
    and parent training for disruptive
        behavior, 123–124
Home visits, 161
Homework, 39, 238, 246, 249
Hospitalizations, 41
HSQ-ASD. *See* Home Situations
    Questionnaire-Autism Spectrum
    Disorder
Hyperactivity
    on behavior questionnaires, 157
    parent-mediated interventions for, 20
    and parent target problems, 51
    as symptom of autism spectrum
        disorder, 5

ICD–10 (*International Classification of
    Diseases*), 117

IDDs. *See* Intellectual and developmental disabilities
Imaginative play, 87
Imitation Battery, 94
Imitation skills
    assessment of, 95
    in parent-mediated interventions, 19
    and parent training for social communication, 86, 87
Implementation (evidence-based interventions), 262–263
Implementation science, 263
Impulse control, 118
Incidental teaching, 23
Incontinence, 204, 207
Incredible Years program, 11
Indirect assessment, 49
Indirect functional assessment, 125
Individuals With Disabilities Education Act, 12
Infectious disease, 41
Informant-based assessment, 122–123
Injuries, 41
Instruction, 203
Instructional supports, 210–211
Intellectual and developmental disabilities (IDDs)
    and parent engagement, 67–68, 70, 72
    and parent training for elopement, 234
    and parent training for toileting difficulties, 204, 224
    and sleep disturbances, 151
Intelligence quotient (IQ), 119
Interagency Autism Coordinating Committee, 233
Internal locus of control, 122
Internal validity, 262
International Classification of Diseases (ICD–10), 117
International Classification of Sleep Disorders, 154
Interventionist role, 73–74
Interviews, 239
In vivo strategies, 240
IQ (intelligence quotient), 119
Irritability, 118

Jaquess, D. L., 180
JASPER (Joint Attention Symbolic Play Engagement and Regulation) program, 20, 97–101, 103–107
Johnson, C., 185
Johnson, C. R., 152, 154, 161, 178, 188
Joint attention, 87, 93, 95, 97–99
Joint Attention Symbolic Play Engagement and Regulation (JASPER) program, 20, 97–101, 103–107
Joint engagement, 87, 95, 97
Juice, 215

Kaiser, A., 102
Kasari, C., 20, 100, 102
Kazdin, A. E., 11, 67
Kuschner, E. S., 178

Lagerway, M., 179
Language samples, 94, 96
Lawton, K., 100
Learning
    factors in, 24
    and parent training for toileting difficulties, 204–205
Lecavalier, L., 118, 119
Leiter International Performance Scale, 45
Leslie, A., 134
Levin, L., 186
Limited joint engagement, 85
Limit setting, 40
Linscheid, T. R., 185
Locus of control, 122
Lovaas, Ivar, 23
Low-intensity parent training programs, 15
Low-resource areas, 100–101
Lukens, C. T., 185

MacArthur–Bates Communicative Development Inventories, 95
Magnetic resonance imaging, 41
Maintenance
    in parent training for disruptive behavior, 131
    in parent training for toileting difficulties, 222
Maladaptive behavior
    common functions of, 23–24

Reynell Developmental Language
Scales, 95
Rhythmic movement disorder, 150
Rickets, 178
Rigidity, 174
Risperidone, 21, 132, 133
Rivet, T. T., 234
RLS (restless-legs syndrome), 150
Rodger, S., 179
Role play, 39, 126, 240
Routine
    creation of, 127
    and parent training for toileting
        difficulties, 205, 213–214
    in parent training for toileting
        difficulties, 224
RUBI (Research Units in Behavioral
    Intervention) Autism Network
    Parent Training program, 21,
    132–133, 135–137
RUPP (Research Units on Pediatric
    Psychopharmacology) Autism
    Network, 132–134
Rural areas, 263

Safety
    and controlling the environment, 126
    and parent training for elopement,
        247
    and parent training for sleep
        disturbances, 160, 161
Santucci, L. C., 135
SB-5 (Stanford–Binet Intelligence
    Scales-Fifth Edition), 45–46
Scheduled waking (sleep disturbance
    intervention), 159
School-based services
    and clinical assessment, 41
    overview, 12
    and parent-mediated interventions,
        20
School functioning, 119
School placement, 45
SCQ (Social Communication
    Questionnaire), 42, 45
Screening Tool of Feeding Problems,
    185
Scurvy, 178
SDB (sleep-disordered breathing),
    150, 154

Seizures, 152, 153, 157
Self-blame, 47
Self-injury
    and clinical assessment, 39
    parent-mediated interventions for,
        20
    and parent target problems, 51
    and parent training for disruptive
        behavior, 118
    and parent training for elopement,
        232
    and planned ignoring, 128
Self-soothing difficulties, 153, 161–162
Sensory stimulation
    and parent training for disruptive
        behavior, 120
    and parent training for food
        selectivity, 174, 180
    and parent training for sleep
        disturbances, 161
    and parent training for toileting
        difficulties, 205
Sensory strategies, 161
Serotonin, 153
Severe behavioral problems, 133–134
Shaping (applied behavioral analysis)
    and naturalistic developmental
        behavioral interventions, 24
    in parent training for toileting
        difficulties, 223–224
Sharp, W. G., 180, 188
Simons Simplex Collection, 118
Single-subject designs, 261
Skill acquisition, 130
Skipper, B. J., 180
Sleep diary recordings, 155, 156
Sleep-disordered breathing (SDB),
    150, 154
Sleep disturbances
    clinical assessment of, 41, 50,
        153–157
    and parent engagement, 62
    and parent training for elopement, 233
    and parent training for toileting
        difficulties, 205
    as symptom of autism spectrum
        disorder, 5
Sleep efficiency, 155
Sleep hygiene, 158, 161
Sleep onset delay, 149, 154, 159–162

Sleep questionnaires, 153–155
Sleep-related breathing disorder, 126
Sleep restriction, 159
Sleep–wake cycle, 152–153
Sleepwalking, 151
SLPs. *See* Speech-language pathologists
Smith, L. E., 18
Snell-Johns, J., 63
Social communication
    clinical assessment of, 41, 46, 94–96
    and deficits as symptom of autism
        spectrum disorder, 4
    and parent engagement, 62
    in parent-mediated interventions, 19
    parent training for. *See* Parent
        training for social
        communication
Social Communication Questionnaire
    (SCQ), 42, 45
Social functions, 235–236
Social learning theory, 4, 22–23
Social Responsiveness Scale (SRS-2),
    42
Social stories, 159–160, 243
Social support, 63, 71
Social workers, 17
Socioeconomic status
    and parent engagement, 65
    and parent training for social
        communication, 100
Sofronoff, K., 21, 134
SPA (Structured Play Assessment), 95,
    103
Speech, 86
Speech-language pathologists (SLPs),
    181, 182, 187, 194
Speech therapy, 5, 41
SRS-2 (Social Responsiveness Scale),
    42
Standardized tests, 94, 96
Stanford–Binet Intelligence Scales-Fifth
    Edition (SB-5), 45–46, 136
Stepping Stones Triple P parent training
    program, 21
Stigma, 241
Stimulus fading procedures, 191
Stimulus transfer procedures, 222–223
Stoewe, J., 66
Stores, G., 154
Structure

creation of, 127
in parent training for food selectivity,
    189, 190
Structured Play Assessment (SPA),
    95, 103
Suarez, M. A., 178, 179
Surgeries, 41
Symbolic play, 87, 97–99

Tangible function, 235
Tantrums
    and clinical assessment, 39
    functions of, 24
    parent-mediated interventions
        for, 20
    and parent target problems, 51
    and parent training for disruptive
        behavior, 117, 118
    planned ignoring of, 128
Target age groups, 15
Target behaviors
    and clinical assessment, 49
    and parent training for disruptive
        behavior, 122–123
Task analysis, 220
Technology, 100, 101
Telehealth programming, 101, 263
Therapeutic relationship
    and defining parent training, 4
    for parent engagement, 65
    and parent training for
        elopement, 240
Time-out from reinforcement, 129
Time-outs, 128–129
Toileting difficulties
    and parent engagement, 62
    parent-mediated interventions
        for, 20
    parent training for. *See* Parent
        training for toileting
        difficulties
    as symptom of autism spectrum
        disorder, 5
Token economy system, 130
Tracking devices, 244–245
Treatment adherence
    and parent engagement, 66–67
    and parenting stress, 65
    and parent training for elopement, 240
    to session content and assignments, 63

ABOUT THE EDITORS

Cynthia R. Johnson, PhD, is the director of the Cleveland Clinic Center for Autism, Cleveland, Ohio, and is on the faculty of the Lerner College of Medicine at Case Western University. She has been awarded National Institutes of Health–funded and numerous other grants. A member of The RUBI (Research Units in Behavior Interventions) Autism Network, Dr. Johnson's recent research has been on the treatment of frequently co-occurring/associated problems in autism spectrum disorder, including disruptive behaviors, sleep disturbances, and feeding problems. Dr. Johnson is a licensed psychologist and a board-certified behavior analyst.

Eric M. Butter, PhD, is a clinical psychologist with specialization in autism spectrum disorder (ASD), attention-deficit/hyperactivity disorder (ADHD), and other neurodevelopmental disabilities and is an associate professor jointly appointed in pediatrics and psychology at The Ohio State University. Dr. Butter's research has focused on the biomedical correlates and potential etiologies of ASD and ADHD, as well as the disorders' psychological and medical treatment. He has been continuously involved in several autism research networks since 1999. Dr. Butter is the chief of psychology at Nationwide Children's Hospital in Columbus, Ohio, and continues to work on implementing and expanding parent training interventions for children with ASD.

Lawrence Scahill, MSN, PhD, is the director of clinical trials at the Marcus Autism Center in Atlanta, Georgia, and a professor of pediatrics at Emory University. He is a recognized leader in the design and conduct of clinical trials in children with neurodevelopmental disorders, such as autism spectrum disorder and Tourette's disorder. Dr. Scahill is an editor of *Pediatric Psychopharmacology: Principles and Practice* and coauthor of *Parent Training for Disruptive Behavior in Children With Autism Spectrum Disorder*. He has played a central role in the Research Units on Pediatric Psychopharmacology Autism Network and the Research Units in Behavioral Intervention.